The English Friend

A life of William de la Pole first duke of Suffolk (1396–1450)

Susan Curran

with photographs by Mike Dixon

First published 2011
by the Lasse Press
2 St Giles Terrace, Norwich NR2 1NS, UK
www.lassepress.com
lassepress@gmail.com

Also published in electronic versions

ISBN-13: 978-0-9568758-0-8

Typeset in Frutiger, Garamond and Stone Sans by
Curran Publishing Services Ltd, Norwich, UK

Manufactured in the UK by LPPS Ltd, Wellingborough, Northants NN8 3PJ

The English Friend

Above, Church of St Pierre, Dreux
Cover, St Lawrence's Church, Norwich

Chascun doit estre bien enclin
Vers la paix, car certainement
Ella departira butin
De grans biens a tous largement.
Guerre ne sert que de tourment:
Je la hé, pour dire le voir!
Bannie seroit plainement,
S'il en estoit a mon vouloir.*

Charles duke of Orleans, a ballad for the duke of Burgundy

Also that every man in faithful wise
Be warned thus, that no man hinder other,
But love his fellow as he were his brother.

William de la Pole, first duke of Suffolk

* *a very rough translation:*

It is for every man to lean
To peace, for it is true to say
From this there will for sure be seen
Great blessings for them every day.
War brings them nothing but torment:
I hate it more, the more I see!
It should be banished, hellward sent
That's what I'd do, were it up to me.

Trinity Church, Vendome

Author's note

Much becomes muddied and lost after 600 years, so it would be foolhardy to call this a true story. But it is not fiction; no dialogue or incidents have been invented, and where guesswork has had to fill in the historical record, I have tried to make it clear.

Physical things change as well. Stained glass is reset, buildings are repaired, farming practices change, even coastlines alter. So the pictures herein are intended to give a sense of the England and France that Suffolk knew, but it can be little more than that. The buildings and glass are mostly roughly contemporary with the story; a few are later but in the style of the fifteenth century.

No portraits survive of Suffolk, and few of the other characters in this story. Except where indicated, the pictures of people are also intended as broadly illustrative, no more. Much of the stained glass shows religious scenes and individuals of religious significance; no disrespect to that function is intended in my reusing it in this different context.

For more information visit the companion website: www.theenglishfriend.com

Contents

Maps

Genealogies

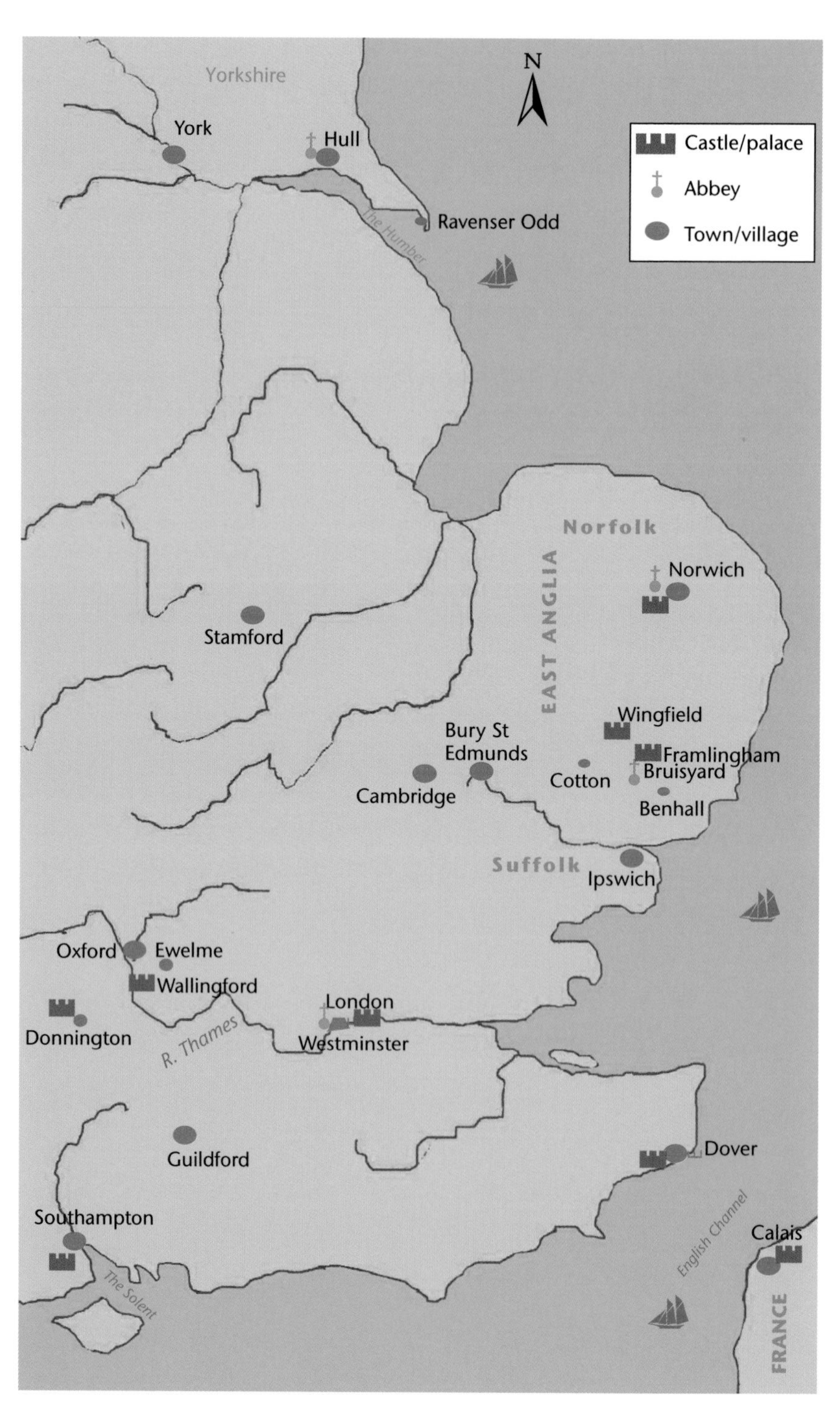

Eastern and southern England

1
The Echo Tower

By June of 1429 William, earl of Suffolk must have known Jargeau well. His troops had captured the little town on the upper reaches of the Loire the previous October, easily enough that the damage to its walls had soon been repaired. Then he had stayed only days, but the next May he had returned, this time with a sizeable contingent of the Lancastrian army. Perhaps 1,500 men had joined up with the small garrison. They crammed into the houses within the walls that those inhabitants who fled had left empty, and filled the suburbs around the rue des Moulins where the mills lined the river, and the roads south to Orleans and the swamps of the Sologne. They manned the five towers and the three gatehouses, and spread too into the buildings of the collegiate church of Saint-Vrain. Suffolk stationed a contingent across the river in the straggle of houses known as the faubourg St Denis, and guards to control the glory of Jargeau, the fine stone bridge, a hundred years old, with fifteen piers and sixteen irregular arches, which curved in a shallow ellipse towards the main road north. The bridge at Orleans, a few miles west, had been half-destroyed during the siege that had just been lifted, so this was the only fixed crossing over the river – which was almost as broad as the town itself – for many miles.

Then he had sent his heralds off to the duke of Bedford, who as regent was in overall charge of the Lancastrian campaign in France, and waited for further instructions. This over-sized garrison could not squat among the sullen French shopkeepers for long, but they had to be cautious, since there were a large number of troops supporting Charles of Valois in the field against them.

The Lancastrian army had split into three divisions after they had abandoned the siege of Orleans, and the Valois had split up their own forces too. Some of them had followed Suffolk's men, and there was a vicious skirmish or two, in one of which the captain of the Jargeau garrison, Sir Henry Bisset, was killed, before the Valois withdrew. This left Suffolk in sole command. He must have spent many hours pacing the top of the walls, stopping to talk with the men stationed in the towers, pausing at the Porte du Pont and checking that the guards were maintaining a close lookout upstream and downstream, and towards the north bank too. He would have sent out foraging parties, and perhaps gone with them, to find food and firewood from the farms and villages in the broad flat valley of the Loire.

One of the towers was called the Levantine Tower – perhaps a crusader had built it, or a merchant from the East. And another, a small round watchtower to the west of the city, was called the Echo Tower, probably because men had found that their words echoed around its stone chambers.

The weather had cleared after the thunderstorms that had chased them from Orleans, but it had been a wet spring, and the deep ditch around the walls was close to overflowing.

Suffolk must also have spent many evenings by candlelight with his captains, debating what the Lancastrians might best do now. They were experienced men; many had been fighting in France for as long as he had himself, almost fourteen years. Two of his three brothers were among them. Sir John de la Pole had been in France for perhaps ten years, and would have would have offered plenty of advice; Sir Alexander was younger.

Jargeau was on the southern border of Lancastrian-held France, and Suffolk, always a realistic rather than an optimistic commander, must have known that now the Lancastrians had failed to take Orleans, it would be difficult for them to continue to hold

Overleaf: from Evreux Cathedral

it. But they would do so as long as they could, naturally, and it was by no means certain the Valois would make an attempt to take it from them, particularly while this army remained billeted there.

Suffolk had a woman at Jargeau, Malyne de Cay, who had broken the vows she had taken as a nun, and he will have spent some time with her too during these hot dead days and cool nights within stone walls.

Around supper time (in those days, mid-afternoon) on 11 June word came to him that enemy troops were approaching. They were bringing the big cannon that had been used at Orleans. The greatest of these, the *Bergère* – the shepherdess – was so heavy it needed thirty-six horses to lug it overland, and bridges had had to be strengthened before it could cross. The baggage wagons and the cannon travelled slowly, so it was a couple of hours after the scouts first saw the army that it reached the suburbs of the town. By then it was apparent that this was not just a division of the Valois army, but the whole of it. Suffolk's troops were facing perhaps 8,000 men.

The Lancastrians had won battles with worse odds, but his men were outnumbered sufficiently that there was no real argument for riding out to engage this army. Suffolk would have sent off messengers as soon as he knew the Valois were approaching, with orders to find the other English commanders and ask for assistance. Meanwhile, his natural choice was to sit tight and leave the Valois to dig in for a siege. There was a third option: to surrender Jargeau. But he would not have chosen to do that immediately, when there was a good chance that Talbot or Scales and their men would come to his aid and give him enough support to see the Valois off.

His men had plenty of gunpowder, because Jargeau was the main Lancastrian store on the upper Loire, but they did not have large cannon. With the Valois chasing them, they had had to leave those outside Orleans when they abandoned their siege fortifications. So it was their own guns they would be facing now, and with little to counter them. This was not good; although Jargeau was walled, these were not the broad high walls of Orleans. But the other Lancastrian divisions were not so far off, and they would probably have to hold out for days rather than weeks.

At the core of the Valois army were well-ordered ranks of mounted men at arms and crossbowmen, but there was a rabble with them too: men from Jargeau who had headed for the woods when the English came back, men from Orleans downstream, bandits, hangers-on – any and all of the French who wanted the English gone from the Loire. And they could see the white standard with its picture of Christ in majesty, which told them the Maid was still with the army. This was the girl Jeanne d'Arc, whom Frenchmen said heard voices of the saints that told her to rid France of the English. Suffolk had received letters from Jeanne at Orleans, and his

Bridge over the River Loire at Beaugency

heart probably sank at the prospect of getting more of the same rants now.

He could expect the Valois commanders – the duke of Alençon, the bastard of Orleans, he and his men could read the standards – to follow the rules of chivalry, but the girl and the rabble were worryingly unpredictable. And indeed the rabble pressed forwards, when all the professional men at arms knew there should have been a parley, offers made and considered, accepted or rejected, before any attack began. Suffolk and some of his men headed out and confronted them. This drove them back, and when a degree of order had been restored, the heralds rode out from the Valois ranks, and he had them let in to the town.

The demands they brought had the stamp of Jeanne on them. 'Surrender this place to the Heavenly King and to gentle King Charles, and you can go. If not you will be massacred.'

This was both exasperating and worrying. The girl was wrong-headed, of course, in her naive conviction that God was on her side. Gentle King Charles, indeed! Not only was Charles of Valois not the rightful king of France – Henry of Lancaster (in other words, King Henry VI of England) was that, and not this runt his own mother had disowned – he could not even fairly be called gentle. He was no great fighter, true, but he was not a man of peace either; on the contrary, all men knew him for a murderer. Why would the dead saints uphold such a man? Only a crazed visionary could imagine it.

The worrying part was the tone of the proposition. Without the Maid, Suffolk could confidently have expected the Valois captains to come to decent terms: say, accepting an offer

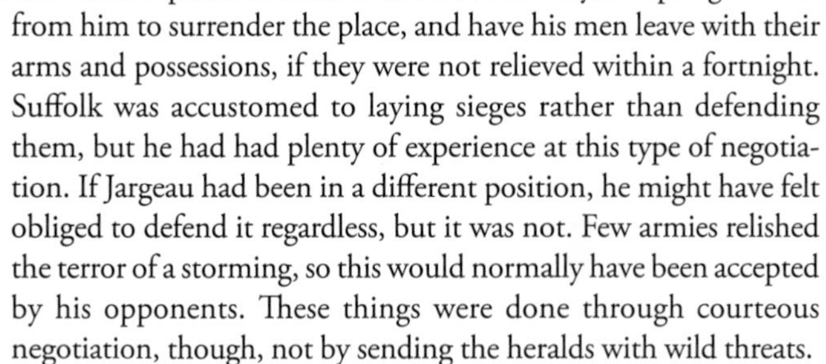

from him to surrender the place, and have his men leave with their arms and possessions, if they were not relieved within a fortnight. Suffolk was accustomed to laying sieges rather than defending them, but he had had plenty of experience at this type of negotiation. If Jargeau had been in a different position, he might have felt obliged to defend it regardless, but it was not. Few armies relished the terror of a storming, so this would normally have been accepted by his opponents. These things were done through courteous negotiation, though, not by sending the heralds with wild threats.

He will have conferred with John, Alexander and his other captains, as was the usual practice. Probably some of the men were for holding out, or for engaging with the enemy – John, for instance, seems generally to have lacked Suffolk's caution – but his own choice prevailed, and they agreed on the terms they should propose. Then the Lancastrian heralds went with the Valois heralds to convey them to the adversary: fifteen days.

The response came straight back. His men might leave with their horses within the hour, or not at all.

That was not an offer to even be considered. In an hour, with next to nothing, and heading on to evening!

No sooner had his heralds given his refusal than the Valois trumpeters sounded the signal, and the rabble – and the professional troops too – headed into the attack. Suffolk probably had not expected this. But his men had had warning, and were

Church of St Peter and St Paul, East Harling, Norfolk
Photo Mike Dixon

experienced at scrambling into action. He kept back some men back to hold the town walls and the towers, and sent the rest out into the suburbs to engage with the Valois.

This was no open battlefield, though, where the English and Welsh longbowmen would have had the advantage. They were fighting around the fields and hedges, the mills and inns. The Lancastrians were outnumbered too heavily. They fought as they were trained and used to do, but still they lost ground as the Valois masses pressed on. Suffolk had to recall them, to save them from a massacre, and it cost them the suburbs and the bridge.

Still, they held the town within its walls, the towers, the strong stone church.

Then the *Bergère* let rip, and its first large stone ball sent half a tower crashing to the ground.

The cannon fired all night at the walls of Jargeau. These primitive guns were slow to fill, to aim, to fire. After each flash and crash long minutes passed before another flash erupted from another part of the French line, followed by the thud of a cannonball hitting the walls, the creaks of the protesting stone, the shouts of the men. Enough damage was done for Suffolk and his men to know they could not have held out for a fortnight, even had one been on offer, which it was not. Come dawn, the Valois men at arms attacked again.

They set their scaling ladders in the ditch at the points where the cannon had driven breaches in the walls, and headed up them, with the Maid in the vanguard. An Englishmen aimed a stone at the girl, smashing her helmet, but the fiend hardly hesitated even then. 'Our Lord has condemned the English,' she cried out. 'At this hour they are ours. Have courage!' She launched back into the assault.

The broken walls could not be held, so Suffolk and his men pulled back, to the surviving towers, the gatehouses, the church. They fought with swords, with axes, with stones and maces. And still the Valois kept coming. They fought in the streets and alleys, in the narrow houses. Those inhabitants who had not fled joined in and fought against them with hammers and picks. In the melee Suffolk lost touch with John and Alexander, and he knew that men, many men, had fallen. He was still standing, but he knew too that the day was lost. There was no merit in losing still more. He shouted to the men around him to head for the bridge. The south bank was all Valois territory, so they could not find safety there, but the Lancastrians held much of the land to the north. If they could get over the bridge and hide in the forest, they had a chance of escape.

It was three hours since the girl had headed up the first scaling ladder, and Suffolk and his men must have been numb with exhaustion by the time they had fought their way up to and through the Porte du Pont. There was the broad Loire, and there was a solid troop of Valois soldiers guarding the bridge across it.

There was no hope that the Lancastrians could get over the bridge. No man eagerly chooses surrender, but Suffolk was one who preferred it to death. He reversed his sword and held out its pommel, then lifted his visor so he could speak to the man who stepped forward from the Valois ranks.

'Are you a gentleman?' he asked this man. He was indeed, the Frenchman answered; his name was Guillaume Regnault. 'Are you a knight?' Suffolk persisted. No, said Regnault, he had not been knighted. 'Then you must become one,' said Suffolk, 'before I surrender to you.' He turned his sword again, and tapped the man on his shoulders with the blade.

Then he held the sword out pommel-first once more, and became a prisoner of the Valois.

Much of that afternoon he must have spent on the banks of the Loire, huddled with the other prisoners, with townsfolk and soldiers holding them at pikepoint. The Frenchmen will have stripped them of their armour and surcoats, tied them up and left them in their shirts and breeches. As the Valois secured the town and hunted down the last resistance – they did not sack it, this was their own place they were reclaiming – others will have joined the captives, bruised and bloody from the fighting.

Word spread of Suffolk's doomed chivalry on the bridge, and there must have been plenty of jokes among the Frenchmen about 'Sire' Guillaume. Regnault probably took it in good part; he would have figured out by then that his captive was a lord, and good for a very sizeable ransom. The commanders would take most of it, but a reward would come to him too. Suffolk himself was probably too preoccupied to care. He would have been watching and waiting to see if John or Alexander was among the men shoved stumbling into the huddle. Neither of them came.

Nobody much wanted the common soldiers, who had little to offer in return for their lives. After Alençon, the bastard of Orleans, the girl and the other captains had come and taken out the men they thought worth holding, the rank and file soldiers and the townsfolk were left to squabble over the rest. They settled the quarrel by killing them all.

So it was to howls and death-screams that the remaining live prisoners were pushed into the shallow barges that plied the river. The banks were too unsafe for this valuable human booty. The barges set off as night fell, heading downstream to Orleans. Once they left Jargeau behind them, it must have been quiet on the broad dark river.

Most of his men dead, and his brothers almost certainly among them. His reputation as a commander in tatters, his liberty lost, his lands liable to be sold to pay his ransom. It was a bad time for the earl of Suffolk. Adversity on this scale can break a man; and when it does not, it changes him permanently. It changed Suffolk.

He was kept prisoner throughout a long autumn and winter. This gave him plenty of time to think not only about his own situation, but about the Lancastrian venture in France, the part he had played in it, and the part he might play in the future. He had spent the first half of his adult life as a man at arms, fighting with King Henry V and his brothers to claim France for the Lancastrians. They had won much, and had continued to secure territory even after Henry's death. But they could gain no more; Suffolk must have been clear on that. Orleans would never be theirs; the great expanse of central and eastern France south of the Loire would never be theirs. Henry on his deathbed had ordered them to keep at the war till they held the whole country, but to Suffolk, haggard in defeat, that was not a realistic option. It was time to secure what they now possessed, and come to terms with the Valois.

The quest for peace would dominate the rest of Suffolk's life. And in the end it would destroy him.

Church of the Holy Cross, Caston, Norfolk

2 The merchants of Ravenser Odd

The fortune that went to pay Suffolk's ransom came from his great-grandfather, and since it had a large impact on his life, we must begin with this first William de la Pole, a Yorkshireman.

The shores of the Humber estuary, which divides the old English counties of Yorkshire and Lincolnshire, have always been changeable. In the thirteenth century Ravenser Odd, which was tucked into the stretch in the lee of Spurn Head, the gravel spit at the north-east end of the estuary, was a small port, and home to a family who, in the style of the times, were known by their trade. The brothers Richard, William and John worked 'at the pool' (the harbour). If the name their descendants were known by sounded Norman, that was no doubt deliberate. There were families of similar name elsewhere in England, some of them quite grand, and men might if they wished believe the de la Poles of Yorkshire to have noble ancestors. They did not; their forebears were probably fishermen, as so many men of the Humber were.

By the brothers' time, the family had begun to diversify into trade. The harbours of the Humber were the natural outlet for the wool from the sheep of the Yorkshire dales and moors, which in those days was shipped to the rich towns of Flanders for spinning and weaving into cloth, and for lead from the mines in Derbyshire, farther west. Seeing that Ravenser Odd would not fit their growing ambitions, or perhaps suffering from the erosion of its harbour (later that century it disappeared beneath the waves, church, graveyard and all), the de la Poles moved farther west to the growing town of Hull, and apprenticed themselves to a bigger merchant, John Rottenherring.

Rottenherring taught them well, and by 1316 they made it into the historical record, acquiring a house from him, for which they paid £4 a year – a sizeable sum in those days. They went on to outstrip him, building warehouses on land and ships to roam the North Sea and the English Channel. (As well as ships to carry their own trade goods, they built some sizeable ships for the King, most notably one called the *Trinity*.) They owned their own brickyards. They began to trade in wine, which was brought to England from the vineyards of Aquitaine and Gascony. They ran ferries across the Humber: there was no bridge (nor was there to be one for hundreds of years), and it was more than a day's journey to round the estuary by land. Later on they went into banking.

The brothers worked for King Edward III, with Richard becoming his chief butler (that is, his supplier of wine), and William lending him money for first the Scottish, then the French, wars he fought in the plague-ridden

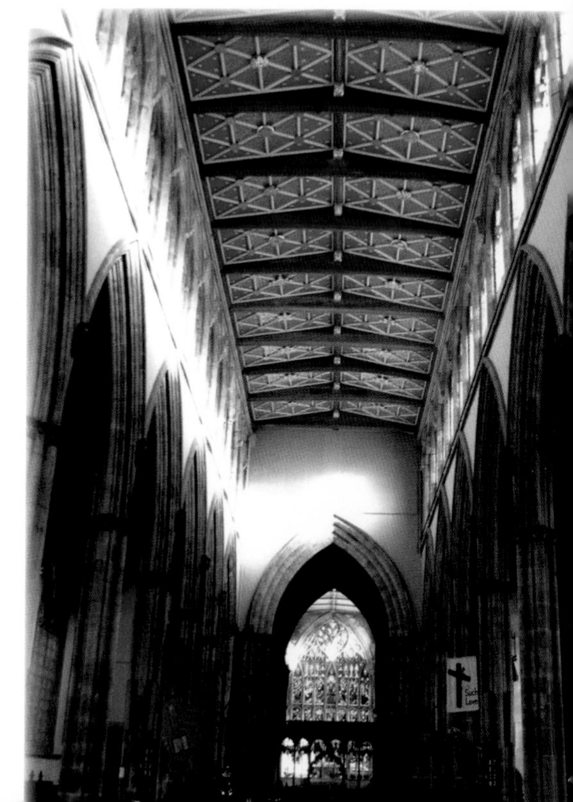

Holy Trinity Church, Hull

days in the middle of that century. The French war in particular saw great successes for the English, with massive victories at Crècy in 1346 and Poitiers in 1356 enabling them to make large demands in the Treaty of Bretigny that ended this phase of it. It gave the king control over a large proportion of south-west France, and a sizeable territory in the north-west around Calais.

Richard and William de la Pole both played their part in the public life of Hull, and when the town was given a charter by the King (it became known as Kingston upon Hull), William became its first mayor. Both brothers represented the town in Parliament. By the mid-century they owned a huge complex of warehouses near to Hull docks, and they were also acquiring land to the west of the city: some of it in Aton, within the town walls, and some in the borough of Myton, just outside. Richard moved to London in about 1328, although he and William still worked closely together (John fades from the record; perhaps he had died), and it was William who built a vast house of brick and stone, with a tower, on part of these holdings. At the time it was known as Court Hall. With a great hall 60 feet long and 40 feet wide, another chamber 60 feet by 20 feet, plus many further rooms, its own chapel dedicated to St Michael, half an acre each of courtyard and kitchen garden, and an acre of flower garden, it must have been by some margin the grandest house in Hull. Another part of the land William set aside, intending to ensure the salvation of his immortal soul by endowing a hospital, and later also proposing to found a religious house for the Poor Clares. The family also had three more great houses in Hull, all built of brick and with towers.

It was a slow and expensive business to turn money into land in the fourteenth century, but that was what men did who wished to see their families rise in the world, and William and Richard slowly pieced estates together: buying some land, acquiring some in return for favours done to the king, by whom all titles to land were ultimately granted. William eventually outstripped his brother: he seems to have been a canny businessmen and at times a ruthless one. By his middle age he was one of the richest men in England. The king's failure to pay his debts shook William's business to its foundations – and battles to get his money back saw him sent to prison in the early 1340s – but he survived to get much of what he was owed repaid to him, and to acquire the great house of the Italian banking family, the Bardis, in Lombard Street in London when they were not so fortunate. It was said that at his peak, William could travel from Hull to London without stepping foot outside the lands he owned. He owned estates in Durham, in Yorkshire, in Nottinghamshire and Lincolnshire; an inn in Stamford, and a dozen shops in London, plus a fine residence there, near the Thames.

William married, of course; his wife was Katherine of Norwich. The city of Norwich is about midway between

From Strutt's *Dress and Habits of the Peoples of England* (1799)

Hull and London, though well to the east of the direct route between the two. Katherine must have had links with the area, and this began the family's long connection with the East Anglian counties of Norfolk and Suffolk.

William and Richard were the first of several generations of de la Poles to be blessed with a multitude of children. It is not known now how many were born, let alone how many survived to adulthood, and only the eldest of William's sons, Michael, plays a real part in this story. But Michael had at least three brothers, and three sisters too.

It was necessary for a man whose estates were worth more than a reasonable sum (£40 a year, according to a proclamation of 1335) to provide men and do service in the king's army. William did so, becoming known as Sir William in later life, and acquiring a coat of arms: *azure, a fess between three leopards' faces or* (that is, a blue shield with a gold stripe across it and three gold leopards' faces). But there was a difference between a knight and a lord, and it was not usual for a man who had made his fortune in trade to rise to the nobility. William was probably wise not to seek it for himself, but he sought it for his son Michael, and got it. No other family of their era was to make the same rise.

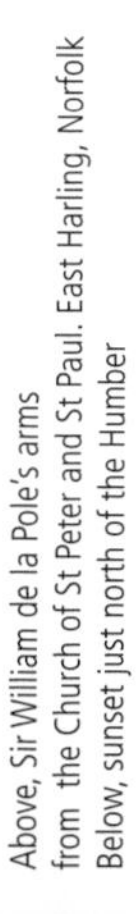

Above, Sir William de la Pole's arms
from the Church of St Peter and St Paul. East Harling, Norfolk
Below, sunset just north of the Humber

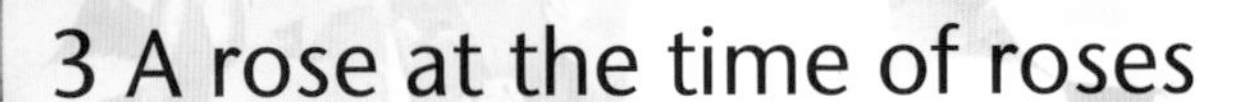

3 A rose at the time of roses

Sir William de la Pole died in 1366. He had lived just long enough to see his son Michael become a knight banneret. Though not yet a lord, this gave Michael the right to ride with his troops to war under a square banner, and not the tapering pennon his father would have flown, and to be summoned to Parliament in his own right. Sir William himself had never had that; when he had been to Parliament it was as a representative of the men of Hull.

Katherine lived another sixteen years. William had obtained a dispensation for her to marry again without the king's permission were she to outlive him, but she never did so. She moved too fast to reinforce her claim to the estates at Myton for the king's liking, and had to pay a fine of £10, no small sum, as a result. But the king then confirmed her lease of them: the fee was a rose at the time of roses, if it should be so demanded, yearly.

The years Katherine lived as a widow saw her eldest son rise much further in the world. Although men claimed he was more at home in the counting house than on the battlefield, Michael de la Pole made his early career as a man at arms, serving mostly under John of Gaunt and the Black Prince, two sons of Edward III. He did well enough as a soldier, although this was after the great victories of the mid-century. He was captured and imprisoned twice, though, and had to pay heavy ransoms to secure his freedom. He came to more prominence serving the Black Prince's son, King Richard II, who inherited his throne as a small child, and never led his troops in battle. As the king grew up, Michael – nearly fifty years his senior – rose in his favour. He served as the king's ambassador, travelling to Milan and Germany. When he was captured by brigands somewhere near the Alps, the king sent his own herald to negotiate his release.

Michael married an heiress from Suffolk: another Katherine, daughter to Sir John Wingfield, one of his comrades in arms. He would have been considerably less rich than his father had been without her inheritance, because as well as the ransoms, Sir William's wealth had been worn down by lawsuits in his later days, and some of his estates had been granted to his younger sons, and used to provide dowries for his daughters, who themselves made good marriages. The Wingfields were a well-established landed family, but not part of the nobility, so this marriage was an appropriate rather than an arrogant step upwards socially.

Sir John Wingfield died of the plague in 1361, and many of the Wingfield estates passed to Katherine and Michael. (They had to wait longer for some, until Katherine's mother died.) Chief among them was the manor of Wingfield, the village in north Suffolk from which his family took its name. It was to be Katherine and Michael's main home for the rest of their lives.

Michael and Katherine produced another large family. Five sons of theirs lived to be adults – Michael, John, Thomas, William and Richard, all born after Sir William died – and so did two daughters, Anne and Margaret.

Michael's greatest achievements came after his mother died, so she never saw him appointed chancellor of England, one of the great offices of state, or learned that the king had granted him an earldom. He became not the earl of Hull, but the earl of Suffolk; we can wonder what his parents would have thought of that.

Inquiries held after his mother's death outline some of the lands she held at that time: in Hull, in Cottingham, Newland, Hesill, West Elvede, Ferriby, Colthorp, Bykerton, Sellebergh, South Couton and Smitherton. She had land in Appilby, but it was hard and stony, and had been left uncultivated. Her holdings included meadows, woodland, two gardens in Hull and a windmill. Michael inherited most of this estate, and moved forward his father's plan to build a religious house in Myton, although he turned it from a nunnery into a more prestigious Carthusian monastery.

He buried his parents in Holy Trinity Church, Hull, probably in the great stone tomb that survives there today. William's effigy wears the merchant's robes in which he had made his fortune, with an outer cloak buttoned close at the neck, a standing cape and buttons down the sides. A dagger hangs from his breast, and at his feet is a lion. Katherine wears a gown buttoned at the waist, with a petticoat under it, and a veil above. Her headdress is mitred in the fashion of the day (William faced eternity bare-headed), and at her feet is a little dog.

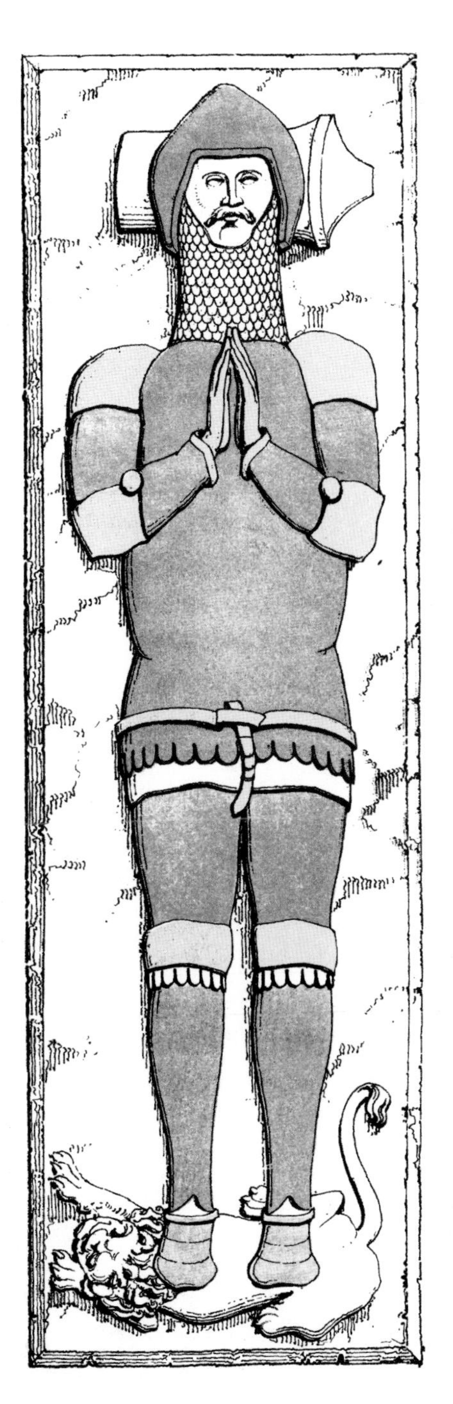

Sir John Wingfield, based on his tomb effigy in St Andrew's Church, Wingfield, Suffolk
Adapted from Napier, *Historical Notices of the Parishes of Swyncombe and Ewelme* (1858)

The de la Pole family

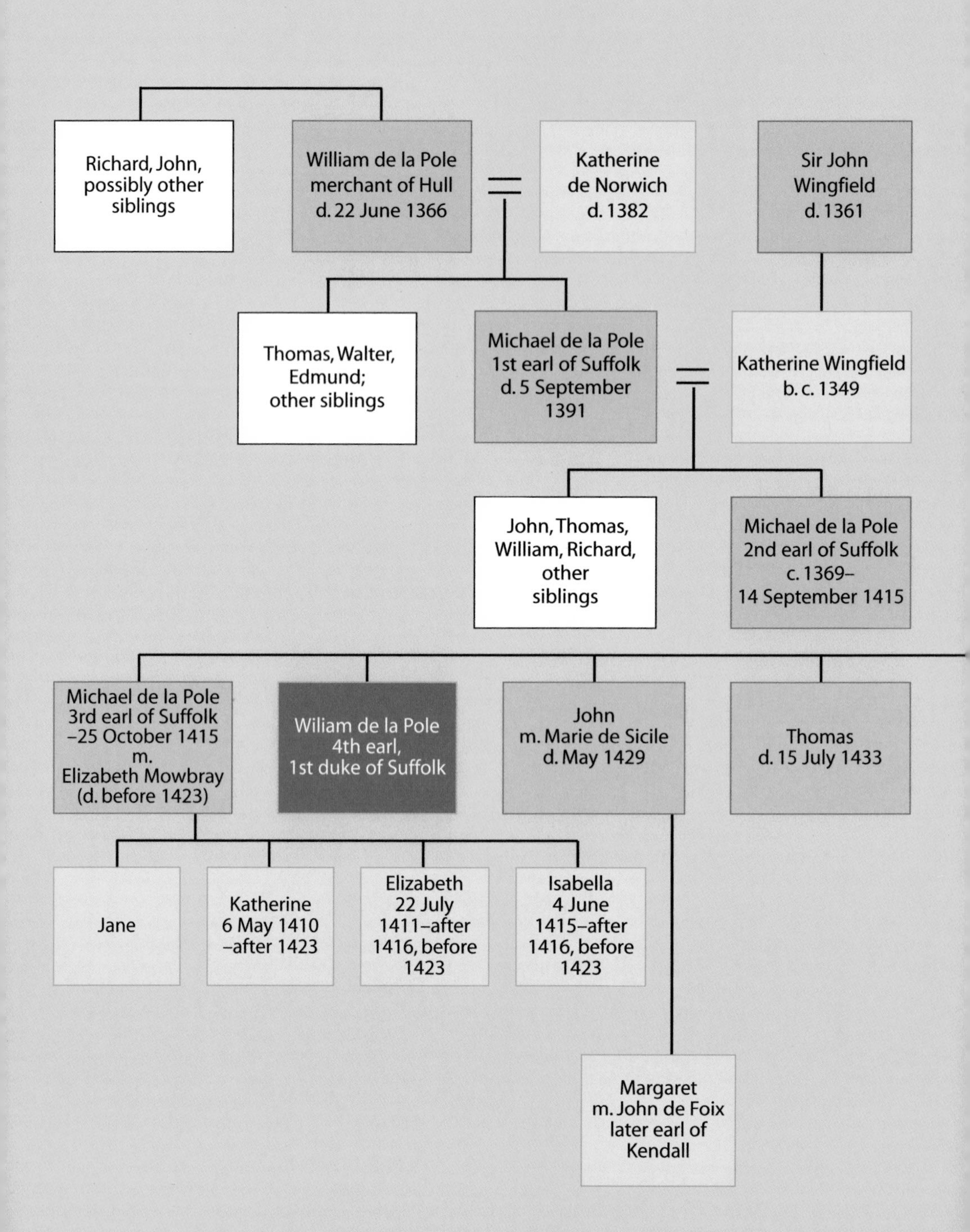

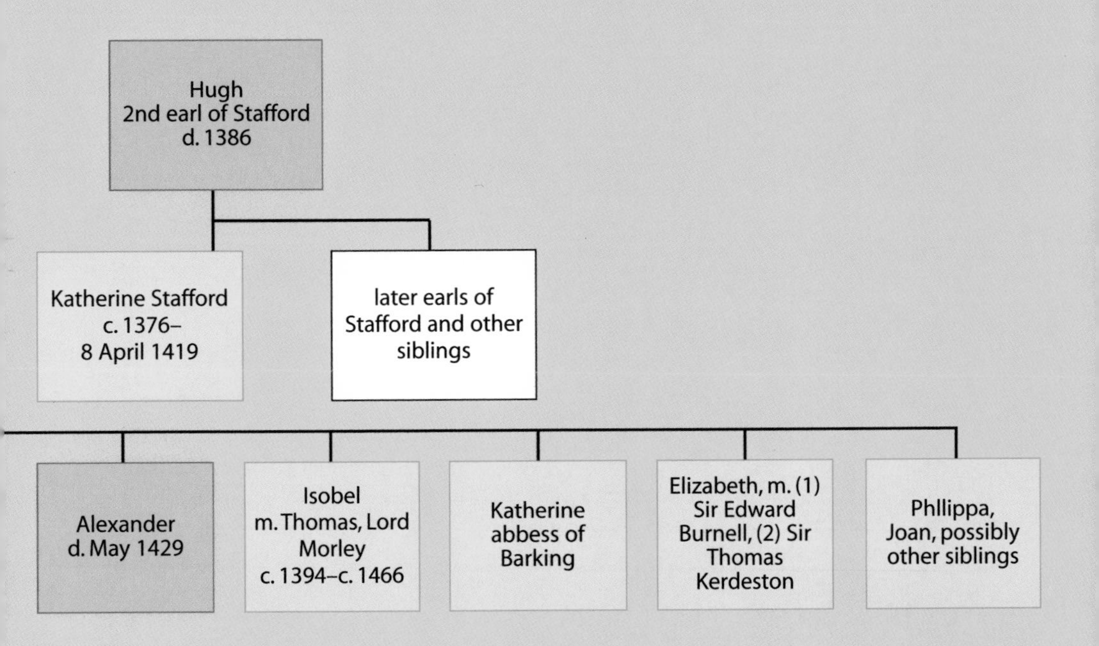

Hugh
2nd earl of Stafford
d. 1386
Katherine Stafford
c. 1376–
8 April 1419
later earls of
Stafford and other
siblings
Alexander
d. May 1429
Isobel
m. Thomas, Lord
Morley
c. 1394–c. 1466
Katherine
abbess of
Barking
Elizabeth, m. (1)
Sir Edward
Burnell, (2) Sir
Thomas
Kerdeston
Phllippa,
Joan, possibly
other siblings

4 A beardless man and a basket of capons

It is not easy to serve a weak master, or a penniless one. Even when no longer a child, King Richard II was both. He was not given to fighting, and it was by his choice that his chancellor pursued a policy of peace. It was a pragmatic choice too: the country could ill afford to continue Edward III's ruinously expensive wars. It was not a policy that won favour with many of the English nobles, however.

To criticize a king was a dangerous thing, but the first earl of Suffolk was a handy alternative target, so he took the brunt of the annoyance that men felt as the glory days of the battle of Crècy slipped into the past, and the English holdings in south-west France were nibbled away by their enemies. His grandfather had been a fisherman, his father had owned ferryboats and brickyards and amassed inordinate wealth, and now this man was chancellor of England, earl and royal favourite. The old nobility were a tightly knit clan, jealous of their privileges of birth and rank, and many of them were clearly not sorry to see him struggle. From 1385 Suffolk and his associates were fighting off allegation after allegation.

His enemies accused him not only of failure to protect English interests, and of poor performance as chancellor, but of using his office for personal gain. It is hard to believe that the son of one of the richest men in England can have needed to divert small annuities for his own benefit, but fortunes do not last forever: taking into account his long-lived mother, his ransoms, his brothers and sisters, aunts and uncles, perhaps it was true that by this time he could barely afford to maintain his high position. He had been taught by a father who had been ruthless, perhaps even criminal at times, and had probably applied some of the lessons he had learned. At any rate, men found complaints to lay against him, and he could not find answers to all of them.

He had kept the trust and friendship of King Richard, but the king needed to placate his enemies and ensure that Parliament continued to grant him funds. In late 1385 Parliament insisted on impeaching Suffolk – that is, trying him on the charges that had been laid against him – before they would agree to a tax being levied.

Men have argued ever since to what extent he was guilty, but his peers found him to be so, although in part the charge was found against the entire king's council. They fined him heavily, and he was imprisoned briefly, but the king soon saw him freed and taken back into favour. Incensed at this, and wishing to drive the king back into line, his opponents went further, and a group of them who became known as the lords appelant forced through charges of treason against Suffolk and several other of the king's close advisers.

Rather than face the uncertain justice of his time, the earl chose to flee across the channel. His wife was dead by then. Most of their surviving sons and daughters were still children; he did not take them with him. He chose a part of France controlled by the English king, and of the two options – Calais and the south-west – he opted for Calais. It was not only the nearer, it was the logical choice for him because his brother Edmund, who had also

Left and above, Tours Cathedral
Right, Le Mans Cathedral

done well as a man at arms, was captain of Calais Castle.

Suffolk cut his hair, shaved off his beard, and disguised himself as a Flemish poulterer. Carrying a basket of capons, he talked the guards into letting him in to the castle. He then had some trouble getting his brother to recognize him.

When he learned what had happened in England, Edmund hesitated over his brother's plea to be given refuge, then passed it on to the governor of Calais, who turned Suffolk down and sent him back to London.

The king allowed him to go to Hull, where he spent a stressful Christmas. Learning that a serjeant had been sent by Parliament to arrest him, on 27 December he fled again. Eventually he came to Paris. He was in exile there when in 1388 the Merciless Parliament found him guilty of treason in his absence, and stripped him of all the lands and wealth that it could take from him.

The earl had managed to escape with a sizeable sum of money, but he spent it all in attempts to win support and regain his title. None of them worked. He died in exile without ever returning to England.

Parliament had agreed that entailed lands (those passed down automatically to the main heir) should not be subject to forfeiture, so his eldest son was left with a handful of the family estates: probably Wingfield, some other lands in East Anglia, and a few of the estates in and around Hull. It was little enough, particularly when his brothers and sisters had to be provided for too. This next generation had neither their grandfather's great riches, nor their father's great title. And they were tainted by the shame of being the descendants of a traitor.

5 A christening, torches, a storm

Sir Michael de la Pole, the eldest son of the Michael who had first been, then ceased to be, the first earl of Suffolk, was married before his father's disgrace, when he was a young boy, and his wife still a child. His father and mother chose carefully: his wife (a third Katherine) was a daughter of the earl of Stafford, so this was an alliance made to fix the family more firmly in the ranks of the aristocracy. It was a sad irony that there was now no title for him to inherit. Nothing could have been done about that while his father was alive and in exile, but after his father's death he had the opportunity to petition the king – though not the right – to have the earldom restored.

It would have been easier if his wife had been rich, but the marriage for status had not also been made for money. Katherine had brought some with her (a thousand pounds, payable in instalments), but not a great fortune by the standards of the nobility, and nor did she ever look likely to inherit more, since she was one of a large family too, with five brothers and perhaps two sisters.

Sir Michael had been old enough in his father's glory days to know what they had lost, and it ate away at him. The fight to regain the title, and the lands that went with it, dominated much of his adult life.

Meanwhile, this second Michael and this third Katherine did as their forebears had done, and proceeded to have a large family.

To judge by his tomb effigy, Michael was a tall and well-built man, whose slightly mournful face was dominated by a drooping moustache. He was about thirty-four, and Katherine possibly in her mid-twenties, when she gave birth to her second son on 10 October 1396. She was at the time at Cotton in Suffolk, where the family owned a manor. Cotton was a few miles to the south-west of Wingfield, and several of their children were born there.

Katherine's first son had been named Michael after his father and grandfather, so her second took the name of his famous great-grandfather. Once his mother was recovered from the birth and the baby strong enough, little William was christened at Cotton Church.

Cotton is a lowland village, nestled amid fields and forests, but the day of the christening was stormy enough for the wind to whip around its huddled houses and its solid stone church. East Anglia is a region filled with great churches built using the proceeds of the wool trade. Cotton's was by no means the largest or finest, but it provided a handsome setting for the service. It has two aisles, set off from the nave by columns that lean inwards just enough to be slightly alarming, and the font that stands there today, with eight cowled monks round the stem, and stone flowers beneath the bowl, is old enough to have been used at William's christening.

Katherine's Stafford relations would not have come from their estates in the Midlands in winter, and few others would have travelled far for the christening of the second son of a man who had yet to regain his father's title, but it was a service of aristocratic standards.

Two bearers with lighted torches led the procession from the manor house to the church. They must have struggled with them in the storm. Baby William had two godfathers. Sir William de Burgate gave him a large gilt cup with a cover, and William Wingfield (doubtless a relative) gave him a silver bell. They gave his nurse twenty shillings and six and eightpence respectively, which suggests she was a formidable servant. The baby had a godmother too, but her name has been lost. There were probably other relatives present: many of Michael's aunts, uncles, brothers and sisters, nephews and nieces lived in the area. Young Michael, William's brother, was then about two, and he had at least one older sister, Isobel. (Probably some of his other sisters – Elizabeth, Katherine, Philippa and Joan, and possibly also Margaret – were older than him as well.) But family life in 1396 was not as it is now: they might not have been at Cotton with their parents, and if they were, they might not have come to the church.

The de la Poles had brought all they needed from the manor: a silver ewer of warm water, a basin, two silver gilt flagons of clarey and malmsey wine, and four silver cups with gilt covers. The torches and candles will have flickered in the draughts as the servants poured water from the ewer into the basin for the baby's sponsors to wash their hands. The priest performed the service and gave him the sacrament, and William was received into the church, saved from the threat of a death unchristened and eternity in limbo. Then the servants poured the clarey and malmsey, and the cups were passed around for Sir Michael and Lady Katherine, the priest, the godparents and the other guests to drink to the baby's health.

He was a healthy child; he thrived.

All photos: St Andrew's Church, Cotton, Suffolk

6 A boy in Suffolk

A child's world swims into focus circle by circle, like a stone thrown into a pond. Nothing is known of William's childhood except for its broader circumstances, but those are enough to give some sense of what it must have been like.

He was an autumn baby, so his first awareness would have been of the chill of approaching winter: the icy draughts of houses in an era before window glass was common, the warmth of a log fire; the blackness of a country night, the soft light of a candle. He would have known the warm smells of mulched leaves and mould. At the centre of his life, first of all, was his wetnurse: aristocratic women did not nurse their own babies. Then there were the other servants of the household; for most of the time not his parents' household, but the household in which he was boarded, since that was the usual practice for rich families of his era. He would have come to know the men and women who worked from dawn till dusk, cleaning the house, minding the fire in the kitchen and cooking the supper, feeding the animals and tending the household's strips of land. If his parents lived in luxury, their children probably did not; they were cared for by women in moderate circumstances, respectable but not affluent. Once weaned, he tasted soggy-centred wrinkled apples, hot broth, fish from the stew-ponds, meat on feast days.

William almost certainly grew up in the county of Suffolk: perhaps in Cotton, perhaps in another of the villages or small towns that dotted a well-populated region. A child of a rich family, he would have lived comfortably. Everyone knew cold in the winter, but William would not have known long spells of hunger. He would not have known solitude; there would have been servants to tend him most, if not all of the day.

As the winters and summers of his early childhood passed, he would have come to know the wide skies of Suffolk; the changeable weather, more dry than in most parts, of eastern England; the huddled wattle and daub houses of the villages, the strip fields planted with vegetables, the orchards, the horses, carts, pigs and chickens of the smallholdings. People lived tight, in small communities, encircled by woodland and pasture, most of it owned by lords or the king himself, and out of bounds to the common villagers.

He would have known churches, dominant in every village, their towers clustered thick in every town; come to know the multitude of priests, monks and friars, with their different hues of rough dark robes. Once old enough, he would have sat with the chattering villagers through masses; if he was lucky, heard song. He would have seen death, of animals and of men, women and children too: from sickness often, from old age for the fortunate, from accidents and violence. He would have felt blows; the practical learning of early childhood would have been cuffed and buffeted into him. He would have learned to fear God, and go through the rituals men went through to try to please Him; and come to believe in the heaven that awaited him, were he to be good, in the life after this one, and in the hell in which he would burn if he died a sinner.

He would have learned, young enough, that his family was grander than the ones in which he was boarded; he would have been brought to meet his parents, though probably not frequently. We can think of him, a child in a cart, bumping over the ruts of a country track, with a good escort of horsemen to protect him, headed for Wingfield, up to the great gatehouse of the castle that was his parents' chief home. It is a low-lying place, set amid trees, so the gatehouse emerges with suddenness as you approach. It must have been a daunting sight to a small child, with its great towers, sixty feet high, built of dull dark flint, with inset panels where the stones had been cut and knapped into a black sheen, and

Wingfield, Suffolk

Wingfield Castle

inlaid with paler stone in an elegant flushwork pattern, all of it shakily reflected in the waters of the encircling moat. Perhaps it was his mother or father who first held him up and traced out for him the coats of arms of Wingfield and de la Pole, set in the stone.

They would not have told him, in time this will be yours, because that was not what they hoped for. He would have met Michael, his big brother, and learned soon enough that there was an importance to Michael that did not attach to him. He was valued to an extent, but not the heir, and increasingly as he grew, just one of a horde of children. His mother must have been almost continuously pregnant, since perhaps a dozen of her children survived infancy. As well as his sisters and his elder brother, William was to have at least three younger brothers, John, Thomas and Alexander.

Past infancy, he perhaps spent more time at Wingfield, and came to know it well. His parents were not at Wingfield much of the time, though: they travelled around their other manors, from Yorkshire to London and back again. His father spent time at court – often at Westminster, but elsewhere too, as the king himself moved around the country – and travelled abroad, in the king's service. But William would not have travelled with him, and would not have known this wider life till he was grown.

Wingfield was, and remains, a sprawling village: it is about a mile from the castle to the village church. Its origins perhaps lie in the Saxon era, so it was a long-established village in William's time, with many houses that were a hundred years old or more.

Parts of the castle were old too, but much of the building William was to come to know was new: it had been built largely by his grandfather, the first earl, about twelve to fifteen years before his birth, after permission to crenellate it – to turn it from manor to castle – had been given by the king. Though built in a grand style, it was more of a country house than a stronghold: a square of buildings set in the moat – towers at each corner, the gatehouse, a hall, servants' quarters and private rooms – around a central courtyard. When the family were in residence they had a large retinue of servants with them: personal servants who tended their clothes and saw to their toilet, household servants, chaplains, kennel boys and grooms, and more. There would have been visiting stewards, lawyers, bailiffs and other retainers, who handled affairs on their estates; visiting priests, from the college of monks next to the church that Sir John Wingfield had set up; visits too from the other great families of the county.

It was probably his mother who taught William his first letters, songs and prayers. She seems to have been a strong-willed woman, perhaps a little forbidding to her young children. Some of her servants' wardrobe records survive; they write of her as 'The Lady', as if there could be no other. The family owned a number of books, including primers, prayer books also used for learning to read, and a handsome book (most likely a missal, a religious book) that Katherine's father the earl of Stafford had given her, with gold and silver paint used in the illustrations, and a coronet on the cover. William must have looked at this many times; till he was older, he would not have been allowed to touch it.

He would have learned to ride horses, learned to train hounds, and hawks and falcons; learned to hunt, probably while he was still very young, since this was a great aristocratic pursuit, a major pleasure in life for those fortunate enough to have the opportunity to enjoy it. The woods and meadows that the villagers might not enter were open to William's family, since they owned them. All around Wingfield was a great park, which also encompassed two neighbouring villages, Stradbroke and Sternfield. This too had been created by his grandfather, with the permission of the king, on the land that was not reserved for the king himself to hunt on. The deer and the boar, and the rabbit too, were the food of the rich. They and their servants would catch them, kill them, bring them back to the castle kitchens. There would have been quiet days when William headed out to the meadows with his brothers, their servants and their hawks; busy days when men from miles around gathered for a hunt with hounds. It was perhaps on hunting days that William saw most of his father, and came to know the other knights and lords of Suffolk. But this was not a child-centred society: the role of a young boy was to listen and to serve.

St Mary's Church, North Tuddenham, Norfolk
Photo Mike Dixon

The very rich often used tutors for their sons, but perhaps by the time William was old enough for booklearning he had taken it in that his family, though much richer than the common village folk, were reduced in status from what they had been a generation or two before. Most likely there were no tutors for him and Michael, but they were sent to school; sent away to school, since there was no school in Wingfield or Cotton, and the village children there would have had little or no formal education. His brother Alexander was sent a few years later to board with a schoolmaster in Ipswich, so much the same was probably done for William. It would have been a small group, of boys from affluent families, though not all as high in status as his own: lads destined to be lawyers, merchants and men at arms, learning together the seven liberal arts that formed the core of education at this time: the trivium based around speech – grammar, logic and rhetoric – and the quadrium based around number – arithmetic, geometry, music and astronomy. William could well have been a quick student, because he grew to be a well-educated man, but his learning would have been beaten into him all the same.

A generation or two earlier the lessons were conducted in French in schools such as this one, but that had changed before William's time. English was the first language of educated men as well as those of lower degree, although many – William included – learned to speak and write both French and English, and acquired something of the Latin that was still the language of the lawcourts.

Out of the classroom, he would have begun to learn to fight. He would have known from very young that his destiny was to be a man at arms. His younger brother Thomas went into the church; William might have been given the choice of that, but more likely not. He would have begun with the sticks and wooden swords of childhood, learning to fence with the other boys, to handle a lance as he rode, and tilt at targets. As he grew, he would have graduated to proper weapons. He would have watched tournaments and jousts, and in time taken part in them. The battleaxe, the mace, the sword and lance were among the main knightly weapons. Common men learned to handle the great longbows, six feet high, that provided the backbone to the English armies, but this was not a knight's weapon, and since its mastery demanded hours of practice daily, William probably did not use it.

As well as learning to wield his weapons and control his horse, William would have learned the lore of chivalry, the complex code by which warfare was conducted in his era. He would have learned to recognize the shields and devices of the great lords (and the lesser captains), the formalities of offering battle and agreeing terms.

Ipswich was the county town of Suffolk, and a thriving port, set on the wide estuary of the Orwell. Suffolk has always been a quiet rural area, with good farmland, and small towns grown rich on the wool trade, such as Long Melford and Lavenham. Norwich was the greatest city in the region of East Anglia, and at the time one of the largest in England, but it was a good day's journey to the north of Wingfield; Ipswich, perhaps half the size, was a similar distance to the south, far enough away that William would not have made the journey frequently. Roughly halfway between Wingfield and Ipswich was Framlingham, the huge castle that was the main seat of the dukes of Norfolk.

William would have spent much time in Ipswich, and grown up familiar with the muddy estuary and the flat coastline of Suffolk, as well as the rolling inland countryside. If he was not quite a child of the sea, still it was familiar to him from a young age.

He would have known the thirteen churches of Ipswich, the sounds of their bells, the cries of the

Ipswich

shopkeepers and the hawkers. He would have known the quays and the ships large and small that travelled along the coast of England, and across the Channel to France and the Low Countries, carrying wool from the Suffolk and Norfolk downlands, and bringing back wine, cloth and other goods. He would have watched the fishing boats come into port, and eaten their catch. He probably did not travel abroad as a child, but perhaps he spent some time mucking about with the other boys on the small boats of the Orwell and the coastline round about.

For a young child, life is as it is; it is only later that children realize it could be, has been, other. In Suffolk, as elsewhere, there would have been houses left to fall to ruin, entire villages deserted, abbeys where every monk had succumbed to the sickness and nothing was left but the graveyard, lands no longer tilled as they once had been. In time William would have learned that this was the result of the multitude of deaths a half-century before his birth, when the great plague of 1348 and 1349, and the smaller but still devastating epidemics that followed it, had reduced England's population (indeed, almost all Europe's population) to perhaps little more than half what it had been in 1300. He had been born in the dog days of a cruel century; and throughout his lifetime, and for generations after it, men would fear the return of the silent, invisible bringer of death.

In time, too, he would have learned of the first Sir William de la Pole, and his descendants. He would have learned of the title so hard-won by his grandfather, and so bitterly lost; and of the long struggle by his father to regain it. Sir Michael was made the second earl of Suffolk by King Richard II in 1398, ten years after his father had lost his title, when William was only two years old. It did not last, though. King Richard was deposed shortly afterwards, and Henry of Lancaster seized the throne, becoming King Henry IV, and founding the Lancastrian dynasty. The new king annulled all Richard's final acts, and Michael had to begin again. The ripples this caused would have spread through his relations, servants, retainers. If William did not then understand the full meaning of this, he would have sensed, surely, his parents' fury and despair.

And he would have become aware in the years that followed of the long hours of attendance at Westminster, the pleas and petitions, the courting of powerful men who might press the family's case. It was not until 1405, when he was a boy of nine, that the title and at least some of the family lands were permanently returned. Even then, there were other lands that the king had granted elsewhere, and that could not be given back. For his family – as for many – the first years of the fifteenth century were not a time of glorious ease, but one of struggle and uncertainty.

7 The silver wings and the leopards' heads

The county of Suffolk in the early fifteenth century must have been as good a place as any, and better than most, for a young boy to grow up. England was a comparatively peaceable land: it had not been invaded for many generations, and most of the wars that Englishmen had fought had been pursued elsewhere. Although the major towns were walled, the villages were not; there must have seemed little need. The churches were built with large windows to let in the light, not like fortresses for refuge in times of trouble.

There was no major road that ran near, let alone through Wingfield, and although Ipswich was much larger and busier, still it was a small town. William was not a child of cities and courts, but his horizons would have expanded, soon enough.

The second earl, William's father, was abroad on the king's service between December 1408 and August 1409, as the senior English representative at the Council of Pisa, a conference aimed at ending the schism that had left Western Christianity with two rival popes. He was then most likely in England until 1412, when he sailed back to France with a small army headed by the duke of Clarence, the king's second son. So his older sons probably saw most of him in the years of William's middle teens. He was thirteen when his father returned from Pisa, sixteen when he left again for France. If the earl took them up to Hull, or down to London – as like as not he did both – it was probably during these years.

The mud flats of the Humber are not very different from those of the Orwell, but Yorkshire is in many ways a harder county. The north wind is colder there, the open spaces wider. Men spoke there in a harsh-edged accent, that those from farther south might have struggled to understand. To Yorkshiremen, their county is the centre of the world. William would have seen the great tomb of his great-grandfather, the houses that the first Sir William de la Pole had built, the monastery his grandfather had founded, the shipyards, brickyards and ferries. But perhaps he understood too why a family that wished to advance at court would have shifted its focus to the gentler county of Suffolk, so much nearer to London.

Church of St Peter Hungate, Norwich

He probably went to the court at Westminster with his father – not often, perhaps once or twice, to see and be seen by the king. In this era a boy's investment as a knight had lost some of the religious significance it had held in earlier centuries, but it was still an important ceremony. Men at arms might be knighted at any time in their careers, but the son of an earl would not have had to wait until he achieved feats in battle: William was probably knighted by the king himself, at the conventional age of fifteen. This signified a real change in rank, and his was a society where a man's rank determined much of the pattern of his life. His father's experience was enough to teach him how much men valued their position. In a society where formality was deeply ingrained, men thereafter would have called him Sir William.

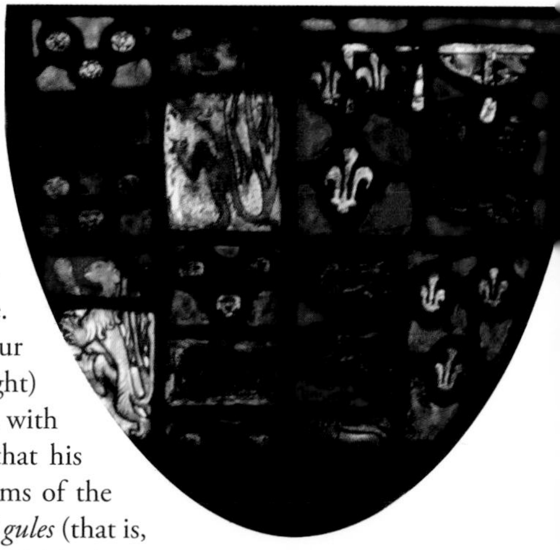

A knight acquired a coat of arms, which identified him not only in battle, but throughout his life. William's shield was quartered: divided into four sections, two of which (the top left and bottom right) carried the arms of the de la Poles, the blue shield with the horizontal gold band and the leopards' heads that his great-grandfather had been granted, and two the arms of the Wingfields, his grandmother's family: *silver on a bend gules* (that is, a red diagonal stripe) *three pairs of wings silver*. (Men of this time were fond of puns, so the wings on the shield were a deliberate echo of the family name.) He did not carry the Staffords' arms, perhaps because unlike with the Wingfields, there were others who did so. (The stained-glass shields shown here have been patched with glass from other sources, but the one above – from Iffley Church in Oxfordshire – is basically William's son's arms, and the shield left, from Wingfield Church, shows William's own arms on the left-hand side.)

King Henry IV was a close contemporary of William's father, so in the years when William was growing up he was by no means an old man. But his reign had become a dour one, dominated by his efforts to secure the crown he had usurped and do down his enemies – in Wales, Scotland and England itself. In its later years it was also marred by his ill health. In the early years of the new century the king suffered repeatedly from serious attacks of an unknown illness, and he was disfigured by a disease that might have been leprosy. He probably seemed a forbidding character to a young lad, but his court was the centre too for his four sons, much closer in age to William, and possibly William met the king's heir, Prince Henry, or Thomas of Clarence, the prince under whom his father was to serve.

He probably also spent some time at university. His brothers Thomas and Alexander were both to do so a few years later, and although Thomas was a destined churchman, and so obliged to face a long schooling, Alexander was not, so it was most likely what the second earl and his countess chose for all their sons. Thomas went to Oxford and Alexander to Cambridge, so this gives no clue which of the two was chosen for William. He would have gone to the university in his mid-teens, younger than students today, and most likely with no intention of staying for years. He would have lodged at a hall or college that accepted laymen (many were only for the clergy) or in the town, listened to lectures, debated with the academics and his fellow students; perhaps worked hard, but probably also enjoyed the freedom from his schoolmaster's and his mother's careful watch. Both here and at court, he would have met the other young men from prominent families with whom he would deal throughout the rest of his life. Even at college, he would have been attended by a valet and other servants.

Norwich Cathedral

He perhaps spent some time as an esquire in the home of another noble family, but no details of this survive. And not least, he would have learned something of his mother's family. Their homes were well distant from East Anglia in the English Midlands, so he would not have known them as intimately as he knew the de la Poles and Wingfields who lived in Norfolk and Suffolk, visited with his mother and hunted with his father.

The Staffords in this era had been no luckier than the de la Poles. William's uncle Ralph, his mother's eldest brother, had been murdered by Richard II's half-brother in Yorkshire in 1385, and it was said that his anger and grief had contributed to his grandfather Hugh, the second earl, dying on pilgrimage at Rhodes in 1386, the same year that the first earl of Suffolk had fled into exile. Three of Ralph's brothers in succession had then inherited the earldom, and none of them had lived long to enjoy it. By 1403 all three of them were dead, and the earldom had been inherited by a baby.

Even by the standards of these tough times that was a cruel sequence. It must have hit Lady Katherine hard. Perhaps it was no wonder if she had learned to repay life in the same hard coin. And it was a blow for the rest of the family too: these were their only noble relations, and in this era there was no powerful and well-established earl of Stafford to support their causes at court or in the king's Parliament. But perhaps at university William met another Stafford, a slightly more distant relative. John Stafford took holy orders, studied law at Oxford in 1413, and had already received the patronage of the archbishop of Canterbury. This man, perhaps eight or nine years William's senior, was to rise high in both the church and the king's administration, and be an important ally of his in the years to come.

8 Two sad families and three marriages

Between boarding out, school and university, William would have seen comparatively little by modern standards of his sisters and youngest brothers, and perhaps not a great deal even of Michael and John, the brothers closest to him in age. But his family was in its way a tight-knit one, and these relations were of course important to him.

When he was a growing lad, and the battle to regain the earldom had been won, one of his parents' main preoccupations would have been to make good marriages for their older sons and daughters, and in particular for Michael. Though obviously less occupied by this himself, still William must have been aware of the lengthy negotiations that typically led to a wedding of an heir to an earldom.

The troubles of both families had taught Earl Michael and his wife to tread cautiously, and perhaps their temperaments led them this way too. The earl seems never to have aspired to do as his father did, and forge a great career for himself at court. He was looking to consolidate the family's fortunes, and since he and Katherine had a comparative lack of contacts elsewhere in the country, they looked to achieve this in East Anglia.

They would have wanted to find a match for young Michael from among the nobility: their position within it was very important to them, and needed to be strengthened. It was not a large group in those days. There were around 50 lords in England, who were in the main markedly more affluent and powerful than those other men entitled to bear arms. By no means all would have had daughters of the right age and qualifications. And they would not have looked for a bride with royal blood, something that might have left them open to criticism on the grounds of over-ambition.

The de la Poles found Michael's bride from the neighbouring family of Mowbray. Elizabeth was the daughter of Thomas, the first duke of Norfolk, a man who had had just as bad fortune as the first earl of Suffolk towards the end of Richard II's reign. After a quarrel with Henry of Lancaster (the future King Henry IV), he had been stripped of his dukedom and exiled from England. He died in Venice of the plague in 1399. His son Thomas was allowed to resume the family's lesser titles, the earldoms of Norfolk and Nottingham, but not the dukedom. Disaffected and quarrelsome, he fell out with Henry IV and joined a rebellion against him. He and his colleagues were captured by the king, who had him summarily beheaded at York in 1405. The family lost their lands as a result, including their castle of Framlingham, at least for a while: at this time it was granted to Prince Henry, the king's eldest son.

Effigy from St Mary's Church, Burgate, Suffolk
Glass from Abbey of l'Epau, Le Mans, France

Another Mowbray brother, John, inherited the title from Thomas, but the two disasters had been enough to all but break the family. Once much grander than the de la Poles, they were now in as bad shape, if not worse, so this was an alliance of two great families fallen on difficult times. But each side must have calculated that both in time would regain their position, and that this union would benefit them in working to do so.

Elizabeth must have been about the same age as Michael, and they married young – if not as children, then as very young adults. When William was in his teens, his brother, scarcely older, was becoming a father. There may have been a daughter Jane, born about 1409, when her parents could only have been fifteen or sixteen. Katherine was born in 1410, and Elizabeth in 1411. All girls: not fortunate, in an era where inheritance was normally through the male line. But Michael and Elizabeth must have expected sons to follow.

These events would have distanced William from his older brother to some extent: though close in age, their lives were becoming very different. The earl gave the young couple a manor of their own, Benhall, which was a few miles to the south of Wingfield, near Saxmundham, so Michael would have spent much of his time there with his wife, and this too would have meant that William saw less of him.

If the earl and his wife tried to find good matches for their younger sons too, they did not succeed. William did not marry young as Michael had done, and nor did any of his other brothers.

At least some of his sisters married in these years, though. Isobel, the eldest, was married perhaps as early as 1403 – although they too would both have been children if this was the case – to Sir Thomas Morley, from a substantial East Anglian family whose main estate was at Hingham in south Norfolk, half a day's journey or so to the north of Wingfield. Morley was about three years William's senior, and they were to fight together many times in the years that followed. Elizabeth married another local man at arms, Sir Edward Burnell. The third sister, Katherine, became a nun, and in later years at least, she was at Barking Abbey in Essex. Barking had been patronized by kings and princes since its foundation in the seventh century. It was regarded as the premier religious house for women in England, so she was in no sense shunted off: her parents paid a good sum to get this covetable position for her. But as nuns are, she was lost to her family, and after she entered the convent William probably saw her only very rarely, if ever.

Church of St Peter Mancroft, Norwich
Photo Mike Dixon

9 King Henry, King Henry, and a king made of glass

By the time his father sailed to France in 1412 with Thomas of Clarence, the second son of King Henry IV, William was old enough to take some interest in the events that had sent him there. This was not only for his father's sake. He was approaching the age when he needed to start to make his own way in the world, and if this was to be as a man at arms, it was of real importance to him whether, and where, the king planned to fight a war in which he might take part.

Any war would almost certainly be with one of England's neighbours: the great era of the Crusades was long past, and the English had fought the Welsh, the Scots, the Irish, the French, in weary repetition throughout the centuries. Of these, the best option from a man at arms' viewpoint was the French: in wars with the French there was a chance of real gain, while there was little of that from the battles in Britain and Ireland. So even if he had had no more than the average intelligent lad's interest in politics, William would have learned something of the tangled web that linked and divided England and France.

Fifty years earlier – in 1360 – the Treaty of Bretigny (which closed the phase of war that the first Sir William de la Pole had helped to fund) had marked a high point in the long war the English had been fighting intermittently against the French. By it King Edward III had gained possession of large regions of south-west France and some land in north-west France, held clear of any obligation to the French king. But there was still other territory in France to which the English kings had a claim: not least, the duchy of Normandy, from which William the Conqueror had come to England three and a half centuries earlier. There was no French duke of Normandy: the English kings had the only claim to that title. But a claim is not possession, and even at his peak Edward III had not controlled Normandy.

And to get what he had obtained, at Bretigny Edward had agreed to surrender his claim to Normandy, and the still larger claim that the English kings had long made, to the throne of France itself.

But the treaty had not held, and subsequent phases of the war had lost Edward much of the land he had been granted by it. His successor Richard II had regained none of it, and nor, by 1412, had Henry IV. As a result, it could be argued that Bretigny was far enough distant, and well enough broken as a treaty, that it could justifiably be ignored by a different English king from the one who had made it.

In spite of his usurpation of the English throne, Henry IV had a credible claim to the throne of France. The laws of inheritance were not clear in that era, and generations of intermarriage made

From the de la Pole tomb, Holy Trinity Church, Hull

it possible for there to be rival claims which could be pursued with conviction, and some justice too. But King Henry was a sick and ageing man, and men must have known that nothing would be done to press the Lancastrian claim until after his death. More, England was not yet recovered from the plagues, its population was still sparse, and its crown was far from rich. But issues such as these had never yet deterred the English from making war.

The situation in France was chaotic, and it provided opportunities for the English to interfere, to make trouble, to fight for gain. This was broadly what Clarence, the earl of Suffolk and their fellow men at arms had set out to do. Nor was this wholly negative. When the French were strong they endangered English trade and raided the English shoreline. Naturally the English wished to keep their neighbours weak so these inconveniences did not afflict them.

Claim what the English kings might, there was of course an incumbent king of France, and he did not come from the house of Lancaster. But he was not just weak, he was mad. This was Charles VI, the contemporary representative of the house of Valois. He held fairly firm control over northern and central France, and had claim to the south, although the Valois kings rarely travelled far below the Loire, the great river that curled across central France. His madness had come on him in 1392, quite spectacularly. Riding through a forest, he had attacked and killed four of his own entourage, and tried to kill his nephew too. Since then he had had moments of sanity, but they were increasingly few. In his mad phases he would run, howling like a wolf, down the corridors of his palace of the Louvre; he would think himself made of glass, and accuse his courtiers of trying to shatter him.

France had no coherent royal council that could govern in his place. Instead there was a battle for power between the great dukes of the country: Burgundy, Orleans, Alençon, Bourbon and others. Unlike English nobles, whose titles were largely ceremonial – the earl of Suffolk did not own, or claim dues from, the entire county of Suffolk – the dukes of

Church of St Peter and St Thomas, Stambourne, Essex
Photo Mike Dixon

France had substantial control over the regions after which they were named. There were also lesser but still powerful lords, courtiers and captains, and the queen, all fighting in the vacuum that the king's madness had created.

The queen of France, Isabeau of Bavaria, was by this time little better thought of than her husband. She was largely estranged from him, and had set up her own – rather shabby – court at Troyes, to the east of Paris, while the king in his mad phases remained neglected in the capital. They had had many children, but most of them were weaklings. Son after son became dauphin, heir to their father's throne, only to die a year or two later. Their seven daughters were almost equally sickly. If the youngest few were less feeble than the rest, that was because, men whispered, these ones, born years after the king's madness had come upon him, were not Charles's children at all.

The greatest of the dukes were richer and more formidable than this pitiable king. Of them all, the most powerful was the duke of Burgundy – known as John the Fearless – who controlled two great sweeps of land: Burgundy in east-central France (stretching from Savoy in the south-east to Auxerre in its north-west corner), and much of the lowlands that bordered France to the north, including the Artois (the territory around Arras) and Flanders. Opposed to Burgundy, and fighting to keep him in check, was a rival faction which came to be known as the Armagnacs: its leaders were the count of Armagnac and the duke of Orleans, who held sizeable lands in southern and mid-central France respectively.

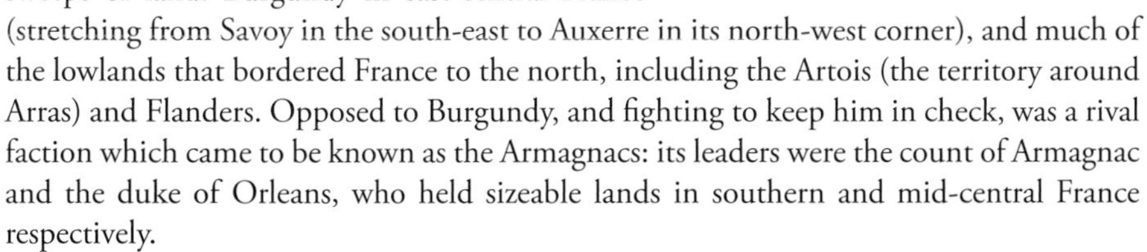

Trinity Church, Vendome, France

In 1407 Louis duke of Orleans had been ambushed and killed in Paris, and John the Fearless had admitted responsibility. Since then, the enmity between the two factions had reached the pitch of a civil war. It was the Armagnacs who turned to the English, hoping that this mutual enemy would help them fight off the threat from Burgundy. An English army gleefully took up the offer and rampaged through France, but before they could do too much damage, the Armagnacs lost their nerve, came to a tentative reconciliation with the Burgundians, and paid the English off. It cost them, in hostages as well as wages: the younger brother of the duke of Orleans (who was the son of the man who had been killed by John the Fearless) was despatched to England for that purpose.

So this venture had achieved little for the French, but it had been profitable for Clarence, and for the earl of Suffolk too. His sons probably hoped there would be more such sorties, with the French proving less squeamish next time. When Henry IV died in the spring of 1413, not long after the earl of Suffolk had returned home, and his son Prince Henry took the throne as Henry V, the odds of this happening much improved.

Men knew it had been predicted that the king would die in Jerusalem. He did, in a sense, but not on crusade: he died in the Jerusalem chamber of the Abbot of Westminster's house.

William was then 16, and the new king was only ten years his senior. Although there continued to be other claimants to the English throne, Henry IV had done a solid job of making it safe for his eldest son, who was a bright, forceful, well-regarded young man, and one step farther from the taint of usurpation. His three brothers – Clarence, John of Bedford and Humphrey of Gloucester – were all older than William, but not by much. They were all strong, healthy, good fighting men. They wanted a war as much as William did, and knowing first-hand from Clarence of the disarray at the French court, they knew it was a good time to pursue one in France.

There was pragmatism here, but there was more than that to it. Henry V believed sincerely in his claims to France. It was his family's homeland, and his ancestors had been its rulers. It was his obligation to defend the French territory the English still held, and this called for aggression if it was not to be scratched away by the French nobles. It was his duty to try to regain the lands that had once been his family's, and it was the duty of his English lords to support him in doing so.

Coming to the end of his childhood, and approaching the time when he could join his father and his elder brother in fighting with and for the king, William must have felt himself to be in a good position. He was healthy and intelligent. His parents were alive, and at least most of his brothers and sisters had survived their childhood, things that could not be taken for granted in these times. The earldom had been restored; the disgrace of his grandfather was receding into the middle distance; the family were comfortably off, respected and respectable. As a younger son he would have known his inheritance prospects were limited. His father might live for many more years, and his brother Michael and his wife were producing a sizeable brood of their own; there

was no point hoping that the earldom would come to him, and almost all the family's lands would go with the title. Anything that could be spared would be spread thinly between him and his sisters and younger brothers. But he had opportunities to make his way, and support while he began to do so. He lived in a land at peace, and had hopes of sailing to another to make war.

Patience was required. The new king could not have gone to war the moment he took the throne of England. He had to establish himself, and plan his tactics; he also had to make efforts at negotiation with the French before he resorted to force. So while William was finishing his education, the king embarked on a round of diplomacy. To begin with, Henry did not mention his claim to the French throne: he concentrated on the more realizable claims. At a parliament in the second year of his reign – in November 1414, when William was just eighteen – the chancellor spoke in his opening address of the king's intention to claim his inheritance in France:

> our most sovereign lord the king desires especially that good and wise action should be taken against his enemies outside the realm, and furthermore how he will strive for the recovery of the inheritance and right of his crown outside the realm, which has for a long time been withheld and wrongfully retained, since the time of his progenitors and predecessors kings of England.

This was a public claim both to Gascony and Guyenne in the south-west of France, and to Normandy and the surrounding territories in the north-west. These words would have been repeated across England. William's father the earl was there at Westminster to hear them, and to pass them on to his sons and his servants.

The king negotiated both with the duke of Burgundy and with the French king's representatives. One significant bargaining counter was his marriage. Though in his mid-twenties, he had not yet taken a wife. He offered his hand to King Charles's youngest daughter: an alliance through her could have made him a credible third force in France. But the negotiations failed, and by 1415 it was becoming apparent that the king would muster his army and press his claims by force.

St Margaret's Church, Herringfleet, Suffolk

10 Out of the fire and out of the nunnery

This story has come down in history, but it seems to date from some years after the death of those who feature in it; some think it to be untrue.

Michael de la Pole, William's brother, and his young wife Elizabeth had a daughter Jane, their first-born child. When she was young, as a result of her nursemaid's negligence she fell into a fire, and although she survived the accident, she was badly disfigured by burns. Her family judged that a girl made so hideous would be unmarriageable, so they had her put in a nunnery. But the life did not suit her, and when she reached the age of discretion she chose not to take vows, but to leave the nunnery and return to her family.

Her family were angered by this; her grandmother, Lady Katherine, particularly so. But Jane was a stubborn girl, and swore that the nunnery was not for her. Meeting a will to match her own, Katherine offered her a compromise. She might stay in her grandmother's household, but she should tell no one whose daughter she was. She was passed off as Katherine's god-daughter, the orphaned child of a poor gentlewoman.

In spite of her family's harsh verdict on her, Jane was found a husband, or perhaps rather she found herself one: the son of an honest and well-off Suffolk yeoman, whose name was William. They had children, and grandchildren; we must hope this made her happy.

It was only much later in her life, when Lady Katherine was dead and her threats gone with her, and Jane was a widow, that she confessed this to a doctor. It was he who told her she should make the story better known. Her story showed the workings of Almighty God, he pointed out: it was her duty to reveal this to the world.

Church of St Peter Mancroft, Norwich
Photo Mike Dixon

11 A muster and a plot

The late spring and early summer of 1415 was the time of the great muster. It would have dominated the lives of hundreds, even thousands of men after the indentures to draw up the army were sealed by the king on 29 April, and Sir William de la Pole was one of them. Negotiations continued with the various French factions even after this date, but meanwhile the English army was being put in place.

There was no great standing army in those days: troops were mustered when they were required. This was done in a rough pyramid fashion: the king gave his orders to his lords, and they in turn signed up captains, who signed up their men. The basic unit was a lance, which consisted of a man at arms, his squire, one or two pages, and normally three archers. These fighting men were supported by servants who did not fight: cooks, armourers, fletchers, chaplains, trumpeters, grooms, heralds and messengers, and many more trades, though some at least of the fighting men also doubled in these roles.

The second earl of Suffolk committed himself to raise 160 lances, and he gave the command of 20 of them to each of his two oldest sons. This was eighteen-year-old William's first command, and he must have been pleased by this confidence his father showed in him, and by finding himself for once on a par with Michael.

His main task in these weeks would have been to sign up the men. He could expect to find willing volunteers, for this was a paid army. The men were not always paid what was promised on time, but what they were promised was good by comparison with civilian wages, and they could hope to supplement it with ransoms from prisoners and booty from places they sacked. Men of all degrees – respected and experienced captains, young ploughhands, drifters and criminals, retainers of the family who knew their duty – would have turned up at the gatehouse at Wingfield Castle, ready to sign on with the earl and his sons. They were not all young men: they ranged in age from lads like William to veterans in their seventies. But it would also have been necessary for William, like his brother and his father, to ride about the family's estates, and to Ipswich and the other

Church of St Peter and St Thomas, Stambourne, Essex
Photo Mike Dixon

Trinity Church, Vendome

towns in Suffolk and beyond, seeking out men he knew, and strangers too – friends from his schooldays, men he had hunted with at Wingfield or Framlingham, men whom the family's stewards recommended to him – and putting them together into a force he could depend on. Naturally the captains competed for the best men, and it was necessary to be active and forceful in these weeks, if he was not to be left with the dregs that no other contingent wanted.

At the same time the rest of the earl's household, and many people beyond it, were helping to assemble the supplies that were needed. The women opened storechests and shook out banners and surcoats, and set to work to sew many more. Experienced tradesmen and those they could round up to help them made arrows and bowstrings, horseshoes, tents for the men to sleep in. The armourers checked over the suits of arms, repairing joints and bashing out dents. The cooks prepared the rations – the men were ordered to bring with them food for the first few days, so meat needed to be dried, fish salted – and the herbalists the medications: armies always brewed sickness.

The armour that men at arms wore at this time was plate armour – the chain mail of earlier generations had become outmoded – immensely heavy, designed to cover a man from head to toe. It was an expensive investment, and it was the men who could not afford their own armour and sword who generally served as archers. They had lighter protection, typically toughened leather jerkins and iron helmets.

The army was to contain nearly every able-bodied fighting man in England, as well as a number of foreign mercenaries, including experts in the more technical arts of war: mining, planning sieges, handling cannon. The only lords to be left in England were the king's brother John of Bedford, and a small council to help him govern England in the king's absence.

Come summer, the men assembled, and in clots that grew into clumps, into crowds, they headed down to Southampton and the ports round about on the south coast, ready for embarkation for France.

The de la Poles' 160 lances gave them about 1,250 fighting men, and at least as many servants, so this was a good portion of the king's army, though far from an overwhelming one: in all, perhaps 25,000 men headed down to Southampton. The men at arms rode their horses, sturdy destriers bred to carry the weight of a fully armed man, but the archers and servants marched, or ambled, down the rutted roads, and there was a train of carts to carry all the bulk supplies. Such a force travelled slowly, so the journey took them several days.

As well as minding his own contingent, the journey and the days after they arrived and set up their temporary camp provided a time for William to renew acquaintance with many other captains who were bringing their men down to the south coast. His and Michael's brothers-in-law, Sir Thomas Morley and Sir Edward Burnell, were among them. The earl of Norfolk brought his men too. And there was news from Michael himself, because Elizabeth had given birth to their third or fourth child shortly before the men set off. She and Michael must have hoped this time for a son and heir, but it was yet another daughter who was born on the fourth of June. They called her Isabella.

There was a wait of many days when they got to the coast, since the arrangements were not yet complete. Not least, the ships were still being assembled. The king had about thirty ships of his own, including the *Trinity*, a successor to the great ship the de la Pole brothers had built for Edward III on the Humber, but these were not remotely sufficient to carry the army to France, so the king's council was requisitioning every merchant ship that could be found.

Suffolk's men might have camped some way from Southampton itself, but at some time in the days of waiting the earl and his sons probably rode to Porchester Castle, and presented themselves to the king, who had made his base there. There were men among the king's large entourage whom the earl knew well, and whom his sons would have known to some extent too. These included Thomas of Clarence, and the king's personal chaplain and confessor, who was an East Anglian: the bishop of Norwich, Richard Courtenay. So they probably spoke with these men as they negotiated their audience with the king himself.

Henry V was then 28. His brown hair was cut into a brutal pudding-basin style, a common fashion at the time, and he was clean shaven and scarred: he had taken an arrow in the cheek at Shrewsbury a few years earlier. He was blessed with charisma and drive, and had been reckless enough as a young man for his father to be rather slow in entrusting him with responsibilities. As a king, everyone agreed he had sobered, almost to a fault. Bishop Courtenay reckoned he had not lain with a woman since he took his crown. This was a king who took personal charge of his army, and a personal interest in his men. His intimates would have guarded access to him jealously, of course, so for the earl of Suffolk and his sons at this point, it was probably only a fleeting interest.

But it was useful too to talk with Clarence, an experienced fighting man like his brother, who had command of a large portion of the army. Suffolk and his men were most likely a part of it, renewing the relationship that had been forged back in 1412. Clarence too was known for his skill as a commander, and – even more

Evreux Cathedral

than Henry – for rashness and energy. Unlike his three brothers, he was a married man: he had married his widowed aunt by marriage and inherited a brood of step-children, although he had none of his own. The third of the brothers who were to lead the army, Humphrey of Gloucester, was younger, and as yet untried. He was gaining a reputation as the most light-hearted of the three, in many ways a typical youngest son. Men admired the king and Clarence, but they liked the company of Gloucester.

Then they waited some more. This must have been difficult for a new young lieutenant, not only because of his own impatience to set sail, but because of the task of controlling his men. True, there were among them resigned old hands who knew that hanging around is a large part of soldiery, and were happy to collect their pay for sitting in the sun in the fields of England. But there were hotheads too, who made the most of the opportunity for mischief. And there was the problem of supplies: they could not eat all the rations that had been prepared for France, but with so many men to feed, it was difficult to obtain alternatives. Practical problems like this would have kept captains like William much busier than their men.

So when the buzz grew in the East Anglian camp that signified news, William must have hoped it was the order to embark. It was not. It was something greatly more alarming: it had been announced that a plot on the king's life had been uncovered.

There were many who were not yet fully reconciled to the Lancastrian usurpation of the throne, and those of that inclination took a keen interest in King Henry's plans to leave England. So in a sense this was no surprise, but still it must have come as a shock.

The details spread throughout the army over the next few days. It was the earl of March, cousin to the king, and heir to the duke of York (the chief rival claimant to the English throne) who had told the king. A small group of men had enlisted him in their plot, and planned with him to fire the ships, kill the king and have March replace him. But March had got cold feet, knowing the penalty if such a plan were to fail, and decided the safer option was to confess it all. With luck he would be pardoned; it was his co-conspirators who would pay the price.

According to March, for these men the long days of waiting had been enlivened by a series of secret meetings, including one on the ferry across the River Itchen. March named three conspirators: Sir Thomas Grey; Lord Scrope, a cousin and trusted servant of the king's; and the earl of Cambridge, the duke of York's brother.

Although the army as a whole was huge, still the king had not so many lords and captains, and William's father would have known them all. Lord Scrope, indeed, was a distant relative: one of the earl's aunts had married into a branch of the family. Sir Thomas was married to a Mowbray, and related through her to Michael's wife Elizabeth. So this came close enough to send a chill down their backs.

It was dealt with briskly, as was all but unavoidable in the circumstances. Clarence was deputed to conduct a brief trial. March was indeed pardoned, and the other men were sentenced to traitors' deaths. They suffered them barely a week later: on 5 August they were hanged by the neck, taken down from the scaffold barely alive, dragged through the streets on horse-drawn hurdles, then disembowelled, their bodies quartered, and their severed heads displayed on pikes.

It was done for show, and thousands of the men watched it. Perhaps William and his men were among them. Even if they were not, he would have heard all the details. This was not an everyday occurrence like a common hanging; it was the talk of England, and doubtless before long of France as well.

The king had driven his lesson home: he would show no mercy to those who threatened him.

William had surely had no such intention. He had no reason for disaffection, and every reason to look forward to the king's great venture. Perhaps the worst part of this for him and his men was the delay it had caused. But with the executions over, the king moved fast – as he needed to, since the summer was wearing on. The army headed down to the Solent, and prepared to set sail.

It must have been a fine sight, the hundreds of ships large and small that had been assembled, and the press of men, horses, carts, crowding the shores and waiting to embark. There were swans swimming between the ships in the sheltered water of the estuary. This was a good omen.

Then a ship caught fire, and with the vessels packed so tight it spread to a couple of others before men managed to contain it. The flames reflected in the water, the shouts of the men, the whinnies of the frightened horses; for a while, at least, it was pandemonium. Ironically, it was an echo of what the dead traitors had envisaged; and another stark warning of the dangers ahead.

But they got on board, crowding into the boats with their animals and their equipment. The sails filled, the oars plashed, and they were off to the open waters of the Channel, and France.

From Jacques Coeur's house, Bourges, France

12 Harfleur and the bloody flux

Few of the men would have known where they were headed on the coast of France, since the king had kept his plans close, and Sir William de la Pole was not one of them. Men speculated, of course. Such a huge force, with so many requisitioned ships, would not make the long crossing to Gascony: they would land somewhere on the stretch of coastline between Calais in the north, and Cherbourg in the south. This was a large enough expanse that there was no danger they would be met immediately by a large French army. Anyway, the word was that although the French must have known from their spies of the muster, they had not as yet raised an army to counter the English one.

There were too many of them for a chevauchée, the kind of swift ride across enemy territory, laying waste and plundering, that had characterized much of the action in the long intermittent war. Most likely they would settle down to besiege a port. The king would have picked a good-sized place, somewhere that could provide a strong base for further campaigning. With luck he would take it quickly, then he would probably eject the townsfolk, and replace them with settlers from England. This was much what had been done at Calais, which had been English-held for nearly seventy years, and there it had served the English well.

If that was the prediction, it was at least half right. The armada took a middle course, and once across the Channel, approached a wide estuary, much of it bordered by high chalk cliffs, some of it by low boggy ground. The ships dropped anchor, and at the signal the captains took to their boats and were rowed across to the *Trinité*, where the king awaited them. He gave them their briefing, to pass on to their men. This was the estuary of the Seine, the great river that rises just north of Dijon and flows broadly north-west, through Paris and Rouen, two of the great cities of central France, and their target was Harfleur, a port with a fortified harbour that sat round a little tributary on the north bank.

They were well distant from any English-held land, so it was clear the king was taking an ambitious course. If he took Harfleur he could at least damage, if not destroy, French trade along the river, and this would put pressure on the places upstream, up to and including Paris itself. He would have bases to both the south and the north of Normandy, and an opportunity to work outwards from them to take more territory. Opportunity – but not the easy option of expanding directly from Calais or from the English-held territory in Gascony.

The army disembarked along the shoreline, a safe distance from the town walls, and set about unloading their supplies. This took several days to complete, since there were so many of them, and a limited amount of suitable land to draw near to. There was no opposition: the townsfolk of Harfleur had withdrawn behind their walls, and the farmers and peasants had either fled or joined them there. Then the men set out across the salt meadows towards the town.

From a mantelpiece in Jacques Coeur's house, Bourges

It was wet underfoot; increasingly wet. Water was creeping across the meadows, lapping round their feet. They must have cursed at that. Men worked out soon enough what had caused it: there was a series of dams controlling the tributary of the Seine on which Harfleur sat – the Lézarde – and the townsfolk had opened the sluices. This cut down the amount of land on which they could camp.

They did not draw close to the walls immediately; they waited well out of range of the cannon on Harfleur's ramparts while the king sent his heralds into the town, to parley with the leaders of the small garrison and the townsfolk. This was the proper way to wage war, and this was a king who did it properly. The heralds told the men of Harfleur that Henry of Lancaster was the rightful lord of Normandy, and they must admit him to their town. Henry would not have expected the townsfolk to agree with this assertion, but once they refused, he was entitled to attack them.

The refusal given, the king and his lieutenants made their dispositions. The earl of Suffolk's men were probably allocated to the seaward side, near the marshes. They found as dry a stretch of land as they could, and William and his father's other lieutenants directed operations as the men set about pitching their tents, choosing sites for their fires, finding grazing for their horses, and generally settling in. Then in the days that had followed they built siege fortifications – banks and ditches to give them shelter from the defenders – and started the investment. Wooden siege engines not far different from those the ancient Romans had known were still used at this time, as well as the newer brass and iron cannon. The king had three huge cannon – the *King's daughter*, the *Messagère* and *London* – which, though too heavy and cumbersome to play a role on the battlefield, were formidable weapons when they could be set up slowly and aimed with care. These were dragged into position, the miners checked out the land for suitable sites for tunnelling – it was a core tactic to try to undermine the walls – and since the business of provisioning was always crucial, the first foraging parties followed the first scouts into the surrounding countryside.

St Martin's Church, Harfleur

Many of the requisitioned ships sailed straight back to England, and the sailors from those that remained were detailed to take control of Harfleur's harbour and the estuary, which they achieved without difficulty.

The basic tactics of a siege had changed little in hundreds, even thousands of years. The town or stronghold had to be surrounded, to prevent supplies from getting in. Then the aim was to starve the defenders into submission, find a way to gain entry by treachery, or weaken the defences sufficiently that it was viable to storm the place. A direct assault on the walls was difficult and uncertain, and often led to very heavy casualties, so it was rarely attempted in the opening stages of a siege.

Many sieges succeeded through one of these routes, though by no means all of them. Sometimes the attackers were not strong enough to force a conclusion, and sometimes the enemy sent a relieving force to engage with them. Sometimes sieges took months. But with a strong army, the king obviously hoped to take Harfleur relatively quickly.

Indeed, some of the experienced men probably grumbled that he had rather too strong an army. A third as many men might have been sufficient for a siege of a place that size, and as it was, they were cramped shoulder to shoulder on every nearby patch of dry land. And when he took the town, what then? For the Valois king to lose a sizeable town to the English would be a blow, but hardly a mortal one. There would still have been thousands of towns and castles kept for him across the rest of France. Would the Valois hold off from joining battle, and leave the English to exhaust themselves besieging stronghold after stronghold? Even if they took a dozen, it might seem little enough for Henry to gain from a season's campaigning with a large army. He would still be a long way from regaining all the territory to which he made claim. Or would the French pride, outrage and hatred of the English push them into a major confrontation?

That was what the English hoped for. That was why King Henry had not divided up his forces.

The battles of Crècy and Poitiers were now at the farthest reach of living men's memories. The memory of them was not encouraging to the French, since it was their armies that had been annihilated. The English and Welsh longbows used in those battles had had the advantage over the continental crossbows, which were at least as powerful, but could only be shot at a much slower rate; and since battlefield weapons had changed little in the intervening years, this was still the case. So there were two strong arguments against the French risking all on a great confrontation, even if the great dukes had managed to drag themselves sufficiently into alignment to jointly raise an army. First, the status quo was to their advantage, so they had no reason to try to change it; and second, the lessons of history told them the odds were not in their favour.

This meant it could not be taken for granted by either side that a large army would come to relieve Harfleur. But the place stubbornly refused to make a quick surrender.

It was a hot August, and the flies and bugs were thick on and above the marshy ground. Thousands of men were living, eating, shitting at close quarters; the stench before long was appalling. The king had the attackers work in shifts, to try to do as much damage as possible. The boom of the cannon and the creaks and thuds of the siege engines, the grunts and yells of the men, continued through the days and nights. So there was little sleep, and there were long hard days of fighting, digging, foraging, debate among the captains.

Church of St Peter Mancroft, Norwich
Photo Mike Dixon

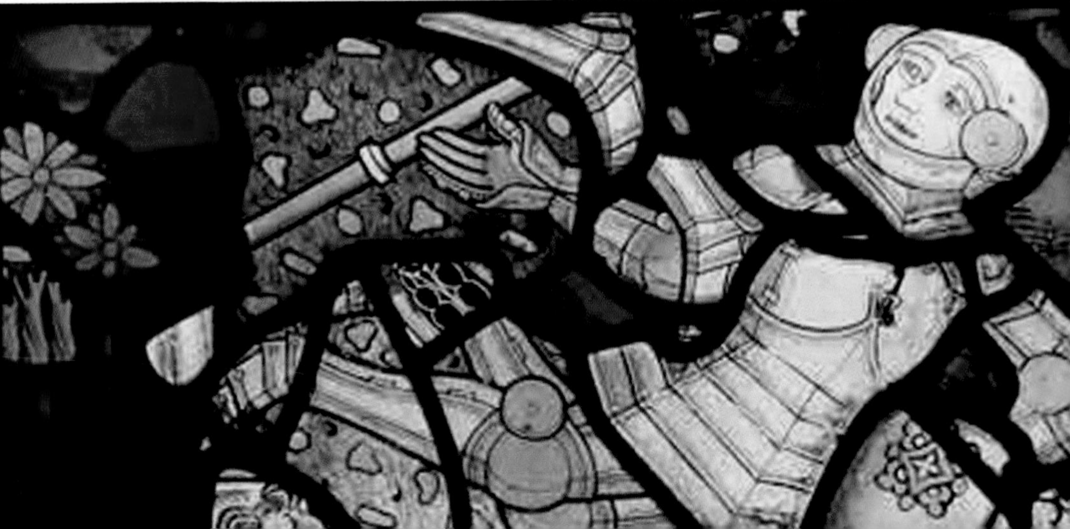

They all knew that disease was often a greater danger in these situations than was the fighting itself. Even so, there was little they could do to prevent it. When the cooks had finished with the animals the foraging parties brought in for slaughter, they threw the bones and leftovers with other rubbish into the river, creating a fetid stew in the shallow water. Food was short, so men ate unripe grapes and other fruit; they fished out shellfish from the stinking mud. If the commanders as usual got the first pick, it was of the rotting meat and the dubious clams and mussels. Within a few days, men were beginning to come down with the sickness they called the bloody flux: not just the common archers and servants, but the princes too. It probably started with cramps in the stomach, bad enough to make a man bend double with the pain of them, and continued with sickness and a diarrhoea that was soon thick with blood. It was no light inconvenience; people had encountered similar diseases often enough to know that even the fittest men could die from them.

The disease was worse amid the men camped amid the salt marshes. By early September, William's father was down with it. William was out of action too, although it is not known whether he had the flux, or had been injured in the siege operations. It is perhaps more likely he took an injury – in a skirmish with men from the town, or while with a foraging party – because not only he, but his armour too suffered damage.

He was probably pulled back to the rear of the camp, where the men too sick to carry on the work of the siege were sent to be nursed. There were servants – those not also sickening – to do what they could for him amid the heat, the noise, the stink. But even so, he almost died.

And for a while at least, he probably knew little of what was happening beyond the sick tents. His servants would have told him he was being signed off the muster, sent back to England to convalesce. They would have told him he was not alone, that a horde of men were in such bad shape that there was no alternative but to ship them home, even including Thomas of Clarence. They probably left it to Michael to tell him the rest.

Their father was dead.

It turned their world upside down. Compared with that, the rest of the news must have seemed almost trivial. Bishop Courtenay was dead too. Sir Edward Burnell was dead, and their sister Elizabeth a widow like their mother. In total, perhaps two thousand men had died, nearly all of them done down by the dysentery and not by the French.

Oh – and Harfleur was theirs. The earl of Suffolk had died in the salt marshes on 14 September, and a couple of days later, the townsfolk had agreed to surrender if they had not been relieved by the following Sunday. That Sunday was past. The king's men had set his throne on the top of the hill opposite the town, Henry had donned the crown he had brought in his baggage for this purpose – the one with which he intended to be crowned king of France – and he had sat there, looking out over the battered walls of Harfleur, while the officers of the garrison, dressed in shirts of penitence with ropes round their necks, trudged up to hand over the keys of the city.

Michael de la Pole, now the third earl of Suffolk, had been there to witness it.

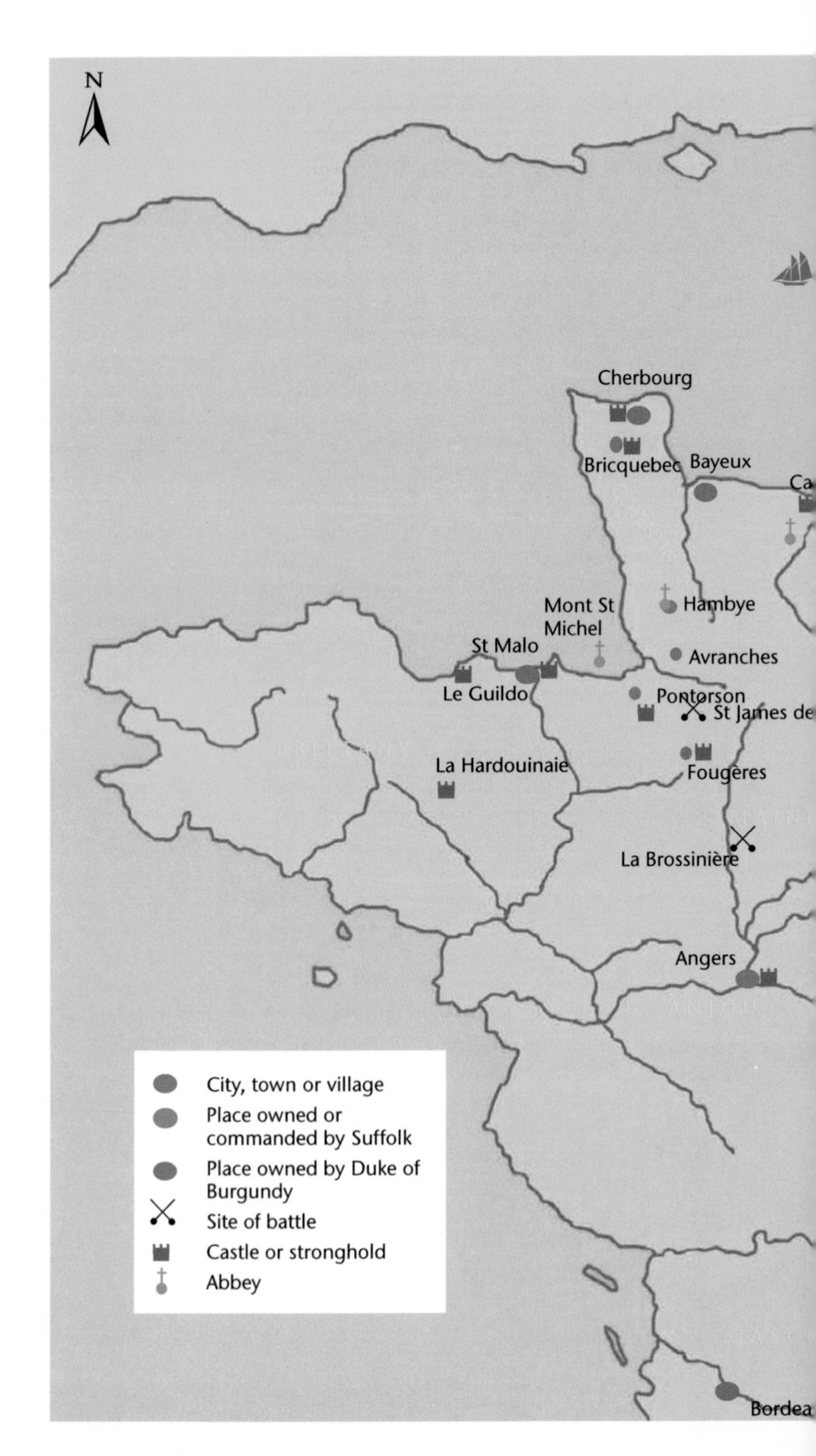

North-west France

Bruges
Ghent
Brussels
Calais
ENGLISH CHANNEL
Agincourt
Le Crotoy
Hesdin
Arras
R.Somme
Aumale
Harfleur
Rouen
R.Seine
Reims
R.Oise
Evreux
Pontoise
Meaux
Verneuil
St Denis
Dreux
Paris
Troyes
Montaiguillon
Montereau
R. Yonne
Montargis
Vendome
Orleans
Auxerre
Beaugency
Jargeau
Cravant
Tours
Blois
Dijon
Bourges
La Roche
Macon

13 Boiled in a barrel

Common archers and servants who died at Harfleur, or later in the campaign, were buried where they fell, but this was not appropriate for a lord. The second earl of Suffolk's body was cut into joints, which were put in a cauldron with plenty of spices, and boiled till they were cooked through. Then the flesh and bones were packed into a barrel, ready for the long journey back to Wingfield.

William most likely left it to Michael to detail two men at arms and four archers to form a guard of honour for their father's body, and Michael, or their men, to liaise with the king's men over the shipping home. He was probably carried onto the ship, with the guard and the bones in their barrel, and the men's horses, and was in a rough state not only during the Channel crossing, but through much of the slow journey up through southern England. Without the corpse he might have lingered on the south coast to recover, but with the need to get it home for burial, he was probably urged along the rutted roads by the escort.

The new earl's herald would have ridden ahead, to take the news to Wingfield. The Lady would have sent priests and servants down to meet the sorry procession, and the last miles from London and through Suffolk would have been at funeral pace, the barrel discarded and the second earl's bones decanted into a coffin covered with his colours, with candles lit and black-clad men singing dirges.

William must have been sick at heart as well as sick in his body. This was not the start as a man at arms that he had wished for.

He spent the next weeks, or months, recuperating in a household full of the silent bustle of mourning. If he was capable of it, he attended his father's funeral, of course. All the family would have done so – bar Michael in France – and so would have their servants and retainers, the priests from the college that their Wingfield ancestors had established, representatives from the Carthusian monastery at Myton in Yorkshire, and many others too. They went in solemn procession along the long mile from Wingfield Castle to St Andrew's Church. It was and is a charming, light-filled building, holding the bones of many of William's ancestors, and dominated by the great stone tomb of Sir John Wingfield. The monks crowded into the chancel, the bells tolled, the women wept.

It was the custom for men who could afford it to arrange for large numbers – hundreds, even thousands – of masses to be said for their souls, so there were frequent services at Wingfield (and in Hull too) in the days, weeks, months and years thereafter. William would have attended his share of them, praying that his father might be spared the flames of hell.

He might well have taken part in the discussions about his father's tomb that surely began at this time, although the effigies would not have been completed until after his mother's death. Unusually, they were carved in wood. They both show handsome, well-built individuals with rather long faces, although there is no guarantee they were much of a likeness of the earl and his wife. The earl wears plain plate armour, and his feet rest on a small lion, just as his grandfather's did. There were niches cut round the side of the stone tomb chest to hold images of his children.

St Andrew's Church, Wingfield

There was of course a will to be read. The second earl had rewritten it that summer, just before he left for France. It was a conventional document, which provided no great surprises. Some of the land was entailed and would pass automatically to the third earl. Almost all of the rest was left to Katherine. She kept the estates at Wingfield, and Court Hall in Hull. Her husband left to her – as well he might – the illustrated book they had had from her father. He left her, but only for life, a 'large primer', with instructions that it be passed on to his heir, 'and so from heir to heir, whom God pleaseth'. Michael was left another small primer, a ring, and an 'image of gold of the blessed Virgin Mary'. William, his other brothers and his sisters were each left 'one ring, with my blessing'.

It was not the greatest of inheritances, but William had probably expected no more. He was still a minor, and unmarried; there had been no reason to make particular provision for him. And the estate had to be kept together, if it was to provide an earl's livelihood. His mother and Michael would ensure his expenses were covered, until he was in a position to pay his own way.

The blessing was doubtless genuine enough.

Lady Katherine was not the only widow. William's sister Elizabeth Burnell had lost her husband, and other men from the de la Pole contingent must have been casualties too, so this was a time of much sorrow.

William and his family also gave thought to the living. Everyone at Wingfield would have been anxious for news from France – especially of Michael and the other men connected with the family – but William would have taken a particular interest, not only for his brother's sake, but for his own. That summer's campaign was lost to him, but what happened during the remainder of it would shape his opportunities in the following years. Would the king have gone on to take other places after Harfleur? Would his men have gone on raids, and devastated swathes of northern France? Might a Valois army have taken the field; would there be a battle? The siege of Harfleur had taken longer than any of them had hoped, and cost more than the king could afford. If he was to continue his campaign in France over subsequent years, he would need another victory of some kind to round off the season.

The summer was by then drawing on into autumn. And slowly, news trickled back to Wingfield, with the third earl's messengers, men from Framlingham, merchants from London. They would have learned first that the king had chosen to do at Harfleur what had been done at Calais, eject most of the French inhabitants and call for English men and women to come and settle there. The requests for volunteers were probably read out in the church, and men from Suffolk were among those who chose to head for a new life in France. The king left a garrison to guard his new possession, but the bulk of his army marched off, heading north-east through Normandy. Men still ask themselves now, and doubtless asked themselves then, what the king's purpose was in doing this. Perhaps it was intended to tempt out the Valois army; perhaps it was simply to assert the king's ability to cross Normandy unhindered, and emphasize his claim to this land.

There was another month, perhaps, of waiting before more news came. The French had stirred themselves at last to raise an army. The warring dukes had not fully united to do this: neither the duke of Burgundy nor the duke of Brittany joined it. King Charles VI, the sorry madman, was not capable of fighting, and his sons did not join the army either, so it was headed by men from the Armagnac faction. Messengers and spies traced its route westwards, towards the English army.

The next news was bad. They must have known this as soon as the messenger rode up to Wingfield Castle and over the drawbridge, and they gathered round with grey foreboding in the courtyard to hear what he had to say.

There had indeed been a battle. The two armies had met between Harfleur and Calais, just north of the mouth of the Somme and near a small village called Azincourt. The French had outnumbered the English, perhaps as many as ten times over, and the English were wearied and short of rations.

A disastrous defeat? No, it was far from that. The English were good professional troops, and disciplined, set against arrogant French nobles and unruly French peasants. And they had their longbows, which had defeated the French at Crècy. They were to do it again, and win a great victory. King Henry V would go down in history as a legendary fighter, the inspiration of his men. Thousands of Frenchmen had been killed, and not just the peasants. The dukes of Alençon, Brabant and Bar, 90 counts, 1,500 knights, and perhaps 5,000 French men at arms: all of these were corpses now in Flanders. Two of the great royal dukes, Orleans and Bourbon, had been taken prisoner, and in time huge ransoms could be demanded for them.

All this was marvellous, and there had been only a handful of English casualties. But among them was Michael, third earl of Suffolk.

Church of St Mary and St Walstan, Bawburgh, Norfolk
Photo Mike Dixon

14 The fourth earl

It is a truism that is great good luck to inherit a fortune. But many fortunes come with ties, and a medieval earldom was certainly one of them. Before the messenger arrived at Wingfield, William had been a young man relatively light on obligations, recovering steadily from the sickness or injury that had brought him home from Harfleur, and probably thinking of little beyond getting back on his feet and returning to his position in the army. Now he was the fourth earl and the head of the family, and responsible not just for the family estates and the men and women who worked on them, but for a newly widowed mother, a newly widowed sister, a newly widowed sister-in-law, three younger brothers, a clutch of other sisters and another clutch of nieces. It would have been no wonder if he was daunted by it.

Church of St James the Great, Castle Acre, Norfolk

If Lady Katherine tried in her own way to be supportive to him, she also fought to retain her own position, which was all the stronger because the new earl was still legally a minor. (He had just turned nineteen.) It was quite possibly not an easy relationship.

At first, of course, the focus was on Michael – Michael dead, that is. He had held his title barely six weeks; he had fought in just one battle. His bones too arrived back in Suffolk in a barrel, although what then became of them is not clear. Perhaps the family was exhausted by the weeks of obsequies for the second earl, for although they surely grieved over Michael's early death, there is no indication that they made a similar great display to mark it. There is no stone tomb surviving for the third earl of Suffolk; it is not even clear where he was buried.

He had fought well in the battle of Azincourt (or Agincourt, as the English came to know it), or at least this was the message that came from France, and they would all have wished to believe it. The heralds wrote that he had been 'as strong, as active and as daring as any member of the court'. Over the next weeks the surviving men from his contingent of troops returned to England, and many of them would have come to Wingfield to pay their respects to Michael's mother, and tell her of his bravery. Some of them went to Benhall too, to see the third earl's grieving young widow and his brood of daughters.

They sought out William as well, and offered to serve under him in future, pressing home what he already knew, that he no longer had to build his future on a ring and a blessing. He had acquired a great position, and men expected him to fill it.

In name, it was his mother who took all the public actions over the coming weeks – as was proper and necessary – and we cannot judge now what part William privately played in them. In the weeks that followed Lady Katherine moved, or ordered her stewards and lawyers to move, to do all that was necessary to secure the family's position. The de la Pole lands were extensive, the terms of their holdings complex; many men would have coveted them, and it was important to act fast and decisively. The second earl's executors

were still with the army in France, but their names were joined to the petitions she made to the king. (Of course the king was in France too, but they could be lodged for his return.) Lady Katherine requested control of all the family's lands, and asked in addition that since her husband and eldest son had died in the king's service, she should be absolved from making the usual payments to the Crown. The king granted all this on 8 December 1415, only a few days after he had returned to England.

The king needed every lord in his realm, and William was confirmed very quickly in the title. By 1416 the king's grants to him (part of the lengthy official business that followed the deaths of his father and brother) were addressed to 'our beloved and faithful William de la Pole, earl of Suffolk'. (This formal phrase does not imply that he was any particular intimate of the king.) Men will have addressed him as my lord of Suffolk, and Suffolk is what he will now be called here.

All Saints Church, East Barsham, Norfolk

By the spring of 1416 Suffolk was probably strong enough to fight again. But he could not do so until there was another campaign in which he might take part; and meanwhile, there was plenty for him to do in England. Not having expected to inherit, he would not have been taught about the family's interests to the depth that Michael had. Now he had to work to get to know in detail what lands they held and what roles the earl was expected to fulfil, in Suffolk, in Yorkshire, on the lands that remained to the family between their two great centres of activity, and in London as well. As he continued to recover, and the long winter gave way to spring, he probably chose to spend less time with Lady Katherine on her dower estates, and to establish his own household, moving between the manors that had passed to him with the earldom, and of which he would take full control as soon as he came of age.

He would have built up a group of trusted servants, most if not all of them men he already knew: men who had come with him, his father and brother to Harfleur, and men who had stayed in England as well, working to keep things running in their absence.

Beyond an inner circle he chose for himself, his father's agents and retainers continued in place. It was common for generations of a family to serve the same lord, so the men who collected rents and dues, kept order in small ways, and ensured that the family's interests were properly represented in the choice of justices of the peace, members of parliament and other local officials, were many of them from families who had worked for the de la Poles in Yorkshire, the Wingfields in Suffolk, for a century or more. The Heydons and the Tuddenhams – both solid families, affluent in their own right – and many others were firmly established as the retainers of the earls of Suffolk. As servants do, they would have done things in the way they had learned and were used to doing them, and if Suffolk had the formal authority, he perhaps did not yet have the influence to change their ways, even had he known what he wished to change. He could not realistically choose these men; they were effectively bequeathed to him with his lands.

He most likely turned to his surviving brothers for support and companionship in these strange and disruptive months, although the sudden change in his fortunes would have altered his relationship with them. John was perhaps still finishing his education. He too was set to become a man at arms, and would have been anxious, like Suffolk himself, to know what the king planned to do next in France.

Thomas was at Oxford. He was headed for a life as a priest, and the bishop of London, Richard Clifford, had provided for his education. The bishop, an eminent man and king's councillor, had made some steps towards establishing a new Oxford college (although they petered out without any lasting result), and Thomas was perhaps one of the students at Burnell's Inn, which the bishop rented from Balliol College. Bishop Clifford died in August 1421, and it must have been a disappointment to Thomas to lose this powerful patron. Lady Katherine was also supporting Thomas, as we know from the expenses detailed in her surviving wardrobe records: in 1417 she paid his tutor, Thomas Rowebury, and sent her son eight shillings 'for play and his small expenses, together with one purse to put his money in', plus two and a half yards of violet cloth.

St Margaret's Church, Herringfleet, Suffolk

The youngest brother, Alexander, was studying under Master William Bury at Ipswich (probably at the same school as Suffolk had been to himself). There is a record of John Heydon, a family retainer, riding with men to fetch him when he was brought back to Wingfield in the summer of 1417.

Suffolk's sisters had to be considered too: both the ones still single, and the newly widowed Lady Elizabeth Burnell. Isobel, Lady Morley, was perhaps a help rather than a responsibility. Her husband Sir Thomas had inherited the title of Lord Morley when his grandfather died in 1416, so he too had more importance now, and was to be an useful associate of Suffolk's, both in the army and at court. Katherine was in her nunnery, so her future was also secure.

Lady Katherine seems to have taken the lead in caring for her other daughters, and Suffolk was perhaps glad to leave these tasks to her. The family account books mention shoes and cloth bought for Lady Elizabeth Burnell. She would have inherited some lands from her husband, so this was perhaps less financial support than her mother's attempt to cheer her up. Philippa was not yet married, and probably still a young girl: the records show her staying with her maid at the Benedictine priory at Bungay, and making occasional visits to Wingfield.

Another sister, Joan, was given money to meet her costs in travelling from Wingfield to London in February 1417, a nasty month for a journey down bad English roads. She spent 26 shillings and eightpence, so she must have taken plenty of servants and baggage. She was also advanced 100 shillings for seeing to the repair of Suffolk's armour. Presumably this was the damage – clearly considerable, for that was a large sum – that he had done to it at Harfleur. Joan sounds from this like a maiden aunt in the making, pluckily running errands for her brothers and sisters. Nothing is known of her afterwards.

Elizabeth, Michael's widow, might still have been a minor; or if she was not, she must have lacked the character or the inclination to compete with her mother in law. She was a dowager countess now, and had lands and money of her own. But she had no son to inherit, and that weakened her bargaining position. Nor did she have full control over her daughters; the right to arrange their marriages went to William.

Elizabeth went to the abbey of the Poor Clares at Bruisyard, near to her family's main seat at Framlingham, and not far from Wingfield, and took her daughter Katherine with her. Perhaps at first this was a temporary refuge, but she remained there for the rest of her life. Her other daughters, Elizabeth and Isabella (and perhaps Jane too) were boarded out at houses and convents around Suffolk. This was not intended as cruelty: it was the way things were done in their time, and the few surviving records show that good care was taken over the girls.

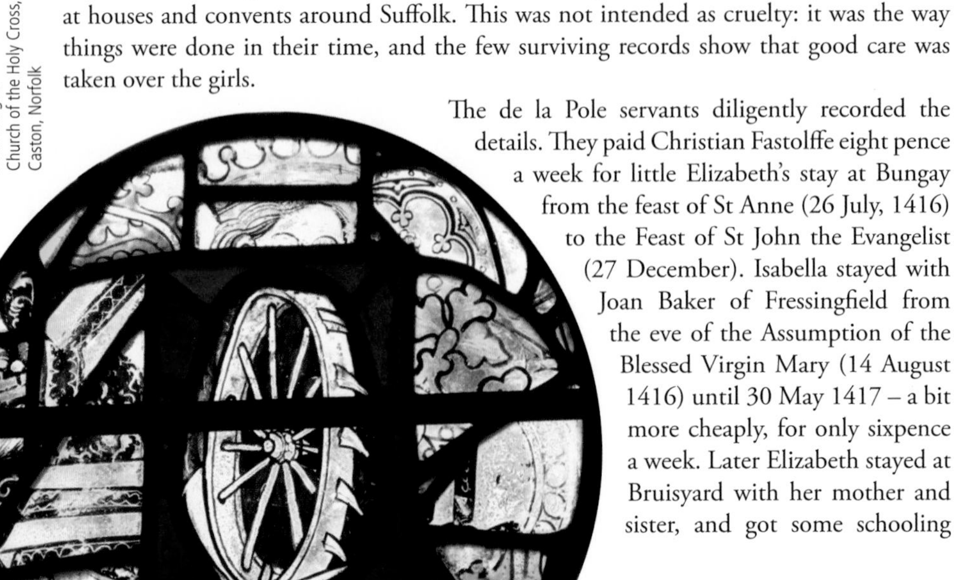

Both images: Church of the Holy Cross, Caston, Norfolk

The de la Pole servants diligently recorded the details. They paid Christian Fastolffe eight pence a week for little Elizabeth's stay at Bungay from the feast of St Anne (26 July, 1416) to the Feast of St John the Evangelist (27 December). Isabella stayed with Joan Baker of Fressingfield from the eve of the Assumption of the Blessed Virgin Mary (14 August 1416) until 30 May 1417 – a bit more cheaply, for only sixpence a week. Later Elizabeth stayed at Bruisyard with her mother and sister, and got some schooling there, as Katherine maybe did too: the Lady's servants paid a friar called 'le President' for his labour in teaching her. The girls visited Wingfield, but none too often: though it was not far distant, it was a sizeable operation to bring them there. When John Heydon rode to collect young Elizabeth, he took a group of men and seven horses with him.

To take the trouble to educate girls was unusual in their time, but these were the daughters of an earl and the granddaughters of a duke; they might have grown into women of importance. Sadly, it was not to be. By 1423 Elizabeth, Isabella and their mother were all dead, and Katherine had taken vows as a nun at Bruisyard.

Men – and his mother – must have suggested to Suffolk, once the first deep mourning for the dead earls was done, that he should think of a marriage for himself. But Lady Katherine had plenty to do without searching out a wife for her son, and it does not seem to have been Suffolk's own priority. Although many children of aristocratic families married young, not all did: the king and his two single brothers were proof of that. And Suffolk had good heirs in his own brothers, so there was no need for him to marry to get one. He knew from what he had seen that the life of a man of arms was one not easily shared with a woman, so if he married he and his wife would probably spend long years apart. Anyway, his fortunes might improve. He might gain loot and preferment on the king's next campaign, and then he would be in a better position to bargain a rich marriage.

For all it had cost Michael his life, William probably regretted having missed Agincourt. Battles as large and decisive as that happen barely once in a man's lifetime; those who had been there would still be talking about it on their deathbed. It had benefited the king hugely in terms of reputation and bargaining power with the French, but the men at arms and archers probably grumbled that it had benefited them very little. The king had decided that his two greatest prisoners, the dukes of Orleans and Bourbon, should remain in captivity for the time being and not be ransomed; he wanted France weakened more than he wanted the huge sums they would have to raise to pay for their freedom. And there were relatively few lesser prisoners, because in the later stages of the battle he had ordered the killing of most of the French captives when he feared that the English were too stretched to hold them securely. (He had excepted the nobles, but some of them had been killed by mistake.)

It was not unheard of to do this, but it was not routine either; men might justifiably think it cruel. Frenchmen, that is: Englishmen had learned by now that this was a king who did not brook criticism.

15 A lord at court

During 1416 and the first part of 1417, Suffolk must also have spent some time in London and Westminster. Being there now would have been a very different experience from his stays in the capital when he was younger. Then he had been a boy of no great importance, tagging along with his father and older brother; now he was one of the lords of England. As well as having business to deal with in London, he was welcome at court. Not just other lords, but the king and his brothers too would have looked with interest on him, both as a likely commander in future military campaigns, and as a potential ally in the political intrigue around the king's council.

London was by far the largest city in England, but it was not then the sprawling metropolis it later became: most of it was still crammed within the old Roman walls, which enclosed an arc of territory on the north bank of the Thames. To the south was the suburb of Southwark; to the west, quite separate from the city (though linked to it by a long straight road, the Strand) was Westminster, dominated by its royal palace and its abbey. Even within the walls there were open spaces, most of them attached to churches and monasteries; and in the south-east corner of the city there was the looming bulk of the great fortress, the Tower of London, the military stronghold which held the king's troops, his armoury, his prisoners of state, and the royal menagerie.

The de la Poles no longer ran the banking business set up by Suffolk's ancestors, and they probably did not still own Bardi House, from where Sir William de la Pole had run it. Later Suffolk was to buy a manor known as the Rose, in Dowgate Ward in the centre of the city, but it is not clear where the house that he used in this era was located. It was probably near to the Thames. Most of the houses of the lords and rich bishops were close to either the northern or southern shore, from where they could take their barges upstream to Westminster, avoiding the mud and stink of the narrow city streets.

Kings travelled from manor to manor, just as their lords did, and Henry V was not always at Westminster. But Suffolk probably chose to come to the city when the king and his court were there, perhaps in the summer of 1416, when the king was entertaining Sigismund, the Holy Roman Emperor, who had come to England on a diplomatic mission with a huge entourage. Later in his life he would have come when Parliament was called to Westminster, but as a minor still he was not summoned to the Parliaments of 1416 and 1417.

It was a court stiff with formality, but that would have come as no surprise to a man of Suffolk's era, where rules and rituals governed life at every level, although they were particularly intense and demanding among the nobility. Not just the different ranks of the peerage, but the men within each rank, knew their position of precedence, and life-long feuds had developed when these were disputed. Since Suffolk's own earldom was a relatively new creation, it ranked below older titles. But as an earl he ranked above the barons, so Lord Morley (whose title was a barony) was lower in precedence. He ranked below those of royal blood, and below the rare dukes and marquesses who did not have royal blood. And there were other positions that conveyed rights and influence too, such as membership of the king's ruling council, or of the great order of chivalry that had been set up by Edward III, the Garter.

These things dictated where a man might stand in relation to the king and others present, or even whether he might stand at all. They dictated where he might walk in procession – to church, for example – and where he might sit on arrival. They also dictated to whom he might speak. Even an earl would not have approached a prince without invitation, so to talk with Thomas of Clarence, for instance, was not a matter of going up to the man, albeit Suffolk already knew and was known by him; it was a matter of angling with attendants, catching eyes, waiting to be called to a conversation. This had been so even on the campaign in France, but it was more so at Westminster.

Nor were these things trivial, because a man's position did much to shape his opportunities in life. True, there were rare men like the first Sir William de la Pole who rose in the world, but the great majority remained in the station that their birth had brought them. As an earl's younger son, Suffolk would have had the opportunity to make a solid career as a man at arms, but he could not have expected early command. As an earl, he could be confident that such commands would come to him. Ability played a part, but only a small part. A young man from a wealthy and noble family, who from his birth onwards had been deferred to and flattered by servants, retainers, men and women of any and every kind whose rank was lower than his own, Suffolk would in any case not have been lacking in confidence in his own abilities.

He clearly saw his future as a man at arms, and his main interest would have been in the king's plans to return to France, and build on his success at Agincourt. So he must have met with the men who might tell him how the diplomacy and the military planning were progressing. He had a few contemporaries who had also inherited their titles young, including his sister-in-law Elizabeth's brother, the earl of Nottingham and Norfolk (he had yet to regain the greatest of his family's honours, the dukedom of Norfolk). Lord Morley, Suffolk's brother in law, was on good terms with the king. Lord Stafford, his cousin through his mother, was younger than him, still a boy; and he had no other close relations among the nobility: none of the younger de la Pole sons from the previous generations had reached this level. But there were men who, though not his relatives, had shared experience, and might become (in some cases already were) his friends. One such was Ralph, Lord Cromwell, who was only two or three years his senior, and whose father had

15th-century noblemen, from Strutt, *Dress and Habits of the People of England* (1799)

died in 1416. Cromwell had been Thomas of Clarence's man for some years, and as well as going on Clarence's expedition to France in 1412, he had been at Harfleur and fought at Agincourt. He too was coming to be known as a friend of the king's.

Suffolk would also have looked to older men; even an earl needed patrons if he was to gain well-paid positions and build his fortune. There was a powerful older generation, chief among whom were the king's uncles, the Beauforts, and which also included influential churchmen. But much of his focus would have been on the king and his brothers. They too came from a family that had known reverses: if they were princes now, they had grown up as the sons not of a king, but of an exile. They were all of them intelligent men; all of them cultured, at least to some degree. He could learn much from them, and he was probably wise enough to know it.

The court at this time was dominated by men at arms, but it had its share of festivities, of music, and of churchmen. The king had a fondness for ceremony – not unusual in his time – and having missed the great displays when the army returned to London after Agincourt, Suffolk perhaps enjoyed the feasts and pageants that were put on for Emperor Sigismund. But he was probably glad too that the diplomatic initiatives failed to bring peace, and that by the start of 1417, the king was preparing for another campaign in France.

Before the autumn of 1415, few men can seriously have believed that Henry would conquer France; to deter its pirates from raiding the English ships and coastline, and to secure the lands that Edward III had held, must have seemed more than ambition enough. But more was possible now, perhaps much more. It would have become clear to those who kept their ears open at court that the king's next aim was to take more land in Normandy, building outwards from his bases at Calais and Harfleur to dominate the north-west of France. The Armagnac faction at the French king's court had been devastated by their losses at Agincourt, and the duke of Burgundy, who had not fought there, was more concerned to gain ascendancy in Paris over the Armagnacs than to fight the English. King Henry agreed a short truce with Burgundy, and with that done, was ready to launch his next expedition.

Two of his brothers were to go with him. (John of Bedford, the third of Henry IV's sons, was left as regent in England, as he had been two years earlier.) Suffolk probably knew Thomas of Clarence the better: it was Clarence whose man his father had been, Clarence under whom he and his family had served on the king's previous campaign. Like Suffolk himself, Clarence had been invalided out of Harfleur and had missed Agincourt, so this was a shared disappointment. However it was not Clarence, but Humphrey of Gloucester under whom Suffolk and his men were placed when the king's muster was drawn up.

Suffolk had had little time to get to know Gloucester at Harfleur, but he must have met the prince on that campaign, and perhaps had come to know him better during these visits to the court. Humphrey had all the traits of a last son: the charm, and the irresponsibility that went with it. Although Bedford collected finely illuminated missals, it was Gloucester who was the great reader, who loved music and patronised musicians, who had an eye for women. He was the prince who was loved by the common people, who were coming to speak of him as Good Duke Humphrey. Perhaps this charm seduced Suffolk too, and to serve under this man, not much his senior, was what he had chosen.

It was perhaps only at this time in his life, stepping into the earldom that his father and grandfather had held, that Suffolk began to get a sense of how others had seen these forebears of his. And at the same time, men would have begun to judge what he was like himself, and how he might play the hand that had been dealt to him.

From six hundred years of cobwebbed distance, it is difficult to reconstruct their verdicts. Men of their time rarely wrote of their impressions of others except in generalized terms – a brave warrior, a devout man – and perhaps did not even talk of them. But here is a suggestion of what they might have found.

Following on from two generations of exceptionally energetic, forceful, cunning men, who had found a way to cut through the dense worsted weave of the English class system and rise high, William's father seems to have been a less driven character. He had only succeeded in regaining the earldom after years of struggle in which he had never quite found the cracks he might widen, the doors he might prise open. Made earl in his turn, he had filled his position honourably, but without great distinction. His experiences encouraged him to be cautious, but there is little evidence that he was naturally inclined to be anything else. His wife comes across as the more forceful of the two: it was she who, born like her husband into wealth and high position, had been honed by waves of misfortune into someone hard, clear and determined. She had kept the family together through its disasters, ensured her children thrived and were educated, held onto her focus when her husband and eldest son were killed. It was perhaps her living shadow that her second son most needed to step away from at this point in her life, and not his dead father's shade.

Suffolk himself had had an easy childhood, by the standards of his time. Only in these past few months had he known misfortune. He had survived it so far, and as soon as he might, would return to France to fight some more. Of course that was expected of him, but he did not duck it; indeed he did more than was needed, then and later. He was an intelligent man, as far as we can judge, and with some at least of his ancestors' sharp cunning; he was to discover a taste for the

Westminster Abbey

intrigue of the court, spying and diplomacy. He was cultured, a lover of music and poetry; when he had the resources to, he kept fine musicians among his household, and later he wrote poetry and cultivated the friendship of other poets. He was a loyal brother, and worked to help John, Thomas and Alexander thrive alongside him. He loved women rather than men: only a few of them, as far as we know, but not always wisely.

If he had some of his mother's hard steel, it never crossed into cruelty: the worst men could say of him, later, was that he sometimes let his servants be brutal for him. They would call him greedy for money and position: he had a sense of what his family had gained and then lost, and the motivation to regain all of it and more. He had some of his father's caution: indeed, too much of it to be a great captain at war. He was motivated to survive, and though no man ever called him a coward, neither was he first into the breach, sacrificing himself in the process. And he had some of the charm that had brought his grandfather a high position at court. The next phase of his life would be as a man at arms, but perhaps he already realized that it was at court that he would find his true metier, and there that, in years to come, he would rise as high as his grandfather, or even higher.

Trinity Church Vendome

16 The white walls of Caen

After Suffolk went back to France in 1417 he was to remain there for most of the next fourteen years, but he could not have foreseen that when he said goodbye to his mother, his brothers and sisters, the stewards and bailiffs he had begun to get to know. He knew the king was planning a longer campaign than the 1415 one, hoping to have his army winter in France and not make the expensive return to England at the end of the autumn, but he probably expected to be abroad for not much more than a year. That would have sufficed for his own immediate goals: to put the disasters of Harfleur behind him, and win some success at arms.

The men who mustered at Southampton in the summer of 1417 were similar in number to those who had assembled two years earlier, so it was again a formidable army. Suffolk contributed thirty-one men at arms and ninety archers; not as many men as his father had provided the previous time, but still a solid number. Muster rolls (the lists drawn up by the king's administrators, to control the payment of the army) survive for this expedition, so we know that his men included a number of older East Anglian knights with well-established reputations. Some, perhaps all, of these men had been among the de la Pole contingent in 1415, and although Suffolk must have missed his father's presence and his advice, he could turn to them for counsel when he felt the need.

Though still very young, he must have felt more confident this time, not only in taking command, but in his awareness of what the king was planning. He probably knew in advance that they would sail back to Harfleur. The town was far from completely secure, so the king needed to reassure its nervous English settlers, and he also had the opportunity to use it as a base for supplies. Harfleur was not large enough to provide winter quarters for an army of this size, though, and one early objective was to take a place sufficiently big to serve this purpose.

It was no more practicable for a single English army to try to take France stronghold by stronghold than it had been a couple of years earlier, but that was probably not the king's aim. He would take sufficient places to drive home the lesson, then seek to negotiate with the French king or his lords. There might be a coup, similar to the one that had put his own father on a throne, or perhaps Charles VI would agree to abdicate, or failing that make Henry his heir. Or one of the warring French factions might come out in support of Henry and help him finish the job – as men like Lord Morley and Lord Cromwell had most likely discussed with Suffolk, there were various ways in which it might turn out for the best. And if it did not – well, if Henry had a firm claim to a coherent stretch of territory in Normandy, he could negotiate to hold on to it. The places he took would also provide booty, which was important too. Almost as soon as they landed the men began to grumble that their wages had not been given

Church of St Peter Mancroft, Norwich
Photo Mike Dixon

to them, and that was largely because the king did not have the money to pay them, so he needed find sources of profit.

The French had enlisted a Genoese fleet to try to prevent the English from taking full control of the Seine estuary, and there was a naval battle (in which Suffolk probably did not take part) before the coast was clear for the invasion. So the main English armada set sail late in the season, on 30 July. They made their landing at the mouth of the river Touques, which runs between Deauville and Trouville, on the southern side of the estuary, a little to the southwest of Harfleur on the north bank. The king sent out troops to hold the roads and prevent surprise attacks, and they took over the nearby villages and hamlets. Then the entire army settled down to a major joint endeavour, to attack the city of Caen.

Half the army served under Clarence and the other half directly under the king. Humphrey of Gloucester was put under one of his older brothers, and Suffolk and his men in turn reported to Gloucester.

Their first task was to take the two abbeys outside the walls of the city, the Abbaye aux Hommes and the Abbaye aux Dames, Both were huge complexes, built by William the Conqueror and his wife Matilda in the strong white local Caen stone, which had also been used for the city walls. The aim was to turn them into bases. They were not to sack them, though, Henry instructed: they could turn out the monks and nuns, but they must treat the buildings as places of God, and show particular respect to the Conqueror's tomb in the Abbaye aux Hommes. If some of the rougher men needed to be told this, Suffolk and the king's other captains probably did not. Like the king, they were God-fearing men, anxious not just to achieve feats of arms, but to do so in a way that honoured the rules of chivalry, and preserved their immortal souls.

They took the abbeys readily enough, and the men crowded into the cloisters, the churches, the dortoirs and refectories. Then the heralds went out under their banners, and made the invitation to surrender. It was refused, as it had been at Harfleur. But this time the king was determined not to be drawn into a long siege, and his brothers perhaps also urged him to try a different tactic. So the message went out to the captains, to be handed down to their men: the cannon would be used first, to create breaches in the walls, then as soon as there was an opening, the army was to storm the city.

It all happened at a breathless pace: there was less than a week between their landing at Touques and the order to begin the direct assault on Caen. This must have been deliberate: to attack a walled city is a terrifying business, easier done in the swirl of continuing action than after weeks sitting in trenches. And it was preferable too not to give the defenders the time to make full preparations to resist the attack.

The men had first to head across the open ground around the city, to the moat and the battered stone walls, carrying bundles of faggots (that is, firewood) to throw into the water to create a dry way across, and scaling ladders for climbing the walls. The captains led, urging their men to follow. They knew, of course, that they would be met with all the means available to the defenders to resist: not just crossbows but stones, boiling water mixed with fat, lime and burning rags. They were fully armed, clanking in their cumbersome suits of iron plate, their vision and breathing restricted by their helmets. They must keep their feet on a ladder, try to dodge the missiles, and once they were up, gain a firm footing on the battlements. Then there was hand-to-hand combat with the armed defenders, with a sheer drop from the walls to the streets below for any man who lost his balance. Once they found a clear path,

Church of St Peter Mancroft, Norwich
Photo Mike Dixon

they headed down the stairways to the streets, where they met resistance from both the rest of the garrison, and those inhabitants who had not retreated cowering to their cellars: more stones, more burning rags, more boiling water thrown out of the windows and on to their heads. The place had to be taken street by street, building by building, from men fighting for their lives with knives, sticks, axes and spades, until the last resistance in the town was done, and only the castle held out.

Then they sacked the place. Women and children as well as men were butchered: 2,000 of them, maybe more. The attackers were euphoric, berserk: the king had not forbidden it, and it would have made little difference if he had.

Finally, exhausted, daring to raise their visors, they were met with a scene of death, devastation, blood mingled with the mud in the streets and streaking the white walls. The survivors glared at them with hatred in their eyes. This was the fate of the English in France: they were the goddamns, the rosbifs, the devils.

King Henry was never going to make the French love him.

But he could not have done so, most likely, however his troops had behaved. There was a long and bloody history between England and France: the old enemies, looking on each other with mutual detestation and contempt. The Normans had not offered to accept Henry as their duke; if he wanted the place – if he wanted all France, come to that – he would have to enforce his claim. At best he could hope it would not be necessary to repeat this terrible lesson too often. Men who knew what horrors would follow resistance would be less motivated to resist, or so at least was the theory.

Come to that, men who knew what they and their comrades had done in the storming might have felt queasy once the rush of blood drained away. They did not doubt that it was a glorious calling to be a man at arms; that fighting was a man's proper business, violence – in the context of war, with the opportunity for surrender given and refused – not just tolerable, but right. But the battered bodies of butchered infants, the bleak despair of raped women – if it was inevitable that such things happened, still they were hardly to be glorified. Henry's men stormed no other major place during his campaigns, although he was to face fierce resistance and pursue long sieges. Nor did he storm the castle at Caen once the city had been taken. The negotiations resumed, and the garrison were allowed to come to terms.

Then the English crowded into the churches, and their chaplains held masses for them. They needed both to give thanks to God, and to atone for the sins they had committed. Confessed, shriven, they could hold their heads high.

Suffolk must have given particular thanks. This was his first major action, and he had come through it unscathed.

Once Caen was securely theirs, the king divided up his army. Gloucester took command of a division of it, and with Suffolk and his men, headed west. They took the city of Bayeux, then focused on the reduction of the Cotentin, the promontory that stretches out to the west of Caen. The men were blooded now, and the inhabitants had learned the hard lesson of Caen. Bayeux surrendered to them with little resistance, and over the next few months they took the towns of St Lo, Carentan, Coutances, Avranches and Pontorson, and a number of strongholds including Valognes, St Saveur and Bricquebec.

This was a solid record of success. Gloucester played his part creditably in the king's great campaign, and so did Suffolk. No one was to hail either of them as one of the finest commanders of the age, but these two men, similar in many ways and very different in

Chateau of Clisson, France

others, appear to have worked well together at this time. Perhaps Suffolk's caution tempered Gloucester's rashness, and vice versa; perhaps too, they were both sufficiently conscious of their inexperience to take advice from the older men who served under them. In these months they must have come to know each other well, and they seem to have forged the basis of a good relationship. Suffolk probably warmed to Gloucester's exuberance, and enjoyed the conversation of a man who was eager to know the great thinkers, writers and musicians of his age – and was already in contact with more than a few of them, beyond England as well as within it. If older men muttered that Gloucester needed to learn good judgement, that he had yet to prove reliable in harder situations than the relatively easy victories of these months – Suffolk might have heard them, but he had no reason to act on what he heard, and many reasons to excuse the prince's faults, and glory in his friendship.

There were other things that he must have seen, but perhaps did not choose to think too hard about in these months of gain and glory. If some places surrendered easily, others only after strong resistance, there was no relieved welcome from Frenchmen sick of a weak regime and the squabbling nobles in Paris. Although King Henry claimed the crown of France, there were not many Frenchmen who believed he was their rightful king. He was an English king with an army of English invaders – including some Flemish, German and Spanish mercenaries, but few if any Frenchmen. As the soldiers foraged for food, burned buildings, looted goods and took captives for ransom, the hatred the French felt could only deepen.

By the summer of 1418, Gloucester, Suffolk and their men were ready to besiege Cherbourg, a small fortified port. The place was strongly defended, and they did not try to storm it. It was a slow siege, so they sat out the summer in this far extremity of western France. This war-ravaged country was hard territory for an army to live off by then: they had to send their men out to forage in threes.

Cherbourg only fell in October, when their second winter in France was coming on. Still no French army had come to engage with them. There was resistance from the garrisons, but none from Paris. It was no wonder: while Henry was besieging the towns of Normandy, the French dukes were continuing to fight among themselves. That autumn the duke of Burgundy was besieging Paris. The Armagnacs had held the capital since 1413, but now that they were at a low ebb, their commanders killed or imprisoned at Agincourt, there was an opportunity for Burgundy's opposing faction to regain ascendancy at the Valois court. If Burgundy still had a treaty of sorts with the English, they would not have deluded themselves that he was fighting in their support; what he was doing was done for the duke of Burgundy. In May 1418 his troops took the city, and proceeded to ransack it.

St Mary's Church, North Tuddenham, Norfolk
Photo Mike Dixon

17 The lord of Bricquebec

Of course the victorious English captains expected rewards, and Suffolk got his share. In 1418 he was appointed lord and captain of two small towns that he and Gloucester had taken in Normandy, Hambye and Bricquebec: that is, he was given these places as his possessions, and also garrisoned their keeps for the king. (The garrisons were expected to do as garrisons had always done: extract taxes and dues sufficient to provide for themselves, and produce a profit for their captain.) A chronicle of the time refers to the king giving these places to 'his favourite, William earl of Suffolk, who was to render him in return a shield of the arms of St George annually'. It was a normal grant rather than an exceptional one for a lord in Suffolk's position, but by this time the king would have known him personally, and perhaps did indeed favour him.

The Cotentin peninsula, the area of western Normandy where Suffolk had been campaigning with Gloucester, is set between the bay of Mont St Michel to the west and the bay of the Seine to the north. At that time it was a remote and isolated area. A band of marshland ran across the peninsula, cutting off the higher ground to the north, and making it all but inaccessible in the winter. (It was sometimes described in those days as an island.) Bricquebec lay in this northern part of the Cotentin. It was set safely inland, a few miles to the west of Valognes and south of Cherbourg.

The Cotentin had always guarded its independence, and it had only belatedly (in the mid-tenth century) become a part of the duchy of Normandy.

The lordship of Bricquebec brought Suffolk a substantial castle, which had been built by the Bertran family in the eleventh and twelfth centuries. He probably visited it once he had been granted the lordship, and admired the octagonal stone donjon sitting on its motte, and the solid buildings that surrounded it. This was a large enough place that he could station his troops there in winter when they were not campaigning.

The manor of Hambye was farther south, in the valley of the little river Sienne, between Granville and St Lo. It had been owned by the same family (the Paisnels) as Bricquebec in the late fourteenth and early fifteenth centuries, which perhaps explains why the two passed together to Suffolk. Hambye was noted most for its sizeable Benedictine abbey. This too was old by Suffolk's time; it had been built in the twelfth and thirteenth centuries. It had been at its peak in the thirteenth century, but had suffered like all of Normandy from the ravages of the long war with England, and was in slow decline when Suffolk acquired the manor. Much of it remains even today, however.

Chateau of Bricquebec

Suffolk had little or no time to enjoy his new possessions, though. While Gloucester and his men were still waiting for Cherbourg to fall, the king sent for them, because he needed his troops to unite in a larger campaign. That autumn, every man in the English army who was not needed to garrison an English-held stronghold gathered around the walls of Rouen.

18 Useless mouths

It would have taken many days to travel from Cherbourg to Rouen, along the coast of north-west Normandy, the men at arms riding their horses, the archers and servants trudging alongside them, the carts rattling over the ruts. It was most of it territory they had taken that year and the year before: past Bayeux, Caen, their landing place at Touques, looking across the estuary to Harfleur, then following the loops of the great river inland to the Norman capital. In an era before maps were common and reliable, Suffolk and Gloucester would have depended on their heralds and poursuivants – their messengers – to show them the road.

This was a time of year when all the men would have been hoping to withdraw to winter quarters, if they were not to sail back to England. But the siege of Rouen had been in place since July, and had to be brought to a conclusion first.

Much had been achieved already, and the English were in control of the territory around the city, but it was still wild and dangerous countryside. As many as 20,000 poor people, judged incapable of fighting, had been forced out of the city before the siege dug in, and all the suburbs and small places nearby had been laid to waste by the French to hamper the attackers. Many people were living rough in the area, competing with the army for food. This was a time to keep the troops tight together and the baggage well guarded, and set a strong watch when they paused for the night. Nearer the town they needed to keep off the fields for fear of chausse-trappes, the three-pronged iron mantraps the French had sowed them with. They passed trees hacked to stumps and pasture turned to blackened stubble, then as they came closer to the city, the ruins of the burnt and broken-down houses, inns and workshops.

Both upstream and downstream, the English had built temporary wooden bridges across the Seine. There were two permanent bridges in Rouen itself, but none across the stretches of river immediately to the east and west of it. The heralds led the troops across the bridge downstream, since they had come from the south-west and the city is to the north of the river, and probably showed off the defences the English had set: strong chains stretched from bank to bank, above and below the water, to ensure that no boat could

slip through in darkness to bring food into the city. There were no boats moored along the river, because every one had been sunk, even the two royal galleys that were normally kept in Rouen. Gloucester, Suffolk and their men would have circled the walls, keeping at a safe distance from the cannon, and heading for the convent of Notre Dame de la Rose, a short distance east of the city, which the king had taken as his headquarters.

Notre Dame de la Rose, Rouen, from Cook, *The Story of Rouen* (1899)

From the higher ground – this region is hilly, with high chalk cliffs like those around Harfleur – they could look down on the spires of Rouen, a city which had made much of its wealth from weaving, goldworking and trade. This was a far larger place than Caen, Cherbourg or Harfleur. It had a fine cathedral, three grand abbeys, over thirty convents, and almost forty parish churches. There were nearly five miles of walls, and within them was a strong garrison. Now that he had taken control of Paris, and was in the ascendant at the Valois court, the duke of Burgundy had thrown his lot back in with King Charles VI of France, and had sent the city several thousand men to swell its defenders. There were Parisians too, and men who had retreated from places such as Caen that the English had already taken, so perhaps in all there were 25,000 men defending the place, and two or three times as many of the common inhabitants still within the walls.

Henry's besieging army was even stronger. Including all the non-fighting supporters, there might have been as many as 50,000 men camped in the ruined suburbs, the fields and on the clifftops. He had supplemented the main English force with Gascon, Spanish and Lombard mercenaries, Welsh longbowmen, and Irish footsoldiers: ragged, often barefoot men who fought with enormous knives and bundles of darts. The cannon fired continually, from the walls onto the attackers, and from the strongpoints the English had established onto the city. Both sides used older siege engines too, hurling stones and arrows from trebuchets and ballistas. Gibbets stood silhouetted on the higher ground: discipline had to be kept tight in a long hard action such as this one, so harsh justice was applied, and hanged men were left to rot in the open as a warning to the rest.

Gloucester and Suffolk met with the king, doubtless. It was probably the first time they had seen him for months, since they had been fighting a good distance from Rouen. Like them, he had had many successes over the previous two summers, but by this time he must have been weary and frustrated at his failure to make a breakthrough in the siege. Henry had directed it in person from the start, so this was not only a city he needed to take for tactical reasons, it was also one he was determined to take for personal ones. He must have been glad to gain this solid tranche of reinforcements, and to have his younger brother alongside him once more.

There were many other captains in such a large army, and Suffolk and Gloucester will have met with them too, and been briefed on the events since the investment began. The man who had made the biggest impact was Thomas Montacute, the earl of Salisbury. It was he who had taken the steep hill to the east of Rouen, on which stood the fortified monastery of St Catherine and a small fort, St Michel. Suffolk probably already knew Salisbury to some extent, but he was to come to know him much better over the next few years, since Salisbury became the commander he fought alongside for much of the time, perhaps by his own choice. A skilful, thoughtful man, though with a streak of brutality – he had been known to drag his captives to their dungeons at the end of a rope – Salisbury was about eight years older than Suffolk, and had held commands throughout Henry's campaigns. His family, like Suffolk's and so many, had been devastated by the end of Richard II's reign and Henry IV's usurpation: Salisbury's father had been killed in the unrest at that time, in 1401.

Men like Salisbury were protective of their positions in an action such as this, and coming late to the siege, even Gloucester could not expect to do more than play a supportive role. The king put him and Suffolk in front of the Porte Sainte Hilaire. This was to the east of the city, by a little stream, the Robec, so they were between the walls of Rouen and the king's headquarters, in a position to communicate easily with the king. Suffolk's men took the south side of the stream, and with the winter coming on fast, would have busied

Rouen Cathedral

themselves setting their tents and doing what they could to protect themselves from the cold. The king had no plan to storm Rouen, it was too large and too strong. Unless the Valois managed to get together another army to challenge them, they would sit it out until the city starved.

Their spies and the men they captured trying to break through the lines would have told them how things were in the narrow streets of Rouen. Even a few weeks into the siege, bread had become the main currency in the city. Later, dogs sold for ten shillings, rats for sixpence, eggs for thirteen pence – sums only the rich could afford. The men in the Lancastrian army probably repeated these tales to cheer themselves, because although they had better supplies than this, theirs too were very tight. There was nothing left to forage for, so the king had sent to England. When ships drew up at the temporary bridge to unload their cargo of wine and beer that November – butts of tyre, romency and malvesy wine, pipes of ale and beer, and courtesy of the citizens of London, 2,500 mugs to drink them from – they must have brought cries of delight to drown the cannon.

The cold began to bite hard, and still the siege wore on. The captains had to try to cheer their men, the king to try to cheer his captains. Perhaps the greatest of Henry's qualities was his clarity and resoluteness: he never seemed to doubt that what he did was right, and had the strength of heaven behind it. Rouen had to be taken, he would have repeated to Suffolk and the rest; they could not stand down. Normandy was his province, and he needed to be in control of this city, or none of their other conquests would be safe. He was the rightful master of the city, and the haggard men who fired their cannons at his troops were traitors, no better, refusing to allow him entry into a place should have been his to command.

He was their king, and they had to believe it.

In early December there was a commotion. The gates of Rouen opened, and out of them stumbled all those who were unfit to defend it: poor women and children, the old and sick. The French (and the English too) called them with brutal accuracy 'les bouches inutiles' – the useless mouths. There were more of them, and more, and more: about 15,000 sorry souls spewed out under the spikes of the portcullises and into the broad ditch that surrounded the walls.

They would have gone further, but Henry ordered his men to stop them. They hefted their pikes and drove the old men, the women with babes in arms, the skinny kids, back into the ditch. They must have known they could do nothing else. There was little enough for them to eat, without this tattered horde as competition. They had to be cruel or die.

So the bouches inutiles were trapped. The gates had closed behind them, and the starving defenders of Rouen would not open them again. The English lines had closed, and the king would not open them either. They begged, screamed, pleaded for food, for sanctuary, for shelter from the December wind and rain. And the English did their best to stop their ears.

To sack a place was brutal enough, and Suffolk had done that now. But that was short, and done in the heat and exhilaration that followed a storming. This was slow. Over hours,

Church of St Maclou, Rouen

Rouen Cathedral

days, weeks, the cries rose from the multitude of sorry humanity in the ditch. Over hours, days, weeks, their pleas had to be resisted. The cannon continued to fire, and down in the ditch, the cries grew weaker and the old men, the women, the children slowly starved to death.

It was not his fault, the king insisted. It was the duty of the Rouennais to care for their own. If they could not do so, they should have surrendered. If they were mulish enough to ignore this obvious truth, he could not be blamed for it.

A couple of weeks after the poor were thrown into the ditch, the Porte Sainte Hilaire opened again. This time a troop of armed men marched out, 2,000 or so of them. Shouts went up from the English army, and there must have been a scramble in the camp for men to get their weapons and make formation.

It was the first time the English had fought a sizeable action for months, and taken by surprise, at first Suffolk and Gloucester's men were beaten back. But more of the English, Welsh and Irish piled in, and soon they managed to regain their ground. They were still fighting when the word began to spread that this was a feint; a bigger attack was planned from the west of the city, where the castle stood. Once the French who were set against them had been downed or fled, Suffolk and the other commanders gave the order to march to the west. They never reached there, though, because the heralds intercepted them en route. Head north instead! The bridge over the moat at the castle gate had collapsed, and those defenders who had not gone tumbling into the ditch had turned back. Men were needed at the other gates, to stop them if they tried to attack from another point.

By the time Suffolk's men had marched half-way round the walls, the English stationed to the north were in control. The gates had shut behind the defenders, and the English killed the men trapped outside them, but they did not get into the city; so it had gained them nothing. There were fewer people in Rouen to share the dregs of the supplies, and the stench from the corpses rotting in the ditch was worse than ever.

By Christmas, the English were all still camped around Rouen. Rumours were circulating that the duke of Burgundy planned to send an army to raise the siege; that King Charles VI or the dauphin, his heir, meant to send an army; but once again, no army came. They did what they could in the English camp – and no doubt in the French city too – to celebrate the season. The king had his minstrels with him, so there was music, at least for his captains; there was food from what supplies they had left. There were masses celebrated in the echoing spaces of the nunnery church. Whether it was the king's own idea, or his

priests that persuaded him to it, Henry agreed that something should be done for the starving in the ditch, so the priests headed out with baskets of food, and threw them down to the sorry heaps of skin and bones. Perhaps it would have been kinder to kill them faster.

Much of a winter had gone, and they were still shivering in their tents on the fields around Rouen. After Christmas there can have been few kind words for the French in the English camp.

On the eve of New Year's Day one of the gates opened once more. This time a group of envoys came out of Rouen under a flag of truce. The English were beyond jubilance by then, sunk in chill and weariness. The word spread round: make them suffer.

For two long humiliating days the Rouennais tramped from tent to tent, while the English stood and jeered. They did not attack these starving wretches – a flag of truce was not to be flouted – but they were damned if they would help them. When the envoys found their way to the convent of Notre Dame, it was to face a king who did not hide his anger at their long resistance. If they had surrendered when they ought, he told them, he might have shown them clemency. No more. He would have Rouen remember him 'until the Day of Judgement'.

The men of Rouen were willing to negotiate, they said, but not to surrender if the terms were not right. So negotiations had to be arranged. They were held on the land between the king's headquarters and the Porte Sainte Hilaire, where Suffolk's men were stationed, so it would have been they who cleared a space in their camp and provided a tent for the two sides to meet in.

The king demanded terms so harsh that at first no agreement could be reached. The envoys retreated back through the Porte Sainte Hilaire, but soon they ventured out again. They all knew – Henry's men, the citizens of Rouen, its sorry garrison – that no relieving army was coming, and that the surrender had to be made.

They negotiated then through the short winter days and the long winter nights. Henry

Rouen, houses and the cloister of St Ouen

held out, and in the end the end he got his submission. The men of Rouen would pay the English 300,000 gold crowns, a sum so enormous that it took them eleven years to find it. They would give the king a large site within the walls to build a palace. The garrison were allowed their lives, but nothing else. When they filed out under the flag of truce, the English soldiers stopped them and stripped them of everything but the clothes they wore.

This was an occasion for King Henry to show his love of pomp and ceremony. If he was taking the keys of a city where more than half those still within were corpses, that was no reason not to do so in splendour. His servants brought out his throne and dressed him in cloth of gold for the surrender. The keys of Rouen handed over, the French and Burgundian men at arms marched off, and the king and his captains led the procession through the gates they had been staring at from the outside for so long. The English standards rose on the battered walls. The surviving inhabitants watched them. There was no sack. This was a cold, hard victory.

The troops stayed for a while, to make sure the place was firmly theirs, before the bulk of them withdrew to other winter quarters. Suffolk's men were billeted in the abbey of St Ouen. It was most likely little warmer than their tents had been. The French had been rebuilding the abbey, which dated back in parts to the sixth century, even before the life of the saint whose bones it held, so the soldiers took over a mishmash of half-raised buildings made more battered still by the cannon. There was the makings of a huge, fine, forbidding stone church, with a choir, chapels, and at least part of a transept. There were the monks' living quarters into which the men swarmed, and there was a solid tower centuries old, the Tour aux Clercs, from which Suffolk could probably see the Porte Sainte Hilaire.

This beautiful, haunted city with its stench of death was to be the English headquarters in Normandy for the rest of Suffolk's time there. Even when the English took Paris, they continued to administer Normandy from Rouen. Suffolk would have come there regularly, and for some time at least, he held onto the abbey complex and lodged his men there, although he probably later requisitioned a house to serve as his own quarters. Four years later, the incoming archbishop could not lodge in the abbey before being invested because it was so full of English soldiers.

19 An admiral and a queen

Rouen changed the war, and it changed the men. It had been brutal before; now it was bitter too. Suffolk and his contemporaries had lost the last traces of merry boyhood, and were lean, toughened, cold-hearted to those who opposed them.

With the city secure, Suffolk's men probably headed back to western Normandy, raiding those farms and villages that had not yet been sacked en route, and doing their best to build up some winter supplies. The takings were almost certainly thin, but still they were better than anything that had been available in Rouen. Then at last they could sit out the remainder of the cold weather, around their fires within the thick walls of Bricquebec castle.

It was perhaps there that the news came from Wingfield in April 1419. Lady Katherine, Suffolk's mother, was dead.

Lady Katherine's tomb in St Andrew's Church, Wingfield

Her funeral would have taken place before he even heard of her death. If he went back to England in its wake – to pay his respects at the tomb where her body lay next to his father's, sit through some of the masses in their memory, claim her dower estates for his own, check on the running of his lands, visit his sisters – then he did so only briefly, since in later years he was to say that he was continually at this time in France. Perhaps he settled for lighting candles and saying prayers for her in Bricquebec.

He could have claimed Wingfield now, and dominated much of Suffolk from it; claimed Court Hall, and set himself up as a power in Hull. He could have done both. Or perhaps he could not: he was a man at arms, he served his king, and if his king felt the need of him in France – where his king continued to campaign, neglecting his own responsibilities in England – Suffolk probably felt he could do nothing other than stay there. He was not alone in this: there were many English lords who remained in France while the campaigns continued, although there were others, including Humphrey of Gloucester and Lord Cromwell, who returned to England not long after the taking of Rouen.

Although John of Bedford – and after Bedford in turn came to France, his brother Gloucester who replaced him – did his best to rule England with the help of the king's council, England felt the lack. For a lord to send his servants messages through his heralds and poursuivants was not the same as for a lord to ride across his lands, see their condition for himself and listen to the tales of the men who lived on them. There was no war in England, but there was not the king's peace either; instead there was a vacuum.

Suffolk probably gave little thought to this. He was focused on the king and his campaigns; his life at this time was in France. It was not all a matter of fighting. The king now had reasonably firm control over a large area of Normandy. It had to be administered and controlled; it had to be brought back to peace and normality. In Caen, Rouen and the other towns and cities that the English had taken by force, garrisons had to be maintained and supervised, broken-down walls and wrecked houses rebuilt, English settlers enticed and French inhabitants accepted back, provided they took an oath of loyalty to Henry. (There were not so many of either of these, however. England had not enough spare inhabitants to repopulate the whole of Normandy, and perhaps half of the native French chose to leave their homes and head north, south or east, rather than submit to life under the invaders.) There was work here for men such as Suffolk. And there was opportunity here too, in many ways more so than in England. There were appointments to be made, estates to be granted to new lords, and he could expect to gain his share, or even more than his share, if he remained in the favour of the king.

Suffolk's brother John had been destined from the outset to be a fighting man, and at some point during this period he followed Suffolk to France, and began to forge a career for himself as a respected captain in the king's army. Alexander did the same when he was grown. Thomas remained in England. He was in holy orders, and had his own path to follow. That June he gained his first appointment in the church, as a prebend – a type of canon, drawing income from the manor of Brownswood in London, and serving at St Paul's Cathedral. He remained in this post for the rest of his life. The management of his English estates was a task Suffolk entrusted not to any of his brothers, but to the servants who had been his father's before him, men such as John Heydon, who would have written assuring him that all was well at Wingfield.

Meanwhile in France, Suffolk was beginning to gain appointments of his own. In May 1419 he was made admiral of the duchy of Normandy. There was no standing fleet controlled by the English in Normandy, and only a few of the actions over the next few years involved naval blockades, but it was an honour and a responsibility nonetheless. In June he became captain of Pontorson, and in August captain of Avranches, a sizeable town. These places were to the south-east and south of Mont St Michel, so both were only a short distance from

Church of St Peter Mancroft, Norwich
Photo Mike Dixon

The French royal family

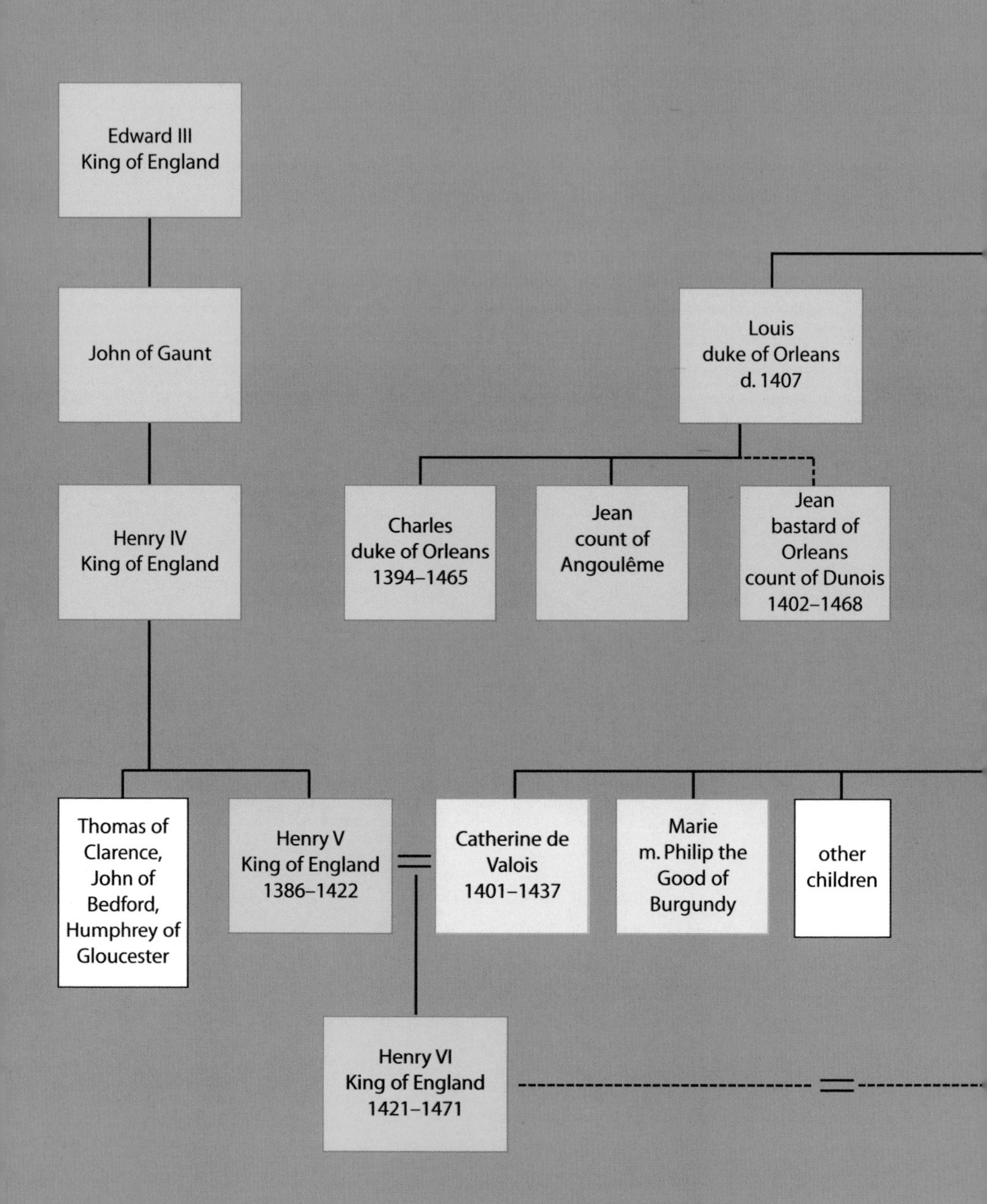

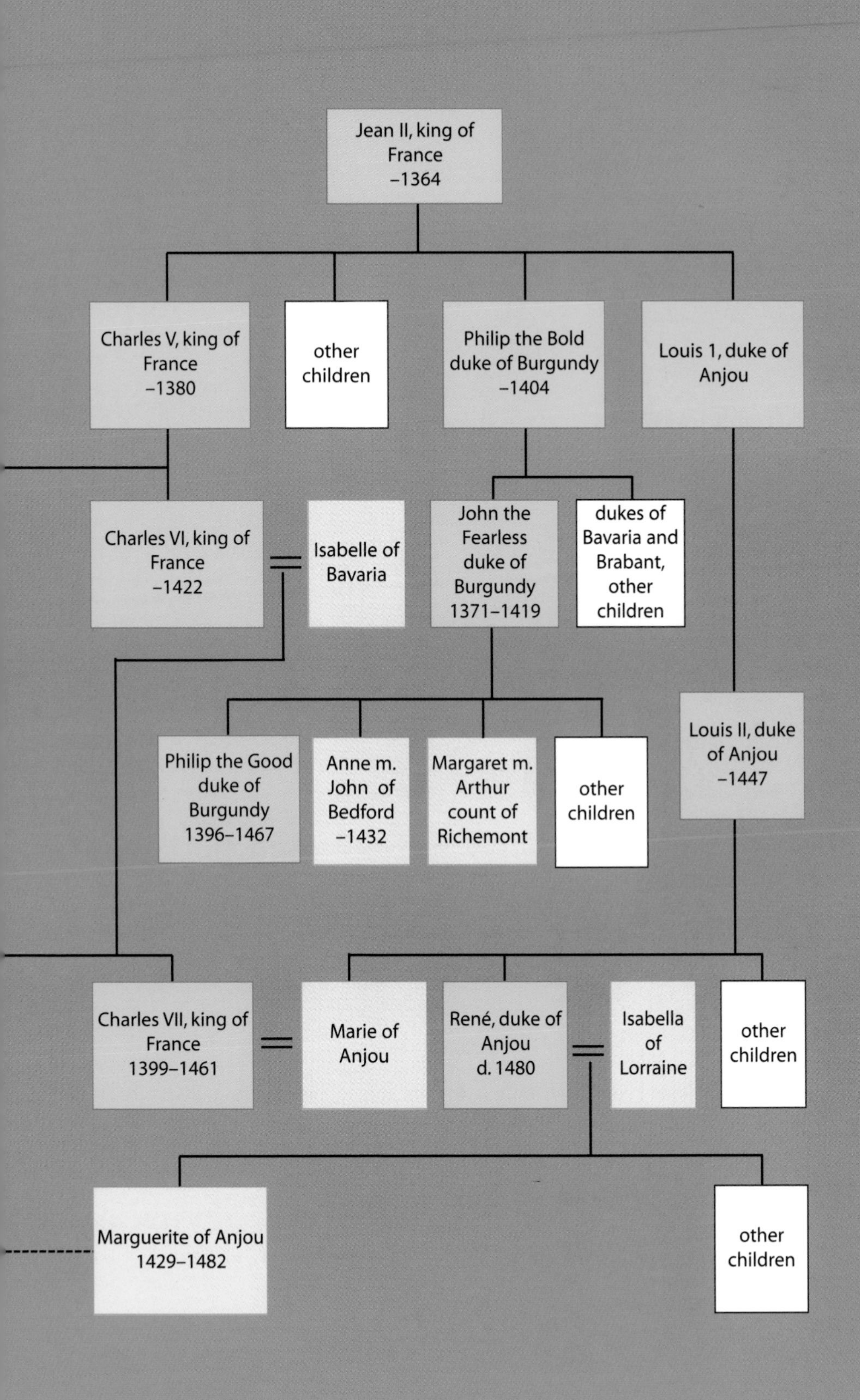

Jean II, king of France –1364
Charles V, king of France –1380
other children
Philip the Bold duke of Burgundy –1404
Louis 1, duke of Anjou
Charles VI, king of France –1422
Isabelle of Bavaria
John the Fearless duke of Burgundy 1371–1419
dukes of Bavaria and Brabant, other children
Philip the Good duke of Burgundy 1396–1467
Anne m. John of Bedford –1432
Margaret m. Arthur count of Richemont
other children
Louis II, duke of Anjou –1447
Charles VII, king of France 1399–1461
Marie of Anjou
René, duke of Anjou d. 1480
Isabella of Lorraine
other children
Marguerite of Anjou 1429–1482
other children

Hambye. Many similar appointments were to follow in the succeeding years. If the posts were more than one man could fill, that was no matter; it was usual to appoint lieutenants to do much of the actual work, give them part of the fee, and retain the rest. So his career was progressing steadily: perhaps not quite spectacularly, but as well as he could reasonably have wished. He was growing into his role as a great lord.

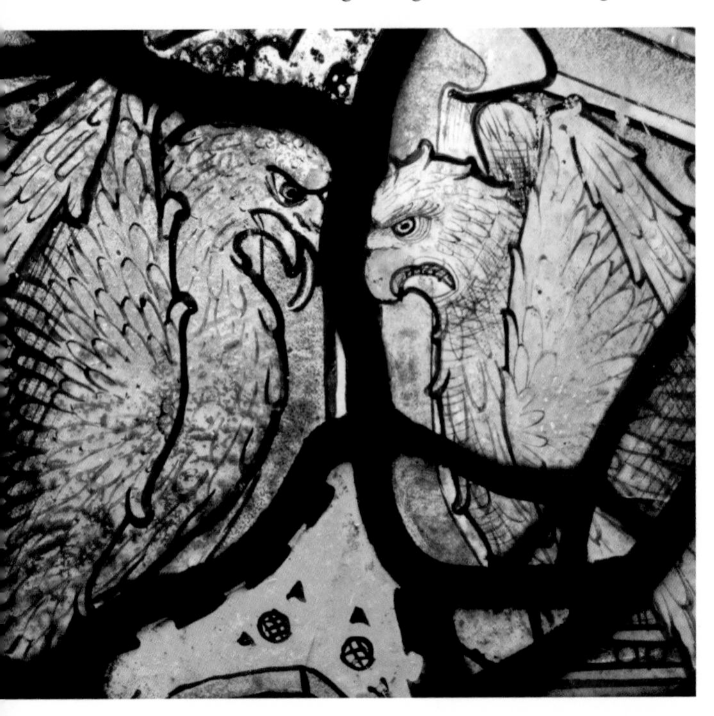

Inevitably, though, as a young man he was more of a supporter than a leading figure in the events of the next few years. He was at the king's side for at least some of the time; he had his new estates and positions in France to maintain; he continued to play his part in the military actions, though as yet he had relatively little opportunity to shape them.

In the wake of the taking of Rouen, things went well in France for the English, so this must have been an exhilarating time to be one of the king's captains. When they resumed campaigning in the spring of 1419, castles and towns surrendered rapidly to them. Some isolated places still held out for the Valois. The English had made no attempt as yet to take Mont St Michel, for instance, and Suffolk probably realized that since his own possessions surrounded it, he was being marked out for the thankless job of besieging the immensely powerful island stronghold. But enough was in Lancastrian hands that the king's captains might regard themselves as lords of Normandy.

Humphrey of Gloucester did not return to France, and Suffolk served for the next few seasons under the king, the earl of Salisbury, and Thomas of Clarence. He must have travelled repeatedly (with a strong escort) between the places that he commanded, checking on their garrisons. He spent much of his time with the men under his command who were delegated to take further towns and strongholds, setting directions for the sieges, but leaving the men often to pursue the work of them under his lieutenants. And he will have travelled to Rouen and elsewhere to meet with King Henry, Clarence, Salisbury and the other commanders, and learned directly from them, as well as from his own heralds and from what he saw on his travels, how the wider war was progressing.

He not only listened; increasingly, he contributed to the discussions. He was not a formal member of the king's ruling council, but there were plenty of informal conversations that he could take part in. He was past the stage now when his focus was on what the

Above, St Mary's Church, North Tuddenham, Norfolk
Right, cloister of St Ouen, Rouen

war meant for him and his brothers; he was acquiring a strategic sense, and his discussions with men such as Salisbury and Clarence must have helped to focus his thoughts.

Although the fighting was going well, the diplomacy was more problematic, and there must have been some long hard discussions between the king and his advisers. If Henry was to be accepted as the duke of Normandy, let alone as king of France, he needed the support of at least some of the major French lords. But the brutal actions had widened the gulf between the English and French, and none of the great French dukes, or even the counts, had leapt the chasm.

The mad king, Charles VI, had now lost all but one of his sons, so the youngest, another Charles, had taken the title of dauphin and become his heir. The man who might have been the leader of the Armagnac faction, the duke of Orleans, was still in captivity in England, as he had been since he was taken at Agincourt, and King Henry still had no inclination to release him. So the Armagnacs were the weaker of the two parties at the Valois court, and they had lost Paris as a result; but their grouping was by no means extinct. Indeed the dauphin himself, though a spindly runt of a man, was steadily emerging as their new leader. This had the potential to be a problem of itself, however: it meant that the heir of the house of Valois did not stand aloof between the two opposing factions among the French nobility.

The duke of Brittany did his best to keep out of the wrangling, favouring neither faction. The English courted his favour, but he was not the focus of their attention. The duke of Burgundy was in that position. He was the man who had the potential to transform the situation. If the work of the English spies and agents could help to keep Burgundy and the dauphin at odds; if Burgundy could be persuaded that his own position would be better if he chose to support Henry, then the two of them together might bring the French civil war to a close, and see their joint party firmly in control of the country.

John the Fearless was a difficult man to deal with. He could be slippery, devious, even duplicitous. Of course the English could be all these things too, but King Henry was on the whole a straightforward man, clear to both himself and others about his plans and intentions. And he was a man who adhered to the commitments he made. Henry had obviously taken note that Burgundy had sent troops to the defence of Rouen – not the army the Rouennais had hoped for to raise the siege, but a good contingent to strengthen the garrison. There was still a truce in force between England and Burgundy, which had been agreed before the invasion. It was worrying that Burgundy had broken it so lightly.

Seen from the right angle, however, John the Fearless' policy became more apparent.

Burgundy was richer and more powerful than either of the rivals for the French throne; he knew it, and had no intention of taking a subservient role. He was not motivated to help put a strong man on the throne of France; it suited him far better when the French king was weak, and the real power lay instead with him. And he was a proud Frenchman, instinctively antipathetic to the English; he wanted to keep the support of the other French lords himself, and could see no advantage in becoming the first of them to cross to Henry's side.

If the English also asked themselves – as they must have done – what they least wanted to see happen at this stage, then the answer was plain. If the dauphin decided it was in his own interests to offer Burgundy all that he was seeking, and managed to carry the Armagnac party with him, and the duke and dauphin then jointly bolstered their depleted troops with a good contingent from England's other enemy, the Scots: that could have given them enough heft to fight back in earnest against the English.

It was this possibility that needed to be prevented at all costs. So in parallel with the military actions, there was intense activity from the spies and diplomats, trying both to court Burgundy's favour, and to keep dissension in the French ranks.

Church of St Peter and St Paul, Salle, Norfolk

July 1419 was a crucial month. The English truce with Burgundy expired at this point. If it had proved to be worth little in practice, still it had real diplomatic significance. Henry would obviously have chosen to renew it, but when his agents brought the news that Burgundy had instead agreed a truce with the Armagnacs, he had to decide how to respond to this new and dangerous situation.

He chose to do so with a show of force. He set his men to attack a Burgundian stronghold: Pontoise, a town to the north-west of Paris. The English took the place without difficulty, and this gave them some strategic advantage. But there must have been doubts among the king's advisers as to whether it had been the wisest policy. True, some might argue that it would send Burgundy the message that the English were so strong that he would be unwise to turn away from them. But others would argue that this was a message that would encourage him to do just that.

We cannot know whether Suffolk made this analysis, and was dismayed by the situation in which this put the English. If he thought so, he certainly could not have said it. He probably did not yet feel able to put a proposal to the king while policy was being discussed. And once the king's decision was made, it had to be supported. Even the most powerful English lords – even his brothers – did not tell the king he had made a mistake.

Nor was the king a man who would admit as much, probably not even to himself, and certainly not to his captains. So when the messages came from the spies that the dauphin and the duke of Burgundy were arranging a face to face meeting, the English probably responded with bluster and mutual reassurances: they were strong enough now to hold their own against a united French opponent.

Underlying this, though, there would have been real concern. Would the French actually manage to put their bloody dissensions behind them? It was twelve years now since John the Fearless had had a hand in the murder of a duke of Orleans: was that long enough to forgive and forget a crime that had never been avenged? Suffolk, and the other commanders too, would have given their heralds instructions to bring them any news as soon as it arrived. Over that summer, there must have been many such messages. The French lords would meet in Paris; no, they would not, it was neither secure enough nor neutral enough. They would meet outside the city, on the south or the east, well away from the English at Pontoise, and the army under Clarence that was forging a way through the towns and strongholds to the west of the city. They had fixed a venue: Montereau, a small town at the confluence of the rivers Seine and Yonne, in the secure Valois territory to the south-east of the capital. The Burgundians could assemble north of the bridge at Montereau, the Armagnacs to the south, and the two would meet, symbolically, in the middle of the river.

The next news was stunning indeed. John the Fearless of Burgundy had met the Armagnac delegation on the bridge at Montereau, and the dauphin's supporters had fallen on him and murdered him.

What luck that was for the English! King Henry might not always make the right choices, but he had something even more valuable than good judgement: he had good fortune. The tide that had been flowing with him was now a flood. The Valois had been thrown into a disarray from which they could not, would not, recover for years. The dauphin was claiming it was none of his doing, the heralds reported: he had not only not taken part, he had not ordered or sanctioned the murder. But the men who had done it were of his party, and that was enough to damn him.

The hole in John the Fearless' skull had created a great rift between Burgundy and the Armagnacs. Henry took advantage, of course. With one duke of Burgundy dead, another took the lands and title – John the Fearless's son Philip, who came to be known as Philip the Good – and the English approached him: first privately, but as the feedback reached them, and it was all promising, in public and in full defiance of the dauphin. Surely now the Burgundians would throw in their lot with the English. They might not feel warmly towards Henry, but their antipathy to him was nothing compared with the hatred that Philip the Good now felt for the Armagnacs.

The fighting continued meanwhile, and went well for the English: by September Clarence's army was at the gates of Paris.

Almost certainly Suffolk had never met John the Fearless, and at this point he had not met his son

Church of St Pierre, Dreux

Philip either. Come to that, he had not met King Charles of France, or the dauphin, or most of the lords, men at arms, churchmen and administrators who made up the French king's court. Not only was not he not well acquainted with these men, he had never crossed swords with them, never negotiated with them, or stood alongside his king or another man while they did so. These were things he shared with other captains of his own age, but not with the older generation, many of whom had met at least some of the leading Frenchmen. Clarence, for instance, had negotiated with the Armagnacs in 1413, and other lords had taken part in the diplomacy before and between the king's two expeditions to France.

Bourges Cathedral

Suffolk had met plenty of Frenchmen during the two years since the 1417 invasion, but almost all would have been men of lesser degree: captains of provincial garrisons, burghers who negotiated surrenders, tradesmen who took the oath of loyalty in front of him when the king was not present. All this was now to change, and change dramatically. Although he did not play a central role in the negotiations between Henry of Lancaster and Philip of Burgundy, he played a supporting role, as did all the king's lords in France. He met Burgundian envoys; in time, met the duke himself. And the agreement that was forged over the next few months between England and Burgundy was to alter the entire character of the Lancastrian venture in France, and his own experiences with it.

All the English lords would have been curious about this new duke, and there were men – the heralds, merchants who had dealt with the Burgundians before the war, past negotiators – who could tell them something at least of what they wanted to know. Philip of Burgundy was barely a couple of months Suffolk's senior. He was not just richer than common men, but far richer than lords such as Suffolk himself. Like Suffolk, he had come early and suddenly to his high position. In many ways a cautious and at times a devious man, he was also one given to feuds and rages. He had a weakness for women, which was already becoming well known: men counted more than thirty mistresses over his lifetime, and he sired a stream of bastards. Duke Philip talked often of fighting, but rarely came actually to do it. In all this he was the antithesis of King Henry. Their slow rapprochement, fuelled by Henry's ambitions and Burgundy's furious grief, must have intrigued all of those who witnessed it.

At first it was handled through intermediaries: messages spoken by heralds and ambassadors, then as the proposals began to solidify, messages written as well. Only months later did the king and duke meet face to face.

Both men needed to gain from what was decided. What Philip wanted – spurred by his widowed mother – was revenge for his father's death, and assurance that the dauphin would never become king of France and his own overlord. He also hoped to gain lands and power; he was not a man who acted on principle alone. One of his strategies was to alienate the dauphin from his parents. Charles VI was still only intermittently sane, and could be relied upon for little, but his queen Isabeau could be leaned on to act in her husband's stead. Philip's wife at this time (he was to have three) was Michelle, one of Charles VI's daughters, and she too was encouraged to sow divisions in the French king's family in the duchy of Burgundy's interests.

Henry, meanwhile, wanted not just Normandy, but what it suited Philip so well for him to claim – the throne of France. What he had to offer was, first, his highly effective army, which could continue to campaign and assert his claim with force; and second, his hand in marriage.

Many men must have privately criticized King Henry for his slowness to marry: he was in his thirties now, no longer young. His own failure had probably held his brothers back too, and more than a few men would have thought Humphrey of Gloucester, in particular, might have been better off tied to a sensible woman. But it was to the king's advantage now that his marriage was a bargaining card. The possibility of his marrying Charles VI's daughter Catherine had been discussed on and off for years. Now with Isabeau leaning on Charles, and Philip leaning on both of them, it could be brought about. Then Henry would be married to Burgundy's sister-in-law; and he offered too to marry one of his brothers to a sister of Burgundy's, to further tighten the bonds between the Lancastrians and this powerful dukedom.

The English must have assumed at first that this would be the deal Henry would settle for: a truce with Burgundy, marriage to a French princess, effective control of France while Charles was alive, and the prospect of grabbing the throne with Burgundy's support once the mad king went to his grave. The dauphin would be sidelined, if Philip of Burgundy managed to bring other French lords to support the Lancastrians. But as the messages passed from Burgundy's courts in Bruges and Dijon, to the English in Rouen and Isabeau in Troyes, it became apparent that they could get still more. Queen Isabeau, sickened by her son's complicity in the murder of John the Fearless, and indebted to Philip the Good for help both practical and financial, was willing to let it be suggested that the dauphin was not the king's son. This paved the way for his disinheritance. And then with Catherine's hand, Henry could become heir to the kingdom of France.

It took till the spring of 1420 to wrap it all up. On his marriage to Catherine, Henry would become regent of France until the death of her father. Then when Charles VI died he would take the crown, with the provision that France must remain separate from England, with its own laws and government, and be in no way subservient. The ambassadors drew up a treaty to confirm all this, and Henry and his counsellors travelled to Troyes, the city southeast of Paris where Isabeau had set up her court, to ratify it that May. The king of England and the princess of France were betrothed and then married there, in the cathedral.

While the common men at arms continued to hold the places the English had taken, and mark time in besieging those they hoped to take next, the lords of England who were in France headed for Troyes for the king's wedding. King Henry needed to put on a fine display; he chose to bring them all, to set against the French and Burgundians who would also come to Troyes.

Troyes was a small town, tight-walled in the shape of a champagne cork, and fizzing to bursting with the men – and women too – who had arrived there for the ceremony. Henry did his best to impress his new allies. Queen Isabeau could be depended on for little, and it was not Burgundy's role to plan the ceremonial, so the English took charge of it all. The king had had eight white horses brought over from England to draw the bride's carriage. He ordered his men to dress splendidly, determined they should outshine the French, and told them to give offerings at the marriage service on the English scale – much more than Frenchmen would have given. They must stay sober too, and not disgrace him with soldiers' rough manners. The order went out that none of the English should drink the rich wine of the Troyes region unless it was well watered first.

So it was a clear-headed earl of Suffolk who met the French and Burgundians at these festivities. He was particularly useful to the king because he spoke good French. Many of the English did not: their lives even in France were spent mostly among other Englishmen, and if they had learned the language as boys, it was rusty now, or so Anglicized that the French themselves could not make sense of it. According to some reports King Henry himself barely spoke French at all. Queen Isabeau, Duke Philip and the rest had little or no English, and the same was true of the bride, so there would have been nods and smiles, leavened with interpretation from the heralds and chaplains – or men such as Suffolk – when it was needed.

Philip the Good had plenty of Valois blood in him – all the French nobility, indeed all the European nobility, were much intermarried – and it showed in his long nose and weak chin, but he was a sharp-witted man, with none of the French king's taint of madness. He was also a proud and haughty one. Suffolk would not have expected to make a close friend of this man; it was enough to be noticed by the duke. He spent more time, and just as much trouble, with men of the Burgundian court who were comparable to himself in degree. If he was eager to play a part in the diplomacy, this was his opportunity to make contacts who could pave the way. Now that the Burgundians were allies, he could – and did – start to exchange letters with some of the duke's councillors, and encourage Burgundian men at arms to join his troops.

As well as the marriage, there was the truce to be signed, and Suffolk had his part in this. He was named as one of the conservators of the truce, the men who took formal responsibility for ensuring that it was adhered to. This was the first such role he had played.

St Mary's Church, North Tuddenham, Norfolk
Photo Mike Dixon

He must have been curious too about the bride, this sister of the disinherited Charles of Valois – and of Philip of Burgundy's wife, and indeed of Richard II's now-dead second queen – who was set to be the mother of the next Lancastrian king. Of course, he would no more have expected to become an intimate of hers than he expected it with the duke of Burgundy. Princess Catherine was closely chaperoned her mother and by the Englishwomen whom Henry insisted replace her French attendants, and Suffolk had no wife himself who could be set to befriend her.

The chroniclers and heralds praised Catherine's beauty, and claimed that the king had fallen in love with her at first sight. Theirs was not a cynical age, so perhaps Suffolk believed this too. The girl was pleasant-looking in her own way, a pale woman with a long neck, a thin face with a long nose, and eyes set deep in their sockets. She was eighteen when she married, old enough to get a child quickly. If Suffolk tried to converse with her, he probably realized that she was less well educated than his own sisters and nieces. She had been taught a little at a convent in Poissy, but few praised her for her accomplishments. And she had that disreputable mother and insane father, though those were things the English would not have mentioned even in their guardrooms late at night over a few cups of wine.

The second marriage that had been agreed in principle – between one of Henry's brothers and of one Philip of Burgundy's sisters – did not take place at the same time, but it was not forgotten. The chroniclers did not try to praise Anne of Burgundy's beauty: they all agreed she was notably plain, and the cruel said she looked like an owl. It was perhaps as well that Henry's unmarried brother in France at this time was not Humphrey of Gloucester but John of Bedford, the most cautious and unshowy of the four sons of Henry IV. He was a better match for Lady Anne than his brother was, the English captains agreed, and fortunately Bedford got on well with her.

The respite for all of them was short. A couple of days after the marriage was solemnized, Henry dragged his men back to war. What was the point of playing at tournaments, he remarked, when there were real places to be attacked? Catherine and her mother came too. For the next few months, they tagged along with the army as the king continued to besiege the towns and cities of central France. Henry did his best to please his bride, in a somewhat soldierly way: he arranged accommodation for her and her ladies far enough from the sieges that they were not disturbed by the noise of the cannon. And every day, at sunrise and at nightfall, a band of eight or ten musicians was called to play for her.

St Peter's Church, Ketteringham, Norfolk
Photo Mike Dixon

20 Two Garter knights

Up till the king's marriage and the truce with Burgundy, the English lords must have been very aware that they led an English invading army in France. But that had changed now there were Frenchmen allied with them. They were no longer the English side in the war; they were better called the Lancastrian side, the men – and women – who supported Henry of Lancaster as regent and future king of France.

The Armagnac faction was also changing its character: it came to be known as the Valois party, since it was dominated more and more by the dauphin, and continued to uphold his right to inherit the French throne as the representative of the house of Valois. It still held much of France, particularly in the centre, the south and south-east, and the north-east. But the Anglo-Burgundians had much of the north-west, east and south-west – and since Burgundy's men had taken it the year before, they held Paris.

Suffolk, like all the English lords, must have been eager to visit this great city that could now be regarded as friendly territory. That December, when the campaigning season was over, King Henry brought Queen Catherine to Paris. They had a large escort, so Suffolk was probably part of the party.

Paris had for centuries been the largest and finest city in France, and it was so still. The great buildings on the ile de la Cité, around the cathedral of Notre Dame and the Sainte Chapelle, were among the glories of the Western world. The royal palace of the Louvre sprawled across the right bank of the Seine; the grim fortress of the Bastille dominated the eastern side of the city. Paris held one of the world's great universities; it was a religious centre; it was a centre of trade and commerce. The lords of France maintained huge palaces there. But it had been ravaged by wars and rebellions for decades, and the battles between the Armagnacs and the Burgundians for control of the city had done it considerable damage.

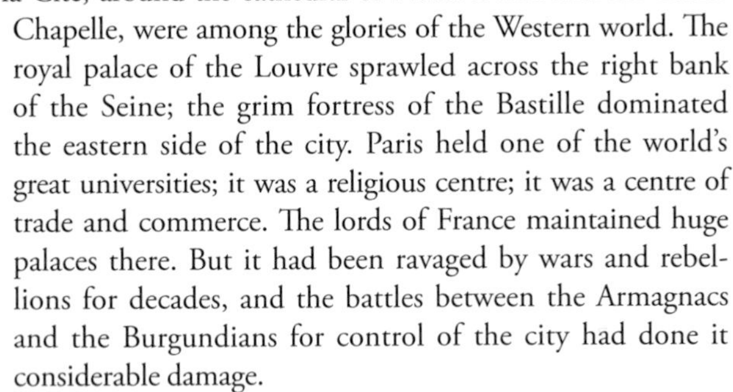

Natural disasters had played their part too. In 1418 it had known a plague so terrible that it was said 50,000 people had died in less than five weeks. And the wars in Normandy and elsewhere in the north of France had destroyed the supply routes to the city. The fields that should have been tilled were deserted, as perhaps half the population had fled, and the remainder were too scared to work out in the open. What harvests there were had been commandeered by the troops, and even the reduced population of Paris was hard pushed to find enough food.

1420 had been a good year, however, with an early spring bringing good crops: roses had been in flower by Easter, and the corn almost ready for harvest by May. Charles VI had recovered sufficiently from his malady that December

Le Mans Cathedral

to play a part in the procession, so two kings and two queens led the host that rode into Paris. The burghers of the city met them 'in full noble array'. But under the fine façade, supplies were running low again, and the entry of the huge Lancastrian party sent prices spiralling. The poor people could no longer get bread or salt, and were reduced to eating cabbages and turnips; the poorest could not afford even those, and died of hunger. A Parisian diarist wrote of sorry piles of ten, twenty and thirty children at a time, dying of cold and starvation on the rubbish heaps. Wolves roamed the streets of the suburbs.

St Martin's Church, Hindringham, Norfolk

If it felt at that moment as if France was theirs, the France that Henry was now regent of was no rich and prosperous land; it was a sorry wasteland clogged with misery. And if the Parisians cheered the kings and queens and their courtiers in their rich robes, it cannot have been difficult to read the resentment and wariness that lay curled beneath. Suffolk, Salisbury and the rest were still Englishmen. Even those who spoke good French had English accents and used the Anglicized vocabulary they had learned in their grammar schools. They had not yet brought peace: there was still a hard war to be fought if they were to defeat the Valois party. And although the Parisians must genuinely have longed by now for peace, they were aware that a Lancastrian victory would bring even more conquering English with it.

The English lords were not only in Paris to fill out the procession; there was work to be done, if they were to overcome this wariness and forge a convincing new administration. Henry was eager to get back to the war as soon as he decently could, but Suffolk, and others, could persuade him that although they too needed to check on their garrisons and set their men to besiege strongholds not yet taken, there were also good reasons for them to spend more time in Paris. They could not take Burgundy for granted; the duke still needed to be courted and charmed. The other French lords of the Burgundian faction had to be courted too, and so did all those men who were needed to run the city, and the country, in the Lancastrian interest.

Women too could play a role in this rapprochement between the two parties of the Lancastrian persuasion. At the king's wedding Suffolk must have met more women of his own class than he had seen since he left his sisters and came to France, and the court at Paris had plenty of women attached to it. Henry's queen had ladies to attend her – English women, many of them the wives of the English captains. The intention was for the queen to be taken to England for her coronation there, so these women would not stay in Paris, but other captains were talking now about bringing their wives to France. One of them was the earl of Salisbury, Suffolk's commander and friend. He remarried at about this time – he had been a widower with a daughter but no sons – and his new wife Alice was the cultured and beautiful daughter of a merchant, Thomas Chaucer, the son of the poet Geoffrey Chaucer.

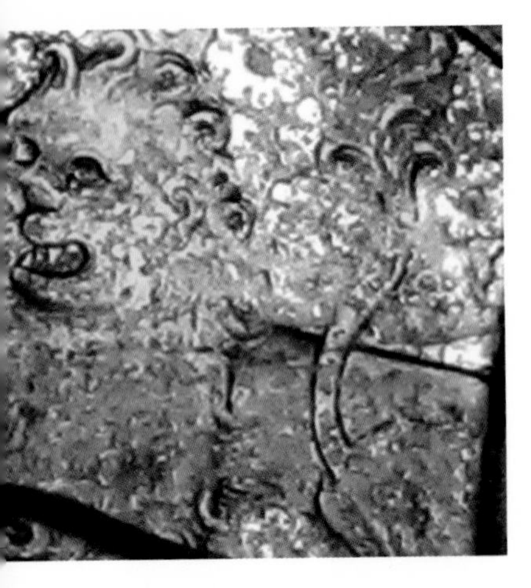

Church of St Mary the Virgin, Ewelme, Oxfordshire

Perhaps Salisbury suggested to Suffolk that he too might look out for such a wife. True, he had no mother in England now to arrange the match, but Lady Morley and his other sisters could have helped him. And many of the lords in France had sisters and daughters, so if he had expressed the desire, a wife could readily have been found. But if he perhaps considered it, Suffolk took it no further.

Paris was hospitable enough to a single young lord, in any case. The duke of Burgundy owned a vast palace there, the hotel d'Artois. He was becoming known for his lavish parties, where there was music and dancing till dawn. This was not King Henry's style, and although he worked to remain on good terms with Duke Philip, the two men were too different for friendship. Suffolk seems to have liked music and dancing, though. He was among the men whom the king detailed to try to get close to Burgundy.

Although the parties were enjoyable, it was not an easy assignment. The English were learning how vain and arrogant Duke Philip could be. They were also becoming aware that he had an agenda that was by no means identical to the king's. Philip was willing to support Henry, true, but he was not willing to pay out to ensure that the Lancastrians took firm control of France. He expected the English to do that. They might recruit his men at arms to their army if they wished, but they would have to pay them. Looking round the ravaged city, the Lancastrians must have asked themselves where the money to do this might be found. The Parliament in England had agreed to taxes to pay for the first phases of the war, but they did not expect, and were not willing, to be presented with an endless stream of requests for funding. It was necessary to make France support the Lancastrian administration. But it was sadly apparent that the starving Parisians – like those Rouennais who had stayed in their ravaged city, and the men and women in the other places the English had taken – were not only as unwilling to be taxed as most people are, they simply did not have the money to hand over.

The duke of Burgundy also expected English support for his own ambitions. Having agreed to support a strong regent in France, he had turned his own attention to the Low Countries, the richer, more comfortable territory that lay to the north-west of France, so Suffolk was among the men who had to learn fast about the politics of this region. He was making friends among the Burgundian lords – Hue de Lannoy, a councillor and court official, was among the most important of these contacts – and they will have briefed him on how the Burgundians wanted to see events unfold.

In particular, the duke of Burgundy was looking hard at Hainault, to the south of the lands he held in the north-west, and Holland and Zeeland to the north of them: territory that was all held by a young heiress, Jacqueline of Hainault. Henry had once thought of Jacqueline (who had been married to a son of Charles VI, but only briefly, since he died young) for Bedford's wife, but John the Fearless of Burgundy had muscled through and got her remarried to his nephew (and her own cousin). The boy was a weakling, and neither use nor pleasure to Jacqueline. Her uncle, John of Bavaria, was contesting her claim to her lands, and her husband seemed incapable of supporting her in her battle to retain control. At about this time she left him, a scandal that was doubtless much discussed, particularly among the Burgundians. Jacqueline did not come to Paris: she headed from her own territory to Calais, and from there petitioned the pope to grant her an annulment, since she and her cousin were too closely related for the marriage to be legal, and applied to go into exile in England.

The queen expressed a desire to have this plea from her one-time sister-in-law granted. Henry was inclined to agree, but he did not want to offend Burgundy, so Suffolk and the other lords had to take soundings. Burgundy was not happy, but he would tolerate it, they reported back. Perhaps he felt that with Jacqueline absent in England, there would be scope to increase his own influence in her territories. So when the king and queen set off through the Lancastrian-held territory to sail to England, they scooped up the countess of Hainault and took her with them.

Suffolk did not go with the king and queen when they returned to England. He was one of the commanders appointed to take charge in Normandy in the king's absence, and he was probably not sorry to instead have this opportunity to expand his role in France. This was a time when the English needed to keep up the momentum, and there was as always much to be done.

It was the first time the king had left France since his second invasion in 1417. But although his men must have missed him, they had a good substitute chief commander in Thomas of Clarence. The long campaign did not pause. There was territory that needed to be taken both in the île de France – the area to the west and east of Paris, which was not yet firmly held by the Lancastrians – and in Maine and Anjou, the regions south of Normandy, leading down to the river Loire.

There was diplomacy to be conducted too. Other French lords needed to be persuaded to follow Burgundy into the Lancastrian camp. The first target was the Bretons. The duke of Brittany's brother, Arthur of Richemont, had been taken prisoner by the English at Agincourt, and held in England ever since. A deal was put to him: if he managed to persuade his brother to sign up to the Treaty of Troyes, he would be set free. The Bretons had always kept on reasonable terms with the English, and had never firmly committed to either of the warring parties of French lords. Richemont agreed to the proposition, the duke agreed, Richemont was given passage back to Brittany, and in February 1421 Suffolk was named as one of the conservators of the truce that was duly signed. So he will have travelled to Rennes and met the Breton duke and his brother.

Chateau of Bricquebec

Duke John was cautiously friendly, but his brother was less so. Richemont was famed for his bad temper, and it had not been improved by the wounds he had taken at Agincourt, which had scarred his face and made him look like a frog, or the five years he had spent in an English prison. It was a running sore, too, that the English had refused to grant him the earldom of Richmond from which he took his name: it had gone to John of Bedford after his father had died. The Bretons probably made it clear to Suffolk and his colleagues that Richemont's freedom would not be enough to keep them loyal indefinitely; they were looking for this English earldom, and for other land and favours from the English as well. But Suffolk and the rest had no authority to make them promises.

In time, if Henry was to be king of France, he would have to release the other French nobles in English captivity, not least the dukes of Orleans and Bourbon. But these men were not in the same position as the Bretons; they were firmly associated with the Armagnacs. Their lands had not been taken by the English, and Orleans in particular was still regarded as an enemy of the Duke of Burgundy. The dauphin was putting together troops by now, planning to fight back against the Lancastrians, and men from the captive dukes' territories were joining them. It was clear that to release the dukes would be too much of a risk.

Church of St John the Baptist, Mileham, Norfolk
Photo Mike Dixon

Clarence, Salisbury and their men headed down into Anjou that season, but Suffolk did not join them; he probably continued in Normandy, overseeing the garrisons according to his command, and fulfilling his role of admiral too. Perhaps his brother John supported him in these tasks. John was also now a landowner in France: in 1419 the king had granted him the manor of Moyon, 'for the good and praiseworthy service performed, and to be performed for us, by our beloved and faithful knight'. Moyon was in the lower Cotentin, only a short distance from Suffolk's own estate of Hambye, so the brothers were close neighbours.

There were places still held for the Valois that would need to be invested by sea as well as by land if the Lancastrians were to besiege them successfully. Mont St Michel was one; Le Crotoy, a stronghold at the mouth of the Somme (not far from Agincourt) was another. Harfleur too needed to be guarded, and the Seine estuary patrolled. The dauphin had come to an agreement with the Scots, and their fighting men were heading to France; the Channel was busy, and Suffolk needed to help ensure that the English maintained some control there. But there was little or no money available for this purpose, so it was necessary to beg, to requisition, and even then to carry out this job with thin and scrappy resources.

He was in Rouen perhaps, or Pontorson or Avranches, when the heralds came with terrible news. Thomas of Clarence had been killed.

Phases of good fortune do not last indefinitely, and death was a commonplace among the Lancastrian troops. But this was no common death, for Clarence was both their commander and the king's heir. It was a major jolt to their campaign, and a real blow to Suffolk, who had grown close to Clarence during his years in France.

Worse, it seemed to have been a stupid, pointless action that had ended Clarence's life. He had been drawn into a skirmish during his campaign in Anjou, on impulse dragging out his men after supper to hunt down Franco-Scottish troops that his spies told him had come within range. Though the English had the advantage when they could set a battle line and use their archers, they had none in running fights, and finding themselves outnumbered, they had lost control. Clarence's lieutenants, the earls of Huntingdon and Somerset, had been captured; and Salisbury had reached the scene in time only to retrieve the duke's corpse.

This little battle at Baugé, north-east of Angers, was not one to set with Agincourt; if it had not been for Clarence's death, the chroniclers would barely have mentioned it. Of the handful of men who had taken part, not all had been lost; quite a few had escaped back to Normandy. But it was a disaster on a human scale. Clarence was the first heir presumptive to the English throne ever to die in battle. The Valois were jubilant, of course; the English were left stunned and grieving.

Masses were said for Clarence in Rouen, and his bones were sent back to England. John of Bedford was still in France, overseeing the Lancastrian administration, and would have sent to tell the king it was not necessary for him to return. But they must all have known that Henry would hear a different message, and would be back with them within weeks.

Deaths leave vacancies, and amidst the grief, Thomas of Clarence's brought Suffolk personal benefit. On 3 May 1421 he was appointed to the Order of the Garter.

This was, and still is, the greatest order of chivalry in England. Started by Edward III, it had then been active for around seventy years. To be appointed was no empty honour: the Garter knights had regular meetings, including a feast on St George's day, 23 April each year, so membership provided opportunities to build friendships and share private information with other powerful men. The knights wore distinctive and elaborate robes, blue velvet mantles with a garter on the left shoulder, lined with white sarsnet, and scarlet hose with a black velvet garter around the thighs. When not in full regalia, they wore a badge to signify their membership, so other men – the French lords and administrators, not least – would now see at a glance that Suffolk was one of the elite twenty-six. Men were chosen to fill vacancies (the number of Garter knights was firmly fixed) by the existing members, although the king played an important role. The core criterion was outstanding military service to the Crown, especially in France; the Garter was a symbol of diligence, courage, honour and loyalty. (Of course, rank played a role as well: this was not an honour given to the low-born, as a rule.) The wives and widows of Garter knights

Trinity Church, Vendome

were also sometimes granted the right to wear the robe, but they seem not to have played a very active part in the Order.

Garter king of arms, the herald who served the Garter knights, would have called on Suffolk and made all the formal arrangements. Each knight was allocated a stall in the chapel at Windsor, which remained his till his death or disgrace. (Suffolk's grandfather had never been a knight of the Garter, so he had had no place to lose on his impeachment. Nor had his father, so he was the first of the family to gain this honour.) Above the knight's stall were placed his arms and crest. Suffolk had used his arms since he was first invested as a knight, so the devices that were put there were the quartered de la Pole and Wingfield arms that he and his men knew well. The crest that surmounted his shield was of a man's head gules, beard and hair gold

Suffolk's Garter plate, taken from Napier, *Historical Notices*

Church of St Peter and St Paul, East Harling, Norfolk
Photo Mike Dixon

with a gold and jewelled circlet (so the head in the illustration was probably not intended as a portrait of him, it was simply a heraldic device, though even so we might wonder whether Suffolk himself had such a nose). After a knight died or left the order, a plate with his arms and crest remained there in perpetuity. Suffolk was allocated stall N13, the thirteenth stall to the north of the chapel at Windsor.

In 1421 no fewer than six vacancies arose in the ranks of Garter knights. Of the other lords and men and arms who filled them, the one probably best known to Suffolk was John Mowbray, earl of Nottingham and Norfolk.

Suffolk did not go back to England for his investiture; he did not need to. Garter king of arms saw to the dressing of his stall at Windsor, and he was given his robes by the king after his return to France.

21 The bridge of boats is swept away

With the queen left back in England, the king's court was a masculine one again, and the campaigning of that summer of 1421 was what they had all come to know well. There were sieges, and skirmishes with Valois troops; no great battles, since there was no great army to oppose them. Although they missed Clarence, the king was in good heart; all being well, a new heir to the throne would be born that winter. In the meantime John of Bedford was next in line.

Like his king, Suffolk probably spent time with his brothers: or at least with John, since Alexander might still have been too young to join the army. John de la Pole married at some point during this period: his wife was Marie de Sicile (that is, Marie from Sicily), though nothing more is known of her. He probably met her in France, and they settled at Moyon, although John would have been absent most of the time with the Lancastrian forces. They had a daughter, whom they called Margaret.

The king had brought more troops from England, to supplement those who had remained in France throughout his absence. He met up with the duke of Burgundy at Montreuil, just south of Calais, and they proceeded to campaign together. Suffolk was with them that autumn, 'employed to discover the country'. In September 1421 he received another preferment, becoming warden of the lower marches of Normandy – that is, the southern borders of the duchy.

The French had made major efforts to retake Harfleur, and Paris was once again the site of battles between what were now the Anglo-Burgundians and the Armagnacs. The king set off to relieve the capital, then besieged and captured Dreux, before heading south and taking Vendome and Beaugency. This took him for the first time to the Loire valley, so most of the upper third of France was now in Lancastrian hands. Suffolk did not go with him: he continued his role in Normandy, ensuring the coast was protected and the Lancastrian-held places – Harfleur included – remained secure. He joined the king that October, though, when they settled in to besiege Meaux, a town and stronghold in the Marne valley, a short distance to the east of Paris.

St Mary's Church, North Tuddenham, Norfolk
Photo Mike Dixon

Although Meaux was not a great city, it was in a strategic location, and the Lancastrians needed control of it. It was apparent from the start that this would be a difficult siege. The town was set in a strong position: on three sides the river looped around it, and on the fourth was a canal. As well as the main defences, there was a fortified suburb, the Market, which was also firmly held by the Valois. The tag-end of the enemy forces from much of northern France had taken refuge behind the walls. The land around the town, where the English set their camp, was exposed and damp, and Suffolk could see it would turn into a bitter winter siege unless they took the place quickly. The king had assembled a strong besieging force, and some of the new Breton allies under Arthur of Richemont had joined it, although it was said there were also Bretons among the defenders. The attackers were set to work constructing wooden siege engines to supplement the cannon: they flung not just stones, but rotting animal carcases too into the town, to try to foster disease there.

It was a wet autumn, and before long the water meadows were in flood, adding to the besiegers' misery. The king had the men build a bridge of boats across the river Marne, but when the rains caused the river to break its banks they were swept away, and the men on either side of the river had no easy way to communicate with each other. They did their best to weaken the defences, but the strong garrison kept the damage repaired, and it was apparent they were making little headway.

As if this was not miserable enough, with the first sharp frosts came not only dysentery, but smallpox too. Perhaps the rotting cows had brought the infection. Most of the men were taken sick to some degree, and many of them died. One of the men who had been invested with the Garter with Suffolk, Lord Clifford, was among them.

Suffolk escaped the worst of it this time, but the king did not. He retreated to his quarters, and the rumour began to circulate that it was the smallpox he had been taken with. None of them could confirm that, because they were not allowed to see the king. But they knew the sickness had to be serious, since Henry was not the man to keep to his bed if he had the remotest alternative.

A physician was sent for from England. That was a bad sign. The commanders – Richemont, Suffolk, the earls of Warwick and Exeter – send messages to the king that he should leave them to conduct the siege, and withdraw to more comfortable quarters. But the message came back that the king would not do so. Nor might they raise the siege, and try again to take Meaux come the spring. Henry had never yet lost an action, and he would not allow his men to lose this one.

The king emerged from his sick tent at last. It seemed it had been the flux he had suffered from, and not the pox, but he was haggard, thin, a shadow of what he had been.

They were still camped outside Meaux in December, when better news came from England. The queen had given birth, and the king had a son, a healthy child. He had been named Henry, after his father and grandfather. There were celebrations in the English camp over this.

The heralds added the gossip too. The baby's godmother was to be Jacqueline of

Hainault, the Flemish countess who was in exile in England. Jacqueline was very well liked at the English court, they said. She was a good friend to Queen Catherine, and she had also come to be on very friendly terms with Humphrey of Gloucester. Indeed they were on such good terms that Humphrey had sent to his brother the king to ask for permission to marry her.

Friends of Gloucester – Suffolk must have counted himself as one – would have seen the appeal in this. Evidently Countess Jacqueline was charming, as well as having a strong claim to large and rich lands. And although King Henry had found a bride for himself, and lined one up for John of Bedford, he had not picked out one for Humphrey, who was not so young now, and might well wish to marry.

Norwich Cathedral

So it could have been a fine match – were it not that Countess Jacqueline was already married to her cousin. True, she had applied to the pope, asking him to annul the marriage, but the pope – leaned on, doubtless, by her husband's relations in Burgundy – had refused. The messengers reported that encouraged by Humphrey, Jacqueline was now applying to the antipope, in the hope that he would give her a more satisfactory answer.

In the later part of the fourteenth century there had been two rival popes, one at Avignon and one at Rome. By this time the French had abandoned the Avignon pope – Benedict XIII, not to be confused with a later Roman pope who took the same name and title – and reconciled themselves to the rule of their church from Rome, but the Avignon pope, a fiery Spaniard, had declined to submit, and still held out with a few supporters. Some called him the pope, but more called him the antipope.

It must have been clear to Suffolk and his comrades that neither Humphrey nor Jacqueline were acting wisely. Even if Benedict had granted her petition, many men would have judged Jacqueline to be still legally married. The duke of Gloucester, the king's brother, third in line to the throne even now that Henry had an infant son, was not a man who could reasonably contract a marriage of dubious legality, one that half Europe would refuse to recognize. And there was the reaction of the Burgundians to be considered. Philip of Burgundy had not objected to Jacqueline retreating quietly to England, but he would certainly object if she got herself a powerful new husband there, one who might help defend her lands against the rival he himself preferred.

Indeed, this was so obviously not a sensible request that they must have wondered why Humphrey had troubled to make it. He was already known to have some of the same rashness that had cost Clarence his life, but this was not so much rashness as a rank misjudgement. It was no surprise to the English lords to learn that Henry had sent the message back to England that his brother should do nothing of the kind.

The new year came and passed, and the siege dragged on. In March the English took most of the town of Meaux, but the defenders withdrew to the Market, and held out there until May. When the place finally surrendered, King Henry had the commander of the garrison beheaded.

After the cold winter, a cruelly hot summer was beginning to set in. There was little rain, and the crops were not doing well. It slowly became clear that the king was not recovering as his men might have hoped. Perhaps it was more than the flux that ailed him, though his physicians did not know what else was wrong, or how to cure it.

After the siege had been lifted the king headed for Paris. Suffolk perhaps went to check on his lands and men in the west, visit Hambye and call on John and Marie, but before long he probably joined the king. That June the queen sailed over from England, leaving behind her baby son, whom the king had still not seen. John of Bedford had come to France with her, and the English had found more troops to accompany them.

Paris was scalding, stinking and filthy. The king was still unwell, and keeping mostly to his quarters. The Parisians were wary and grouchy. The queen was little compensation. Her sister Michelle, Philip of Burgundy's wife, died that July. It would have been important to Catherine to know that Michelle too supported the Lancastrian cause, that she was not alone in opposing her brother the dauphin, so this loss of one of her last remaining siblings – seven of her brothers and sisters were now dead – was a painful one in many ways. The link between the two sisters and their husbands had been important to all the Lancastrians. The duke of Burgundy was in mourning, and there was no music, no fine parties, no dancing.

It was probably apparent to Henry's lords too that if the king and queen had made a fair appearance of being lovebirds two summers before, they were doing so no longer. Catherine had been summoned to France because she was needed to conceive again, to doubly secure the succession, but the king showed no great pleasure in her company.

So it was almost a relief when news came that the dauphin had embarked on a new campaign. The Scots troops who had killed Thomas of Clarence had as yet achieved little else, but now they and the Valois were targeting the Burgundian province of Nevers. This was to the south-east of Burgundy's possessions, and south-east of Paris too: not far distant from the Valois-held city of Bourges, where the dauphin had established his court. So this campaign was convenient for the dauphin, but more than that, it was clearly intended to concentrate Philip of Burgundy's mind on the choice he had made.

They would ride with their troops to support Burgundy, the king announced. His men would have said there was no need for him to come, they could readily counter this Valois army without him. They would not have said he was too weak to campaign, but they could all see that this was the case. But the king insisted he must lead his army to meet up with Burgundy's. And what the king insisted, the king did.

So men were raised – the king's escort, the men Bedford had brought, and spare men from the garrisons round about, enough of them to provide a good stiffening to the Burgundian troops. Supplies were gathered, and they all set off on the road to Corbeil: the king, Bedford, Suffolk and many of the other Lancastrian commanders. It was not clear exactly where

Le Mans Cathedral

the Valois army was, but if they headed towards Nevers, they could expect to meet with Burgundy's army en route, and the duke's scouts would be able to brief them.

Henry was too sick to ride, and had to be carried in a litter. His brother Bedford had probably been complaining even before they left that it was insanity for the king to come, that he needed to rest and regain his strength. He carried on complaining till they got to Corbeil. Then Henry himself admitted he could go no further.

They were near the castle of Vincennes, a royal fortress. Henry agreed to retreat there. The army need not pause, though, he told them: they need only detail a small escort to accompany him. Bedford should lead the rest of the men, and carry on to meet up with Burgundy's troops as they had arranged.

It is not clear what Suffolk did, but most likely he rode on with Bedford. It was a stifling August, the crops brown and shrivelled in the fields. This was unfamiliar territory, on the border of Burgundy's lands, fought over much by Burgundians and Armagnacs, but not until now by the English.

They cannot have been sure where the news would come first, from Vincennes behind them, or from the south, where Burgundy's men were, and the Valois army. They went on for some time: a day, perhaps two. Then a Burgundian herald rode up with his escort. The dauphin had retreated with his men, he said. Bloody dauphin: for once they had thought he might actually fight. Was Burgundy pursuing the Valois troops, the English must have asked? Well, no. The duke of Burgundy was no great fighter either. He had decided he might as well return to Nevers.

So it was all for nothing. They need never have left Paris. The Valois army would have been far enough away by then that it was useless to try to chase it. They turned back towards Vincennes.

The castle was set in a forest, so the last miles would have been along a wooded path, with birds calling from amid the trees, and perhaps the sight of a couple of deer, frightened by the clanking of the troops and bounding across the path. Vincennes had been a hunting lodge once, but over the centuries it had been rebuilt into something far grander. There was a quadrangle of thick walls, built of smooth pale stone, and within them a massive keep, 52 metres high, the tallest in all of Europe. It was handsome, but forbidding.

The men at arms, the archers and servants would have waited in the yard, while the captains headed into the keep. With the cool of the stone, they came into the formality of the king's court. The king himself was in the great chamber in the keep, and the anterooms will have been full of his courtiers.

Suffolk and his companions could see that the king's counsellors had been summoned from Paris. The queen was not at Vincennes, however. Apparently she had gone to visit her mother: they were at Senlis, east of Paris and not so far distant, but the king had not asked that she be sent for. He had sent instead for his chaplains and for all the men to whom he needed to give instructions.

They knew what that meant, but it could not be said. So the next few days would have been spent in the strange limbo of a death anticipated but not yet acknowledged or fulfilled.

No arrangements could be made – except by the king himself – because they must pretend – and hope – that Henry might recover. They could not hunt, or laugh, or play at dice, or even ride out in search of Valois troops, supplies or booty. They could only wait.

The king was lucid and determined, weakened in body but not in spirit by his illness. Bedford would have gone in to see him first, but over the days that followed all of the captains who were at Vincennes were given an audience with him. So at some point Suffolk would have been summoned from the room where the lords waited, and ushered into the great chamber, where the physicians, the chaplains and the king's personal servants hovered in the shadows. He approached the huge bed where the king lay, and was perhaps given Henry's hand to kiss. And he would have been told what all the men were told. Although Henry would not live to take the throne of France, nevertheless it must come to the Lancastrians, in the person of his baby son. The king's death must make no difference. They must fight on, till all of France was theirs. There was more – the will that the king had already had drawn up, dispositions for the men – but this was the core of it. Suffolk was told to swear he would do as the king commanded, and he did so.

Then he withdrew, and waited again. In the courtyard and the outbuildings, the army waited. In Paris, in Rouen, and throughout the rest of Lancastrian France, men who had heard the news waited too.

Until it came to pass. King Henry V died at Vincennes on 31 August 1422, in the middle of the night. He was thirty-five years old. And the mad King Charles of France was still alive.

Abbey of l'Epau, Le Mans

22 The hammer of the Gauls, and his baby son

For all they had been anticipating it, they must have been numbed, stunned, and not a little despairing when the news was finally brought from the great chamber. The king is dead; long live King Henry VI!

Hell, not much to cheer for, they must have thought. It was bad enough that Henry was gone; worse, however they looked at it, that the infant they none of them had seen (save Bedford) was now the king in his place. If it had been Bedford himself, or if Clarence had lived, or even Gloucester …

But they were honourable men, by their own lights. The baby king was diligently cared for over the months and years that followed.

Meanwhile, the dead king had been a lover of ceremony, and his men had to ensure that his funeral lived up to his expectations. The mourning began at Vincennes. It took till the feast of the Exaltation of the Holy Cross, 14 September – two weeks after the king had died – to prepare his body to be moved, and to arrange the great procession that would see him home. His coffin was carried on a cart drawn by six black horses. Over it was set an effigy, larger than life, of the king in his robes of state, carrying a shield lined with silk that had belonged to his father. A hundred black-clad mourners with torches escorted the coffin. The bells tolled, the dirges were sung, all along the lengthy route that carried the king home.

Suffolk's brother in law, Lord Morley, was among the men who shouldered the coffin for the journey. Suffolk had not been as close to the king as Morley, or some of the others. He probably wore his Garter robes, and rode in a guard of honour with his fellow Garter knights.

They took the coffin first around Paris to St Denis, the great basilica north of the city, where the kings of France had been buried since time immemorial. They held Henry's funeral there on 15 September. Henry had been the king of England, regent but never king of France. He had not chosen to be buried at St Denis; this first of two funerals done, they were to take his bones back to England.

The duke of Burgundy did not come to the funeral.

Queen Catherine was not at the funeral either. She joined the procession at Rouen, where there were more obsequies. Suffolk perhaps left the procession at or before this point: Lancastrian France was vulnerable in the wake of the king's death, and the captains needed to get back to work. Garrisons had to be visited, men reassured, plans made for the next phase of the war.

Those plans were constrained by what they had sworn. The war must be continued until all France was theirs, and the new king was acknowledged as such by all the men who stood under him. It was crucial that they keep the support of the duke of Burgundy, so he was to be given first refusal of the regency of France, the role that Henry had held himself. John of Bedford was to guard the new king's interests in France, administer Normandy, and be regent of France should Burgundy refuse. The dukes of Orleans and Bourbon were not to be freed until there was peace. Gloucester meanwhile was to be regent in England, and take charge of the infant king. Queen Catherine had not been mentioned.

Meanwhile, the heralds reported from England. Henry had dictated the wording for his tomb, and his brothers saw it put in place in the Abbey of Westminster. 'Henry V, hammer of the Gauls, lies here. Henry was put in the urn 1422. Virtue conquers all. The fair Catherine finally joined her husband' – they left the date, to be completed later. And finally, 'Flee idleness.'

News came from Paris too. On 21 October, less than two months after King Henry V of England had breathed his last, King Charles VI of France followed him to the grave.

Over that late autumn and winter Suffolk must have met up with his brother John, and perhaps with their younger brother Alexander too. With the campaign in abeyance, there was time to spend on their own and each other's lands. They would have spent days hunting, in the woods and meadows of the Sienne valley around Suffolk's estate of Hambye and John's of Moyon, and the pastures that surrounded Bricquebec Castle. It was necessary to be careful in the open: although this territory was firmly held by the Lancastrians, there were plenty of brigands and outlaws, dispossessed French who had refused to live under the English, deserters from the Lancastrian army, and criminals on the run, scratching and scrabbling for a living in the forests and marshlands. But game was needed for the kitchens, and to hunt was also a pleasure they would not willingly have denied themselves. France was their home now, Suffolk's for more than five years. The Lancastrians did here, as far as they could, the things they would have done in England.

They would have spent evenings in their strongholds: evenings alone together, when with the hiss and crackle of the fire, its flames throwing just enough light to see each other by, a cup of wine or cider in their hands, their dogs at their feet and a guard or two outside the closed door, they could feel as safe as they ever felt in France, and could talk freely. Perhaps Lord Morley joined them: he was family, they could have trusted him. There was nobody else whom Suffolk could have spoken honestly with, not even men such as Salisbury, whom he had known well for years, and certainly not the lieutenants who served under him.

There was plenty a man might wish to talk honestly of in these times. The hard truth could not be avoided, albeit it could never be spoken in public. King Henry V's death had changed everything. Was it realistic now to win France for the new baby king?

It had been the late king's rare luck, or skill, to see things hard and clear, right and wrong, what he must do and he did do. For other men they took on shadows. For a small child to reign over one country was hard enough for those obliged to uphold his claims. For him to reign – in title, at least – over two was close to impossible. And it was a major disaster that Henry V had not outlived the French king, and not been able to take the throne for himself, and be crowned with the crown of the kings of France, anointed by the French bishops. This weakened his baby son's claim.

Left, Chateau of Bricquebec
Right, the Sienne in flood at Hambye

The son of Charles VI who had been so casually disinherited was a young man growing into his own. Perhaps he would never be a great man at arms, but not all Valois armies would turn tail and slink back home like the one on the road to Nevers. The dauphin – as the English still called him, though the Valois supporters now saw him as King Charles VII – had the support of most of the lords of France, and he had Scots troops as well, buoyed by their hatred of the English.

What the Lancastrians had to set against him was their own sense of duty (honed by the fear of committing treason), and their desire to protect the lands they now controlled. Hundreds of Englishmen had their own equivalent of Hambye and Bricquebec, valued those possessions, and would fight to keep them. They had Burgundy's hatred of the men who had killed his father, which would lose its edge over the years, but would, they reckoned, be sharp enough to keep him implacably opposed to the dauphin for a good time to come. This did not mean, however, that he would show enthusiasm for the Lancastrian cause. Even in this first winter after Henry V's death, it was apparent that he would not.

The Bretons were even worse. Richemont was a fine captain, true, but he had been nagging the king at Meaux for rewards. Henry had offered him a French estate, but had refused to grant him the title of count of Richmond, although the Breton had made it clear that this was his price. John of Bedford held that, and he was not prepared to surrender it. Nor had Richemont earned it, by Henry's standards: he needed to fight longer and harder for the Lancastrians, and push much less for his own interests, if he was to do that.

It was impossible to bribe even these few French lords with money and goods to hold to the Lancastrians, because the king's council had not the resources to do so. As for lands and titles, there were Englishmen (and Welshmen and Irishmen) who also coveted those, and had as much claim to be granted them. And there were also French holders of those titles, men they needed to see as their own supporters, and not as exiles fighting with the dauphin.

So it was difficult to see how a full conquest might be achieved. But this was what Henry V had commanded them to do, and Bedford and Gloucester had made it clear they intended to honour the promises they had made to their brother. Suffolk had made those promises too. And in time the new king would grow, and judge his lords on what they had done during his childhood. No man could risk his saying, you failed me, and failed my father.

There was no choice for men such as Suffolk but to support the king's uncles, and continue the war as if nothing had changed.

23 Aftermath

Of the four sons of Henry IV, Suffolk would have known John of Bedford at this time less well than he knew, or had known, his brothers. He had served under Henry V, Humphrey of Gloucester and Thomas of Clarence, but rarely if ever directly under Bedford. Since it was Bedford who had been entrusted with the Lancastrian interests in France, it was now a priority to get to know him better.

Most men who knew the royal dukes well agreed they were lucky to get Bedford and not Gloucester. He was a sensible and intelligent man, and a competent commander. He had much of the king his brother in him, and most of it the earnest, pious part. He would both lead his captains and consult them.

And he was a man who would, they all knew, obey his dead brother's instructions to the letter. So he offered the regency to the duke of Burgundy. It was no great surprise when Burgundy turned it down. Bedford did not argue, although he did pursue the plan to marry Burgundy's sister Anne that had been agreed in principle at Troyes. It had been suggested that another of Burgundy's sisters should marry Arthur of Richemont, so the Lancastrians could hope this would create a new web of close contacts to replace the ties that had been lost.

As had been intended by Henry V, Bedford set up two major administrations. A council in Rouen ran affairs in Normandy, while there was a government in Paris to administer the rest of Lancastrian France. Both contained Burgundian and French officials as well as Englishmen, and tried to follow the established French forms of administration. The agreement at Troyes had been that the king should have a French administration in France, and not treat it as conquered territory, and Bedford did his best to honour this condition.

The lesser English in France meanwhile quietly did their best to temper it. They did not want to see all the great appointments in the king's administration, the estates he had to gift, go to Frenchmen. Suffolk hoped for, and expected, more rewards in the years to come. This was even more important to men like his brothers.

Bedford set up households of his own in both Rouen and Paris, and Suffolk probably did the same for himself. Of the two, Bedford favoured Rouen the most. His base there was not the castle for which Henry had demanded land, which held the Lancastrian garrison, but a palace that he called Joyeux Repos – joyful rest. Of course Bedford had not taken part in the siege, and did not have the same memories as Suffolk and the others who had been there that winter.

It was in Rouen and Paris that Suffolk would have met with the regent, and with other

men who could give him news, although his own herald and messengers also travelled regularly between England and France, and between Rouen, Paris and the places that he commanded. So he learned that it proved more difficult to implement the arrangements Henry V had dictated in England. The king's council – which included men like Henry Beaufort, bishop of Winchester, the rich and powerful uncle of Bedford, Gloucester and Henry V – and Parliament made it clear that they were not willing to grant Gloucester full powers as regent. They would accept him as protector, defender and principal councillor, but would not agree to his taking complete control.

Gloucester had ranted and raged, men said, when he learned that his brother had refused him permission to marry Jacqueline of Hainault. He ranted and raged at this too, which confirmed the men who had denied him in their conviction. Bedford stood by the council, and Gloucester was forced to back down.

Suffolk seems to have been as well regarded by Bedford as he had been by Henry V, and in October 1422 he had his first appointment from the regent, as guardian of the Cotentin, the area around Cherbourg that he already knew so well. He probably delegated this command to a lieutenant from the outset, because in the months and years that followed he was rarely in the Cotentin, but spent most of his time in Paris and Champagne, the territory to the east of the city. His men continued to carry out sieges under his command, and for larger actions they fought still with the commander Suffolk knew best and probably admired the most, the earl of Salisbury.

He must also have briefed Bedford on his own attempts to build links in the Burgundian court, and been encouraged to build on them. Among the Burgundians he brought into his service was one of the finest musicians of his day, Gilles Binchois, who was then in his early twenties. This was a happy double benefit: Suffolk could look to get information through Gilles' relatives in Flanders, and he also got to enjoy the man's music.

There was music in the military camps, but that was heavy on trumpets and clarions. Binchois was a composer of chansons as well as masses and religious music: many of his songs are still performed today. With titles such as 'Adieu, m'amour et ma maistresse' (Goodbye love, goodbye my mistress), 'Je vous salue, ma maistresse' (Greetings to you, my mistress), and 'Lune très belle, clère lune' (Beautiful, clear moon), they speak of a gentler, more feminine world than the harsh one of sieges and battles. This was the world that Suffolk lived in during his times in Paris and Rouen. Bedford's Burgundian duchess, Salisbury's English countess, and other women too set their stamp on the life there. Perhaps Suffolk had a woman himself – a mistress, for he still made no move to marry – but if so, we do not know her name.

Paving, Abbey of St Benoit sur Loire, France

24 A song by Gilles Binchois

Amours merchi

Amours merchi de trestout mon pöoir,
tant que je puis, quant il m'a fait choisir
tres douchement et tout a mon vouloir
agatié m'a un tres riche plaisir.
Cescune fois que j'en ay souvenir
le cuer de moy devient tout joieux:
prendre ne puis nul espoir doloreux,
si richement l'ay choysi a mon gré,
et par Amours que le m'a comandé.

A very rough translation:

I thank you, Love, and that most sincerely,
It's to my advantage that you should have chosen me.
Sweetly and softly, and just as I might,
You've brought to me pleasure and real delight.
Each time I remember all that I've gained,
My heart leaps up, with joy unconstrained.
I think no more of sorrow and pain
Love's told me never to do that again,
And I've chosen this world in which pleasure will reign.

Above, St Edmund's Church, Emneth, Norfolk   Photo Mike Dixon
Left, Church of St Mary the Virgin, Yaxley, Suffolk

25 Berserk courage

All the Lancastrian commanders in France would have agreed with Bedford's priorities in his first years as regent: to work closely with the Burgundians, and to try to take the few places still held by the Valois in north-west France. Mont St Michel, Le Crotoy at the mouth of the river Somme, and a handful of other strongholds had not been taken by the English largely because they were difficult targets. Bedford gave Suffolk and his brothers the task of reducing them.

This called for a blockade by sea, and there were not enough ships at Suffolk's command to encircle more one place at a time. Sir John had been marked out by Bedford to try for Mont St Michel, but he protested that it was impossible to attack it without many more men and ships. Suffolk must have agreed. He took his own men north to invest Le Crotoy, where he spent the spring and early summer of 1423, and let John take his troops south instead to Anjou on a chevauchée, a raiding expedition. This was a task better suited to John's talents, and one that would cheer his men too, which besieging a fortress that had never been taken throughout its long history was scarcely likely to do. And they needed booty. If John came back with enough to pay their men for the season, Bedford would surely not complain.

Sitting out what looked set to become another long siege cannot have appealed much to Suffolk either. When word came from Salisbury that he needed more men to the east of Paris, where the dauphin threatened to bring his army, he left the task of taking Le Crotoy to one of his lieutenants, Sir Ralph Boutellier. Enough men stayed to keep the landward side encircled and the little port cut off from supplies; the rest went with Suffolk on the long march east.

Suffolk found Salisbury and his troops at Montaiguillon, a stronghold near the small town of Villiers-St-George; or rather outside Montaiguillon, since they had settled in to besiege the old fortress. Salisbury updated him: there was indeed a Valois army in the field. The dauphin was not with it, he was sitting comfortably in his chateau at Bourges. But his forces included both Frenchmen and mercenaries, experienced men who expected to have to earn their pay, and would not evade the Lancastrians. There were the Scots who had killed Clarence two years earlier; that was something all the English were keen to avenge. There were Aragonese from Spain, and Lombards from northern Italy. The Lancastrians had some such men too, but fewer, since they did not come cheap.

This army was now in Burgundian territory, and for the previous five weeks or so it had been besieging the town of Cravant, in the valley of the Yonne, just south of Auxerre, and some distance south of Montaiguillon. It was a place that had already been taken by Valois supporters and retaken by Burgundians; the walls would be crumbling in places, its inhabitants weary and bitter. The word from the garrison was that the town was desperately short of food, with its inhabitants reduced to eating their horses, cats and even mice. It needed to be relieved as soon as possible.

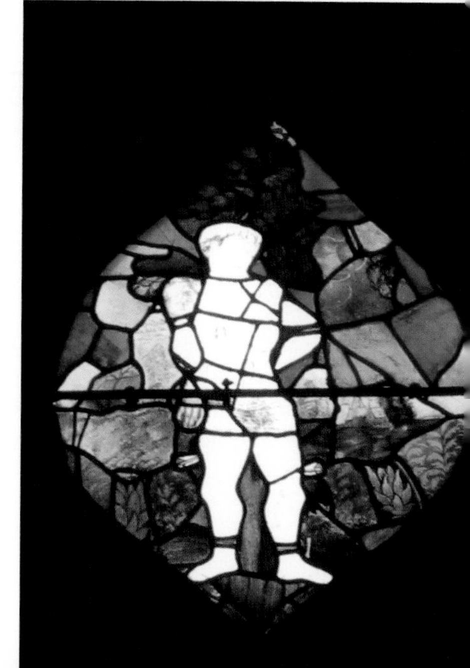

Church of St Pierre, Dreux

They would be joining Burgundian troops: Duke Philip might not be doing much outside his territories, but he was willing enough to defend his own towns. So this would be a chance for Suffolk to use his existing Burgundian connections and forge new ones. And some new English troops had sailed from England that spring, headed by Lord Willoughby. The arrangements had been made: Salisbury's and Suffolk's men, Willoughby's men, and the Burgundians would rendezvous at Auxerre.

St Mary's Church, North Tuddenham, Norfolk
Photo Mike Dixon

So they left a token force to pursue another slow siege, and set off down the road to Auxerre. They found when they arrived that there were fewer Burgundians in Auxerre than they had hoped, and there was no sign at all of Philip the Good. Still, that was no fault of the men who had come. The commanders met in the gothic cathedral of Auxerre. There were perhaps Burgundian captains Suffolk already knew among them, and there were other men he was glad to meet, such as Jean de Waurin, a herald and man at arms who was writing a chronicle for the duke. Waurin was clever, thoughtful, a good man to be in contact with.

Salisbury probably began by outlining the situation and his proposals, with the heralds translating for those men who did not speak English. Their primary aim was to relieve Cravant, and although it was possible the Valois army would abandon the siege when they approached, they must assume this meant a pitched battle with the besiegers. Salisbury would have overall command; the Burgundian captains conceded this. He detailed equal numbers of English and Burgundians to form the advance parties to scout out the terrain, and appointed English and Burgundian marshals to keep the body of the troops in order. And since these were unfamiliar troops, he went painstakingly over the methods the English used to win their victories. There must be firm discipline among the men, with no breaking line. The men at arms must not attack until the archers had had an opportunity to weaken the opposition. And no one must take prisoners until he gave the word that they might do so.

Suffolk knew all this, of course, but only in theory. He would be twenty-seven that autumn, had been a man at arms fighting in France for eight years, and had been in plenty of sieges and skirmishes, but he had never yet fought a pitched battle. He would act as Salisbury's lieutenant at this one, with Lord Willoughby given command of the other wing of the army; that made sense, considering his inexperience.

The arrangements agreed, the rest of the army came into the cathedral. There were perhaps

The River Yonne at Cravant

six thousand men in all, so they filled the great high spaces: the nave, the aisles, the transepts, standing shoulder to shoulder. Many of them would be dead within a few days. Every priest in Auxerre must have helped to celebrate the mass. Suffolk probably thought of Michael, and his first and last experience of battle. Perhaps after the service he lit a candle for his brother. Many men must have done the same.

The next morning they set off. They took their supply carts with them, loaded with food, not just for themselves but for the starving inhabitants of Cravant, and sharpened stakes for the archers: they would hammer these into the ground and station themselves behind them to shoot. Many of the archers, and the grooms, cooks and valets, would have walked the nine miles or so from Auxerre to Cravant; the men at arms rode. There was work to do for men such as Suffolk, not just keeping his eyes on his own men, but also liaising with the other captains. He had Salisbury's news already, but Willoughby's was fresh – from Westminster and from Paris – and it was particularly important to speak with the Burgundians. There was a psychological battle to be won here, as well as a physical one to follow.

With Willoughby and Salisbury – though not with the Burgundians – he would have discussed not just the significance of Philip the Good's failure to join his army, but the even more problematic Breton situation. Bedford had negotiated a defensive alliance between Brittany, Burgundy and the English at Amiens that April, but it was reported that the duke of Brittany had also signed an alliance with the dauphin. Many men judged that their new sister-wives would not succeed in keeping Bedford and Richemont on good terms. The Breton lord knew by then that Bedford would not surrender the English title he coveted. The English captains must have known that the dauphin would approach him with promises; perhaps he had already done so. Perhaps they could live with that, if Richemont's brother the duke did not follow him into the Valois camp.

It was midsummer, still and very hot, and the valley around them was silent, but for occasional birdsong: the farmers had fled or hidden, and taken their livestock with them. The river Yonne here was broad and rather sluggish. Salisbury brought them to a halt perhaps a mile short of Cravant, and the men waited till the advance party came with reports.

They had found the Valois army. The small town of Cravant was set on the east bank of the river, with about a hundred yards separating the water from the nearest stretch of wall. There were hills rising sheer behind it. Some of the Valois encircled the walls, but the bulk of the dauphin's troops had taken up a strong position around a break in the hills, almost a gorge, just north of the town. They had clearly chosen it as the best place in which to fight.

But they did not have to be attacked in that strong position, nor even that day, since it was unlikely they would choose to move to meet the Lancastrians. We can wait, Salisbury announced, and make them wait too.

So the Lancastrians made camp. They set their guards, and the other men got what sleep they could. Come dawn, the men put on their armour. This was a long slow job for a fully clad man at arms, so Suffolk would have stood for some time while his valet fastened the pieces one by one. The heat was already rising, and the metal plates must soon have been scalding. His valet then tied his surcoat over the metal, so that like all the men at arms, he would be readily identifiable to his comrades – and to their opponents too.

They were on the east bank. They left the baggage there, and the horses, with their servants to mind them, and the men at arms waded across the broad shallow river, carrying their long wooden lances, and the other weapons they chose to fight with: typically maces, hatchets or swords. They did not use shields: no need, since the steel plates covered their entire body. The archers followed them, in their lighter armour, with their stakes, their bows and full quivers; standard bearers came too, and probably the chaplains, since each man wanted to go into battle newly shriven of his sins.

The heat was draining. The men at arms had to stop repeatedly, kneeling in the cumbersome armour, opening their visors and pressing their faces to the earth to cool them. Their sweat mingled with the river water that had seeped through the joints in the metal, soaking the padding they wore beneath the metal.

They tramped right past the Valois army in the cleft among the hills, and the scouts brought them word that the Valois had done what they now had no choice but to do: abandoned their position and followed them upriver towards Cravant. They all stopped when they came level with the walls. Salisbury drew up his troops on the left bank that they had been marching down. They could look out across the river at the small town, which had a tall narrow tower to the north from where the garrison commander was surely watching them, and at the Valois army scrambling to form up on the level land between the walls and the river. There were a lot of them, perhaps three times as many as in the sizeable Anglo-Burgundian force. Suffolk would not have known all the devices, but the heralds did, and could tell the rest of the

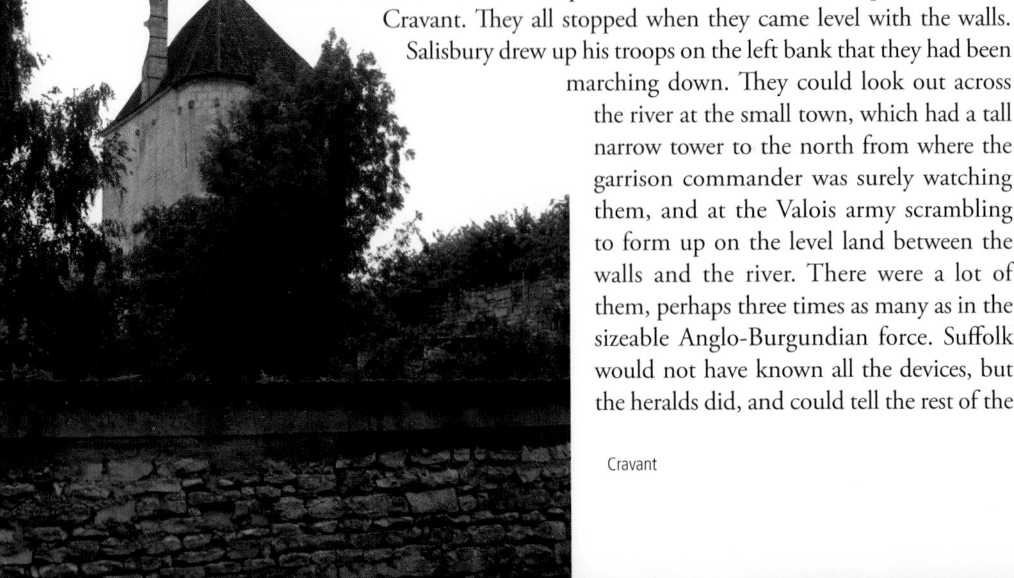

Cravant

men. The commander of the French was the count of Ventadour; of the Scots, Sir John Stewart of Darnley. No princes, no dukes, stood on either side of the Yonne, so however they fared, this battle would not be as famous as Agincourt.

There was a stone bridge across the river, but it was not wide, and they could not realistically all cross the bridge, even with the fire from the archers to protect them. The Scots were stationed at the town end. Willoughby's men should take the bridge, Salisbury decided; the rest of the Lancastrians would have to wade across the river, unless the Valois crossed it first.

The Lancastrian and Burgundian heralds rode onto the bridge, met with the Valois heralds there, and the usual offers were made and refused. The Valois would not raise their siege; they would fight.

The archers on the flanks hammered their stakes into the dry ground, and took up position behind them. At least in the first stages of the battle, they would not cross the river, but keep their place behind the stockade and direct a hail of arrows – each man firing up to fifteen each minute – at the ranks of the opponents. The captains addressed their troops. The chaplains moved among the men, taking confessions, offering encouragement and reassurance. Their cause was good, they were told; the Lord was with them. Then the chaplains withdrew, and the men at arms and archers stood and stared at the French men at arms in their massed ranks, the crossbowmen interspersed with them, the banners held high above their heads, but drooping limply in the sultry heat. The sun rose. This was common, as Suffolk knew. Often it was hours before one side began the attack. It was still possible that neither would do so.

And they would have a disadvantage if they did attack first, since the river had to be crossed. But eventually Salisbury gave the nod to his trumpeters. 'St George! Banner advance!' he cried. The men knelt, and kissed the dry earth. Then they rose, as the trumpets blared, and set up a great yell. They yelled and yelled till the noise echoed around their steel-clad heads, then they began to move forward.

The captains led, with Salisbury at their centre. The air above them was streaked thick with arrows. They yelled, yelled hard, to keep their courage, and must have felt, rather than seen, the other men follow. They could feel the water seeping into their damp clothing; they had to tread slowly, to keep their feet in the mud and slime. The heavy lances had to be kept level, their points set straight at the enemy. In places the water came to their waists. Some men slipped, but Suffolk was not one of them. He dragged his men onwards, till they were coming to the bank, and the Valois were approaching under the blizzard of arrows.

Berserk courage, Jean de Waurin called it. The first wave of the Valois came onto their lances, their own set to counter them, and they swung the heavy length, trying to find a gap and drive a man down, watch for the sharp points and keep their bodies clear.

With their wet armour in the midday sun, the English would have steamed. They could barely see. Then the Valois were right on them, and it was time to drop their lances and draw their swords.

Men were down already, unable to rise in the melee, other men treading them into the dry ground. Men at arms did not try to penetrate the

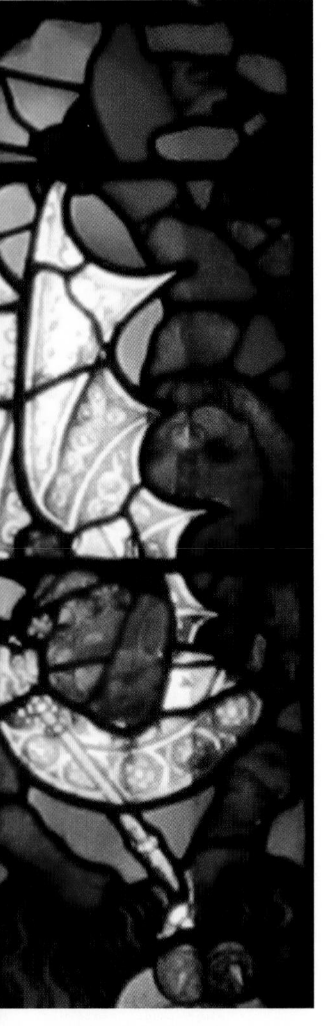

opponents' armour: the aim was to catch them off balance, with a blow to the head, or a hard whack to the arm that made them drop their weapon. With a man downed, the archers could follow after with knives: lift visors, find joints, stab and slash.

They swung their weapons, staggered, recovered, turned; swung again. There were moments when they saw clear, moments when they were dizzied or blinded. Trumpets blared, but much of the time they can barely have heard them. Men fought alongside, but they scarcely registered them. In the thick of a battle like this, though men fought for their comrades, they each fought alone.

Suffolk probably sensed, rather than saw, when reinforcements came: the garrison, staggering out of the town gates, almost too weak to walk, and laying in to the French and Scots from the rear. Then the ranks of the Lombard and Spanish mercenaries broke, and there would have been a moment's air, and the exhilarating knowledge that the day was headed their way. They ran – or as near as they could, in their heavy armour – after the fleeing troops, along the banks, since the hills beyond the town were too steep for armed men to climb. A thrown mace, a stone, a sword clanged on his helmet, could fell a fleeing man from behind.

This was the killing time, till great clumps of bodies piled up around the piers of the bridge, and the water of the Yonne ran red.

When it was clear the victory was secure, Salisbury sent word out: now they might take prisoners. There were many men disarmed now, men fallen, men wounded. They rounded them up, about 2,000 of them. Sir John Stewart had lost an eye. The count of Ventadour gave them his sword too. They could not sack Cravant, it was a Burgundian town, but there would be gains for all of them from the ransoms that men like these would pay for their freedom.

Others were dead. Suffolk had survived, but men he knew well, men who had fought in his contingent for years, must have been sprawled lifeless on the banks of the Yonne. The English and Burgundians had lost about 1,000 men, and their opponents perhaps three times as many.

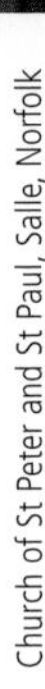
Church of St Peter and St Paul, Salle, Norfolk

So if there was time for relief and joy, when the prisoners were secured, and the men and women of Cravant had surged out of the town to greet their saviours and fall on the approaching wagons of supplies, there were grim chores as well. It was the archers and valets who gathered up the unbroken arrows and discarded swords, pulled armour roughly off the cooling corpses. It was they and the townsmen who dug the graves. But every man must have gone to the masses that followed, and grieved for the comrades whose lives were at an end.

26 The chemin gravelais

There was no need to keep the army together after Cravant was relieved: there would be no other major battle that season, no massive Valois army to make them wary. The Burgundians returned to their capital, Dijon, and a large part of the English army returned to finish the job of besieging Montaiguillon. Suffolk, meanwhile, was detailed to do in the east of France much what his brother John was doing farther west. His men swept down south on a chevauchée, raiding places for booty. He took them as far as Macon, about a hundred miles south of Cravant, and captured several strongholds before the summer was over. By then he was confident enough to divide his men still further, and send a contingent under Sir William Glasdale even deeper south, to take the strong castle of La Roche.

So it had been a fine summer for him. He had money in his coffers, and the prospect of more when the ransoms from Cravant were paid. He was blooded in battle and had acquitted himself well. And the Burgundian alliance had held firm in its first major test.

The exhilaration did not last long. It ended abruptly when a messenger arrived from his brother John, perhaps as Suffolk was headed back north at the end of the season. John was not dead, the messenger would have hastened to tell him – but most of his men were, and he was a prisoner of the Valois. They had been attacked in Anjou, overrun by a larger enemy force. John hoped to agree a ransom, and he needed Suffolk to arrange it for him.

It was something that the Valois were apparently willing to ransom him, since this could not be taken for granted. Just as the Lancastrians still held several of their high-ranking prisoners from the early stages of Henry V's campaign, so the Valois had held onto some of theirs: the earl of Somerset and other men taken with him at Baugé were still prisoners. But John was clearly not thought important enough to retain, and Suffolk would have set promptly about making the necessary arrangements.

The ransom for a knight such as John was high, not as high as an earl's ransom would have been, but still a life-changing sum. In those days a man at arms was paid a shilling a day in wages (to cover himself and his servants); a captain got four shillings, an earl six and eightpence. The details of John's ransom are lost, but the Valois would have demanded several thousand livres, perhaps twenty years' wages. So John could not be expected to find it all from his own resources: Suffolk would have had to raid his reserves and send to England too, to have his stewards forward money to him. Quite possibly they sold some land.

All this took months. Throughout the autumn straggling groups of men who survived the attack would have made their way back north. It would have been winter by the time a

Bourges Cathedral

Hambye Abbey

chastened and much poorer John was free. He must have met up with Suffolk, perhaps in Bricquebec or Moyon.

It was a hard thing indeed, to lose his men and live to know it. Of course, it was not unusual: the Valois coveted ransoms as much as the English did, and they took care to keep alive the men who might provide the largest of them, even as they killed the lesser men. But it must still have felt to John like a disgrace. Bedford would have been angered too, since he had not approved the chevauchée, and he was the duke (in name, at least) of Anjou, the territory John had invaded.

Back in the safety of the Cotentin, they must have gone many times over the details. John's men – perhaps 2,000 of them – had got almost as far as Angers. It was rich territory down there, like the territory Suffolk himself had raided: the fields in Anjou were not choked with weeds like the abandoned ones in Normandy, and there were cattle grazing still in them. Twelve hundred head! If he had got these beasts north, up the chemin gravelais, the ancient route his scouts had found for him, they could have fed the whole Lancastrian army, with plenty spare to sell in Paris or Rouen.

When they had heard of the Valois gathering to resist them, near a place called la Brossinière, close to Segré – a town he had taken and raided – his men had planned a good defence, drawn up the carts in a square with the cattle enclosed within it, dug ditches and banks to shelter behind. But there were so many of the Valois, not just Angevins but men from the rest of France too, all bitter and determined, seeking revenge. This was not an army with mercenary captains, it was a rabble whose hatred steamed off them: farmers whose herds had been taken, townsmen whose wives and daughters had been raped. This blow for André, this for Suzanne! A man fights for such causes with a rage he cannot find to defend a thousand stolen cows. John's men had beaten them off once, but when the French regrouped and attacked on the flanks, they had nothing left in reserve.

In the years that followed, it seems that the brothers chose to work closely together; they did not fight separate actions again.

27 A secret marriage

Suffolk's men eventually took Le Crotoy. Its siege had dragged on all summer and beyond, so Suffolk would have returned, perhaps several times, to oversee its final stages. Burgundians had joined his forces: not the duke, but still, Burgundians. Bedford had sent his best cannon. Encircled by sea, battered from the landward side, the garrison finally admitted defeat. When they rode off under the flag of truce, they left behind them nine veuglaires – a type of iron cannon – two casks of gunpowder, twenty-three crossbows and nine coffers of arrows. Suffolk did not just send to Bedford to report these gains, he must have met with the duke, in Paris or Rouen. It was a small compensation for Sir John's disaster.

Bedford also had other reasons to feel troubled that winter, and Suffolk learned of them, not just from the regent's men, but from his own heralds in England, and contacts there like Lord Morley. Humphrey of Gloucester had married. He had done so in secret, though he had announced it loudly, once done – and he had married Jacqueline of Hainault.

Pity the priest, in Hadleigh in Essex, who had been ordered by Gloucester to conduct the wedding mass. Pity the herald who had brought the news to Bedford. Normally an even-tempered man, Gloucester's elder brother must have been livid.

Gloucester himself sought to defend his actions. He pointed out – loudly, again – that this was no rash marriage for passion. He had had months to consider the pros and cons of it, and he expected other men too to see the pros. Jacqueline had a valid claim to large and rich lands, bordering those that were claimed for little Henry of Lancaster. Would it not be better to have the child-king's uncle in firm control of those lands, lending support to the alliance, than to have to depend on the fickle duke of Burgundy? Envoys from Gloucester came not just to Bedford but to Suffolk and other commanders too, making this case, and suggesting they should aid the duke in enforcing his new wife's claims.

The lords in France must have talked this over, both with and without Bedford. Suffolk, Salisbury and the rest would have appreciated the argument Gloucester was making, but seen the negatives too. The churchmen were complaining that Humphrey and his wife had gone flat against the pope's ruling, and even if Englishmen and Hainaulters were cowed into taking this marriage as valid, the rest of Europe would scarcely do so. And did Duke Humphrey genuinely expect them to move their troops from their fragile southern border, and take them north to fight against Burgundy's Flemish troops, men such as those who had fought at Cravant and manned the cannon at Le Crotoy?

Salisbury's father in law, Thomas Chaucer,

Evreux Cathedral

was a power in the English Parliament, chosen repeatedly as its speaker. He spoke for the merchants in England who dealt with the Flemish clothmakers – and he did not advocate support for Gloucester. The message he sent was reinforced by all the men who reported from England. By doing this, Gloucester had turned the deep differences among the men of the king's English council into an open split. He had set himself up against the bishop of Winchester, his powerful uncle, and dozens of other lords too. The earl of Norfolk was supporting Gloucester, apparently, but precious few others were.

Suffolk probably took Norfolk for a fool. But what could he himself do, and other men in France? They were conscious that Bedford could have no wish, and had only limited power, to thwart his brother. Gloucester might not have the regency that Henry V had intended for him, but his was still the major power in England. These men themselves valued Gloucester's friendship – hell, they liked the duke, and if they were shocked at what he had done, they must have smiled too at the thought of Gloucester and Jacqueline getting themselves up in disguise and riding by night into Essex to find an obliging priest.

They threw ideas around. Perhaps they should assassinate Burgundy, and help Gloucester grab his title and all of the Low Countries? Jacqueline was popular, evidently; Gloucester knew how to make himself liked; and although men called him the Good Duke, Philip of Burgundy was by no means universally admired. All right, that was hardly a viable plan. Should they appeal again to the pope, get men like the bishop of Winchester to put pressure on him to change his mind? That was more sensible, indeed it had to be done. But since few of them believed that Pope Martin V would reverse the ruling he had already made, more had to be done as well. The problem was, none of them could see quite what would improve the situation.

When the campaigning season began in the spring of 1424, Suffolk went back to besieging inland places with Salisbury. This time they set their troops to take Valois-held fortresses to the west of Paris, and that August they were laying siege to Ivry la Chaussé, a stronghold just north of Dreux, when news came that another Lancastrian army was approaching to join their men.

They already knew that the dauphin had regrouped his forces after the disaster of Cravant, and that his army was rumoured to be in this region. With a levy of men from across the territory he controlled, reinforced by another contingent of Scots and more Lombard and Spanish mercenaries, he had mustered perhaps 15,000 men. This had to be a prelude to another battle against the Valois. But when they realized that the lead standard of the approaching troops was the regent's own colours, they knew too that there were good reasons for John of Bedford to have come to meet with them in person.

Bedford and his men – who included a contingent of Burgundians – reached them just in time for the surrender of Ivry, on 15 August. They brought the news that the Valois were thought to be headed for Verneuil, a day's journey to the west. Verneuil was strongly held for the Lancastrians, so it could be assumed that the Valois would surround it for a siege. The Lancastrian forces were to make for Verneuil too, to raise the siege; but before they did so, there were discussions Bedford wished to have with his commanders.

They must have chosen somewhere secure to meet, perhaps within the thick stone walls of a fortified church. This briefing would not have been written down, but it is clear from how events unfolded what John of Bedford said.

Most likely the news that the regent brought came as little surprise: Suffolk and Salisbury would have known, from both their own and Gloucester's messengers, that Gloucester had continued with his plans, that Norfolk had continued to support them, and that word had gone out in East Anglia for men to join the troops he was raising. Gloucester was determined to take his bride back to Hainault and reclaim her lands. He needed a show of force if he was to carry this off. True, the English did not want to offend Burgundy; but Gloucester must have argued that Burgundy in his turn could not really afford to offend the English. Burgundy knew that Jacqueline's claim was valid. Was it not conceivable that he would decide not to support her opponents (her estranged husband and her uncle, John of Bavaria), but to ally with his niece and her powerful new husband, and create a grouping that would be dominant in western Europe?

They could hope for this, but the trouble was, Suffolk, Salisbury, Bedford and the rest did not believe it would happen. They could barely predict how events would unfold. But they must start to move, Bedford must have instructed them; make and implement not just one plan, but layers of plans. The French and the Burgundians had always acted like wily foxes, saying what diplomats said on one level, and doing what suited them best on another. This was no time for English straight talk; they must play that game, and beat the Frenchmen at it.

Their priorities were clear. First and foremost, they must protect the king's interests. Second, Gloucester was one of

Church of St Peter and St Paul, East Harling, Norfolk
Photo Mike Dixon

them, and though they might deplore his actions, he too must be supported and protected – in public to some extent, in private without question. Third, Burgundy was an important ally, but if it was necessary to sacrifice him to protect the king and Gloucester, this was what they must do. The French themselves had used every tactic up to and including assassination; the English must not be squeamish. All these men would surely have preferred to avoid killing Burgundy: they might have killed in battle, but cold murder was a sin. If murder had to be done, though, it would be. It would have to appear an accident; they must not foment another feud. And in public, Bedford must and would stand clear. If they were caught, he could not and would not come to their defence.

It seems to have been Suffolk who got the task, though with Salisbury's support. He saw it as a way, perhaps, of further regaining Bedford's trust and approval after the débâcle of John's unauthorized chevauchée. He had built up fine contacts among the Burgundian troops, and at the duke's court. The father of his chief musician, Gilles Binchois, had served Jacqueline of Hainault. He must use these channels on the surface, and assure the duke of Burgundy of his sympathy and support, just as Bedford was doing through his own intermediaries. But he must use his other resources too, to ensure that if events turned against Gloucester, he would be protected and defended.

Perhaps Suffolk retained men who could have been trusted to carry out an assassination. There could be a joust in Paris, perhaps – the duke of Burgundy was found of jousting – that went tragically wrong. He certainly retained men who knew how to forge letters. There was one in particular, who called himself William Bennet among the English, but could also pass as a Frenchman, Guillaume Benoit. Exactly what Suffolk planned will never be known, but it seems most likely that he played with the idea of a plot to assassinate Burgundy that was largely fake, but could yet be made real if events necessitated that. As his plans were always to be, it was a little too complicated. He thought, at least, of using the unreliable Breton lords as intermediaries. A letter could be dropped, or a man conveniently captured; chaos would spread, men's minds be changed. He must have known he was walking on rotten floorboards. But he probably relished drawing his plans up nevertheless.

Chateau of the Dukes of Brittany, Nantes

28 Captive at the horse's tails

Bad news arrived the next day, probably before Suffolk had had a chance to set pen to paper, or brief William Bennet. The Valois had taken Verneuil.

They had done it through a ruse so well-worn that the men of Verneuil should never have fallen for it – or so the Lancastrian commanders doubtless thought. They had persuaded some of the Scots soldiers to pretend to be prisoners, and tied them up, roping them to the tails of their horses. Then they paraded these men before the town walls, and sent envoys to tell the townsfolk that there had been a battle, they had defeated the English army, and these were the spoils of their victory. Anxious, naturally enough, to be found on the right side, the townsfolk had opened the gates and let them in.

So there was no siege to be relieved. Still, Bedford reckoned the Valois would be up for a battle. It was not certain, true: not after Agincourt, not after Cravant. But the Scots wanted revenge for that latter disaster, the French for the former, and the dauphin needed a sizeable victory, not just the retaking of a small town in lower Normandy. So the regent decided that his men should head for Verneuil, and attempt to win a third great victory, one that would see off the Valois threat for years to come.

St Mary's Church, North Tuddenham, Norfolk
Photo Mike Dixon

It was the feast of the Assumption the next day, and Bedford wanted to celebrate it properly. But someone had to shadow the French army while he did so, so he gave that task to Suffolk. Meanwhile Bedford, Salisbury and their men would march to Evreux, half a day's journey to the north-west, where Valois spies would report to the dauphin's commanders that they had made their devotions in the cathedral.

Bedford sent the Burgundian troops off to resume siege operations farther north. Suffolk probably understood why, though it is hard to understand the reasoning now. Bedford must have known his men would be outnumbered by the Valois army. Maybe he reckoned it was not the best of moments to risk these allied troops in battle. Maybe he did not trust them, and maybe he was right. The Burgundians had fought well at Cravant, but that was in their own territory. Verneuil was in lower Normandy, a long way from any of the territory the duke of Burgundy controlled.

So Suffolk was left with about 1,600 men, to march the fifteen miles or so from Ivry to Verneuil. They must not disclose their position, Bedford ordered – the last thing they wanted was for the Valois army to annihilate this little force before the rest joined them – but they should scout thoroughly, plan where the action might take place, and do their best to ensure that the Valois army did not head out of range.

This they did, successfully. They went as far as the great forest of Piseux, just to the north of Verneuil, and the chaplains celebrated the festival mass amid the trees, while the scouts rode out to, and round, the small town. It was a handsome place, they reported back, one they would be only too glad to see back in Lancastrian hands. As well as good walls, it had a wet ditch, filled from the little river Avre. Valois standards were flying from the towers, Valois tents camped in the meadows to hold the men who could not find billets in the town, so Bedford's intelligence had been correct: this was a large army, and it was all at Verneuil.

There was a flat plain between the forest and the town, which the road from Damville to Verneuil bisected. There was nowhere that they could repeat the tactics of Agincourt, funnelling the Valois soldiers into a clump that could easily be hacked down, so the plain looked like the best location for a battle.

Suffolk maybe rode out to check on the site himself. It was a dry and dusty summer. The scouts were right, as far as he could judge. He sent word to Bedford to bring his men. Then he set plenty of guards, and his men made camp in the forest.

Next day the rest of the Lancastrians marched up. The men and horses kicked up so much dust from the road that the Valois must have seen them coming from miles off. Suffolk's scouts, sent out again, reported that the Valois had clearly done so, and preparations were being made in their camp and in the town. The Valois army would have to fight; they could not all cower behind the walls of Verneuil and eat the rations down, and they could not flee now the Lancastrians were so close.

When the Lancastrian troops emerged from the forest they found the opposing army already lined up, across the road and the fields, about a mile from the walls of the town. Bedford would command the army, of course; as regent, he could have done nothing else. Salisbury would take the second force, and Suffolk would be one of his lieutenants again.

There was no river to wade across this time. And this was a bigger engagement than at Cravant: virtually all the free Lancastrian forces, and the whole Valois army too, would join the battle. Yet again, the Lancastrians were heavily outnumbered. Suffolk and the rest must all have thought, looking at the mass of men facing them, that they could not continue indefinitely to get the better of much larger armies. But perhaps they could do it one more time.

Oxborough Hall chapel, Norfolk
Photo Mike Dixon

Bedford seemed to think they could. More than any of them, he needed this victory. With this he might assert his control, convince men that the loss of Henry V had done nothing to weaken the Lancastrian cause, and gain his own reputation from the chroniclers. With a victory here, won without help from the Burgundians, he might have power enough to hand down orders to both Gloucester and Burgundy, and see the problems in the north resolved.

He made the dispositions confidently, and Salisbury, Suffolk and the rest, most of them thoroughly experienced fighters by now, passed the orders down and saw them carried out. The troops pulled up and the knights dismounted out of arrow shot of the Valois army. The carters, pages and grooms drew up the carts into close formation, and tethered the horses head to tail, with the neck of one fastened to the tail of its partner, so they could not run off if they were frightened. Bedford sent his heralds forward to the Valois commanders – the count of Aumale for the French troops, the earl of Douglas for the Scots. When they came back, he called his commanders to conference, and told them the terms of engagement. The Scots had said they would neither give nor receive quarter, so these men would have to be fought to the death. The French would discuss terms if the day did not go with them, although the English would need a solid victory if they were to claim Verneuil at the end of it. The mercenaries were pragmatic, as usual; given a choice between death and surrender, these men would choose to live.

Although the Lancastrians had dismounted, as was their custom, the Valois troops did not all dismount: they had small divisions of men, mostly Lombard mercenaries, on horseback on their flanks. These men could ride round quickly and attack their enemy's rear, or the reserve that guarded the baggage. But they were vulnerable to fire from the archers; they could be defeated. So Suffolk would have told his men, and those who had been at Cravant or Agincourt, or even heard about those victories, would have believed him.

Once again, it took ages. The summer sun rose and began to fall. Finally Bedford gave the order, and the captains took their places in the line.

It was about two o'clock in the afternoon by the time the Valois front line lowered their lances, and began to plod forward in their armour. Bedford gave the signal. 'Avaunt, banners!' The men bent down and kissed the ground, and gave their reply, 'St George and Bedford!' 'A Clarence!' they cried too. Many of these men had not fought in battle since their old commander had been killed. They raised their shouts, and the trumpets and clarions fought to be heard above them.

The archers stopped just within range, and the men at the rear passed forward the stakes. The ground was baked hard in the summer heat, and the men at arms must have seen that the archers were having difficulty hammering the palisade firmly into the earth. They must have seen the French cavalry charge, seen the archers being swept back. Then Bedford's trumpeters sounded again, and Suffolk and the rest put that knowledge from their minds, and moved to engage with the enemy.

It was a long and bitter battle. Suffolk's men probably fought under Salisbury, on the left flank. Their opponents here were the Scots: not the levies of French farm boys, but trained troops who fought hard. They held their position, but did not advance. But perhaps an hour and a half later more troops joined them – Bedford's men, who had sent the French fleeing – and gave them the advantage. Weary but determined, they set about slaughtering the men who had refused quarter.

They killed and killed, between the blue sky and the flat plain. They killed the Scots, almost to a man: one-eyed Douglas, his son, his son-in-law, about fifty more knights and a host of men at arms. They killed the French, they killed the Lombard mercenaries. They pursued the men who ran for Verneuil, hacked at them on the banks and kicked their corpses into the ditch. Their own men died too, of course; not Suffolk, not his brothers, but as always, men he knew. But he learned of that only afterwards.

Afterwards. The eerie silence of the battle done, the trumpets silent, the men too weary to shout, or too dead. Corpses strewed across the fields, with the blood pooling thick around the cabbage stalks. Corpses in the ditch, on the banks, in the little river Avre, staining its waters scarlet. The heralds counted them: they made the total 7,262. It was the annihilating victory that Bedford had hoped for.

They had killed the count of Ventadour, who had been taken prisoner at Cravant. They had killed Aumale, the supreme commander. They had taken captive the duke of Alençon, the young son of a duke who had been killed at Agincourt. He was good for a large ransom. It took him the next five years to get it together and regain his freedom. Suffolk's share of it must have gone a long way to repairing his losses from paying John's ransom.

Not everything had gone well. The reserve troop had fled from the Lombard horsemen, who had plundered the baggage train, untying many of the tethered horses and setting them free. Well, the Lancastrians could tell themselves, if these men had fought in the main battle instead of messing about at the rear, the Valois might have done better. There were horses that had belonged to dead Frenchmen, dead Scots; this was a loss that could be repaired.

Bedford sent men out to round up the reserves who had run off. This was a joyless task, since they all knew these men must pay the price. And if milder in manner, Bedford proved as ruthless as his dead brother in dealing out justice. The men stood and watched as gibbets were built, and the men were hanged from them. Their captain was hung, drawn and quartered.

Then the survivors headed into Verneuil, now safely in their hands again, and gave thanks that they had come through safely through the curtain of blood.

Trinity Church, Vendome

29 Such a brother, such a wife

Church of St Mary the Virgin, Yaxley, Suffolk

The Lancastrians celebrated their victory not in London, but in Paris. This was their capital now; this was the city that needed to see their triumph. Of course the English celebrated in London and elsewhere too when the news reached them, but for Suffolk, his brothers and his comrades, it was Paris that mattered.

There was euphoria, there was even frivolity in Paris that autumn, and for all their triumphs, these had been rare things in Lancastrian France. At that moment, even the most wary of them must have believed they could wrap up the conquest, see the dauphin surrender, and present the throne of all France to the baby King Henry.

Even the duke of Burgundy seemed to believe it again. He came to Paris and joined in the festivities. There were weddings in Paris that autumn – of Lord Scales, one of Bedford's commanders, and of a Burgundian lord – and there were parties. Philip of Burgundy had always liked a party. He held a particularly fine one at his hotel d'Artois.

Suffolk was there, talking with the duke's councillor Hue de Lannoy and his other Burgundian contacts. He probably talked too with Bedford and his wife. Duchess Anne's sister and her husband, Arthur of Richemont, were not in Paris, however. Richemont had chosen this moment to desert the Lancastrians – as they had all half expected – and take up the dauphin's offer to make him constable of France.

This struck a sour note, and there were one or two others. Burgundy made a pass at Salisbury's pretty young wife, and persisted when she tried to laugh him away. What was Burgundy doing? He must surely have recognized the countess, and realized it would offend Salisbury. Perhaps he had had a perverse desire to do just that.

Some women might have dealt with this tactfully, but clever as she was, Alice of Salisbury did not manage to do so. She made a scene, which caused some embarrassment to the English. Her father Thomas Chaucer was in Paris, so perhaps that was part of it. Although Chaucer was rich, he was a commoner, and he and the daughter he had seen married into the nobility might have been touchy about their status, and quick to respond to what they saw as slights.

Bloody Burgundy, must have been Salisbury's reaction, and Chaucer's too. It was probably Suffolk's as well. He was Salisbury's comrade, he liked Lady Alice, and he had not forgotten the scheming of that early summer. Gloucester was still pressing him for support against Burgundy. Chaucer would have told both Suffolk and Salisbury of the rows between Gloucester and the other lords on the king's council. 'Such a brother you have here,' the bishop of Winchester had written plaintively to Bedford. Chaucer was in sympathy himself with the bishop of Winchester, who was his own kinsman as well as the king's, and all too short on patience with Gloucester. But he probably told Salisbury and Suffolk too that all the warnings and disapproval had not discouraged Gloucester one jot from his plan to invade Hainault.

That information was followed quickly by more news. In October, only weeks after the victory at Verneuil, Humphrey of Gloucester and his wife crossed over to Calais. They took a good force of men with them, including the earl of Norfolk's troops as well as Gloucester's own, and a number of Hainaulters joined the force when they reached Jacqueline's lands. They proceeded unhindered into Hainault, and the spies and messengers tagged along with them. Jacqueline was popular in Mons, its capital, and men greeted Gloucester kindly as well. He was treated like the lord of the land, so they were told in Paris. That was of course what he intended to be.

Bury St Edmunds Cathedral, Suffolk

Jacqueline had still not been granted annulment of the marriage to her cousin, but Bedford let it be known that he had written privately to the pope, urging him to rethink. And he had assured the duke of Burgundy that the English would be grateful, and respect every inch of Burgundy's own territory, if he chose to hold off and let Gloucester claim Hainault.

So they could hope that it might all develop to their advantage. There were plenty of tournaments in Paris that autumn, and nobody caused the duke of Burgundy to suffer a nasty accident. Still, Suffolk was probably reminded by Bedford that it was as well not to be over-confident. They had seen from the incident with Lady Alice how erratic and arrogant Burgundy could be. Pursue your plan, was the message. Do it quietly, and do not involve me; but put it all in place, in case it is needed.

So he did so. In parallel with the public meetings with the Burgundian lords, he spoke with Gilles Binchois, and perhaps sent messengers to Binchois' father in Hainault. He not only spoke with William Bennet, he had the man draw up a set of forged letters, which spelled out – not too blatantly – the details of a plot to assassinate the duke of Burgundy. He assured the Burgundians that he appreciated duke Philip's concern about the events in Hainault, and he worked in secret to ensure that the duke did not act on that concern.

He hoped, most likely, that it would stop there. Burgundy would rage in Bruges, just as the bishop of Winchester had raged in Westminster, but both of them would conclude that they could not realistically prevent Gloucester from doing just as he had chosen. For a while, that was perhaps likely. Then it was still possible. Then it was not possible any more; the spies and heralds alike were reporting that Burgundy had decided to retaliate, and help her uncle to dispossess Jacqueline of her lands.

And now Suffolk would have to put the plan into action.

He set off for Hainault. On the surface it was a diplomatic mission: go to Mons and speak to Gloucester, go to Bruges or Hesdin and speak to Burgundy, smooth tempers, take soundings, make promises. Below the surface it was something else, because he took the forged letters that Bennet had made.

By then it was a grey November. Suffolk did not take a troop of men at arms with him:

the aim was not to inflame Burgundy. He took a fellow knight and the abbot of Fécamp – embassies always involved churchmen, so this was the conventional thing. They had their grooms and valets, of course, and a strong guard. They paused overnight in the village of Breteuil, between Beauvais and Amiens. There was nowhere to stay but a dilapidated inn. They probably went over their tactics after supper.

Then Suffolk went to bed – and the ceiling fell down on him.

It was no joke, though perhaps for a moment his valet dared to find it so. He was not only showered in rotten straw and sodden plaster, he was banged hard on the head by a solid oak beam. When he came to, and found his servants and the abbot standing round his bed, all half-surprised that he was not dead from the impact, he realized that he was going nowhere but back to Paris on a litter. And that none too soon, either; for some time he was confined to the dirty little inn.

Garter king of arms – Bedford's man – came there to call on him. He asked about the letters, and a groggy Suffolk must have told him where they had been hidden. He assumed afterwards that Garter had found them, and taken them off, most likely to be burned.

It was weeks, or even months, before Suffolk was well enough to return to the regent's court. Bedford could hardly blame him for the knock on his head, but he must have been somewhat embarrassed at the collapse of his scheme, and he perhaps suggested to Bedford that he should get Bennet to draw up more letters, and try to revive it. The situation in the low countries was still combustible. Jacqueline's uncle John of Bavaria had died that January, which left Burgundy in a position to try to directly annexe her lands. Gloucester was holding on in Hainault, and the latest suggestion was that he and Burgundy should resolve the claim to the territory by single combat. Duke Philip had agreed with remarkable enthusiasm, considering his normal reluctance to fight with his army. He had employed armourers and fencing masters, and was preparing energetically at his castle of Hesdin.

Gloucester had announced that he would return to England to make his own preparations. Suffolk had probably had messages not just from him, but from Jacqueline too – expressing her sympathy at his injury, but also sounding him out, should his help be needed.

Suffolk cannot have expected Bedford to welcome the single combat notion. Whatever the outcome, a trial of strength between Gloucester and Burgundy would fatally damage one of them. It would wreck the alliance, and even if the Lancastrians were at full flood, they could not readily afford to do that. So he must have been surprised when Bedford told him the situation was under control. Of course, he would have realized with a little thought that Bedford would hardly have sat and waited for him to recover. There must have been other men pursuing other schemes.

And one of them had come to fruition. There was a pretty young girl among the ladies who had been assigned to attend on Countess Jacqueline during her exile in England. Gloucester clearly liked this Eleanor Cobham, and the Lancastrians had realized that this could be taken advantage of. The marriage with Jacqueline was not

Evreux Cathedral

recognized by the pope, so one might as well say that Gloucester was not married at all. If this Eleanor was pushed gently (or not so gently) in Gloucester's direction, and Gloucester nudged in hers as well; if Eleanor went back to England with Gloucester, and Jacqueline remained in Hainault – true, Mistress Cobham was not a great heiress, but given the choice between fighting for his life, or staying in England in comfort, and swapping his troublesome wife for a pretty and obliging one, would it be so unlikely if Gloucester agreed? Bedford would draw in the bishop of Winchester and his supporters, and persuade them that as part of the deal they must grant Gloucester a little more power, and a larger salary to accompany it. Burgundy, meanwhile, would be assured that the English would turn the other way while he marched his men into Hainault. He would be convinced that this was a favour Bedford had done him because the English so valued his alliance with them – and he would not be wrong, at that.

It was a deal that worked for everyone except Jacqueline of Hainault.

St Taurin's Church, Evreux

When Jacqueline wrote again – and it seems she did – it was not to plead for Suffolk's help on behalf of the duke of Gloucester, it was to plead for it on her own account.

Suffolk felt sorry for her, clearly. Most likely he had not yet met the woman, but he had heard plenty about her over the months and years, and most of it was to her advantage. She had done her best with a hand of cards other people had insisted in playing for her, but time and again things had not gone her way. The Binchois, father and son, were probably sorry for her too, and many other men and women felt the same when they heard the story.

Gloucester was not a boorish man or a fool; he had married her in good faith. He probably told himself it was not his own fault that it had not worked out, and that he had been left with no alternative but to bow to the pope. But still, it was hard on Jacqueline, and he knew it. If he got word that Suffolk was thinking of helping her, he might have encouraged it. Then again, Suffolk perhaps felt no need in the circumstances to tell Gloucester what he planned.

He more likely told Bedford, and Salisbury too. Because it seems he headed up to Mons that spring, met up with the countess, and did what he could for her.

This was a woman for whom Gloucester had risked much, a woman who had made herself loved at the English court. She was perhaps not quite beautiful, but her spirit made her seem so. By that spring, it seems that she and Suffolk were lovers.

They could not marry: churchmen might quibble over whether Jacqueline was married to John of Brabant or to Gloucester, but no one doubted she was validly married to one of them. They could not realistically have lived together without marrying. So when she conceived, it was something of a problem.

The best, if not the only, answer was for Suffolk to take the child, a girl, and have her quietly cared for, well away from Hainault. Her name came down in history – Beatrice – and she was heard – or at least rumoured – of later in England near to Suffolk's home. Perhaps he sent her to Lady Morley at first, or to his sister Katherine in her convent at Barking.

There was a story later that in 1428 Suffolk and Jacqueline did marry. By then Pope Martin had declared finally in favour of Jacqueline's second marriage, not her third, and this made her a widow, since John of Brabant had died. However, this could not have been true: in 1428 Suffolk went nowhere near Hainault, and Jacqueline would not have travelled across war-torn Normandy to meet up with him. Anyway, both of them went on to marry other people. This was perhaps a tale put about by his people, or hers, to counter some of the rumours that were circulating about the child. Although it was no great disgrace for a nobleman to have bastards – the bishop of Winchester had been one before his parents later married, and also sired a daughter himself; Gloucester had a couple; Philip of Burgundy had a horde of them – it would have been a scandal for the countess of Hainault to have been known to do so. However much the pair had tried to keep things quiet, nothing an earl or a countess did was entirely secret. There were always people around them, and those people knew such things.

Meanwhile, with the help she was given – from Suffolk; from the Binchois family, from her own servants and troops – Jacqueline continued to fight on spiritedly against the duke of Burgundy. The citizens of Mons supported her for as long as they reasonably could, but they eventually surrendered her to Duke Philip, who brought her in triumph to Ghent as a state prisoner. She disguised herself as a man, escaped from her prison, and got back to her own territories, travelling via Zieriksee to Gouda. Eventually she came to an agreement with Burgundy, signing the Treaty of Delft on 3 July 1428. It made him the legal heir to her territories, but she kept them secure for the rest of her life.

The plot that Suffolk had drawn up did not remain secret either. It is not clear who gave the hint to Burgundy's men, but they learned of it somehow, and when in 1428 they took Guillaume Benoit (or William Bennet) prisoner in Lille, they questioned him about it. That kind of questioning is not readily resisted, and Bennet made a long deposition about the forged letters. That must have been embarrassing for Suffolk. But nothing had happened, after all; Duke Philip lived to a good old age. And he and Suffolk remained on cordial terms, so somehow Suffolk must have managed to explain it away. Perhaps he blamed it on the Bretons.

Evreux Cathedral

30 From Danzig and the Orwell

Perhaps the bang to his head had injured Suffolk in more ways than he realized, because although the next couple of years were by no means entirely disastrous for him, nor were they a time of great success. He had a solid record of achievement now as a captain at arms, and as well as directing his own men in scores of actions, had acted successfully as lieutenant to Henry V, Salisbury and others in larger joint endeavours. This should have been the period when he emerged as a leading commander in his own right, but somehow it did not happen.

The business with Jacqueline of Hainault might have caused him to lose focus. Perhaps it was bad luck, or fate: he was a believer in fate, that men's fortune is written – cryptically – in the stars. Perhaps it was simply that the actions of these years demanded qualities he did not quite possess. He did not have the fine edge of brutality that had made Henry V – and was to make Salisbury, and other rising Lancastrian commanders like Lord Talbot – so feared by the French. He was a thoughtful man, but perhaps he did not think in the clear, fast way that the battlefield demanded, or with the kind of imagination that could wrongfoot the enemy. Whichever combination of factors it was, these were the years when he might have carved a great reputation – and he did not.

Bedford retained confidence in him – as a lieutenant, and as a negotiator. In the next couple of years Suffolk gained a series of new appointments and honours, including a French earldom: of Dreux, to the west of Paris. He continued to act as lieutenant-general of Caen, the Cotentin and Lower Normandy. He continued to ride between Paris, Rouen and scores of other places, across the wasted land from which the English had driven most of the French. He had seen Bruges and the other cities of Flanders now, and knew that they had not just cloth markets and rich merchants, but great music, great art. The duke of Burgundy had a particularly fine painter called Jan van Eyck at his court. Burgundy on his own territory kept menageries and had his craftsmen design elaborate mechanical fountains – he had a fondness for drenching his guests. In Paris the wolves still came out at night, and in Normandy and the île de France there were no herds of cattle to be seen in the fields.

Although the battle of Verneuil had been a brilliant victory, it did not lead to a break-through, a surge that brought them the rest of France. Men more distant might have believed it had weakened the Valois and strengthened the Lancastrians, but men in the thick of the Lancastrian campaign knew the truth was more complex. The English felt their losses hard. It was more difficult every year to find men back in England to take the place of those who had been killed, or injured too badly to fight again, or deserted (there were plenty of those). It would take the Valois a year or two to assemble another large army, but there was no shortage of Frenchmen to join it. Meanwhile, the French were not joining the Lancastrian army. A few Burgundians were part of it, but not many others. Frenchmen did play their part in Bedford's administration, but this did little to disguise the fact that every Lancastrian-held town still needed a garrison to keep its inhabitants loyal. Even the earldom of Dreux was a mixed blessing, because it brought with it more places that Suffolk was now responsible for garrisoning. He must have spent much time, as did his lieutenants, trying to find men to fill these places for him.

These were tedious years, when they pursued the grinding business of taking territory piece by piece, or retaking it, where the Valois troops had fought back. The dauphin had not surrendered, or ever looked likely to. Against all the odds, and unlike most of his siblings, the man lived on, and in his way, thrived.

Suffolk had carried for a couple of years now the black shadow of knowledge that he would have to try for Mont St Michel. It was necessary to conquer the place and throw the Valois clean out of Normandy. Whatever amends had already been made, Sir John still had a debt to repay to Bedford, and this was the way that he and his family had to discharge it.

So Suffolk and his brothers headed in the spring of 1425 for the bay of Mont St Michel, which has the Sienne valley and the southern Cotentin to its north-east, and Brittany to the south and west. It was only a few miles from Hambye and John's estate of Moyon, and nearer still to Avranches and Pontorson, where Suffolk commanded the garrisons, so they had seen the fortified monastery rising sheer out of the shallow waters many times from the shore, albeit they had never walked through its doors. Men called it impregnable; they called it La Merveille. The Archangel Michael had appeared to the bishop of Avranches there, six centuries before. The French revered the place, and the English too cannot have been immune to its mystery and power. Today a causeway links the island with the mainland, but this did not exist in Suffolk's day, when the Mont stood isolated in the bay.

When Sir John had ridden off to Anjou instead, two summers before, Bedford had given the task of taking the Mont to another captain. Sir Nicholas Burdet had spent months building defences for the besiegers, then he was caught in a pincer attack between the garrison on the Mont and a French force that had crept up from the landward side without his scouts noticing. He and most of his men had been captured. This was not the happiest of antecedents.

Still, they must try. Suffolk had already sent out orders for vessels to form the seaward blockade. They came from across Europe: Rouen, Danzig, the Orwell estuary and the Kentish port of Winchelsea. While he and his men were settling into Burdet's old trenches, the ships were taking up their positions around the bay. It had to be possible to starve out the Mont, Suffolk and his brothers must have told themselves. There could not be tunnels to the mainland, it was solid rock. Encircle it with ships, and eventually it would run out of provisions and the men would capitulate.

Eventually did not happen. What happened was a Breton fleet, sailing up from St Malo, and engaging with this motley armada. The duke of Brittany was supposed to be their ally, but Richemont was not an ally any more, and many

other Bretons also were not. This was not an attack they had foreseen, but afterwards perhaps they realized they should have done.

Even if they had, though, more ships could not have been summoned from Danzig at a moment's notice. Suffolk and his men were left standing on the shore, watching the smoke rise as the ships they had commissioned were boarded by the stronger Breton force, the sailors overpowered, the hulls set on fire. A couple managed to evade the Bretons and sail clear; the rest sank into the still waters of the bay.

They could not take the Mont without a seaward blockade. It was impossible to storm the place, it could only be starved out, and unless it was encircled boats would come in each night and reprovision it. Suffolk sent to Bedford with the bad news, and a request for funds to requisition more ships. The answer came back, as he had probably expected, that no funds were available for that purpose. Suffolk must have ridden to Rouen. He spoke to Bedford and the Norman administrators. Bedford repeated that there was no money. Could they not try to take the place without more ships, the clerks in the counting house asked? Well, no. They could sit on the shore in their trenches, but short of a miracle, that would achieve nothing.

He went back to Pontorson, and conferred with his lieutenants. None of them had a stroke of genius that showed them how they might take the Mont. They all agreed they would waste their summer if they sat watching it from the shore, too far distant for their cannon to damage the walls. Bedford might want this to be done, but as far as these men could see, there were only two options: they could fail slowly, or they could fail fast.

They opted for failing fast. On 13 July Suffolk's men lifted the siege and marched away. They could be, and were, useful to the east and south, but half the season had been wasted, and it had gained them nothing.

Worse, it had brought home that the Bretons were once again a problem. Richemont was urging his wife to work on her brother the duke of Burgundy. The English were not as strong as they seemed, she must have whispered: their coffers were empty, their king was still a small child. Just as Richemont had not been given an English title and lands, so Burgundy had not gained much from supporting the Lancastrians. These men did not understand how to bribe their supporters in the French manner. Even Hainault had not as yet come to the duke. Was this not a good time to think again, and consider what the dauphin might offer instead?

Bedford was clear on this: the damned duke of Burgundy would not be given more lands and honours. He must support their cause because it was right, and because he had sworn to it. There was another flurry of diplomatic activity, more letters written, more envoys sent. Meanwhile, the Bretons needed to be taught a lesson.

That was Suffolk's task the following spring. His men were probably only too glad to have the job of giving the Bretons a bloody nose. They rode as far as Rennes on their chevauchées, and took plenty of booty. Suffolk did not have the men to hold this territory firmly, but he could, and did, establish a base in the Breton marches, the strongly walled small town of St James de Beuvron, to strengthen the western frontier of the land he controlled. His men held it that winter: about 600 of them, a good garrison as was necessary in this vulnerable frontier location, but no army. He did not have more men to spare. It was possible, he knew, that the Bretons would try to retake the place. In fact, it was likely. He left Sir Thomas Rempston, one of his best captains, in charge of St James, with orders to send fast for aid if the Breton army arrived.

In March 1426 – when he was in Avranches, perhaps, or Bricquebec – he was brought

Church of Notre Dame, Chateau l'Hermitage, France

word from Rempston's messenger. Richemont had mustered an army, and brought it to besiege St James. There were maybe 16,000 Valois, the messenger reported: a sea of men at arms, from Brittany and well beyond. But no fear, Sir Thomas would do his utmost to hold them off.

Arrangements were in place for this contingency, and Suffolk put them immediately into effect. Men were peeled off from his garrisons, the forces who wintered at Bricquebec marched down the lanes of the Cotentin, and they all assembled ready to head to Brittany. Hell, though, 16,000 Valois! He could not muster even a quarter this many men to set against them. If Rempston held out till they arrived, and the Valois engaged with them, it would be another battle like Verneuil and Cravant, with each of the Lancastrians set against many more of their opponents. Still, if he could pull this off, it would be the victory he craved, one that was his alone, which the heralds would report in Paris and London.

He sent scouts ahead, of course. Was the Valois army still there, surrounding St James? Was Rempston still there, holding out in the town, or even just in the keep?

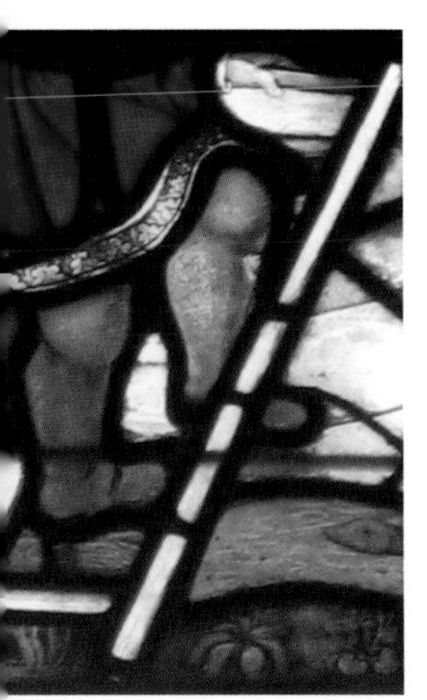

Trinity Church, Vendome

No, and yes, the answer came back. There was no sign of the Valois, but it was Lancastrian banners that flew from the towers.

How? Why? When the men got to St James, filed unopposed through the gates, and saw to their amazement that there were large cannon set on the walls, cannon they had not seen when they were last at St James, they learned it all. These were, said Rempston, Valois cannon, and the Valois had used them against the defences. Suffolk's men had held off the initial attack, but they had realized they would be foxes in a hole if they did not find a way to fool the French into believing they were about to be relieved. So Rempston had left just a handful of men on the walls, and led the rest out through a side gate during the night. They crept round the French in the dark, and before dawn they attacked in the rear. They blew every horn and trumpet they could find, banged swords on their steel-clad knees, yelled their hearts out. The French troops had scrambled out of their tents, panicked and fearing for their lives, and ran. The Lancastrian had run after them, and caught a bunch by the nearby lake. Many had drowned, but they had taken around fifty as prisoners. Just as useful as the ransoms was the rest of their booty: the cannon – fourteen of them – plus barrels of gunpower, jars of wine, and crates of biscuits, dried fruit and dried herrings.

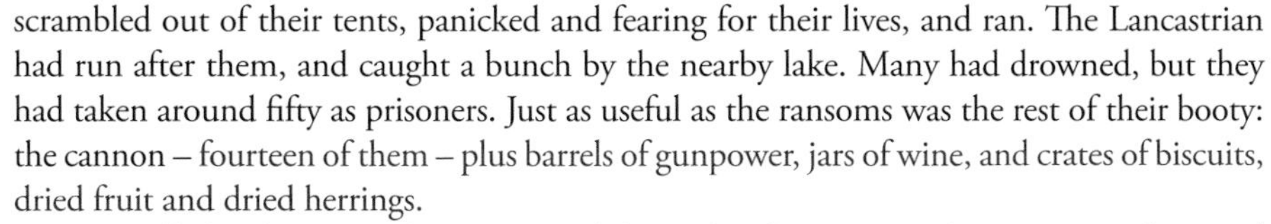

They called it the Rout of St James. It did wonders for Rempston's reputation, destroyed Arthur of Richemont's, and gave them all a fat spring. Suffolk must have wished he had been there himself, though.

John of Bedford sailed for England that year. Suffolk would have known from his heralds and correspondents that while Bedford's administration was working well in France, in Westminster the king's council was still bitterly divided. At the core of the problems was the tussle for power between Humphrey of Gloucester and the bishop of Winchester. The bishop was given a red hat by the pope at this time, and became a cardinal, something that Henry V had always opposed – fearing it would divide his loyalties, and encourage him to support the pope against English interests – but that Bedford and Gloucester could not realistically prevent. Bedford saw off some of Gloucester's and the Cardinal's supporters, promoted his own men, and enforced an uneasy truce, though he could not resolve the underlying issues: Gloucester's rashness, Cardinal Beaufort's greed for wealth and power, the long years before the king would come of age.

In the months while the regent was gone, it was Suffolk who led the negotiations with the Bretons. Duke John was at heart a peaceable man, and had always tried to stand clear of the conflicts that had riven the Valois court. He had no wish to see the cannons captured at St James used against his other strongholds. Suffolk agreed a truce, and paved the way for Bedford to turn it into a peace treaty. The Bretons would not fight for the Valois – or at least, most of them would not; Richemont continued on his own course – although the Lancastrians could not expect them to fight against the Valois either.

Bedford brought other men back from England with him, and a determination to lift the pace of the war, and finish the conquest of northern France. The earl of Warwick, a veteran of the Crusades who had acted as guardian and tutor to little King Henry, was among them, and in the spring of 1427, Suffolk and his brothers rode west to join Warwick in trying to take the town of Montargis. To the south-east of Paris and east of Orleans, it was on the southern fringe of the Lancastrian-held territory, north of the dauphin's court at Bourges.

Montargis was and is a charming town of canals and lakes, sitting on the confluence of several small rivers including the Loing and the Ouanne. It was no rocky impregnable site like Mont St Michel, but the lakes made it difficult to attack, and like the other places north of the Loire that held out for the Valois, it was well defended. Its inhabitants had strengthened the walls, and had plenty of cannon.

The Lancastrians had enough men – about 6,000 – to divide their army into three. Warwick took one division, Suffolk commanded another, and Sir John de la Pole was given the third. They would not storm the place, they agreed: it would have cost them casualties they could not afford. There were enough of them to completely surround the town, and wait while the townsfolk ate down their stores.

This took all summer, and it did not go well. The men holed up in Montargis were veterans of many sieges, there were plenty of them, and they tried ruses as well as sallying out repeatedly to skirmish with the Lancastrians. The Lancastrians caught one man, and persuaded him to show them a way into the town. It was not till they got through a side gate, and found a troop of Valois soldiers moving to block their way out again, that they realized it had been a trap, planned by their opponents from the start.

This was not on the scale of Richemont's disaster at St James, but it was a blow, and the other schemes Suffolk and Sir John hatched did not work either. Warwick was old and cautious, a good man in his way, but no Salisbury. (Salisbury himself was now back in England.) They all needed a victory at Montargis, but this was turning into another bitter siege like Meaux.

The word from the spies was that the dauphin was working to raise an army to lift the siege. He had commanded Richemont to do

Montargis

this, but his men had insisted they would not march to Montargis until they had been paid, and the Valois were finding it as difficult as the Lancastrians generally did to generate the funds. Then there was word that another troop was approaching, headed by not Richemont, but the young bastard of Orleans, half-brother to the duke who was still a captive in England. This was a defended supply train, not a huge army – about 1,600 men at arms, and perhaps three times as many crossbowmen – and with the wagons to defend, it would move slowly.

The Lancastrians had time to plan their moves, to try to capture the supplies. Warwick had his ideas; Sir John had his, so did Suffolk. They had to expect the defenders to devise an ingenious way to get the stores into the town. The supporting troops would not simply drive the wagons straight at them. They were still working through the options, and ways to counter them, over lunch on a hot summer day, when the trumpets blared.

St Mary's Church, North Tuddenham, Norfolk

The bastard had left his carts in the forest, and brought most of his men forward to launch a surprise attack. They were on the Lancastrians while they were still scrambling for their weapons and armour. Then as the first swords clashed, the gates of Montargis were flung open and out rushed the garrison. And not just the gates: the sluices opened too, and the water from the canals came pouring across the water meadows.

It was chaos. Suffolk and the others were calling to their men to group and resist, fight as they knew how to do, but the Valois were laying into them from both sides, the timbers of the bridge across the Loing screamed and it crashed in ruins into the flood, and they were lost almost before it had begun.

They fought, of course; fought hard, in the flooded meadows. They had always had the best of the Valois in hand to hand combat. But they had not expected this; they were not used to the French showing flair and aggression. Suffolk got his men together, and they put up a defence, but they could not get across the Loing, with the waters pouring out of the canals and the bridge in ruins, to help the men trapped on the other side. Sir John was among them. The townsmen were heading out of Montargis now, with their staves and their axes; if they did not run they would be overwhelmed.

Suffolk called to his men to give up the fight. They got to their horses, and pelted down the road to Nemours, till they were clear of the last pursuing Valois, and could pull up and group, ride to a Lancastrian-held place, and send messengers to find out what other men had got free, and measure the scale of the disaster.

And a disaster it was. The siege was in ruins, a summer lost. Men had been downed in the first rush, knocked over by the floodwater, or simply stayed too long before making a run for it. The Valois killed about 1,500 men, more than the Lancastrians had lost at Agincourt or Verneuil. They took another 600 prisoner, including Sir John.

31 The window over Orleans

It was probably the bastard of Orleans who held Sir John. All the English must have been uneasy about dealing with him. This was a man whose half-brothers had been kept captive in England for years on years, heading now into decades. The duke of Orleans had been held since Agincourt – twelve years, by then – and his brother Jean of Angoulême had been taken as a hostage when Thomas of Clarence's campaign ended back in 1413. It was not unacceptable for the English to continue to hold them, if they thought it wise, but it was undoubtedly hard on both men. There was no obligation on the bastard, in these circumstances, to ransom his English prisoners.

But the bastard proved to be fair and not vindictive. A ransom was agreed, and Suffolk had to spend much of that winter raising it. Sir John needed to keep Moyon, since it was home to his wife and daughter, but he must have lost any other lands he held in France, and Suffolk lost some of his own as well. Still, by the next season John was free once more.

He returned to a situation which, from a political perspective, was better than might have been expected. For all the uncertainties that surrounded it, the Breton alliance was holding firm. In the autumn of 1427 Bedford and his duchess travelled to Arras to meet with Philip of Burgundy, and they renewed that alliance as well. Gloucester had settled down in England with Jacqueline of Hainault's former lady in waiting, and the situation in the Low Countries had been resolved. The king's English council had been pacified by Bedford's strong hand, although it and the English Parliament had resisted his pleas for more money for France. They thought the French territories should be meeting their own expenses by now.

But Salisbury in his turn had gone to England, and his efforts at court, plus the expenditure of much of his own money, produced some reinforcements. He came back to France in the spring of 1428 with 2,700 more men. It made up for the losses the summer before.

Could they take the rest of France with these men?? Hardly. But Salisbury argued that they should go on the offensive, and since he had paid out for the men, he got his way. The northern and western borders were reasonably secure now, so they would try to take a string of towns along the Loire valley, to either side of and including Orleans.

Bedford was later to claim he had had reservations about this proposal; Suffolk probably admitted to them all along. They all knew how many men had been needed to win Rouen, and how long it had taken. With a peacetime population of around 30,000, Orleans was not much smaller. They did not have enough men to invest it properly; they would be hard pushed even to find enough men to garrison it once it was taken. Also, it was at the far end of long supply lines, and a siege would create logistical nightmares. There was a chivalric objection too, which could not be taken lightly. It was against the rules to target places that owed allegiance to the duke of Orleans without giving him the opportunity to pay a ransom and get free to defend them in person. This mattered to Suffolk, and the knowledge that the men of Orleans had treated John fairly would have underlined that lesson.

His experiences at Montargis must have weighed heavily on him as well. The bastard of Orleans' action there had been the most impressive they had seen from a Frenchman since Suffolk had first come to France. It would almost certainly be this man who defended Orleans for the Valois.

After the disaster at Montargis, though, Suffolk probably chose to keep a low profile, and not make these points too forcefully. And he must have been glad that Salisbury was back.

Above, replica of Jeanne d'Arc's banner in the church of Ste Catherine de Fierbois
Right, Chateau of Sully, on the Loire near Orleans

They scraped up spare men from the garrisons across northern France, and brought the number of troops up to about 5,000. Some Burgundians joined them: not the duke's whole army, but a useful contingent. It took till midsummer to put this together. Then they headed down to the Loire valley, and set about erasing the memory of Montargis.

From mid-August, when the campaign started, through to mid-October, the Lancastrian army took more than forty towns and fortresses: some by assault, some by surrender. They won towns such as Beaugency and Meung downstream of Orleans, and Jargeau just upstream of it: places that were small by comparison with the city, but even so far from insignificant. They all had strong walls, and donjons that could be garrisoned to give them a secure hinterland. They all provided booty, and helped Sir John de la Pole to repay his debts. Then with all this achieved, they invested Orleans.

The city sprawled across the northern bank of the great wide river, with its shallows and islands. It was very well fortified: its walls in places were thirty feet high. And it was well defended too. There were more men at arms inside the city than outside attacking it. There were seventy-one guns on the walls, and some of the stone shot they fired weighed nearly 200 pounds, and could travel close on a mile. If the bastard of Orleans had brought out the men of the city and pushed it to a battle, it could have gone roughly with the Lancastrians. Perhaps he argued for it, but there were plenty of other Valois who had learned to be nervous of battles with the English, and the Orleanais stayed within their walls.

The French had left nothing standing on the south bank, not even the churches; the city's suburbs were a wasteland. The Lancastrians dug in amid the ruins. They did not have enough men to surround the city, but there were targets they could attack from these positions, the major one being the bridge across the Loire. It was solid stone, 300 years old, with nineteen arches. At the southern end was a drawbridge. There was a fort that guarded the drawbridge,

called les Tourelles, and there were banks and ditches to the south of the river. The gunners trained their cannon on the fort, and the engineers began to tunnel, trying to weaken its foundations. The Valois at first resisted strongly, then they evidently decided this outpost was not defensible, and withdrew across the bridge. They broke down a couple of the arches after them, leaving the little fort isolated above the river, and in English hands.

It was a fine start to an impossible task. The Lancastrians must all have been jubilant. Perhaps they had had reverses the summer before, but Salisbury was the kind of man to make them all believe in miracles. And had they not defeated French forces again and again? Didn't actions like Agincourt, Verneuil, even Rempston's amazing escape at St James de Beuvron, prove that God was on their side? With a righteous cause, they would eventually succeed in taking France for the king. They must have told themselves so; they must even, at that moment, have believed it.

Let's go and take a good look, Salisbury said to his captains. We'll get a better sense of Orleans from the top of the Tourelles. He took a group of them – most likely Suffolk, Sir John, and a handful more – and strode out towards the newly won fort. They climbed the winding stairs, and in the upper room, Salisbury headed for the window that looked out over the city. The window must have been larger on that side than the one opposite, since the Tourelles had been built for Orleans' defenders and not its besiegers. Leaning forward, Salisbury could indeed see down the length of the bridge, over the walls, to the roofs and towers of the city.

We can train the cannon –

A thud, a crack. They all jumped back, as the iron bar that formed the lintel sprang out of the wall, knocked out of place by the force of the cannonball that had slammed into it. There was a moment, perhaps, before they took it in. Then they saw Salisbury, hands to a face that was not his face any more, but a battered mask of blood. The bar had whacked straight into him.

They must have known straightaway he could not survive the wound. Somehow they got him down the stairs, back beyond the banks and ditches, and onto a wagon. They detailed an escort, and told the men to drive off. Salisbury had to be taken to safety; but it was more than that, perhaps. He was taken to Meung, ten miles off, not least so that his army would not witness his slow, painful death.

At some time in the next few days, Suffolk probably rode there himself, and said his goodbyes. Salisbury did what King Henry had done; he ordered them to keep at the war to the end. They promised him that.

It took eight agonizing days before the earl of Salisbury died from the effects of his wounds.

The command of the army went to Suffolk as soon as Salisbury was injured; it was confirmed by Bedford when he got the message about Salisbury's death. It must have been a bitter appointment. No man takes pleasure in stepping into a dead friend's boots, and it is worse when he cannot share his dead friend's conviction that the assignment is both right and achievable. Suffolk clearly thought it was neither.

He would have conferred with his captains, including his brothers. John needed a successful and profitable action even more than Suffolk did. Alexander, their younger brother, had not yet made a name for himself, and must have been anxious to do so. But these men knew as well as Suffolk himself that there was no chance of an easy win in their current situation. They would be blamed if they raised the siege, and they would be blamed equally if they pursued it through the winter, and still failed to take Orleans.

Suffolk sent to tell Bedford what the regent already knew, that the 5,000 men he had were not sufficient to surround and starve out the city. Although he perhaps did not tell Bedford this, he must have been painfully aware that men had been deserting from the start of the campaign, and with Salisbury's death many more had melted into the dark autumn nights. These were men who perhaps also told themselves they had no business besieging Orleans when its duke was a prisoner; they were men who had been at Rouen and Meung and could not face another winter siege; they were men who, as always, despaired of getting their long-overdue pay. Some would become bandits, some by now had wives and children elsewhere in France, some would head for Calais or Harfleur and beg a shipman to take them back to England.

Suffolk asked for reinforcements, although he knew he would not get them. There were no more men that Bedford could have sent. He strengthened the fortifications on the south bank that were now held by the Lancastrians, and set a troop to defend them. Then he pulled back the rest of his army into winter quarters in the neighbouring towns. It was a holding operation, but it spoke more of withdrawal than of pressing onwards.

With these arrangements complete, he most likely went to Paris, to share his thoughts in person. He was not now the boy who had listened while greater men talked; and Bedford, though regent, was not the king. He had to be treated with deference, but he could be spoken to. Suffolk would have pressed the case he had made the summer before: that they should pull their men back to Normandy, secure the territory they already held, try to repair some of the damage, get fields reploughed and herds rebuilt, work on making the conquered territories liveable once more. He would have heard when in the city, if he had not heard previously, that Bedford was having problems with the Burgundians. Their duke

Church of St Peter and St Paul, East Harling, Norfolk
Photo Mike Dixon

as always offered too little and wanted too much in return. It seemed not unlikely that those Burgundians who had come to Orleans would be pulled out of the action. Suffolk must have worked to find a tactful way to remind Bedford of this, to hint at the problems that continuing the siege would present.

Perhaps Bedford listened, but he did not agree. He probably repeated to Suffolk the oaths they had all made on Henry V's deathbed. Of course it was difficult, but they must find a way to secure all of France for his son. Orleans had to be taken. In the wake of this, he detailed two other commanders, Lord Talbot and Lord Scales, to join Suffolk in what became a three-way captaincy of the siege. If it was a humiliation, well, Suffolk had all but asked for it. And given these orders, he did what he could not avoid doing: he went back to Orleans, and through the rest of that winter of 1428 and into the spring of 1429, he worked with Scales and Talbot, to do what they could to put the city under pressure.

It was a cold and grim winter, because they had no realistic hope of taking the city quickly. Perhaps by now Suffolk had met Malyne de Cay, the woman who was later with him at Jargeau, and he had some respite in the hours he spent with her.

The Lancastrians set up a camp round the church of St Laurent, to the west of the city on the north bank, and began to set a line of fortifications circling round to the north. They established another base at St Loup, to the east of the city, and also began to fortify outwards from this. Then orders came to the Burgundian contingent to quit the siege. Bedford's negotiations had broken down.

By the spring of 1429 they still had not managed to cut off Orleans from its supply routes, and had no realistic prospect of doing so. They had not run chains across the river to halt the shipping, as they had done at Rouen a decade earlier. Perhaps they should have done, if only to forestall the criticism they got later from men who claimed they had forgotten. All of them, forgotten? They would probably have answered that the broad, shallow Loire was not the Seine with its deep channel and steep banks. The expanse of water was too wide, the islands made it too inconvenient, the boats that plied the Loire were shallow-bottomed barges, not royal galleys, and if they had encountered obstacles, they could have been hauled onto the banks and dragged past them. Anyway, if men had failed to bring in supplies by boat, they could readily have brought them in by land, through the gaping holes in the Lancastrian lines.

Storming the city was not an option: they were far too weak to consider it. They could neither starve Orleans into submission, nor pound it into submission, and none of them had any ideas for how they might dupe it into submission. All they could do was carry out the familiar actions of a siege, without any concept of how they could bring it to a conclusion.

The Frenchmen in Orleans stayed put and watched them do it.

But while Suffolk and his comrades were sending messages to Bedford, and through Bedford to England, the bastard of Orleans

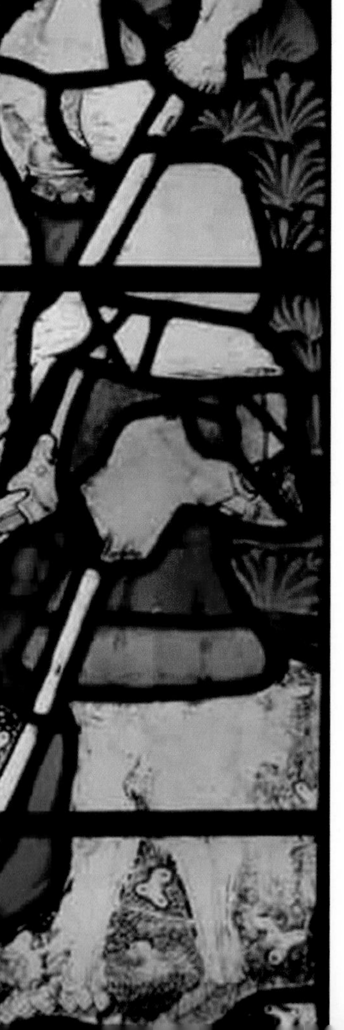

St Peter Mancroft Church, Norwich
Photo Mike Dixon

and the other Valois commanders were sending messages to the dauphin. They made it clear that they could not live indefinitely with the humiliation of an English army pinning them in the city. Charles of Valois had to act.

In the spring, he did so. He mustered a relieving army in Blois, forty miles downstream – mostly Frenchmen under the count of Clermont, with a few Scots and other mercenaries – and sent it towards the city. It paused en route to engage with the armed escort of an English supply train, which was bringing herrings, beans and other commodities down to the Loire. The Lancastrians fought back – they had no choice, since they could not afford to abandon all the supplies – and although they were outnumbered, through a mixture of disastrous Scots tactics, English resolve and sheer good fortune, they routed the French. Small miracles, at least, could still happen for the Lancastrians.

'JHESUS MARIA
King of England and you, duke of Bedford, who call yourself regent of the kingdom of France; you, William de la Pole, earl of Suffolk; John, Lord Talbot, and you, Thomas, Lord Scales, who call yourselves lieutenants of the said duke of Bedford, acknowledge the summons of the King of Heaven, and render up to the Maid who is here sent by God, the King of Heaven, the keys of all the good towns you have taken and violated in France. She is come here by God's will to reclaim the blood royal. She is very ready to make peace, if you will acknowledge her to be right by leaving France and paying for what you have held. And you, archers, companions of war, men-at-arms and others who are before the town of Orleans, go away into your own country, by God; and if you do not do so, expect news of the Maid who will come to see you shortly, to your very great injury.'

It was on the Tuesday of Holy Week, 1429 – 22 March – that this message (in French, of course), was brought by the Valois heralds to Suffolk and the other Lancastrian commanders. They had probably already heard from their spies about the girl, Jeanne d'Arc, in whose name it had been written. They knew the dauphin had agreed not just to receive this crazed child, but to muster another army under the duke of Alençon (who had been taken captive at Verneuil, and was newly released by the English), and let her ride with it to Orleans. The dauphin had given her armour, which she wore as if she was a man at arms. He had given her a personal standard, white canvas fringed with silk, showing a field of lilies (the fleurs du lis, the royal flower of France), on which was painted a picture of Christ in Majesty flanked by two angels, with the words 'Jhesus Maria' at the side. She carried a sword she claimed to have retrieved from under the altar of the convent of St Catherine de Fierbois, which had once been owned by a crusader, and was decorated with five holy crosses.

Theirs was an age in which men believed not just in the power of God, but in the power of the devil too. They did not doubt which side this 'visionary' was on. God's justice, to them, lay with King Henry V, who had made his rightful claim to inherit the throne of France, and with his son, King Henry VI, whom they regarded now as its king. The dauphin was a feeble bastard, disinherited by his own mother; a girl who claimed him as her inspiration could not be other than a fraud. Of course they took seriously the news that another relieving army was on its way, but they could hardly have taken seriously the news that its inspiration was a young girl.

Abbey of l'Epau, Le Mans

It was the Lancastrians, after all, who had had the great victories. And the last of them just a few weeks earlier: men were now describing the tussle between the Valois army and the Lancastrian supply train as the Battle of the Herrings, and they laughed at the thought of the Valois troops slithering around on a field of spilled fish and beans. Leave France and pay for what you have held! When they still held it! Not likely!

But under the laughter they were not far from despair. It was five months now since they had invested Orleans, almost as long since Salisbury's death. They were no nearer to taking the city. Desertions had continued throughout the winter, and Bedford had not managed to persuade the Burgundian troops to return. Perhaps it was the Valois who were losing the war, but the Lancastrians were wading in mud rather than winning it.

And if they wanted to be pessimistic, Suffolk and his brothers perhaps even thought that the combination of Alençon – joining a French army where few dukes, and no kings or princes, had fought for many years – and the bastard of Orleans, leavened with a bit of visionary hokum, might well cause the Valois to lose it more slowly.

It shocked them, even so, how fast the situation changed. This Valois army brought supplies into the city. Orleans had been provisioned right through the siege, but this was not just a few men with sacks on their backs, it was a supply train. And it was an army too: tripping in with style, under their noses, with the kind of touch they had seen from the bastard at Montargis, but not seen much of in the long months since. They set scouts to catch it, sent men to try to intercept it, and the French sneaked around them. Then this Valois army ventured out, and attacked the Fort St Loup. There was only a small force of Lancastrians to hold it, and it took some time to bring more of the troops around the city to support them: by the time they got there, the garrison were out on their ears and the Valois standards were flying from the ramparts.

Jeanne had so many priests with her, the heralds said, that the soldiers' knees were rubbed bare from kneeling at mass. She had banished the camp followers, and she fined men who swore. But the Valois were putting up with it. No, more than that: they were fired by it, enthused by it, persuaded by this girl that they had both the right cause, and the strength to uphold it.

Next the Valois targeted the Tourelles and the earthworks that guarded the end of the bridge. Alençon's army came round and attacked from the south, the Orleans defenders from the north. The Tourelles garrison resisted hard, but they were hopelessly outnumbered. The Tourelles was lost in a matter of hours, and its captain, Sir William Glasdale – a long-standing lieutenant of Suffolk's – was drowned in the river.

Evreux Cathedral

The bulk of the English army were still crouched in their ditches. These enemy forces had wrapped up their attacks before they had had a chance to get out and intercept them.

Suffolk, Talbot and Scales met up, and debated how they should respond. They all agreed: if the Valois wished to fight, they should have their fight. But it should not be done in swift raids like this; they would offer a pitched battle. God stood on the English shoulders in battle, and they would damned well show the French so.

So they ordered the men to prepare for battle. On 8 May 1428 – just five days after Jeanne, Alençon and the Valois army had reached Orleans – they filed out into the no man's land between the English defences and the walls of Orleans. They set up their lines, and sent off the heralds, to challenge the Valois to do battle with them.

They waited for some time. Then the gates of Orleans swung open, and the Valois troops came out. They too formed up in battle array. With the townsmen, there were many more of them than of the Lancastrians. But it had been so at Verneuil, at Agincourt, at Cravant as well; the English who had fought these battles were not deterred.

The girl Jeanne was with the Valois army, and when they were placed in their lines, she came forward with a group of priests. They led the men in hymns and prayers. Some of this was normal before men risked their lives. The Lancastrians always prayed too, although they made less fuss about it, and they had never been led by a girl. They turned to their own chaplains, and doubtless raised their voices higher.

Church of St Mary the Virgin, Saxlingham Nethergate, Norfolk
Photo Mike Dixon

The Lancastrian chaplains finished their blessings, and pulled back. But the Valois priests did not. A portable altar was brought onto the field. They said a mass. That was more than was normal, more than was needed or right in these circumstances. Then they said another mass. The Lancastrians watched this, exasperated by now. The day was wearing on; it was time they began to fight. But they could not have attacked while the French priests were droning on in the dead space between the two armies; they waited, shuffling and stamping their feet, till the second mass was done.

The priests packed their altars away. And as they did so – still before the Lancastrians could decently attack – the first Valois troops turned and began to file back into the city.

Were the bastard and Alençon too scared to attack? Or were they wise in deciding not to? The Lancastrians must have argued about that, in the days that followed.

Still, it was clear there would be no battle now, and they had not the stomach to repeat the whole charade the next day. Suffolk, Scales and Talbot gave the orders. Raise the siege; get in columns; march away.

32 A prisoner in France and two prisoners in England

Suffolk took his men to Jargeau; and to defeat at the hands of the Valois army.

Then he came back to Orleans, but not as a conqueror. He came as a captive, in the dark, in one of the flat-bottomed barges that plied the broad, shallow river. Past the burned-out buildings of the suburbs the men of Orleans had fired a year earlier; past the banks and ditches that the Lancastrians had created to protect the besiegers, past the debris from the camp they had deserted, up to the battered bridge with the ruins of the Tourelles and the arches that had been broken down so the river could not be crossed. Into the city, and to a stronghold, where he and the other prisoners were kept under guard until the Valois decided what to do with them.

Perhaps fifty of the English who had been in Jargeau had survived out of the 1,500 or so Suffolk had brought from Orleans, and the small garrison that had remained there throughout the siege of the city. He must have been close to many of the men who had died there: not just his brothers, although that was more than loss enough, but men he had fought with for all of the thirteen years he had now been in France, and some he had known before that in England as well. He had been responsible for every last man.

He might have wondered briefly if it was to the girl that he would be given as a prisoner, but some things, at least, in this strange Valois army followed the conventional pattern. The commanders shared the prisoners out, with Jeanne d'Arc getting none of them, and Suffolk was allotted to the bastard of Orleans.

To be a prisoner could be a grim affair in 1429. But although it is never pleasant to be deprived of one's liberty, and it could not have been pleasant either to contemplate the huge sum he would have to raise in order to regain it – many times more than had been demanded for Sir John, since ransoms rose steeply with the rank of the prisoner – Suffolk would have known he could expect a degree of comfort once his captivity settled into its pattern. It was never likely they would kill him, once the town was safely theirs; he was too valuable for that. It was not likely either that he would be thrown into an oubliette in chains. The rules of chivalry – though not always followed – dictated that a nobleman as prisoner should still be treated as a nobleman. He would be presented wi th a bill for the luxuries he enjoyed, but still he might enjoy some luxuries. He would sleep in a comfortable bed; he would have men to attend to him, as he was used to have – although these would be Frenchmen and not his own servants. But life would not be as he was used to it being. Ever since he had come to France, he had been in charge of other men, and he had always been busy. Even in the longest, slowest siege there was much for a captain to do. In the weeks and months that followed, there was little or nothing demanded of him.

The bastard's men saw him to his prison – a stronghold on or near the Loire, we do not know where – then departed to continue with the campaign. It might be ended for Suffolk, but Talbot, Scales and other captains still fought on for the Lancastrians. The girl Jeanne was determined to win enough territory to get the dauphin to Reims and have him crowned there, and the Valois captains were helping her – or she was helping them. So there was no

Church of St Mary Magdalene, Gedney, Lincolnshire

prospect of a quick end to this imprisonment. He would have to wait for weeks even to speak with the bastard and to agree terms, and then he would have to spent months, he knew, raising his ransom before he could hope to be freed.

This was assuming, of course, that his captor would be willing to come to terms, as he had done for Sir John. That could not be taken for granted, since it was not only the Lancastrians who sometimes held onto their captives for years. The earl of Somerset had been taken at Baugé nine years previously, and was still not free.

He must have paced the stone walls within which he was confined, till he knew every last crack, every last spider's web, every last way the light slanted in from the narrow window. He must have thought much – about John and Alexander, Sir William Glasdale drowning in the Loire, Salisbury's last agonies with his face torn away, and other losses, other things witnessed and felt, of which we know nothing. He must have thought about his own situation, all he had done in the last thirteen years, and what he might do in the future. There were probably moments, or more, when he wished he had died on the battlements of Jargeau. He must have prayed. A priest – a Valois priest – would have been provided if he had asked for it, and held a mass for him; and perhaps he prayed alone as well.

And he wrote poems.

It was not what all men did in prison, but it was not unknown. There were men who had become famed for writing poetry in these circumstances. The chief among them was the duke of Orleans.

Suffolk knew this. The captive duke's poems were fine works. The minstrels sang them, in France and in England – though mostly in France. Men learned them by heart and recited them. Gilles Binchois and his other musicians, Bedford's musicians and entertainers, the duke of Burgundy's – all these passed round the words of the duke of Orleans.

So he was echoing what that other prisoner had done – the prisoner whose half-brother he was now waiting for. Orleans had had a very long time in which to write poetry. Each plea by the French to release him had been refused. He would not be set free till all France

Chateau of Sillé le Guillaume, France

Chateau of Saumur, France

was held for the Lancastrians; that was what Suffolk and his fellow lords and captains had sworn to Henry V on his deathbed.

He must have thought these things, as he asked for pen, ink and paper and began to fill in his days with verse.

He wrote in English, and in French as well. He wrote with care, and competence. Paper was valuable, especially for a prisoner, so he will have composed these works in his head, sounded them over many times before he set the words down. They were not private works: his jailers knew he was writing them, and he let them be copied and passed around, among both the Valois and the Lancastrians.

Charles of Orleans' best poems are works of genius. Suffolk's are not. All writers hope that what they set on the page will echo in other men's souls, and sometimes Suffolk came close to that, but by no means always. He kept to it, though, in those long weeks while the summer flared and faded.

He did not write about politics; that would not have been wise while he was a prisoner. He wrote, conventionally, mostly of love. But plenty of misery comes across too in the poems which his men copied and handed around, noting that they were 'made by my lord of Suffolk whilst he was prisoner in France'. This is one of them, written in English:

Compleynt

Walkyng allon, of wit full desolat
In my spyrytes turmentyd to and fro,
And wyth mysel fallying at gret debat
That I had power to wythstand my wo,
Knowying fully how fortune was my fo,
And I must nede of verrey force endure
The vttirmest of all myn aventure;

And then anon I gan remembre me
How that I had bene hyndred here byfore,
With-outyn cause, by gret aduersyte –
My troubly thoughts encresying more and more,
My wofull hert constreyned me so sore
That I ne couthe, as by the way of kynde,
Myn heuyness avoyde out of my mynde.

And when I saw ther was non other way
But always styll my fortune to abyde,
The lod of loue anon then gan I pray,
That he vochesafe to be apon my syde.
Wher-euer I went, he for to be my gyde;
And of that thought I sodeny abrayde,
Wyth humble hert, to hym ryght thus I sayde:–

'O god of love, whos noble excellence
May not be told by possybilyte,
Let thys compleynt come to thyn audience,
And se that I sumwhat rewarded be
For my seruyse, though I vnworthy be,
And syth I ment but trouth, as in thys case,
Haue routh on me, and take me to thy grace.'

Much depended, of course, on the character of Suffolk's captor. Suffolk had probably known a little about the bastard of Orleans before he became the man's prisoner, and in these weeks he would have tried to learn anything else that might be useful. He would have got nothing but conventional praise from the Valois who tended him, but at some point his herald would have been allowed access to him, and would have told him more, or been ordered to go away and find out more to tell.

Jean, the bastard, was six years Suffolk's junior; he was then twenty-seven. The illegitimate son of the duke of Orleans who had been murdered by the Burgundians in 1407, he had been brought up in his father's household, together with the duke's two legitimate sons. To call him the bastard was not an insult: it was an acknowledgement that he was of noble birth, and a first cousin to the king. He had escaped the worst of the Valois genes, though, and seems to have been a sturdy, intelligent, competent man.

He could not have seen Jean of Angoulême, his younger half-brother, since 1413, when he himself was ten years old, and the boy (as he was then) had become a hostage following the English expedition that had been led by Clarence and Suffolk's own father. He had not seen the duke since Agincourt. But he would have corresponded with them both – although perhaps not frequently – and in their absence, once grown, he had taken control of the duchy of Orleans. It was not a role he would automatically have assumed, but clearly men judged him capable of filling it. So he had had a larger role in their absence than he would have done if his brothers were in France, but men did not take him to be the kind of man to wish as a result that they might remain in England.

He was one of a new generation of Valois commanders, grown up to replace those killed at Agincourt, in the other battles with the English, and not least, in the civil wars of the French themselves. The dauphin did not lead his armies, so it was men like the bastard and the duke of Alençon who led them for him. They were doing better than their predecessors, at least in these months when they had the girl to bring fire to their men. The Valois won back the bastard's own estate of Beaugency a week after Jargeau was taken, and although Alençon let the English troops surrender and march away, Talbot and Scales lost to a battle to the Valois forces at the nearby village of Patay a couple of days later.

A battle lost to the Valois. This must have troubled Suffolk greatly when he heard it.

He probably got some at least of this news, as he waited and prayed and wrote poems that summer. It was tremendous news from his jailers' viewpoint. A month after Suffolk was captured, Jeanne d'Arc got her dauphin to Reims, with the Lancastrians and Burgundians barely troubling to hinder him, and he was crowned with proper ceremony as Charles VII of France.

For an English lord in captivity, it was disaster after disaster.

33 A winter fruit

Je fu en fleur ou temps passé d'enfance,
Et puis après devins fruit en jeunesse;
Lors m'abaty de l'arbre de Plaisance,
Vert et non meur, Folie, ma maitresse.
Et pour cela, Raison qui tout redresse
A son plaisir, sans tort ou mesprison,
M'a a bon droit, par sa tresgrant sagesse,
Mis pour meurir ou feurre de prison.

En ce j'ay fait longue continuance,
Sans estre mis a l'essor de Largesse;
J'en suy contant et tiens que, sans doubtance,
C'est pour le mieulx, combien que par
peresse
Deviens fletry et tire vers vieillesse.
Assez estaint est on moy le tison
De sot desir, puis qu'ay esté en presse
Mis pour meurir ou feurre de prison.

Dieu nous doint paix, car c'est ma desirance!
Adonc seray en l'eaue de Liesse
Tost refraschi, et au souleil de France
Boin nettié du moisy de Tristesse;
J'attens Bon Temps, endurant en humblesse.
Car j'ay l'espoir que Dieu ma guerison
Ordonnera; pour ce, m'a sa haultesse
Mis pour meurir ou feurre de prison.

Fruit suis d'yver que a meins de tendresse
Que fruit d'esté; si suis en garnison,
Pour amolir ma trop verde duresse,
Mis pour meurir ou feurre de prison.

Charles of Orleans

A very loose translation:

I flowered in the days of childhood past
And in my youth thereafter came to fruit.
I clambered up the tree of pleasure fast:
To juicy folly did I then pay suit.
And for that, Reason, who redresses all,
At his own pace, with no mistaking why,
Had me to rights, and sagely made me fall,
Thrown into jail, and there as like to die.

Inside I've lingered many long hard years,
With no chance of a break for freedom
made,
I'm glad enough, and know for all my fears,
All's for the best. And langour's now put paid
To greater hopes than tarnishing and rust.
The candle's flame has flickered, and I sigh
To think that there's little chance of healthy
lust,
Thrown into jail, and there as like to die.

God give us peace, that's what my hopes
advance,
That I'll achieve a place of greater gladness,
Refreshed and happy in the sun of France
Though sprinkled still with the cold dew of
sadness.
I'm waiting for good times, enduring humbly
Because I hope God cures me by and by.
He ordered this, as all things, think I
numbly,
Thrown into jail, and there as like to die.

A winter fruit is never quite as tender
As summer fruit. In cooking you must try
To temper its green hardness. That's my end
there:
Thrown into jail, and there as like to die.

34 Malyne de Cay

At some point during his captivity, Suffolk was brought word of the woman he had left in Jargeau. She had found she was pregnant in the grey aftermath of the attack.

Malyne de Cay – to judge from her name she was probably French, although she might have come from farther south – had been a nun. The story of how she had come to be with Suffolk is long lost. It was said later that she conceived from their lying together the night before Jargeau fell to the Valois.

It is difficult to imagine Suffolk, with the cannon firing, sending to a convent and having a nun brought across to him, even if nuns had remained in Jargeau after the Lancastrian army arrived. This was not the hot aftermath of the battle, it was the cold night before. If he felt the need of a woman, there were easier ways to find one. And this was one who did not just know his name – every woman in Jargeau would have recognized him – but knew which men to use to carry her message, and persuaded them to do so. They in turn persuaded the bastard's men to pass it to Suffolk.

So it seems more likely that he had known Malyne for some time, and that it was a relationship she had chosen, or at least acquiesced in. Not all nuns embraced their profession with ardour, it was as often a fate decided for them by others. And many women throughout Lancastrian France would have been eager to accept the protection of a powerful lord.

It is a sin, even so, to sleep with a nun. Suffolk was a God-fearing man; he must have loved her to have done it. He would have thought of his sinfulness in these days when God seemed to have forsaken not just him, but all the English. Other men thought of it too.

This was perhaps a reason that he did not continue the relationship with Malyne (if indeed he did not; little is clear). Also, he had probably already decided that his future would lie in England, and while he might have lived with her in France, he could not have done so in Suffolk. But perhaps the largest reason was that he now needed to marry, and could not marry a woman who had taken vows. He needed it both to get an heir, now that John and Alexander were both dead, leaving only one daughter between them, and to repair his fortunes. It was not just desirable, it was necessary for him to find a rich wife.

First, though, he did what he could for Malyne. She had perhaps already made her way to the safety and privacy of Hambye; if not, he would have detailed men to escort her there. She was cared for through her confinement, and gave birth safely to a daughter. They called her Joan. It seems a strange choice, the name of the Frenchwoman who had seen Suffolk taken prisoner, but it was also the name of his enterprising sister, the one who had seen to the mending of his armour. It would probably have been his choice, not Malyne's.

Either then, or later, Suffolk sent the child to England, and had her brought up there – quietly, but as his acknowledged daughter. It was what he had done for Jacqueline of Hainault, and just as it had seemed best to her, it probably seemed to Malyne the best thing to do – for the child, at least.

What became of Malyne after that is not known.

St Edmund's Church, Emneth, Norfolk
Photo Mike Dixon

Church of St Mary the Virgin, Yaxley, Suffolk
Photo Mike Dixon

35 The prebend of Brownswood

At last the campaigning season ended, and the bastard returned home. In time – he had no reason to hurry – he came to meet with his prisoner. Over the next weeks and months the two men must have met many times. There was much to negotiate, and over the course of their discussions they began also to forge a friendship which was to last for almost all the rest of their lives.

The size of the ransom was of course a large part of the negotiations, but there was more. There was the bastard's wish to see his brothers freed from captivity in England. The bastard could have asked Suffolk to swear that he would not fight again for the Lancastrians, for an agreed period, or even for the remainder of his life. And there was the possibility that Suffolk would need to go to England or Normandy in person to raise the sums agreed, leaving a hostage in his place.

Suffolk had probably realized in advance that the issue of Jean of Angoulême and the duke of Orleans would be raised. If the Lancastrians and the Valois had arranged a swap of prisoners, it would have eased the burden on him: perhaps he would have had to pay, but at his leisure, to the English treasury, instead of immediately to the bastard. And the plight of a prisoner resonates when you are a prisoner yourself; he must have had sympathy for the poet whose works he had been reading, and his brother who did not write poems, but had suffered an even harsher fate, since he had not been captured in battle, but given as a hostage, and had spent his entire adult life as a prisoner.

If he had not already sent to Bedford and made these points, when the bastard asked for just this he proceeded to do so. The message came back from the regent: that cannot be done. Bedford stuck, would always stick, to what he had sworn to his brother. The duke of Alençon had been freed because this had not been part of the oath – he had been captured after Henry V's death – and the Lancastrians were eager to get his ransom. But for Orleans and Bourbon, the other duke held captive since Agincourt, there was no prospect of liberty. The king's council in England judged it useful to retain Jean of Angoulême as well, so the answer was no to this request too.

Both men must have bitterly regretted this answer. The bastard probably appreciated that Suffolk had done his best. He seems to have asked instead that Suffolk do what he could for his half-brothers in England. And it seems that Suffolk promised to do so.

They agreed the ransom at 20,000 livres, a massive sum. Suffolk would have to sell lands to raise it, in England as well as in France. There was no one he could realistically instruct to do this for him, so the bastard agreed to accept a hostage in his place.

It had to be a blood relative, so there was no risk at all that he might break the deal and abandon the man. Only a man (not a woman) was feasible in these times of war. Suffolk had no sons, and only one surviving brother, so it had to be Thomas, the priest. Thomas was then – as he had been for years – the prebend of Brownswood, serving at St Paul's Cathedral in London. Suffolk had perhaps had little to do with this man whose life had been so different from his own, or John's or Alexander's. But he sent his herald to London, and waited to hear. Eventually the message came back: Thomas was negotiating leave from his post, and would do his duty.

It would have taken weeks to arrange this, weeks more for Thomas to travel. It was winter by then, and Thomas was no man at arms, used to riding fast over rough territory. Suffolk probably talked often with the Bastard as they waited for his arrival. He might also have got news once or twice from his herald; apart from servants and priests, he most likely saw no one else.

And however much they warmed to each other, he and the bastard would both have been wary. One does not talk too freely with an enemy commander. Even in private the bastard would have professed himself loyal to the newly crowned Charles VII, and Suffolk made it clear he was equally loyal to King Henry. Below the conventional surface, they might have tried to probe how deep this loyalty ran. The answer was, deep enough. All the Valois knew that Charles was not the great king Jeanne d'Arc had imagined; perhaps she had even realized that herself by now. But he was their king, and they could not envisage an alternative – certainly not the boy-son of Henry V. Similarly, Suffolk, an Englishman, could never have resigned himself to leaving France to the man he saw as a disinherited bastard and a cold-blooded murderer. True, he had never met the young King Henry VI, but he had sworn to his father to uphold his claim, and that weighed heavily with him.

But the war had to be brought to an end. And the bastard had a right – indeed, all but a duty – to ask him if he intended to fight again. The answer he gave here was necessarily a diplomatic one, but he probably tried to make it honest as well. So he most likely said that he was weary of war, as many men would be after fourteen long years of it. He had lost too much already, and had no wish to lose more. He hoped to work to bring about peace, but had no idea as yet how that might be done. Meanwhile, if he was free to fight, and ordered by the king or his regent to rejoin his troops, then he would do so.

The bastard did not ask him to swear not to. He had realized, of course, that Suffolk would be an important contact for him in the Lancastrian court, just as he in his turn would be an important contact for Suffolk. Perhaps he judged that Suffolk would be more useful if he was allowed to redeem the disaster at Jargeau, at least as far as that could be done. It would sit better with his comrades if he restored his reputation; it would be important to him personally as well.

Church of Notre Dame, Béhuard, France

So Thomas arrived, and the surviving de la Pole brothers met, under the eyes of the bastard who had not seen his own brothers for so many years. If it was a joyful reunion, it was probably also a difficult one. They would have to talk about John and Alexander. Suffolk would have to go over the events at Jargeau. And however he told them, to himself, to Thomas, to other men in years to come, he was left with the ineradicable guilt of the survivor.

They were neither of them old, but they must both have aged and changed in the thirteen years since Suffolk had left England. Suffolk was scarred, from battles and from the beam at Breteuil. Thomas was perhaps in indifferent health, and had found the journey hard.

Perhaps Thomas had hoped to bury John and Alexander, but Suffolk would have put him right on this. Their corpses would have been looted after the battle, their armour and weapons stolen, their surcoats burned, and the naked remains tossed into a mass grave. But masses could still be said for their souls, and their brother the priest would have ensured it was done.

News from England came with Thomas, and news from Lancastrian France as well, since he must have travelled through these territories. The Valois campaign had run into the sand: not just the usual lull of winter, but a dulling of the sharp edge that Jeanne had brought to it. They had tried to take Paris, but been held off by the Lancastrians. The girl had been injured, a crossbow bolt in the thigh, and it had not been lost on the defenders that the Valois captains had left her to lie in the ditch overnight, and not risked themselves to rescue her. For a while she had been a comet, streaking across their sky, but perhaps now she was fading. The commanders wanted the glory for themselves, and were less and less keen to attribute it to Jeanne. They disagreed with the tactics she argued for. As for the men, they were sick of doing without their camp followers, and being harangued each time they swore.

There was scope for Bedford's men to regroup and fight back. And there was a strong reason to do so, because the king's council were talking of sending the young king to France. If his rival for the throne had been crowned, then he too must have a coronation. Lord Morley was talking of coming with him.

They must have discussed the rest of their family too. Some of what Thomas

Chateau of Montsoreau, France

said was already known to Suffolk, some of it fresh. Elizabeth was remarried, to Sir Thomas Kerdeston: not a grand marriage, but a thoroughly respectable one. Katherine was a power now at Barking Abbey; if she became abbess, she would be one of the most powerful religious women in England. The Morleys had a son and two daughters, all thriving. Suffolk had seen none of these relatives for years, but he would be back in England soon, and these were things he needed to know.

Church of St Peter Mancroft, Norwich
Photo Mike Dixon

Then he left Thomas to sit in a castle on the Loire, and rode north to set about the necessary business. He had to visit Marie de Sicile, tell her how John had died, and reassure her that he would care for her and her daughter – which he did, diligently, all his life. He sold Bricquebec, sold Hambye, perhaps told Marie that he would be little if at all in the Cotentin in future, and persuaded her to sell Moyon. Then or later, her daughter came to England, and if she was still alive (nothing of her is known), Marie probably came too.

He cut down his household in France. Gilles Binchois left his service and went to work for the duke of Burgundy; others left too. Then he went to England, and started to put the arrangements in hand to sell what lands he could there. The core estates were entailed: he could not have sold Wingfield, or Court Hall in Hull. And although his stewards and bailiffs had worked for him in the years when he had been absent, they had probably not worked as hard as they might have done had he been there to push them; there was less to sell than he might have hoped. It must have been much in his mind that he would need to find a rich wife, if he was to maintain his position as an earl.

It took him about three years to complete this business and square his account with the bastard.

Thomas never came home again. At some time during the next few months he died in France. So the bastard had lost his hostage, and Suffolk had lost his last brother. But there was no other that could have been a substitute, and the bastard did not ask Suffolk to return to captivity.

36 To the court in Rouen

Suffolk probably moved between England and France several times during 1430 and 1431. After the silence and solitude of his captivity, this must have been a time of bustle, activity, travel, hard negotiations and hard choices. He had to rearrange his long-neglected affairs in England, but he also had ties and obligations in France, ranging from his appointments under Bedford to Malyne de Cay and her child. However disillusioned he was with the war by now, these ties could not be sundered overnight. And when Thomas died, there were arrangements to make for him, and doubtless guilt felt too: his brother had had his own ambitions, own preferences, and it was not to fulfil these that he had journeyed to France.

By the time he got back to Lancastrian-held territory, the plans were well underway to bring the young king to France, so the court he joined was not at Westminster. He perhaps played a part in the final arrangements for the expedition. It was the largest the English had made to France since well before Henry V's death. There would be seven dukes and earls, thirteen other great captains, and twenty lesser ones, leading an army of perhaps 10,000 men to supplement the garrisons already in France. It would not just be an army: there would also be a large household surrounding the king. Cardinal Beaufort was to accompany the king to France, and John of Bedford was determined to work well alongside him, and avoid the rows that had enmired his brother Gloucester in England. Bedford left the court to Beaufort, and focused on the army, and defence of the Lancastrian territory.

For this he needed Suffolk, and every experienced man he could obtain. Extra efforts had to be made, to ensure that the downturn in the Valois campaign was permanent, and to resecure the territory the Lancastrians held. They still had good control over Normandy and some of the territories south of it and north of the Loire, including parts of Maine and Anjou. They had Paris, and a number of towns and strongholds to its north, east and south, although much of this area was now held by the Valois. Burgundy's lands were mostly safe. And the English held Gascony, but there were no plans to take the king to Gascony. What was needed was to take him to Paris, and if at all possible, to Reims – a city in Valois hands – to be crowned where French kings had always been crowned. It would be a major task to bring this about.

The English forces landed at Calais. Suffolk probably went there to meet up with Bedford, who had come to greet the king, and with other men he knew – men like Lord Morley and Lord Cromwell, who had been back in England for much of the time that he had continued in France, and could give him better information about the tides of influence and conflict at court. This must also have been the first time that he met the king himself.

Henry VI was now a boy of nine. He had already been crowned in England, though he was young for it – mind, there were few precedents for what to do when a baby succeeded to the English throne. Men said he was old enough, and intelligent enough, to play a part in public life, although there was no question of his taking full control of the government. They had been impatient to see this happen: no one wanted the unhappy arrangements of the regency to continue for longer than they must.

But the rows on the council had barely affected Suffolk and the men in France, and his must have been a less partial view. He probably found the king to be a solemn, rather quiet boy, with none of the force and boisterousness that had characterized his father. He perhaps reminded Suffolk more of the wan Queen Catherine. Of course, Henry had been accustomed from birth to privilege and deference: a lord new to his acquaintance would not have chatted freely with him. Suffolk perhaps told himself he was seeing the king at a disadvantage; he would liven up when he was settled in France.

Suffolk did not stay at Calais long, in any case, because Bedford had commissions for him. He took some of the new troops, and perhaps some of his own men, displaced now from Bricquebec, and led the siege of Aumale. This town and fortress was to the north-east of Rouen: it had to be retaken to secure the king's route. It must have been a relief to him when the operation went smoothly: by the summer Aumale was theirs again, and the king's great household began the journey down through Normandy to its capital.

Rouen 1430: it was twelve years since King Henry V had ridden into the town dressed in cloth of gold with his crown on his head. Much of the physical damage of the siege had been repaired. But there were other kinds of damage, less easy to mend: many of the fathers, daughters, brothers, sons of those who had died in that terrible winter still lived within the walls. There were English too, brought over to help with the Lancastrian administration of Normandy, but the population of the city was still probably less than it had been two decades earlier, and many of the flattened suburbs had not been rebuilt.

The Rouennais had only just finished paying the huge indemnity that the Lancastrians had extracted from them. It was a city full of builders: Bedford and his administration had sponsored the continuing work on the great churches and abbeys whose spires spiked the valley between the high chalk cliffs over the Seine. Bedford loved Rouen; Suffolk most likely did not, but this was familiar territory to him, although Beaufort's administration was not what he was used to.

Good news accompanied the king to Rouen: Jeanne d'Arc had been captured. Burgundy's men had taken her, in a skirmish outside Compiegne. Bedford and Beaufort both wanted her to be tried by the English – from their perspective she was not just a Valois supporter, but a witch and heretic, and must be punished for it – and Burgundy did not object. He bargained, then handed her over, and she was brought to the castle in Rouen. The Valois made no attempt to get her freed.

Although the king was in the castle too, he was kept well away from this dangerous influence.

King Henry's mother had come to France, and Suffolk, who knew her from Paris, and the time when she had followed the Lancastrian army, must have renewed the acquaintance now. She had, he knew, proved something of a problem. When previous kings had died leaving foreign consorts, they had generally been packed off back to their homelands, but Catherine could not realistically have been sent away when her son was very young, particularly when her brother was at war with the Lancastrians. So she had stayed with the king, but been marginalized. Henry V had not designated a role for her, and the council did not choose to give her one. They never forgot that she was a Valois.

Top, St Mary's Church, Iffley, Oxfordshire
Below, St Mary's Church, Elsing, Norfolk Photo Mike Dixon

Suffolk had just come from among the Valois. She must have sought him out, and perhaps questioned him on what he had seen. He had not met Charles VII, and could probably tell her little; but he maybe noticed that she spoke of this man as her brother – which of course he was – and that little King Henry had been brought up to regard the Valois king not just as his enemy, but as his uncle, a close relative whom he thought of with affection and respect.

Another woman in her situation might have wielded influence and power, but Catherine clearly did not. She was still a young woman, and would by choice have remarried, but the council had prevented it: they were concerned, not least, that any stepfather might have too much influence over the king. So she was left isolated with her women, in this court of men who had reason to be suspicious of her.

Bourges Cathedral

Wherever the influence rested in the court, it was not with Catherine. But she was a woman in a court where Suffolk knew few women, and he was at a point when he needed to find a wife. Perhaps he confided this to her: she could tell him which women in England might be suitable, while Anne of Bedford and the other women he knew from Paris were in a less good position to do so.

What she said to him, he had perhaps already thought for himself. There is one woman, now free, who might suit you very well: the widowed countess of Salisbury.

Where Catherine had little influence, Cardinal Beaufort had much of it. Suffolk would have met him as a young man, in the months after he had first succeeded to the earldom, but that was many years ago now, so the Cardinal probably seemed little better than a stranger to him. It was important to him to renew and build on the acquaintance. Bedford had probably stressed this to him too: it was men like Suffolk who could work to mend the breach between Beaufort and Gloucester.

The Cardinal was no longer young, though not yet quite old: at this time he was perhaps fifty-five or fifty-six (his exact date of birth is not known). He had royal blood: he was a son of John of Gaunt, and half-brother to Henry IV, although because he had been born illegitimate and only later legitimized, he was excluded from the royal succession. He had the knack of making money stick to his fingers. His bishopric of Winchester was a rich one, and he had been given it young, but it still surprised men that he should have been able to build up probably the largest fortune in the country.

The Lancastrian kings were poor (by the standards

of kings), and they needed Beaufort's money as much as, if not more than, his counsel. It was loaned, rather than given, and Beaufort did well out of the loans, but the fact that he could make them was a recommendation in itself. He was a worldly man, not an ascetic, with at least one bastard to his name. And he had the solid caution that Humphrey of Gloucester lacked.

This too was a two-way exchange, where Suffolk and the cardinal could both be useful to each other. Beaufort's two brothers were dead, and his nephews (his brothers' sons became successive earls and dukes of Somerset; his sister had married a Neville, the earl of Westmoreland, and was to produce a huge and influential brood) were still quite young. So he wanted supporters as much as Suffolk wanted patrons to ease his way into the king's council. The subject of Suffolk's marriage probably came up here too. I have a kinswoman whom you might consider, the cardinal most likely said to him. Her name? The countess of Salisbury.

Both pictures, Rouen Cathedral

Queen Catherine and the Cardinal were all very well, but the king needed companions of his own age too. And if they could find them, this would be an opportunity to strengthen the alliances on which the Lancastrians depended in France. The duke of Burgundy had no son, but the duke of Brittany had several, and Suffolk probably played a part in the negotiations that led to one of them joining the young king's court, since he had had many dealings with the Bretons by now, and must have known the duke quite well.

They got Prince Gilles, a younger son of the duke – and nephew to Arthur of Richemont, the turncoat who was still fighting with the Valois. This was a good arrangement, all of them agreed. As well as its diplomatic usefulness, Gilles turned out to be a lively, pleasant boy. Henry got on well with him. They would have talked together in French – Gilles was a Frenchman, and Henry's mother had it as her first language. Even with this new friend, the king seemed somewhat short of verve. Still, men cannot generally choose their kings. Suffolk must have exerted himself to be pleasant to both of these young boys, and to start to wield a little influence with them.

The duke of Burgundy did not come at all to Rouen.

37 My love, my joy

Another poem of Suffolk's, written while he was a prisoner of the bastard's, this time in French:

Lealement a tous Iours mais
Depieca & plus quonque mais,
Ie sui vostre, & vostre me tien,
Mamour, ma Ioye, & mon seul bien,
Mon comfort, mon desyr, ma pais.

Ma volente, mes dys, mes fais,
Sount tielx, & serround a Iamais,
Cest la lesson que Ie retien.

Ou que Ie suis, ou que ie vais,
Quoy que ie dis, quoy que ie fais,
Vous auez le coer que fuit mien;
Or nous entreauion doncque bien,
Si serrount noz playsirs parfais.

A rough translation:

What is now and will never cease
For the greater and the least:
I am yours and yours I stay
My dearest love, my joy each day,
My comfort, my desire, my peace.

My words, my deeds, what I long for
Are yours, and will be evermore.
That's learning I shall not release.

Whatever I am, wherever I go,
Whatever I say or do, you know
You have the heart that once was mine.
Care for it well, and we'll be fine:
Our perfect pleasure comes just so.

My comfort, my desire, my peace. If the expressions of love in this and his other verses were somewhat predictable, they were no doubt felt too; he was a man who loved women. Of course, marriage in his day had less to do with love than with pragmatic alliance. But Suffolk was not a boy, who could be driven into a marriage not of his choice; he was a man of thirty-four, and the woman he chose to court was also one in a position to decide whether to marry again, and to whom. A little romance was not out of place in these circumstances. Perhaps he had written this poem thinking of Malyne, but now she was ushered off stage – treated kindly, we must hope – and Suffolk re-edited the verses and set them, and his thoughts, towards the countess of Salisbury.

She was the obvious candidate. As like as not, he did not even consider anyone else. She was not a stranger, as other eligible women in England would have been: he must have met her many times when she had been in France in Salisbury's company. She had a background custom-made to help her empathize with his. Her father was Thomas Chaucer, an affluent merchant knight (a dealer in wine and other goods, like Suffolk's

Le Mans Cathedral

ancestors, who had also fought in Henry V's campaigns), and the son of the poet Geoffrey Chaucer. Her grandmother – Chaucer's wife – was Philippa Roet, sister to Katherine Swynford (born Roet), who had been mistress, then wife to John of Gaunt. So Alice was cousin to Cardinal Beaufort, Gaunt and Katherine Swynford's son, and to his brothers and nephews, the Beaufort earls and dukes of Somerset. Chaucer himself was a king's councillor at this time, so this added up to a raft of influential relations.

Alice was cultured and intelligent, and renowned for her looks: Philip of Burgundy had not made his obnoxious pass to an ugly woman. She had been married twice already, and the marriage to Salisbury in particular had increased her contacts and her credentials. It had also increased her estate.

It was not insignificant to Suffolk that she was rich. From her first husband, Sir John Phelip, who had died in the marshes at Harfleur, she had inherited some very worthwhile possessions including the valuable priory of Grovebury in Bedfordshire. Salisbury had left a daughter by a previous marriage, but his will gave Alice half his net goods together with 1,000 marks in gold, 3,000 marks in jewellery and plate, and whatever revenue she was able to get from his Norman lands. And she was an only child, so she would in due course inherit both her parents' fortunes.

She was still young, most likely in her mid-twenties. She had no children. Perhaps – probably – that troubled him a little. Her first marriage had been when she was a child, and possibly was never consummated, but she had been married to Salisbury for some years, with him in France for some at least of that time, and even if he had not had a daughter from his first marriage, no one of their era would have imagined their childlessness could be Salisbury's fault. But no one is perfect, and all in all, Alice Montacute, born Chaucer, was the right woman for Suffolk to marry.

And he was the right man for her. She was not obliged to remarry, but she must have wished to do so, and having gained one noble husband, she would not have settled this time for a merchant or a plain man at arms. So Suffolk must have got a promising welcome when he called on her – probably during his trips to England.

As a widow of an earl, Alice needed permission from the king's council to marry again. It was not quite a formality, but this was not a marriage that would have been forbidden: it was in every way suitable, and the king and his council knew how much Suffolk's family had sacrificed in the king's service. Alice got her permission in November 1430, a civilized two years after Salisbury's death at Orleans. At much the same time, she and Suffolk began negotiations over lands and possessions, as a prelude to drawing up the marriage contract. There was no question of simply handing the Chaucer lands to Suffolk: she and her father had struck hard bargains with her two previous husbands, and they did the same this time. Suffolk would find himself in much more comfortable circumstances after his marriage, but he was obliged to consult and appease Alice; he was not left in a position to dictate to her. Although the elaborate legal arrangements were not completed for another two or three years, she and Suffolk were married probably early in 1431.

The Chaucers and the Beauforts

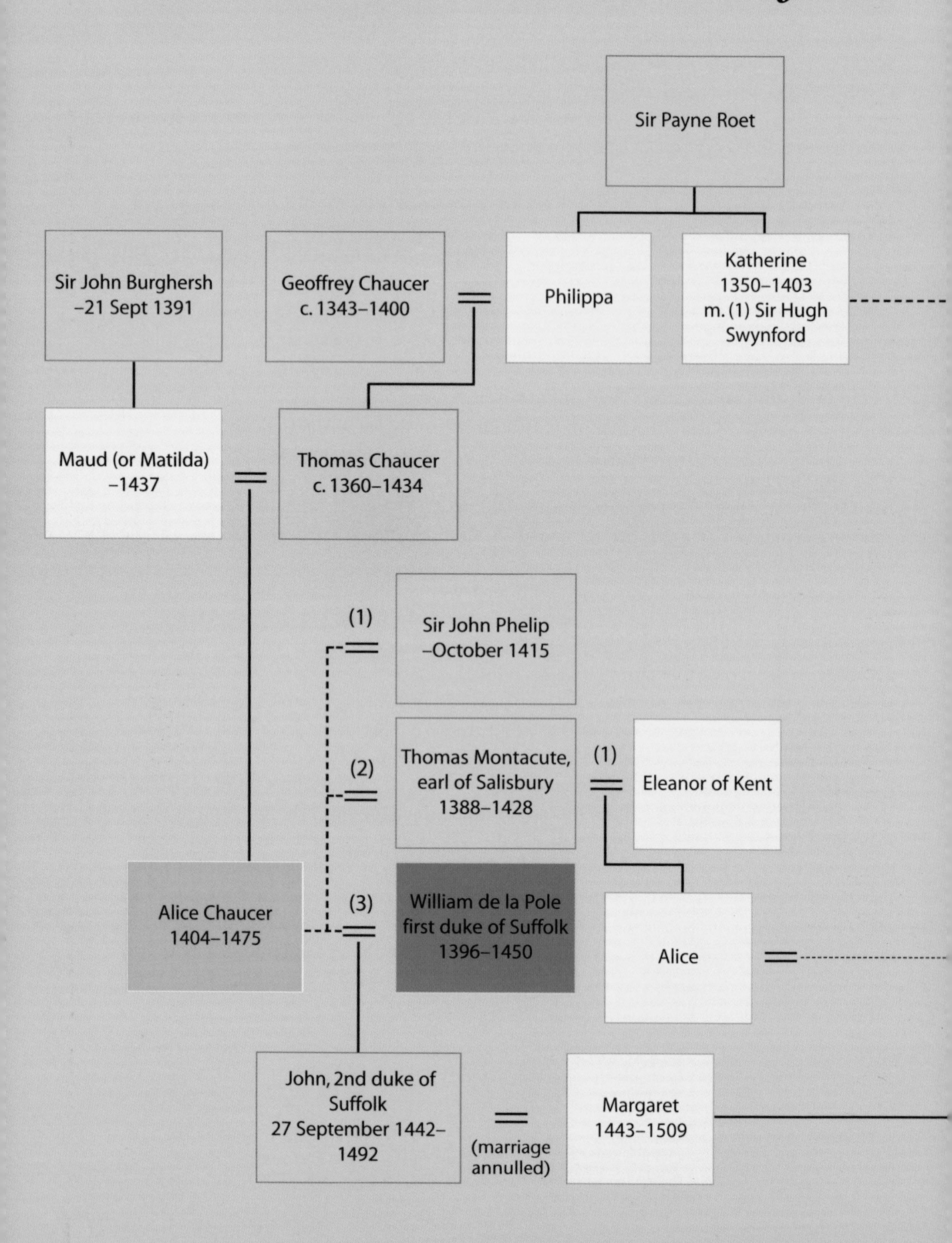

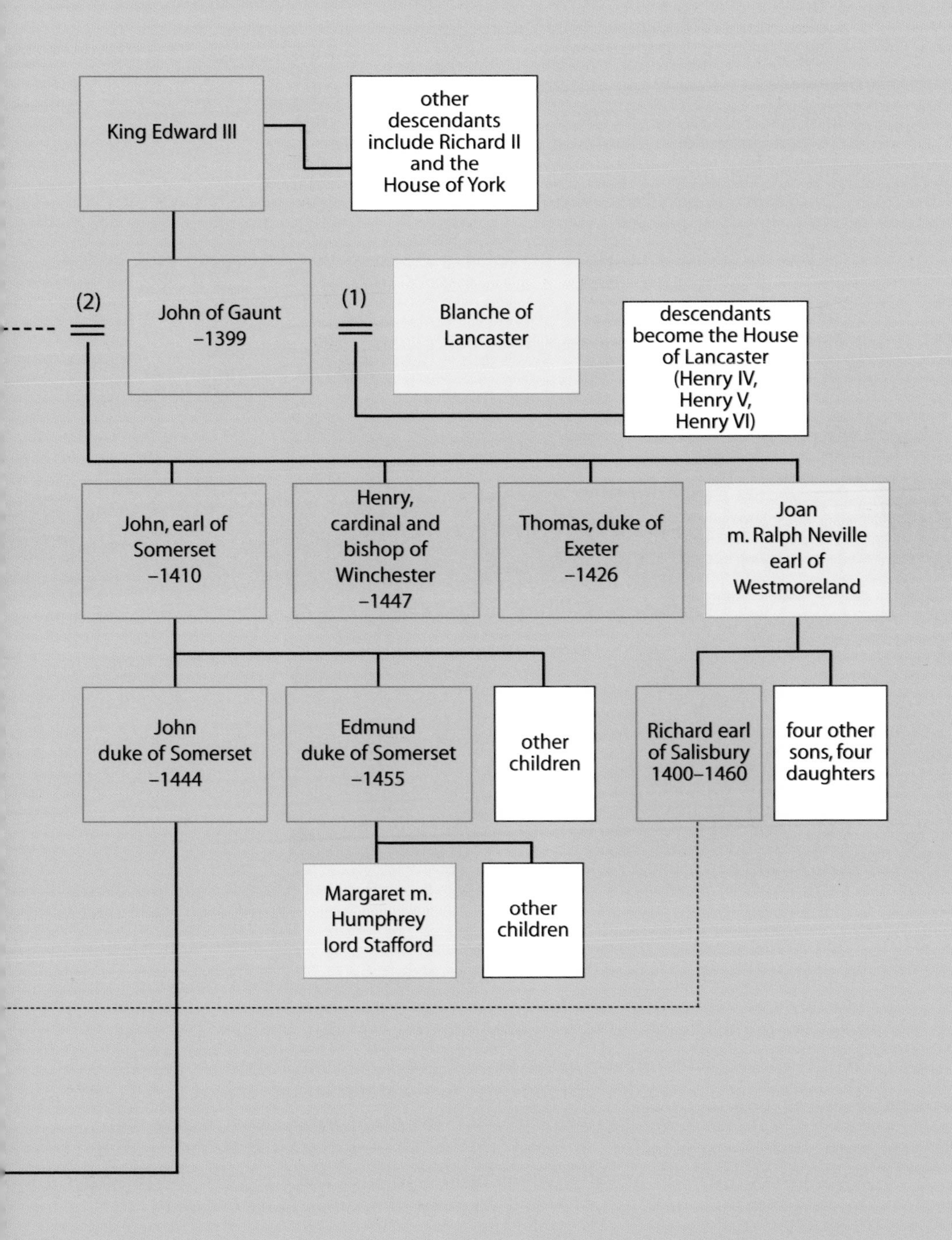
King Edward III
other descendants include Richard II and the House of York
(2)
John of Gaunt –1399
(1)
Blanche of Lancaster
descendants become the House of Lancaster (Henry IV, Henry V, Henry VI)
John, earl of Somerset –1410
Henry, cardinal and bishop of Winchester –1447
Thomas, duke of Exeter –1426
Joan m. Ralph Neville earl of Westmoreland
John duke of Somerset –1444
Edmund duke of Somerset –1455
other children
Richard earl of Salisbury 1400–1460
four other sons, four daughters
Margaret m. Humphrey lord Stafford
other children

38 The second king of France

In the spring of 1431 Suffolk attended Parliament in England for the first time. Humphrey of Gloucester presided; the king was still in Rouen. It was also the last Parliament that Thomas Chaucer attended. They were both perhaps conscious that this would be the case, and indeed Chaucer might well have insisted that Suffolk stay in England to attend it. The negotiations over his marriage were not only concerned with lands and possessions; there must have been much debate too over how he and Alice would live their lives, and what role he would play in the wider world in the future.

Alice seems to have been a forthright, even imperious woman, well aware of her own worth both personal and financial, and her father was a powerful, well-connected man. This was not a disadvantage to Suffolk: he had chosen this alliance, although he was perhaps still feeling his way forward, and discovering how it would work for him.

He would move the focus of his life to England; that must have been clear to all of them by now. Alice doubtless wanted it – she had already lost two husbands to the wars in France, and would not have wanted the same fate for her third – but in any case, Suffolk had begun this process even before he had arranged to marry her. He would not complete that move till the king himself returned to England; they surely agreed on that too. Not only was Suffolk needed in France, to help with the continuing efforts to keep Normandy and the île de France secure, and get the king safely to his coronation, this made sense from the perspective of his future. Beaufort and Bedford were still in France, and so were most of the lords of England. He could stand alongside Gloucester at this Parliament, renew their old acquaintance, put behind him any awkwardness that arose from their memories of Jacqueline of Hainault; but the intention was not for him to be a supporter of Gloucester in a divided king's council. He hoped to help heal the breaches in that council, but if there were to be differences between Gloucester and Beaufort, his path was clear: he would support the cardinal.

From Jacques Coeur's house, Bourges

Thomas Chaucer and his daughter would have made that plain, and fortunately – as with much they made plain – it suited Suffolk well enough anyway. By the standards of noblemen he was thinly provided with influential relatives, and it was all to his advantage to strengthen his connections with these powerful connections of the Chaucers.

But France still tugged; fourteen years of memories tugged, and not least, Bedford and his comrades in the Lancastrian army tugged. He would probably have gone back very soon after this Parliament was closed – on 30 March – if he had not then been taken ill.

He missed the meeting of the Garter knights that April because of it. He was 'seized with the plague' – it is not clear what this was, but it must have been a serious, though not fatal, illness. Perhaps he had married Alice by this time, perhaps they married once he recovered. In either event, he was probably glad to have her support.

And when he did get back to France that summer, she most likely came with him.

The king's stay in Rouen had dragged on for much longer than had been intended. What might have been a brief journey to France for his coronation had extended into a second year now, bogging down the Lancastrian military campaign, and costing the treasuries in both Rouen and Westminster a fortune.

It was not that the king was useful in France, was making connections. This might have happened, true, but it did not. He had Gilles of Brittany at his court, but he did not have visits from Gilles' father the duke, and nor, even now, did he have visits from the duke of Burgundy. This was seriously troubling. All the Lancastrians with Burgundian connections – of whom Suffolk was one – must have been working hard to persuade Philip of Burgundy to come to Rouen and give his allegiance in person to the young king. None of it worked: Burgundy never came. It would not have been appropriate for the king to travel himself to meet these men, even if it had been judged safe for him to do so. He was the king, they his dukes; it was necessary for them to come to him.

Bedford had been mostly in Paris from early in the year, running his own administration and overseeing the military campaign, a good distance from Beaufort and the king. Suffolk probably spent some time there, and some in Rouen. He also assisted at the siege of Compiegne, where the Burgundians had earlier captured Jeanne d'Arc. Alice perhaps stayed in Rouen.

They must have hoped to get the king away from Rouen before the trial of Jeanne d'Arc, but the year wore on, and still there were too many Valois troops, too many strongholds held for their opponents, for it to be safe to escort the king to Paris. Cardinal Beaufort made what arrangements were necessary to deal with the girl, and Bedford supported him. 'A disciple and limb of the Fiend', Bedford called her, who 'used false enchantments and sorcery'. Probably Suffolk would have agreed, though he might have been glad not to play an active part. He was familiar with heretics – they all were – and everyone know what had to be done to them. They gave her a trial of sorts. Then they burned her at the stake.

By October, the end of the campaigning season, the troops that had arrived with the king the year before had achieved at least the first of their

St Peter's Church, Kimberley, Norfolk

tasks. It was safe now to take the king to Paris. They did not hold Reims, and realistically would not capture it that year. The king had already been in France for a year and a half, so it was agreed that the coronation would have to be in Paris. The Lancastrians told themselves there was something to be said for differentiating this ceremony, and not making it a belated copy of the Valois king's. The inhabitants of Paris needed cheering: things in the city were little if any better now than they had been when Henry V had first come there. And they would have a good audience for their great spectacle.

It was just before the king went to Paris that Suffolk joined the king's council. He started to attend it regularly in early November; on 30 November he took the formal oath and became an official member. This committed him to his new course. Two days later the great ceremonial began.

An entourage of several thousand escorted King Henry to his second capital. Suffolk and his countess were almost certainly part of it, and it was a splendid show, one to be proud of. But there were worries too. Perhaps many of the English shared them, because although there was much pomp and ceremony, there was a lacklustre air to the proceedings.

They were more English than French in the king's entourage: not just a few more, but many more. It would have been no wonder if the Parisians watching had silently asked themselves, where are the lords, the dukes of France? Orleans and Bourbon were still in captivity in England. Burgundy had not come, for all the efforts that had been made, and nor had the duke of Brittany. The Valois captains were naturally not invited. Bedford's council had some Frenchmen on it, but they were not the great lords; and most of those around the king were not even these men, but the king's council that had come over from England, Beaufort and the rest of them, now including Suffolk as well.

That the French were not overwhelming supporters of this king's claim did not make it less valid in the eyes of those who did owe him loyalty. But it did make it more difficult to enforce. And Suffolk must have been aware, too (as were others) that in crowning the king they were moving farther down a path with no clear ending. There was no prospect still of winning all France; they were more distant from it than they had been three or four years earlier. At some point, surely, they would have to negotiate with the Valois. And the outcome of that negotiation could not realistically give the throne of France to Henry: he would have to settle for less, as Edward III had once done, as his father indeed had been willing to do in the early days of his campaigns. To crown him now would make that settlement more difficult.

Still, not to crown him would probably be worse.

All Saints Church, East Barsham, Norfolk

The king and his lords came first to St Denis, the great basilica just north of Paris, where the French kings were buried, and Henry V's body had lain in state. They spent two days there, then came the ceremonial entry into the city. The Parisians had arranged much of this, and they did it well. An escort of burghers from Paris in crimson satin gowns and hoods came half-way to St Denis to greet the king. Four bishops, twenty-five heralds and twenty-five trumpeters led the procession into the city. At the first gate the king was greeted by the first of many pageants and tableaux, of the goddess Fame with nine male worthies and nine female worthies, and received the dignitaries of the city. Then he moved down the streets under an azure canopy emblazoned with golden fleurs du lys, carried by four aldermen. He was presented with three hearts to signify the three estates of his realm (the nobles, the commoners, the church), which opened to release birds and flowers, to represent their joy at his arrival. At the Ponceau St Denis male and female savages fought a mock battle, and three women dressed as mermaids swam in a fountain of sweet wine.

Outside the church of Les Innocents a forest had been planted in the street, and a stag was hunted through it right up to the king's horse. He spared its life, then moved on to admire more tableaux, greet more dignitaries and citizens. Later he dined at the Hotel des Tournelles with the members of his court, and passed by the Hotel St Pol where his elderly grandmother, Queen Isabeau, was watching the festivities.

He spent the next fortnight just outside the city, at the castle of Vincennes, where his father had died. It is not clear whether Suffolk accompanied him there; perhaps he and Alice remained in Paris. Then in the chill of midwinter, on Sunday 16 December, the king came back to Paris, to Notre Dame for his coronation. Cardinal Beaufort presided, and sang the mass that followed. The Bishop of Paris felt he should have had more of a role to play, and did not hide his annoyance.

From that point onwards, things did not go well. Few of the French seemed to appreciate the ceremony; it was too English in style, they muttered. The English lords put a brave face on it: hell, what had they got to compare it with? No other king had been crowned in Paris during any of their lifetimes.

Then the state dinner was chaos. The treasury had cut corners, worried about the expense of it all; the administration was a shambles. The dignitaries of Paris, men they needed to appease – they had staged all this ceremony to bind men such as these to their cause – had to scramble to find seats. Much of the food had been cooked the previous week, and even on the top table it was inedible. The French had been looking forward to the banquet; they were loud in their annoyance.

The Parisians had played their part, and it was now the king's turn. They expected him to grant an amnesty to prisoners, and to remit their taxes. He did neither. Suffolk knew Paris and the Parisians: he must have sensed the anger, the bitterness. Surely Bedford did too. But between Beaufort, Bedford, the king himself, the worried officials at the treasury, the scramble of French and English courtiers, none of the things that should have been done were done.

If it had all been meant to win over the men of Paris, they had failed. And now they were leaving these subjects of a child king to a long cold winter and even worse shortages of food. Perhaps they knew, as they rode out of Paris at the end of it all, that they would never come back again.

St Edmund's Church, Emneth, Norfolk
Photo Mike Dixon

39
A homecoming

Although he had been in London the previous year, and perhaps gone briefly to Wingfield and Hull to speak with his stewards and make the arrangements for paying his ransom, Suffolk could not have spent more than a few days in either of these places. But his time in France was over now, his estates sold, his marriage made in England. Now, belatedly, he had come home.

His servants had had plenty of warning to prepare for it. Wingfield had not had an owner in residence since the second countess of Suffolk had died thirteen years earlier. But it was a solidly built place, and with fires lit to take the worst of the chill off the stone, tapestries hung, beds installed, and all the rest of the elaborate preparations demanded by a rich and noble family, it should have been welcoming enough when he and Alice eventually arrived to take up residence – most likely, in the spring of 1432.

After the battered glories of Paris and Rouen, the towns and villages large and small with their stone keeps, their high walls turned to rubble here and there by the cannon, the ravaged fields and half-starved residents, the campaign tents and the billets in abbeys and nunneries, it must have been strange indeed to come back to drowsy, peaceful Suffolk. The fields had been tilled, the barns had not burned down, the priests from the college sang their masses in the chantry, the peasants chatted and squabbled in English, not French, in the muddy streets.

Peace is relative, of course, and to the resident English it probably did not seem the most secure of times. Although some had benefited from the enforced absence of their superiors, many must have regretted it. For years neither the boy king's council nor his distant lords had done much to enforce the law of the land. If there were no French pirates, there were plenty of English bandits. Suffolk was probably no sooner through the gatehouse of his castle than men were queuing up to petition him. Tussles over the ownership of fields and houses, the payment of rents and taxes, fights and injuries – he was presented with all the petty and not so petty business that was traditionally brought to a lord to be resolved.

He had not had a lengthy spell as a resident lord before he had left for France. A few months as a minor, with his mother firmly in control of the estates, was poor preparation for this. And fourteen years of military justice, rough at best and more often no justice at all, cannot have made it easy to gauge the very different expectations of men in England.

He and Alice would both have brought with them the personal servants they already employed, but he now had to deal with the small army of retainers who had maintained his estates and collected his rents in the long years when he had been abroad. The chief among them would have kept in contact with him throughout, but it is one thing to receive a letter from a bailiff or steward in a different country, and another to meet the man and discover for oneself what has been done. These were the men who had worked for his father, or their sons and nephews (and in the wardrobe and the kitchens, their daughters and nieces). He had had little choice in who should work for him fourteen years earlier, and he must have felt he had less choice now. The men who had diligently despatched his remittances when he was in France could not be turned off now he was back in England.

The chief among his servants were themselves men with land and influence, who were of a stature to represent their counties in Parliament. One was John Heydon, probably the man (though perhaps the son of the man) who had travelled between Wingfield, Ipswich and London, escorting Suffolk's young brothers, sisters and nieces fifteen years earlier. The Heydons owned land mostly in north-east Norfolk, particularly around the village of Baconsthorpe. Another was Sir Thomas Tuddenham, an ambitious young lawyer with a difficult private life: his marriage had proved a disaster and he had separated from his wife, who had had a child by another man. He had inherited Oxborough Hall, one of the great houses of western Norfolk. These men acted for Suffolk, and did their best to protect his interests, in the counties of both Norfolk and Suffolk.

There were some complaints about their and their underlings' actions from other men, then and later. But that was inevitable, Suffolk's men must have told him: just as he had had to do in France, he had to defend his own rights, or his men had to do it for him, if he was not to lose ground to more aggressive and unscrupulous men. Indeed, he had lost ground in the years he had been away. The great rivals of the de la Poles for land and influence in Norfolk and Suffolk were the Mowbrays, earls and dukes of Norfolk. John Mowbray, the brother of Suffolk's dead sister-in-law, who had joined Gloucester on his abortive expedition into Hainault, had now regained the family's dukedom. For much of the previous ten years he had been in England while Suffolk had been in France: his men were in the ascendant, and Suffolk's men would have pointed out that in many of the disputes he was told about, it was Norfolk's sworn man who was the complainant.

And if there was some reason for the complaints, well, that was to some degree understandable. He had pushed hard to gain funds in order to pay off the bastard of Orleans, and his marriage would have been expensive too. So there must have been pressure on his servants to maximize their takings, which would have led to pressure on his tenants, which inevitably would have led to grumbles and arguments.

It would have taken half a lifetime to get to the bottom of all these quarrels, and he did not make it his priority. He did what was necessary, but a man cannot do everything, and not every decision can have gone the way of true justice. His own men and their adherents had to be appeased; pragmatism had to play its part. Most lords, he would have reckoned, did just the same.

Suffolk and Alice were only now settling into their marriage, and this was a period, with the relative quiet of East Anglia succeeding the hustle of the king's court and the long journey back from Paris, when they needed to set its patterns. It seems that they did this well enough: as far as can be judged, it grew into a strong and successful partnership.

House and garden in Ely Cathedral close

Although there were many echoes in their backgrounds, their families were quite different. Alice had her parents, to whom she was clearly close, then nobody but the Beauforts, who were important, but must have been considerably less close. They would not have gossiped regularly over wine and cakes with the Cardinal, while that was what had to be done – we must hope they enjoyed doing – with Suffolk's sisters and their families.

The Morleys were perhaps most important to them, because Suffolk had seen much of Lord Morley over the years in France. Morley had not remained there throughout as he had done himself, but had come and gone between France, London and his estates at Hingham. Suffolk had probably seen nothing of his sister Isobel, Morley's wife, so it would have been strange to meet her grown middle aged. She seems to have a been a competent, forceful woman, very much the daughter of their mother. It was perhaps her whom he had entrusted with making arrangements for his two little daughters; she cannot have been grateful, but there was no one in a better position to do it. And if Marie de Sicile and her daughter were now in England, Lady Morley had probably helped to arranged that too.

The Morleys must have asked what Suffolk planned to do now, and been told that he hoped to gain an appointment at court, and to play an active part on the king's council. Morley seems to have been less close to Henry VI than he had been to his father; this king will not be a great one, he perhaps warned Suffolk. Suffolk had probably seen enough of the king by now to judge that for himself. This king was one who would need guidance and support, most likely even after he was grown. But that was a reason for giving it, not the reverse. If Morley was now withdrawing on to his estates, Suffolk did not intend to take the same course.

Isobel perhaps said, you realize, of course, that you are following the pattern of our grandfather? A first career as a man at arms – she would not have said, but she might have thought, no better than variable in its success – and a second as a king's counsellor. And you know how that ended. Suffolk must have thought, and replied, I shall try to ensure that my end is different. He had learned to watch his back in France; a different kind of caution would be needed in England, but he had not forgotten the importance of it.

Suffolk's second sister Elizabeth had also done well, remarrying after her first husband had died at Harfleur. She and her second husband, Sir Thomas Kerdeston, must have been literate people: they commissioned an illustrated manual on hawking, which still in part survives today.

It is less clear what had happened to Philippa and Joan: perhaps they had not survived these years. Katherine was in her convent at Barking. As Thomas had perhaps predicted to Suffolk, she became its abbess in due course, which would have brought her more out into the world; another strong, efficient woman, she was to prove useful to her brother.

They all mourned their dead brothers. Suffolk must have spent much time too dealing with the aftermath of their deaths, settling their business affairs and arranging memorials for them. His sisters were probably glad he had chosen to return to England; with so much lost already, they did not want the family to lose more to France. They would not have spoken of blame to him, but he must have felt guilt still himself, and perhaps worried that they thought of it.

Oxborough Hall (Sir Thomas Tuddenham's estate), Norfolk
Photo Mike Dixon

Suffolk and Alice met with the other great men and women of East Anglia too: at hunt meetings, at weddings and funerals; for Suffolk, on panels to deal with legal issues, and meetings over his business affairs; and for Alice especially, on social outings. He had always handled liaison with others himself; now he had to learn to let her do much of it for him. The Mowbrays, for instance, might be rivals, but they were also relatives through marriage, and must be visited. There was the link through Suffolk's dead brother Michael and the duke of Norfolk's dead sister, and there was a second link that Alice could provide: her stepdaughter (Salisbury's daughter by his first marriage) was married to a Neville, brother to the duchess of Norfolk. They followed threads like these, as they both began to weave a web of connections.

They went to Norwich, perhaps that summer, when many of the great men of the region would have been in the city, and there was much for a vivacious young countess to do. The parties and outings there were not much like the duke of Burgundy's parties in Paris, but perhaps they were none the worse for that.

One was a masquerade party, which Alice arranged. She and her companions dressed up as plain folks, housewives and labourers, and rode out of the city to enjoy a picnic in Lakenham Wood. The wood – not all trees, there was pasture there too – was not far from the city: outside, but within sight of, its walls. Suffolk himself seems not to have joined this outing. Perhaps he was busied with petitions and appeals.

He regretted that, of course, when Sir Thomas Tuddenham brought Alice back rumpled and upset. What happened, he must have asked? Sir Thomas would have tried to brush it away. A stupid incident, nothing that he need trouble himself over. A ditcher had failed to recognize them, and told them to move on.

Alice was not used to not being recognized, not treated with deference and respect. She had told the man who she was, and he had not believed her. True, she was dressed as a burgher's wife and not as a countess, but he should have known better! Sir Thomas had had to intervene, and in the end he had given the man a good kicking. It had frightened her rather to witness the fight, but bravo for Sir Thomas! He had done his best, and kept them all safe.

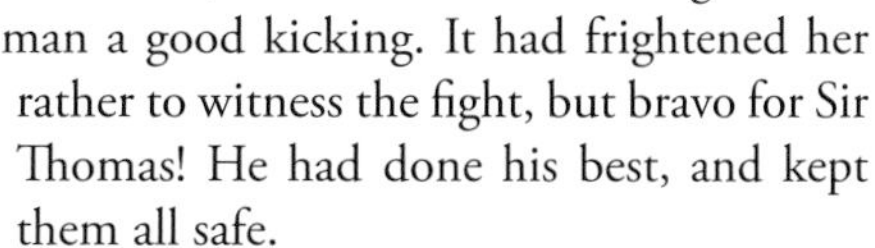

This must have dismayed her husband. He sympathized, of course, but he could remember too Alice's indignation at the duke of Burgundy, which would have been better expressed less loudly, if at all. Tuddenham was their retainer, not quite their equal, but he must have wished she had retained her calm in front of the man. Tuddenham assured him he would follow it up, and make sure the man did not trouble them again. But Suffolk would doubtless have preferred not to feel indebted to him.

40 Bronze-green hose

There have been soldiers in many generations who wrote poetry, but nevertheless it is a minority interest: most men at arms would have opted instead for a brisk ride to hounds. In the aristocracy a degree of learning was more usual, and Suffolk could expect to be admired for his literary efforts. But still there were plenty of men who regarded such tendencies with suspicion.

To write poetry oneself was forgivable perhaps: but to admit that one wished to meet a captive French duke, a man King Henry V had regarded as so dangerous that ten years after the king's death, the English had not let him go free – because he wrote great poems? That was a thing a careful Englishman would tread very cautiously in revealing.

To admit that one wished to meet him because one liked his half-brother, a successful captain in the enemy's army, was still less easy; indeed it was best not done. So that Suffolk succeeded in becoming the custodian of Charles of Orleans by the summer of 1432 attests to a certain degree of tact and skill at negotiation.

The best way to gain access to a well-guarded prisoner was to become the man's custodian, which explains why he took this route. The custodianship of such a man was a lucrative and sought-after position. He could not simply walk up to the duke's current jailer and say, 'Thanks, I'll take him over now.' He had to plan his approach, persuade the king's council, obtain a formal grant of the post. He probably had to rely primarily on his third motive for getting to know Charles of Orleans: and it was helpful, more than helpful, that this was the greatest of the three. He believed that the man could be useful, and that he himself was in as good a position as any man, and a better one than most, to bring to fruition that usefulness.

Suffolk must have given some thought by now to what he hoped to achieve as a king's counsellor, and perhaps he had confided some of his thoughts to other men. There had to be others, he must have told himself, who also wished to see peace between England and France.

There were men who, like himself, had lost more than they could endure to the war. There were also men much in England, but who had come to France for the king's coronation, and had been dismayed to see the state of the country they passed through, in the journeys from Calais to Rouen, from Rouen to Paris. Men who had been shocked at the state of Paris itself, so much less bustling and prosperous than London: the battered walls, the beggars and starvelings, the hostility and resentment of the Parisians, barely disguised beneath their masques and tableaux. Perhaps these men would understand that it was useless to rely upon an ultimate Lancastrian victory, and necessary as a result to seek a compromise.

There was also men who rejected such ideas out of hand. He already knew that Bedford was one: he would never go back on the

Abbey of l'Epau, Le Mans

oaths he had sworn to his dead brother, regardless of whether in retrospect they appeared wise. If Suffolk sounded out Gloucester, he would have done it very warily. It would not have taken much to tell him that Gloucester took the same line.

Lord Morley was not the man for this; he was retreating from the court, not willing to play a larger part, or even as large a one as he had played ten years before. Thomas Chaucer was withdrawing too, ageing and perhaps sick: he offered advice, most likely, but not practical support. Suffolk must have talked to Cardinal Beaufort, and probably found him more receptive, but still at best ambivalent. You realize, of course, that no man can sign away the king's claim to France while he is still a minor? It would be treason, no less, to suggest it. If you wish to try for peace, then you must try for a peace through diplomacy, but not one through compromise. You must get the nobles of France to support our king.

The nobles of France. The duke of Burgundy, by now a well-known and little loved ally. The dukes of Orleans and Bourbon, both in English captivity. The duke of Alençon, fighting for Charles of Valois. The duke of Brittany, tentatively supportive: his young son Gilles was still with the king, in England now, but there was his brother Richemont in the Valois army. The duke of Anjou, rival claimant to a title that Bedford had taken for his own; and others too, though most of them lesser. Charles of Valois had no surviving brothers and few surviving sisters; the French royal family was almost as thin as the English.

Was there any way at all to bring more of this combative, difficult brood onto the side of Henry of Lancaster?

If there was, it had to centre on Orleans and Burgundy; Suffolk must have been clear on that. The feud between the houses of Orleans and Burgundy was at the core of the dissensions in the French court. Dukes of Burgundy and dukes of Orleans had both been killed. But the current duke of Burgundy had not killed a duke of Orleans; the current duke of Orleans had not killed a duke of Burgundy. They must be encouraged to reconcile with each other. And this must be done by the English, and in a way that ensured that if and when they both agreed to support the same king, it would be Henry that they chose.

Suffolk was probably uneasily conscious that by now the duke of Burgundy had learned about the assassination plot he had hatched to support Gloucester. He would be wise to lay low with the Burgundians for a while longer; and he did not use William Bennet again. He found a new man now, a Burgundian, Jennin Cauvel. This man took an appointment as his barber, but later Suffolk also used him to carry messages.

In any case, Bedford was in a much better position to work on Burgundy, first to keep him loyal, and second, to persuade him to reconcile with Orleans in the Lancastrian interest. Surely, Suffolk – and others – must have thought, Burgundy would be more comfortable as a supporter of the child king about whom he seemed so ambivalent, if his allegiance was shared by the other great French nobles. And this would sideline Charles of Valois for good.

Bedford's wife, Anne of Burgundy, was expecting a child: they must pray that she produced a strong, healthy son. That would help to tighten ties not just with Burgundy, but with all her connections: two of her sisters were married to Richemont and to the duke of Bourbon. And Cardinal Beaufort could help too. Philip the Good's second wife was now dead – without giving him an heir – and he had married for a third time, to Isabella of Portugal, who was the daughter of a Lancastrian princess, and Cardinal Beaufort's niece.

Meanwhile, Suffolk's own main task was to win over the duke of Orleans, not just to the English, but to the Burgundians as well. Orleans had never been an ally of the English; but they held him, and they could work on him, to a greater degree than they had done to date. It could be pointed out to him that only with peace could he hope to go free.

Suffolk took soundings, angled, perhaps called in some favours, and obtained the duke's custodianship. Then there was a second stage of approach to plan. Charles of Orleans had learned to be cautious himself, in his long years – nearly eighteen, by then – of captivity. He was still a duke, and there were knotty questions of etiquette to be resolved here: how exactly should a French duke and the English earl who held him captive address each other? Men cared about such matters; he could not afford to get it wrong.

He knew that what he would eventually ask of this man was not something he would find easy to concede. Orleans would need to bury generations of enmity, against both Burgundy and the English. He had to be approached with subtlety.

Men would have told Suffolk about this duke, a man of precise desires, and the capacity to fulfil them. He was fond of a good cup of wine, and had retained in captivity the right to have barrels of it sent from his lands duty free. He was fond of books, and had about a hundred of them, a huge number for his time. Most of them had been gifts from his friends: Suffolk was not the first man who had aspired to that position. Orleans did not favour romances, or the classics, although he made an exception for Seneca. There were the usual missals and prayer books, and quite a few on medicine – a hypochondriac, perhaps? He played chess and tables – what is now called backgammon – so maybe this could be a route to friendship. He was said to prefer mules to horses, have a weakness for Lombard nougat and quince marmalade. His servants assisted him in obtaining the clothes he chose to wear: he insisted on bronze-green hose, the shade of his emblem, the nettle.

The nettle. It stung.

Suffolk probably began with the poetry, and of course with messages from Jean the Bastard. He did not also obtain Jean of Angoulême's custody – the English would not have let the two men from Orleans be held together – but he might have sent messengers, and obtained information that he could give to the duke about his brother. All this careful groundwork paid dividends. He became an English friend of Charles of Orleans.

We can imagine them, in the months that followed, exchanging their poems, or sitting over a chessboard in the duke's stone-walled prison, playing together in amicable silence. We can imagine them talking about politics and France – cautiously at first, but perhaps in private less cautiously, as the weeks and months passed by.

Coutances Cathedral

41 Bella Court

In Rouen and Paris, Suffolk must have heard Cardinal Beaufort's account of his feud with Humphrey of Gloucester. Now in London and Westminster, he had the opportunity to see Gloucester in action on the king's council, and judge for himself. His hope, of course, was to find a way to lance the boil that had erupted on the council, and gain credit for himself in the process. If this was impossible, then he was minded to oblige the Chaucers and support the cardinal against Gloucester; but that was a fallback position, and not his aim.

He probably concluded quickly that Beaufort was right: power did not suit Gloucester. It was understandable that wiser men should have wished to keep him from absolute power in England, but the kind of hobbled half-power that he had been granted suited him if anything even worse. It gave him the opportunity to be rash and petulant, to growl at slights and seethe at Beaufort. But he had to be kept on the council; he was the king's uncle, it was unthinkable to do otherwise. So Suffolk did his best to work with him.

Gloucester was clearly anxious to ensure that the king's return from France, as a twice-crowned monarch, though still a young boy, would not lead to a reduction in his own powers. Suffolk was willing to oblige him there. He seconded a proposal to increase Gloucester's powers, and his pay as well. The chancellor complained that neither was appropriate, particularly when the king's expedition had proved so much more expensive than had been budgeted for, and the treasury needed to make economies. Suffolk assisted Gloucester in getting him replaced, by a man he must have been happy to see in the post. This was John Stafford, a relative of his mother's, whom he had perhaps known at Oxford, or later at court, before he had left for France. Stafford was now bishop of Bath and Wells, and respected as a thorough and reliable administrator. He retained this powerful position for the rest of Suffolk's life.

Outside the council, it was easier: on his own territory, Gloucester showed more readily the charm that had made men love him as a young lad. He owned the manor of Greenwich, downstream from London along the Thames, and was building a great palace there, which he called Bella Court. He patronized thinkers, musicians and writers, such as the poet John Lydgate. He took a keen interest in Italian scholarship and scholars, and corresponded with learned men across Europe. He commissioned translations of Greek classics into Latin. If Suffolk had seen some of this when he had served with Gloucester in France, he must have seen much more of it now. Here was a place where he and Alice could hear good musicians and enjoy literate conversation. There were less high-flown enjoyments too: jesters, gossip, pretty women, men who claimed to be alchemists, fortune tellers.

Suffolk was probably ambivalent at best about Gloucester's duchess. Many people were. There is not much credit in being a lady in waiting who entices away her mistress's husband, and as a man who had loved the mistress, Suffolk would not have been the keenest to scrape some up for her. Nor was this the great diplomatic marriage that Gloucester might have made, one that would strengthen the Lancastrian cause in France: Eleanor of Gloucester's father, Sir Reynold Cobham, was no more than a minor lord. She and Gloucester were the kind of blithe pair, following their instincts in a way few people of their time could afford, that a censorious man – a chaplain of the king's, or even the king himself, come to that – could easily condemn. But Suffolk was not a chaplain, or a king, or a man who had always resisted temptation, and he had a wife who probably warmed readily enough to Eleanor, with whom she had much in common. And the Gloucesters were a couple in love; this generally makes people easy to like.

So the Suffolks worked to build on their common ground with the Gloucesters. It must have been bitter experience that had made Alice touchy and protective of her high dignity: people were by no means always kind to those who had risen in the world, as Suffolk's ancestors too had discovered. Alice could sympathize with Eleanor's distress at the sniffs and sniping that came her way. She could sympathize, too, with the duchess's eagerness to get a child. Both of them must have felt under some pressure to provide their husbands with heirs; both of them must have been disappointed, month after month, when this did not happen. Perhaps they went together to consult the wise women who claimed to offer remedies for such disappointments. There was one called Marjery Jourdemain, whom her enemies knew as the witch of Eye. (She probably came from Ebury, a place near Westminster, though there was also a place called Eye not far from Wingfield.) Eleanor almost certainly used her services, and likely as not Alice did too.

Gloucester had two bastards, a son called Arthur, and a daughter called Antigone. At some point Alice must have learned about the small daughters Suffolk had made arrangements for. If she felt dismay over this – which surely she did, particularly when she was finding it difficult to conceive a child of her own – then this too was something she could share with Eleanor.

If Suffolk enjoyed the music and the serious talk of politics, he also made use of the astrologers, and put some belief in what they told him. Almost all men did so in his time. He knew, for example, that he had been born under the sign of the Scales, that this represented measure, balance, diplomacy; he expected these elements to have a role in his life.

At some point in these years, he had his fortune told. Gloucester had among his men a celebrated society astrologer, Sir Roger Bolingbroke, and perhaps it was he who read Suffolk's hand or cast his horoscope. What Suffolk was told was not altogether cheering, and perhaps afterwards he wished he had not asked. He was told he should beware of the Tower.

There were plenty of towers, of course, in England and in France as well, but to a man of his time, the Tower, said in the portentous tone of fortune tellers through the centuries, meant just one place: the White Tower, the keep at the Tower of London. To beware of this was hardly novel advice; every sane man feared being sent there. It was where state prisoners were kept, where the king's torturers plied their trade. It had provided the last bed before the scaffold for many terrified

St Edmund's Church, Emneth, Norfolk
Photo Mike Dixon

men and women. And any man who knew something of history – whose grandfather, say, had risen to become a great servant of a king, and then endured a harsh downfall – was aware how easy it was to draw down that fate.

Suffolk truly feared it would happen to him.

He knew, too, that although the fortunes that were foretold for men often came to a kind of fruition, this did not mean things unfolded as men expected. Fate was capricious; men's fortunes were full of strange twists and turns. Why, look at old King Henry IV, with his fear that a crusade would lead to his death. He was all too right to fear Jerusalem, but it was in the Jerusalem chamber at Westminster that his life came to its end.

Suffolk must also have spent much time attending on the king. He was coming to know Henry, and be trusted by him. Men like Lord Morley were clearly right: early reports of the king's great intelligence had shown a great deal of diplomatic tact. Some men who did not know him well reckoned the boy an idiot. He was not that: slow in his wits perhaps, but with the careful teaching he had received, he was capable of conversing with ambassadors and courtiers. But the hard truth was that the coronation had showed the best of him. He was happy sitting in furred robes and cloth of gold, waving graciously at lesser men, but the rest of kingship he was much less well suited for. He could be naive, stubborn, and infuriatingly inattentive to others: this would never be a king who travelled his kingdom, listening thoughtfully to his subjects and administering wise justice. Nor would he ever be a man at arms; he seemed to have no martial instincts at all. On the plus side, he was sincerely devout, good hearted, not vindictive, and loyal to those he came to love.

The earl of Warwick was supervising the king's education. He had been the third commander, with Suffolk and Sir John, at the siege of Montargis. That was not a happy memory, but there must have been other, better memories on which he and Suffolk could draw.

Queen Catherine, Henry's mother, was no longer a part of this court. She seems to have withdrawn from Westminster about this time, and it was learned later that in spite of the council's forbidding it she had remarried, or at least entered into a relationship – with a Welshman of no great eminence, Owen Tudor. There was little that could be done about it by then, except to keep them both clear of the king.

There was a change, now, in how Suffolk seemed to be perceived, and part of this was perhaps down to Alice: to her connections, or simply to her pushing him a little more than he had been used to push himself. In France for a long time, he had been just one of the commanders: well regarded by Bedford, given useful commissions, but one of the men the heralds sometimes remembered, sometimes not, when they noted down who had been present at a battle or a negotiation. Now he was noted; now he was looked for.

Alice gained preferment too when the two of them were back in England. In 1432 she received the insignia of a lady of the Garter. Although unlike a man she was not allocated a stall at Windsor, this entitled her to wear the robes of the Order, and it was a very real symbol that she was a woman of power and influence.

42 The mills of Norwich

News came from France: he might not be a part of it now, but the war was still continuing. This was a difficult time in it. There had been a dip in morale after the king had sailed back to England, and many of the men he had brought to France had sailed back with him. Worse, the huge expenditure on the coronation expedition had achieved very little in military terms, and there was no realistic possibility of raising more money in the near future for another army. So Bedford had to conduct a holding operation; and he accepted that in parallel with this, it might be desirable to negotiate with the Valois. A truce would be welcome. If it could be achieved on the right terms, he would also have welcomed peace. Come to that, they would all have welcomed peace.

The trouble was that, as Suffolk knew, there was no basis on which to negotiate. The Lancastrians would have to insist in any negotiations that Henry must be acknowledged as king of all France, and there was no possibility that Charles of Valois would concede this. Charles controlled much of France; he had the loyalty of many of its lords, and most of its people; he too might have wished the war ended, but he had no desire to make concessions in order to bring about its end. Letters and ambassadors were sent; Bedford, Beaufort and Gloucester all played their part; but neither the Burgundians nor the Valois expressed any inclination to come to the negotiating table.

In the winter of 1432, a small disaster struck. Anne of Bedford died in her childbed. There would be no little niece or nephew of the duke of Burgundy to strengthen ties, and Bedford, whose famously plain wife had been much loved, was devastated. He must have seen Philip of Burgundy at her funeral, but neither man can have been in the mood for diplomatic negotiation, and no one could have blamed them.

Suffolk did not participate in these plans for negotiations that he must have seen as something of an empty charade. Perhaps he was not asked to, and he certainly did not press to do so. The time to negotiate, from his perspective, would be when he had won round Charles of Orleans.

So he continued to pursue his friendship with the captive duke. They ate meals together, probably wrote poems together – Orleans had a fondness for poetry competitions, setting his colleagues a first line or a theme – and hunted together too: the duke was allowed this degree of liberty. In time, Suffolk would have raised the political issues he needed to win support on. Orleans was no supporter of Henry as king of France. Suffolk had known that from the outset. He neither accepted the justice of Henry's claim to the throne, nor wished to have this child – of whom he must have heard something, however much his guards censored his news – as his own overlord. He wanted peace in France, though, so Suffolk's aim would have been to persuade him that acknowledging Henry was the best way to achieve it. It would be slow, perhaps, but it would, with luck, be faster than waiting for the king to come of age.

Orleans' attitude to Burgundy was more promising. His long captivity had made

Ewelme Palace, from Napier, *Historical Notices of the Parishes of Swyncombe and Ewelme* (1858)
Glass from Trinity Church, Vendome

the duke phlegmatic, and perhaps he was not naturally a man given to feuds and grudges. Suffolk must have judged that it would be less difficult to create a kind of peace between the men of Orleans and those of Burgundy.

News came from East Anglia too. A petition came from Norwich, which at first might have mystified Suffolk. Why was this Thomas Ailmer, held in the dungeons at Norwich castle? Why were his friends – many of them, too – petitioning to have him freed? And why this note of resentment in the petitions, as if it was all his doing?

Sir Thomas Tuddenham, or perhaps John Heydon, explained. This was the ditcher who had insulted Alice in Lakenham Woods, and tussled with Sir Thomas. Sir Thomas had promised to deal with the man, and he had been as good as his word: he had put him in jail. Ailmer would have to be hauled out at some point, but it would do no harm to let him stew till his lordship chose to return to Norwich, and hold a jail delivery.

Deal with it, Suffolk told him. So Tuddenham dealt with it. He had more men arrested.

More petitions came, more grumbles and pleas. Then Heydon appeared with a grumble of his own. The mayor of Norwich had got him deprived of the recordership of the city. This was a useful position, which provided both pay and influence. He wanted it back.

Deal with it, Suffolk told him. You handled these affairs for fourteen years while I was in France. I have other priorities; handle this yourself.

Perhaps he did not understand, Tuddenham and Heydon said. It was not now a question just of a ditcher; all this had become a cause on which to pin a larger quarrel. The burghers of Norwich were in dispute with the prior and abbey. This was a battle that had rumbled on for years, but if unresolved, it could become nasty. It might he wise if he were to intervene.

Suffolk cannot have wanted to intervene. He told them so. Alice had no wish to return to East Anglia yet, and nor did he. This touches your own affairs, sir, his men must have told him. There are mills on the river upstream from Norwich. There are disputes about the water flow; this is one of the issues the prior and the aldermen are at loggerheads over. One of the mills belongs to you …

Deal with it, Suffolk told them.

More news came from France. Bedford had married again, a scant five months after Anne of Burgundy's death.

Suffolk must have been disturbed and annoyed by this, however much personal sympathy he felt for Bedford. Did this brother of Henry V also have the curse of Lancastrians, the streak of rashness that had cost them so much? It seemed he did. He had not only failed to observe the full period of mourning for Anne, he had married the daughter of a Burgundian lord. Jacquetta of Luxembourg was a pretty girl of seventeen. Her father was a man Burgundy struggled to keep in line, much as he had struggled with the Hainaulters. Burgundy had not given his permission for the marriage, and it can scarcely have needed his contacts at the court at Dijon for Suffolk to know he would be angered by it. This was not the moment to try to bring Burgundy and Orleans together to support the Lancastrian cause.

43 The ape clog

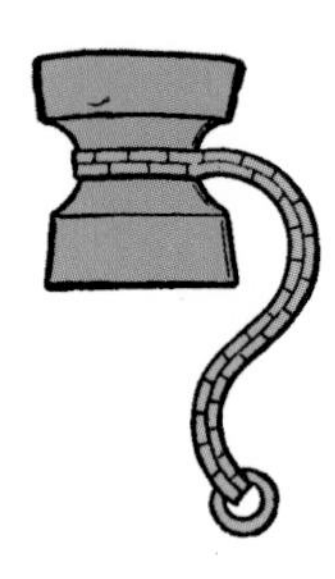

Most great lords of Suffolk's day adopted an emblem. This was not their coat of arms, it was a simpler device that could be made into a badge, to be worn by the men who owed them allegiance. Orleans' nettle, the Lancastrian red rose, the Yorkist white rose, all played this function. Gloucester's was a chained white duck wearing a crown.

Suffolk took as his emblem an ape clog: a kind of bollard, with a loop and a chain. It seems to have been what the name suggests; a weight that was used to keep in place a performing monkey.

The same association appears in the nickname that Suffolk acquired in later life. A monkey was known at the time as a 'Jack of Naples', probably because that was the city through which they were imported as pets into England (although some authorities claim that 'Napes' derives more simply from the word 'ape'). So Suffolk's enemies in later life called him the Jackanapes, a term which is still used today for conceited people who have risen up from humble origins, like Suffolk's family had done.

44 The Burgundian barber

Suffolk would not have given the duke of Orleans any hint that Bedford's rash marriage might have derailed his plans, and he could hope the duke would not realize it for himself. He ensured that Orleans was treated well, but he was treated as a prisoner none the less. When his messengers came, Suffolk's men were present, so he could not receive information or pass on messages that Suffolk did not know of. If he wrote, or received letters, they were read by Suffolk. All this was necessary, however much he liked and admired the duke, because the danger was all too clear: if the duke of Burgundy and the duke of Orleans were to come to agreement, it was not a foregone conclusion that it would be to support Henry of Lancaster as king of France.

Suffolk's barber – the Burgundian he had hired after William Bennet had lost his credibility – had proved useful in all this. He had set Jennin Cauvel to double as one of Orleans' guards. This son of Lille spoke fluent French, of course, and was good company, as he needed to be in his profession. The duke had talked much with him, and Suffolk must have briefed Cauvel on what he was to say. There was much on the fine qualities of the duke of Burgundy.

By early 1433, Orleans was expressing a willingness to play a role in negotiating with the other French lords, in the hope of bringing about a peace that would enable him to gain his freedom. Suffolk would have assured him that he would do his best to ensure Jean of Angoulême was involved as well: this was another inducement he could offer the duke, that the two brothers might meet again at long, long last. He must have been supported in this by Beaufort and the other lords of the king's council.

Orleans agreed he would meet with the duke of Burgundy, if it was thought desirable by the English. He would bury their past differences if Burgundy would also do so. And he also agreed in private with the king's council that if there was a general agreement among the French lords to accept Henry as king, he would fall into line. More, he would work to bring this about.

This was not a public declaration of support, one they could announce to the Valois prior to peace negotiations, but it was all that Suffolk could reasonably have hoped for, and more. He would have been quietly jubilant when Orleans gave him this commitment.

Now they had to persuade the duke of Burgundy to play his part, and end his family's long feud with the house of Orleans.

Bedford took on this task, in partnership with Cardinal Beaufort and Gloucester. He had worked hard to appease Burgundy after his remarriage, and must have been confident he had brought him around. Burgundy's position as a half-hearted ally

Church of Notre Dame, Béhuard, France

of the English, isolated from most of the other great French lords, was not a comfortable one. This was his chance to make it more so, by persuading Orleans and perhaps the duke of Bourbon, the Lancastrians' other great captive, to ally with the Lancastrian cause. With these lords in line, it could be hoped that Brittany would abandon his cautious neutrality and follow, and at long last the Lancastrians would have a sufficiently solid weight of French support behind them to bring about a decisive diplomatic victory.

Burgundy insisted, though, that if there were to be negotiations between these lords, the Valois must be invited from the outset. It would have suited the English better to negotiate with the more sympathetic of the French lords and then present a fait accompli to Charles of Valois, but they realized it was unwise to refuse, so messengers were sent to Charles of Valois and all the great French lords, inviting them to a conference at Calais. The dukes of Orleans and Bourbon, plus Jean of Angoulême and other French prisoners, were prepared to be in attendance, but Gloucester insisted that they would be taken initially only to Dover, and not brought over to France unless it proved necessary.

Philip of Burgundy appointed envoys to attend at Calais. The English ambassadors (headed by Bedford, Beaufort and Gloucester) headed there, and prepared for the conference. Suffolk's own role meanwhile was to arrange for Charles of Orleans to meet with his brother at Dover. It would have been a pleasure for him to achieve this. But if it brought him gratitude from Orleans, he probably knew too that it was not enough. Orleans longed to return to France and freedom, and after the first euphoria of their reunion, the brothers must have been on edge in Dover, waiting for the summons from Calais.

They waited a month, then word came; but not the message they had hoped for. The Valois had not sent ambassadors to Calais, and it was clear now that they did not intend to do so. The Burgundians had made it apparent that they would do and say nothing until there was a formal peace conference, and there could be no such conference unless all the parties attended. So the English ambassadors were now preparing to leave with their retinues, and the prisoners were to be returned to their captivity.

Bedford and the rest clearly felt that Burgundy was showing bad faith in refusing to start the discussions. We do not know what Orleans felt, but bitter disappointment would have been part of it. Suffolk must have been downcast and frustrated too, but he probably assured his prisoner that he would continue to work to bring about a breakthrough, and although he would have known that Bedford and Beaufort had done their best, he believed he might indeed be able to do so. He was writing regularly to his Burgundian contacts, and his herald must have carried many more letters to Dijon and Bruges in the days following his return from Dover.

He probably sensed from his feedback

what the Lancastrians had done wrong. They had expected too much of Burgundy. He was evidently not willing to be the linchpin around whom the other French dukes revolved. He needed to be assured more firmly of Orleans' goodwill towards both himself and King Henry (and indeed of Bourbon's too, although this was the task of other men). And perhaps they had made a mistake in planning so public a conference; this was still a stage at which groundwork needed to be laid in private.

The proposal that Suffolk worked on was for the duke of Burgundy to send envoys to England. There they would meet with the king, but equally to the point, they would meet with Orleans, and establish a more direct contact between the two dukes. It would not yet be face-to-face contact – Philip of Burgundy, the man who had failed to meet with King Henry in France during the coronation expedition, would not come in person to England – but it could be contact via a trusted servant of the duke. For preference, Suffolk probably hoped for his old friend Hue de Lannoy. In some ways that was better than dealing directly with the duke. Lannoy seemed genuinely sympathetic to the Lancastrians, and to Suffolk himself.

At the same time, after the débâcle at Calais, Bedford and Beaufort saw it as a risk to bring the two dukes together, even at second hand, and Gloucester clearly thought it not just a risk, but an unacceptable risk. It seemed all too likely that the Burgundians were playing a double game, and quite possible that the duke of Orleans was doing so too. Gloucester did not trust him, and nor did Beaufort or Bedford, but Suffolk did.

And he got what he wanted: word from Burgundy that the duke would send Lannoy and other ambassadors to England. They wished to meet with the king, and they hoped for Suffolk's good offices in enabling them to arrange this. They hoped, if they might, to meet with the duke of Orleans too.

Word came that Gloucester and Beaufort, plus Bedford and his new duchess, who were coming to England to meet with the king, were to land between Sandwich and Canterbury. Suffolk was among the party that set out for the coast to greet them when they landed. The Burgundians' ship must have outpaced the one carrying Bedford and his colleagues, because en route the group ran into the Burgundian envoys on their way to London. Perhaps Suffolk had planned this, though others in the group would have been surprised by the meeting.

Lannoy reported all that happened to his master the duke, and his reports have survived, so we know in some detail what happened. The Burgundians had brought Suffolk letters from the duke, and Lannoy handed them over in full view of the other English lords. Suffolk was apparently happy both to have the letters, and to have it known that he had been sent them. He was perhaps unwise to make this as apparent as he did. He was grateful to both Lannoy and his duke, he said. Indeed, he was at the duke of Burgundy's command, and felt more beholden to him than to any prince in the world. It was diplomatic overstatement, designed to please the Burgundians, but liable to rile those who had been involved in the failure at Calais when they heard it repeated.

They all returned to London, and Suffolk left the Burgundians to arrange meetings with the earl of Warwick, and with the cardinal. Lannoy reported to the duke of Burgundy that he had found Beaufort 'somewhat stranger than before', and although he must have been more diplomatic to Suffolk, he probably hinted to him too that he was finding the cardinal's attitude difficult. Suffolk could probably understand why. Many men at court must have

Oxborough Hall chapel, Norfolk
Photo Mike Dixon

been wondering why the Burgundians had decided to have discussions in London that they had declined to pursue in Calais. And those who had intended to take control of the negotiations at Calais, and now found themselves marginalized by Suffolk's plans in London, could be forgiven for feeling particularly irritated and uneasy. Beaufort perhaps did not know exactly what Suffolk had done to persuade the Burgundians to come to England, and if he did know, he did not necessarily approve of it.

Suffolk was taking a risk, but he certainly realized the need for caution. He had briefed Cauvel and his other aides. He had no intention of letting Orleans meet the Burgundians when he was not present. Every word spoken, every letter written, must be known to him. The rapprochement might go more slowly as a result, but that was a necessary price to pay.

The king, meanwhile, had gone to Guildford. He had a hunting lodge there, where he spent much time. The Burgundian ambassadors would have found it more convenient if he had been at Westminster, but there were men at court who wished to send a message to the duke of Burgundy, and forcing his ambassadors to travel to meet with the king was part of it.

It was not part of Suffolk's own plan to irritate Lannoy and his fellow ambassadors. So he worked on his colleagues on the king's council, to ensure that the Burgundians received a prompt invitation to join the king at Guildford. He went to Guildford himself too, and probably Alice went with him. She must have been curious to meet Jacquetta of Bedford, and Suffolk needed to try to ensure that the ambassadors were treated well, that the king came across as personable and sensible, and that Gilles of Brittany was much in evidence, as useful proof of the Bretons' support for the Lancastrian cause. Both Suffolk and Alice most likely also looked forward to this chance to enjoy the sport in the king's forest.

The king greeted Lannoy and his colleagues kindly, and Lannoy duly reported back to his master in Dijon that he had found Henry 'a very beautiful child, and well grown'. Intelligent he did not say, but he did describe Gilles as 'a very gracious and clever child'. Gilles asked the ambassador to send his good wishes to the duke of Burgundy. Perhaps he had been prompted to do this. It went down well, in any event.

Back in London subsequently, the ambassadors met and debated with the king's council, and told them that if the king wanted to bring the war to an end 'it would be necessary that he should be assisted by the great and powerful lords of the kingdom of France and neighbouring countries' – and that to get this assistance he would need to 'find means of contenting them'. Practical means, Lannoy meant, such as giving them money or granting them estates. It was not just Bedford's new marriage that had annoyed the duke. Burgundy expected to have his troops paid. He had expected too, when he joined with the Lancastrians, that he would be rewarded with titles and lands. As in Paris after the coronation, the Lancastrians had not been generous enough.

The English were not willing to be generous. That was clear by now. This was not the first such request that had been made. They all remembered Arthur of Richemont's loud demands for an earldom, and the dusty reply – and the result. But they had neither the money, nor the inclination, to bribe the French lords to support their king. If Suffolk felt frustration at this, he must have known too that it was something he could not change.

Bury St Edmunds Cathedral

More privately, Lannoy asked Suffolk where, and when, he might call on the duke of Orleans. At my house in London, was the answer. After dinner would be a good time.

The Burgundians were maybe used to eating early, because they arrived just as Suffolk and the duke were finishing their meal, which they had eaten together. What followed was a mixture of the stiffly formal and the more improvised. The Burgundians made obeisance to both Suffolk and the duke. Orleans took Lannoy by the hand, and asked after the duke of Burgundy. He is very well, he was told; and how are you? Well in my body, Orleans answered, but distressed by my circumstances, as you might expect. I have as you know spent the best part of my life in prison.

Well, said Lannoy, good might yet come of that. Perhaps you can be the mediator of a great peace between England and France.

'Here is my good cousin of Suffolk', Orleans said to the Burgundians, 'who knows how I have always offered myself to the king of England and the lords of his council ... but I am like a sword, shut up in a sheath, of which no man can avail himself unless he draws it.' He needed to speak to his friends in France, he said, and felt that the dukes of Burgundy and Brittany would be particularly useful to this end.

Lannoy assured him that Burgundy wished to help, and Suffolk said too that he had told Orleans often that Burgundy was well disposed towards peace. He did not doubt it, Orleans said, because 'I well know that neither he, nor I, are the cause of the evils which have come upon the kingdom of France.'

This was more than a little disingenuous. It could well have been said that Burgundy's and Orleans' forebears were the cause of many of the evils. And if they were not, then who were? The English? Orleans squeezed Lannoy by the arm, as if he would have liked to say more, but did not feel free to do so – as indeed he was not. This was not an opportunity Suffolk had provided so that the Burgundians and Orleans could join in criticizing the English.

But it had gone reasonably well, he must have thought. When they took their leave the Burgundians asked if they might visit again, and Suffolk assured Orleans that 'they will see you before they leave'. But he needed to make it politely clear that this would be done on his terms. Afterwards he sent Cauvel to the Burgundians. Cauvel explained that the was a guard, and a barber; that he was, too, a good subject of the duke of Burgundy. Men might imagine, he said, that Orleans had reason still to hate the duke of Burgundy. But he could assure them that this was not true, and that Orleans 'wishes nothing but perfect love and friendship with him'. To the end of a better understanding between the two dukes, he made it clear that he would be happy to convey messages to and fro.

The Burgundians returned to Suffolk's house the next day, to take their leave of him and of the duke. Orleans asked Suffolk in front of them if he might be permitted to write a letter to the duke of Burgundy. Suffolk replied, 'My lord, you shall deliberate upon it before night.' It was cryptic and tactful, and it did not mean yes. He sent Cauvel to the Burgundians' lodgings again the next day, to ensure that this message had been received, and to carry a letter to Lannoy from himself. Please do continue to correspond with me, it said. I shall be glad to pass any messages on to the duke of Orleans.

Church of St Peter and St Paul, Salle, Norfolk

45 The white staff

Suffolk got his first appointment in the royal household shortly after these events, in the late summer of 1433, when he became the king's steward. It was probably largely Bedford's doing that this place came to him. He received a white staff of office which symbolized his responsibility for the domestic running of the king's household, much as his own steward would have supervised his servants and domestic establishments; except that since in a sense the king's household comprised his whole kingdom, this was a post with external as well as internal power, and gave him good opportunities to exercise patronage. In theory it was a personal appointment of the king, so it reflected the trust the king was coming to put in him, but in practice the council would have had a sizeable hand in making it.

Bedford got a new treasurer, Lord Cromwell, appointed at much the same time. Suffolk must have looked on this close contemporary, whom he had known since Harfleur or possibly even earlier, as a potential if not a certain ally.

Cromwell ordered his clerks to take a good hard look at the king's finances. This was something too that Suffolk must have supported. He needed, as they all did, to know whether there was any realistic prospect of raising the money to send more troops to France. Or might it be possible to find something to pay Burgundy's men? It was clear that however they approached it, a peace on good terms was not going to come cheap. Could the Lancastrians afford to pay what was needed?

The answer was no. The king's debts after the coronation expedition were £165,000, more than three times his entire annual income. His income itself fell far short of his court's necessary outgoings, including the unavoidable payments for his mother's upkeep. Gloucester was collecting a fat salary, and Beaufort was rich, but the young king was flat broke. There could be no subsidies to the French administration. There could be no paying Burgundy's men to fight with the Lancastrians. There could be no bribes to pliable French lords. And there would definitely be no new great army.

This was dismaying. Suffolk and Cromwell made efforts to reduce King Henry's expenses. They despatched him that winter to the abbey of Bury St Edmunds for an extended stay. It was an expensive honour for the abbot, since he was forced to meet the costs of the king and his household. Beaufort negotiated terms for a new loan to the king, which proved sufficient to send Bedford back to France with a small force to help to keep Normandy secure.

Meanwhile Suffolk himself finally finished paying his ransom to the bastard of Orleans. One of the last things he did to achieve this was to sell the manor of Cotton, the place where he had been born. He continued to write his letters, to send his heralds to Burgundy, to Bedford, and perhaps to the bastard of Orleans as well. He continued to dine with the duke of Orleans, and to keep careful control of the communications – there must have been some – between Orleans and the duke of Burgundy.

46 One man to teach and one to ring the bell

Just as Suffolk needed to spend some time in East Anglia, renewing connections and meeting his obligations as one of the great lords of the region, so Alice naturally would have wished to spend time with her own family and on her own estates. She had been brought up, and her parents mostly lived, in Oxfordshire, to the north-west of London. The Chaucers' core estate was at Ewelme, the ancestral home of Alice's mother, Maud Burghersh, but another estate had been bought for Alice to make her home, at Donnington, near Newbury in Berkshire. This was about thirty miles south of Ewelme, so it was a day's journey on a good horse, or two for someone travelling with a baggage train.

Donnington Castle had been built at much the same time as Wingfield, in the late fourteenth century, but it was more of a fortified castle, with great stone buildings set within large banks and ditches, while Wingfield was primarily a manor house. The Chaucer home at Ewelme was probably also a manor house: there was no castle there, though Thomas Chaucer held the nearby Wallingford Castle for the king.

These were well-placed lands, at the heart of England, within good reach of London and Westminster. Cardinal Beaufort had broad estates in Oxfordshire, which Chaucer administered for him; and John of Bedford owned land in Swynford, the parish adjoining Ewelme. Ewelme was set in gently rolling countryside, not dissimilar to that around Wingfield: the village drifted gently down a slope towards a small brook which was famed locally for its sweet water, thought to have curative properties. Like Wingfield too, it was a small village, dominated by its church and its manor house, and probably inhabited mostly by servants and retainers of the family. It was not near to any large town, but close to it ran the great prehistoric trackway, the Icknield Way, which led across England to Norfolk.

From the brass of Thomas and Maud Chaucer in the Church of St Mary the Virgin, Ewelme
Drawing from Napier, *Historical Notices of the Parishes of Swyncombe and Ewelme* (1858)

Thomas Chaucer had had a remarkable career. He had been chief butler to the King for almost thirty years: the post, involving considerable control of the wine trade between England and the Lancastrian-owned vineyards of Gascony, and plenty of opportunity for patronage, that one of the early de la Poles had held too. He had attended at least fifteen parliaments, and been nominated speaker for a record-breaking five of them. In the 1420s he had sat on the king's council, and he had acted as an ambassador for Henry V in France and the Low Countries. He had largely withdrawn from public life at about the time that Suffolk returned to England, and perhaps by now – he was in his mid-sixties – he was not in good

Overleaf: the Godshouse, Ewelme
Right, Ewelme

health. But he had wide connections, a great fount of knowledge of politics, a shrewd mind, and if he was unable to take part in public affairs any more himself, he must have been eager to hear how Suffolk and Alice were establishing themselves in their turn.

The poet John Lydgate wrote a verse to Chaucer when he went to France in 1417, in which he described him as eclipsing the sun in his ability to run a household and provide an abundance of riches. 'Largesse, joy and all gladness, and passing good cheer with gentleness', was how Lydgate described him. So even in his old age, he would have been able to provide a good supper with a fine cup of wine, and excellent company to go with it. Alice's mother Maud was a few years younger: at this time, in her fifties.

Suffolk and Alice had only a short time left to enjoy Chaucer's company, though: he died at Ewelme in November 1434. That winter was a cold one: there was the greatest chill that men could remember, from St Katherine's day – a week after Chaucer's death – right through to the start of Lent. The Thames and other great rivers were so hard frozen that horses and carriages were able to cross them. The next year the crops failed, and in England and in France too, this was a time of famine.

They buried Chaucer in Ewelme Church. His widow and daughter built for him a great stone tomb, emblazoned with the arms of all the great families to which he was connected. This merchant chose to be remembered for eternity as a man at arms: on his memorial brass he wears the full plate armour of a man who went with Henry V to France and fought at Agincourt, and at his feet is a unicorn, the Chaucer family crest. Maud followed him to the vault three years later.

On her mother's death, the manor of Ewelme came to Alice – as did all her parents' possessions, since they had no other descendants. After that she and Suffolk lived there much of the time. They rebuilt the manor house into one so fine it was known as Ewelme Palace. The main buildings were built of brick and stone, and set within a moat, and the hall was built in a highly modern style, with a roof bounded not with wooden crossbeams but with great bars of iron. A private park surrounded it. When, much later, an inventory was taken of its furnishings, it listed 'several rich beds of cloth of gold, blue satin, and a bed of red sarsnet embroidered with my lord's arms and his crest' and 'a square standard [chest], covered with black leather, and bound with iron with two locks, the one lock broken, and the key with my lady'. In the chapel was an Arras tapestry with the symbols of the Doom.

They rebuilt the church too, in a style very similar to the Suffolk churches that the earl had known from his boyhood. It has flint walls, and a roof set with carved angels. Next to the church they established a school – it still exists today – and an almshouse, which they called the Godshouse. It had lodgings for two priests – one to be master of the almshouse, the other to act as schoolmaster – and thirteen poor men, though they were not to suffer from leprosy or any other 'intolerable disease'. They made endowments to pay these men forever – sixteen pence a week for the man who rang the bells to call the rest to service, and fourteen pence for the others. They were to wear cloaks with a red cross on their breast. All this was set in hand the year after Alice's mother died, so it was intended at least in part as a memorial to her parents.

47 The doom tapestry

In May 1435 Toison d'Or, chief herald to Philip the Good, duke of Burgundy, came to London. (His name meant golden fleece, the name of the great order of chivalry the duke had founded.) He had been despatched there in February, he explained to the king's council, but delayed en route by illness. His instructions were to invite the English to a peace conference that was being organized by the Church under the auspices of the duke of Burgundy, to take place in Arras, one of the duke's cities in northern France.

To be invited late to a meeting that was to take place very shortly was not something to inspire confidence. The English lords must have felt that if Toison d'Or had genuinely been so sick, some other messenger could have been found. And although they might have welcomed another attempt at a peace conference, they naturally would have preferred to organize and control it themselves, and not leave it to Burgundy. Anyway, why was the duke proposing it now? What had changed since the charade at Calais? Suffolk must have known that all his careful shepherding of contacts between the dukes of Orleans and Burgundy had not as yet resulted in a general agreement among the French lords to come out for King Henry. Nor had the English bought Burgundy, in the way he seemed to expect to be bought; they had not delivered on the veiled requests that Hue de Lannoy had made in London. The king was still a minor, and there was, as a result, still no realistic prospect of agreeing a negotiated peace that would grant him something less than the throne of France. So if they could not enforce a peace on the terms they would have chosen, and they could not expect to come to a satisfactory mutual agreement on lesser terms, what exactly did the duke of Burgundy expect to achieve?

The worrying thought was that Burgundy might be planning to come to an agreement with Charles of Valois. The Lancastrians would have known from their spies that Duke Philip had had meetings with the Valois that January in Nevers. Had Charles stepped into the vacuum, and made the kind of offer that Burgundy wished his king to make to him? Reparations for the death of John the Fearless, a personal apology to accompany them, and perhaps a clutch of towns in northern France? Was this a new charade, but designed this time to wrongfoot them and provide Philip the Good with an excuse to break his commitments and change sides? It must have seemed all too likely.

Hue de Lannoy followed Toison d'Or to London. Suffolk would not have asked his Burgundian contact what was happening in quite these terms, but he probably made it clear that the English were concerned. He did not get much reassurance. Lannoy spelled out that in his view, it would be worse for the English if they declined to come to Arras. Then it would be a peace conference between Burgundy and the Valois lords. True, at Calais Burgundy had claimed that unless every party came, there could be no negotiations. But this did not mean he would do the same again.

So the English agreed a delegation. It was a heavyweight one, and headed by churchmen, as was usual for these affairs. Cardinal Beaufort would come to France, although he intended to hold aloof at Calais, and not move on to Arras unless it proved necessary. As well as the general business, he had a more specific issue to pursue. His nephew the earl of Somerset had been a captive ever since the battle of Baugé when Clarence had been killed, fourteen years earlier. The cardinal was naturally anxious to see progress towards getting Somerset freed.

So Beaufort would be a shadow presence, and the archbishop of York would head the delegation. Suffolk was named as next in seniority to the archbishop among the negotiators. Perhaps he had chosen this. If not, he did not argue with the decision. These were not negotiations he would have wanted to lead, since it seemed all too likely they would not turn out well, but he wanted to remain closely involved with the wider negotiation process.

There was some debate about whether and how the Lancastrians might divide themselves into two parties, one representing Henry as king of England, and one representing Henry as king of France; and since it was clearly necessary to bring some securely Lancastrian Frenchmen in support, they enlisted the bishops of Lisieux and Bayeux. They agreed to send the duke of Orleans too. This time he would actually set foot on French soil: he was to wait with Beaufort in Calais. The duke of Bourbon was no longer in their hands, since he had died in captivity the year before. His long imprisonment had ended with his providing neither a ransom nor good will in France; deep rancour was its only legacy.

It was two years now since they had last lined up Orleans to take part in a peace conference, and for those two years he had continued a prisoner. Long acquaintance with imprisonment does not make it easier, and can indeed make it harder. The duke was no longer young, and it must have been agonizing to him to find his life slipping away, with always a faint promise of freedom, but never more. He must have wondered often whether he too was destined to die a captive.

St Andrew's Church, Norwich
Photo Mike Dixon

As his good friend by now, Suffolk knew how desperately he craved freedom. And he knew too that the chances of Orleans proving useful to the Lancastrians once freed were waning steadily. The duke's contacts in France were blunted. Many men he had known as a young man were now dead, and the others were virtual strangers to him. Even the bastard of Orleans, his half-brother, was a man whose face he did not know. There had never been any suggestion that the bastard would support the Lancastrians. The same must have been true of most other men who owed allegiance to the duke. And if Orleans himself counted Suffolk as his friend, and was willing to make compromises in the hope of freedom, still his predominant feeling towards his captors must have been a deep-seated bitterness.

These were good reasons for arguing for an end to his captivity, and there was Beaufort's reason too: that the earl of Somerset was more likely to be freed if this counterpart won his own freedom. Suffolk and the cardinal suggested to the council that it was time now to review the commitment that had been made to Henry V. Fourteen years on, the situation had changed in many ways. Was there not something to be said for agreeing to accept a ransom? Of course, the payment would also be useful in itself; perhaps something could be done with it to appease Burgundy and his rapacious lords.

The council's decision was that a ransom for the duke could be indeed be one of the proposals the ambassadors made. A hundred thousand livres, five times Suffolk's own ransom, was the amount mentioned. But this had to be part of an overall deal; Orleans would not be set free if none was reached. This was something that Gloucester particularly insisted on, since if a peace were agreed, they would not be breaking their word to the dead king in setting their captive free.

And since there was little or no realistic prospect of a full peace being agreed at Arras, they all – not least, Orleans himself – knew that this decision would count for nothing.

There were other problems as they prepared to sail to France. Bedford was sick. He had been in Paris when he was taken ill, but the city was not safe; the Valois had got almost to its gates, and the bastard of Orleans was besieging St Denis. The message came that Bedford had retreated to Rouen. He would not come to Arras, or even to Calais; if they wanted to speak with him, the English lords would have to go to Rouen. Suffolk might have done so briefly, but he had no real reason to talk to Bedford, because he knew the terms the king's council had agreed to offer, and there was no prospect of Bedford changing them. They might – if necessary – offer to cede to the Valois possession of (but not kingship over) all the part of France that the Lancastrians had never even pretended to control. They had phrased it as elegantly as they could, but this was the core of it. This was reckoned acceptable since it did not involve giving away the king's real inheritance. The Valois would realize that this was a titular offer and not a substantive one. There was no question at all of negotiating over the throne of France.

They could also offer a

The duke of Burgundy's city of Bruges

truce; but there was nothing in that to tempt their opponents, when their armies had a slight but real upper hand. They could offer the king's hand in marriage, and be flexible over a dowry. Charles of Valois' daughters had been mentioned, but they were Henry's cousins; this was a proposal that also had evident drawbacks, even if Charles might have been tempted, which was none too likely.

They left Beaufort and Orleans in Calais, and headed on for Arras. It was a border town, between France and Flanders, in the territory known as the Artois. Famous for its weaving trade, and in particular for the tapestries that had become synonymous with its name, it had long been dependent on English wool. But the Flanders weavers had had to learn to diversify their sources over the long years when battles and blockades had made that supply unreliable, and they were not as dependent on the English now.

The Lancastrians arrived at Arras before the Valois or the Burgundians. Preparations would have been under way to receive the ten thousand or so men expected to come to the town for the Congress: they would fill every lodging, and the underlings would have to live in a forest of tents in the fields around the town. It had been a hot dry summer following the icy winter, and it was already apparent that the harvest would be poor, and that many people would go hungry over the coming months.

Burgundy's servants had arranged the accommodation for the ambassadors, the two cardinals (other than Beaufort) who would mediate, and the other important lords who planned to attend. Arras was a double town. Up on the hill was the old town, the cité, which dated back to Roman times, with its narrow streets and walls of the thin bricks that the Romans had built with. There was a gate, the Porte de la Cité, and a ditch with a bridge, which led to the lower town, the ville, also securely walled, with two great marketplaces, the Grand Place and the Petit Place, and the rich abbey of St Vaast where the negotiating sessions would take place. Arras was built on chalk, and there were cellars under the old buildings, and tunnels too. It was a town made for intrigue.

One gate. One bridge. The cité was well separated from the abbey and the ville. Burgundy had put the Lancastrians in lodgings in the cité, while he and the Valois were in the ville.

Philip of Burgundy arrived, with three cartloads of jewels and plate. Although the mediators were neutral – in theory, at least – this was his conference, and he made that very clear. He would hold feasts and tournaments, play the grand host, and take part in the negotiating sessions too.

The Valois arrived. It was perhaps only now that Suffolk and the archbishop learned who was to represent Charles – who would not, apparently, come in person. The senior noble present would be the duke of Bourbon, son of the duke who had died the previous year in his English prison. It was an understatement to call this man hostile to the English; he made it clear that he would not in fact negotiate with them at all.

This left Arthur of Richemont as the main practical negotiator, which was not much better. Suffolk knew Richemont well from the siege of Meaux, and had heard plenty about him in the years since. That miserable siege had done much to end Henry V's life, and although Richemont could hardly be blamed for that, none of them had appreciated his attitude. They had liked it even less when he had crossed over to join the Valois.

The duke of Brittany, Richemont's elder brother, had a separate delegation. The brothers were not on the best of terms, but this was clearly awkward. The duke's son, young Gilles, was back now in France. He was still a great friend of King Henry, and his father was regarded as a Lancastrian ally, but they must have known they could not expect much practical support from him.

There were also delegations from various other lords great and small, and some of the towns and cities of France, but these had no real importance.

There were the usual formal processions and tableaux, tournaments and feasts, then the negotiations began in the echoing spaces of the old abbey. It was a creakingly formal process. The sessions were held in relays, with the Lancastrian, Valois and Burgundian ambassadors sitting in separate rooms, and the cardinals and their servants conveying messages between them.

The English made their offers, and as was expected, they were refused. The Valois also made their offers, which it was beyond the remit of the Lancastrian ambassadors to accept. They did not include a proposal to ransom the earl of Somerset.

In parallel, there were private discussions. Suffolk had men watching and listening, so he knew that Richemont and Burgundy were travelling in the middle of the night to hold candlelit meetings. He must have held some candlelit meetings himself, but not with Burgundy, and certainly not with Richemont. He had to keep working with less powerful men, such as Hue de Lannoy. There were the Luxembourg lords into whose family Bedford had married, and other men too perhaps who were worth sounding out, worth repeating the Lancastrian case to. And he doubtless did his best to charm and flatter the duke of Brittany's men. In the long term this might be useful; at the conference itself, he must have known it would not be enough. The difference between what was being proposed by the two sides could not be bridged, as had been apparent from even before the start.

Worse, the differences between the Valois lords and Philip of Burgundy were all too clearly being bridged. Nothing was said at the negotiating sessions, but word must have spread through the networks of watchers and listeners. Public atonement. A sizeable tranche of north-west France. Unreasonable intransigence on the part of the Lancastrians. A complete lack of realism. What could Burgundy do in the circumstances, but seek peace in the way that seemed most achievable? The cardinals had clearly been briefed on this, the Church would support it, and the English would be left isolated.

At the end of August, when they had been negotiating for a month, and had nothing more to offer, they sent for Cardinal Beaufort. It was unlikely that he could improve things, but it would be helpful to Suffolk and his colleagues to allow him to try. Then Beaufort, at least, could not blame them. Suffolk did not ask that Orleans be brought too. There was nothing the duke could do in this situation, and there was less than no prospect of his being freed, now that there was likely to be no Burgundian ally for him to join with.

Burgundy laid on a lavish feast for the Englishmen, and in the midst of it he took Beaufort and the archbishop of York apart. He berated them for their intransigence, and he all but spelled out what would happen now. It was the Lancastrians' fault, he insisted, that this great endeavour of his had come to nothing. He could hardly be criticized now if he came to his own agreement with the Valois.

Evreux Cathedral

Suffolk kept out of this debate. Perhaps he sat with Hue de Lannoy and watched, as Beaufort became so worked up that the sweat dripped from him in great gobbets. Lannoy was not happy about the situation. He was an honourable man, and he was not convinced that Burgundy had managed to create a justification for what he intended to do. This was a small compensation, though not much of one, Suffolk must have thought. But not all treaties hold indefinitely. Perhaps there would be some new assassination, some feud, that would break the Valois–Burgundian entente. If so, perhaps Lannoy would once again be useful.

They stayed a few days more, conducted another round of talks, spoke privately with everyone again. Then they set about leaving with all the dignity and pomp they could muster. It would achieve nothing to show pique, or complain again that this was unfair. This was as it was, and nothing more could be done.

Suffolk went to Rouen. He learned when he got there that Bedford's sickness had worsened. It must have been clear to Suffolk as soon as he saw the duke that he would not recover. This was a bitter blow too. John of Bedford was by far the best of the lords who controlled Lancastrian England and France. Cardinal Beaufort was not a full substitute, and Gloucester certainly was not.

The king, his court, his countries, would feel the loss; and it was a personal loss to Suffolk as well. If he had not always agreed with Bedford, he had respected and admired, even come to love the man. Bedford must have symbolized all that he had invested in France. It was all coming to an end.

And all he had worked for in England was in ruins too. The years of planning and scheming could not realistically lead now to a great agreement by the French lords to support Henry of Lancaster. They still needed to find a way to peace; there was nothing to be said for more years of war, with Burgundy as well as the Valois lords set against them. But he can have had little idea, at this time, how it could possibly be achieved.

Bedford died on 14 September, a week after the Lancastrian ambassadors had left Arras, and only days after Suffolk reached him. They buried him in Rouen Cathedral. Suffolk took the great silver seal that Henry V had given Bedford, who had used it as a symbol of his power as regent in France. He brought it to Lord Cromwell in Westminster, and saw it put in a leather bag in a great chest in the abbey. Of Henry V's three brothers, only Gloucester was left now.

Word perhaps came to him during his journey that the Congress of Arras had reached its conclusion, with an agreement made and a treaty signed by the French lords who had remained. Hue de Lannoy had been unhappy enough that he walked out of the celebratory mass in the abbey church. This was no use to Suffolk or anyone else, though; he would have preferred to keep the man at the duke of Burgundy's side. Afterwards Lannoy must have thought the same; it was not long before he withdrew his refusal, and swore to uphold the treaty between Burgundy and Charles of Valois.

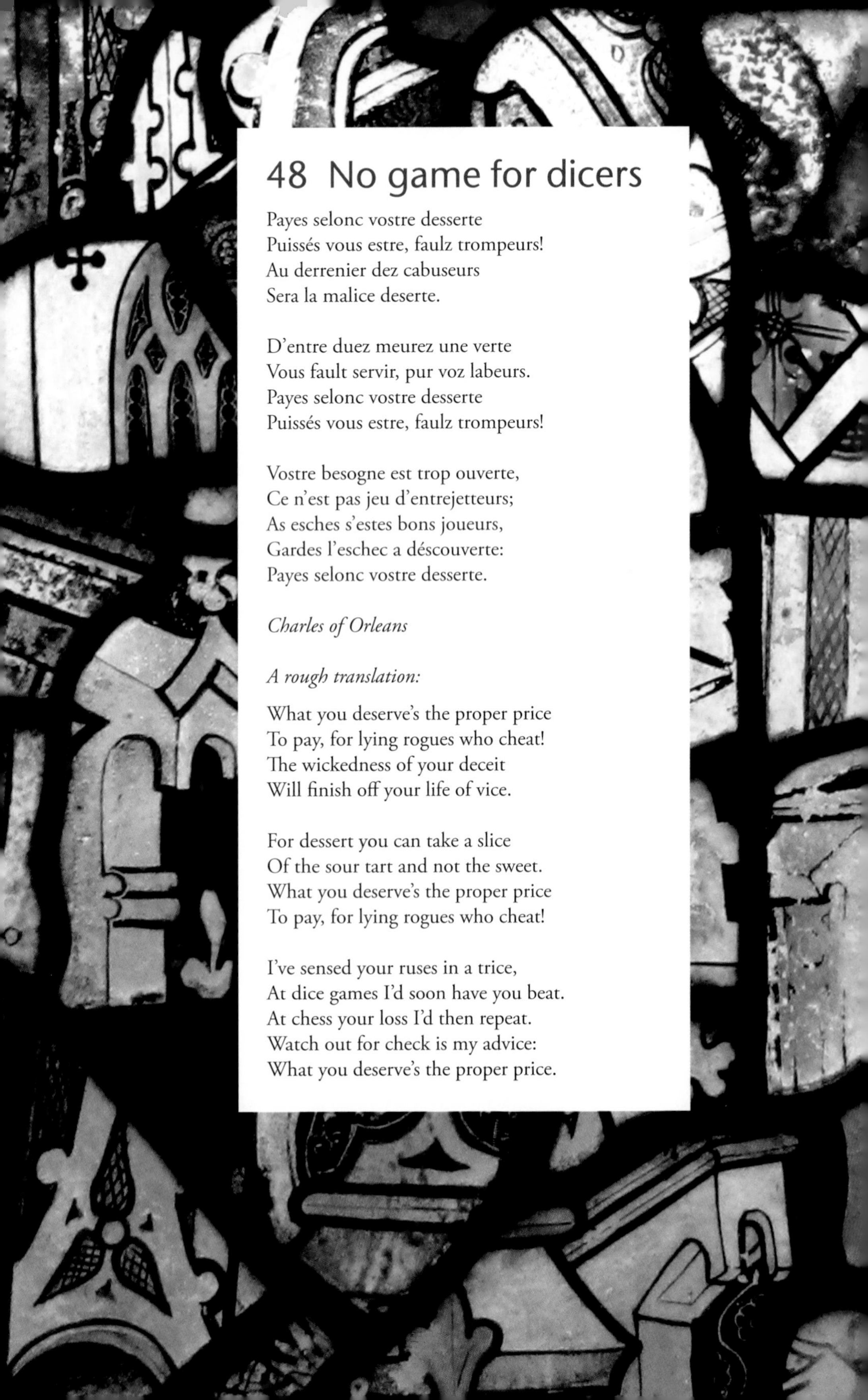

48 No game for dicers

Payes selonc vostre desserte
Puissés vous estre, faulz trompeurs!
Au derrenier dez cabuseurs
Sera la malice deserte.

D'entre duez meurez une verte
Vous fault servir, pur voz labeurs.
Payes selonc vostre desserte
Puissés vous estre, faulz trompeurs!

Vostre besogne est trop ouverte,
Ce n'est pas jeu d'entrejetteurs;
As esches s'estes bons joueurs,
Gardes l'eschec a déscouverte:
Payes selonc vostre desserte.

Charles of Orleans

A rough translation:

What you deserve's the proper price
To pay, for lying rogues who cheat!
The wickedness of your deceit
Will finish off your life of vice.

For dessert you can take a slice
Of the sour tart and not the sweet.
What you deserve's the proper price
To pay, for lying rogues who cheat!

I've sensed your ruses in a trice,
At dice games I'd soon have you beat.
At chess your loss I'd then repeat.
Watch out for check is my advice:
What you deserve's the proper price.

49 Killing cattle and scuppering ships

Coming back to England, with the great seal in his saddlebag, Suffolk was met with riots.

He must have been completely surprised. A trained and experienced man at arms, with a competent escort, he was not really in danger, but he might have had to spur his horse to get away from the angry crowds brandishing their saucepans and spades. And in London, there was more of the same. Burgundians' houses were being attacked, and more than a few were murdered. Lord Cromwell had taken charge, and was doing his best to get frightened men and women safely to the coast and across the Channel. But it was significant that this was needed: the Burgundians, innocent merchants and tradesmen, many of whom had lived in the city for years, were now not safe anywhere in England.

Later, once he himself was safely within the walls of his house in London, thinking over this, and perhaps discussing it with Alice, he must have understood it better. There were two issues that for all his hard thought and careful plans, he had most likely not fathomed at all.

First, there was anger, real anger, among the common people. He could see now that men not connected with the king's council had not understood what would happen at Arras. This was not just the ignorant: pot boys, washer girls, wasters in the taverns. Sensible, intelligent merchants and lawyers who took some interest in political affairs had not seen it either. To them, the course of the war had not looked as it had to him. They had cheered Agincourt, cheered Henry V's coup with the Treaty of Troyes. True, they had mourned the death of the king, but they had not seen it as a disaster for the Lancastrian venture in France, one that could not realistically be overcome, because there had been victories after it, many of them. Cravant! Verneuil! The king's coronation in Paris! These were the stories that had come back to England, been repeated in inns, over supper tables, in shops. A terrible defeat in battle would have registered with them, but few men were as eager to relate the tales of those, and the disasters that had shaped Suffolk's own experiences had barely made an impression at all. Montargis, the lifting of the siege of Orleans, Jargeau: none of these had brought hordes of maimed and starving men, staggering off the ships at Dover and making their way to beg on the streets of London.

Lancastrian France to most people was not the desperate, starving, shrivelled land that Suffolk knew. It was a great English conquest. And for them, this peace conference had been no charade; they had thought it just that. They had believed that the duke of Burgundy, that many Frenchmen, fervently upheld the rightness of King Henry's cause. Perhaps Suffolk had known when he went to Arras that he would not return wreathed in glory, but these other men and women had not seen this. What they had expected was another great triumph, the final, brilliant conclusion to the wars fought for the Lancastrian kings. Failure, and the news that Burgundy was following up the deal he had made with the Valois by moving to claim by force from the Lancastrians the towns that Charles of Valois had promised to him in northern France – St Quentin, Amiens, Abbeville, Montreuil and others – shocked and appalled them. And this was their response.

Suffolk must have found it hard to think of a reply to this. The rioting crowds were not in a mood to listen to cool reason, have it explained to them why peace could never have been the outcome. And even if they had been, he must have known he was not the man to

All Saints Church, Welbourne, Norfolk

do so, or Alice the woman either. Cardinal Beaufort could have done no better. They none of them had an easy common touch, and without that, there was no prospect at all of getting this message across.

The other revelation was perhaps even more alarming. He might get sympathy from Cromwell and some other lords, but he would not get it from Gloucester. On the contrary, in this Gloucester was his opponent.

The appointment of himself and the other ambassadors, the encouragement to Beaufort to go to Calais in support: Gloucester's hand was apparent now behind all the decisions that had seemed to emerge so artlessly from the council. And now that they had failed in a task they had never expected to succeed in, Gloucester was fanning the flames. Good Duke Humphrey had always had the ability to win sympathy from the London crowd. He was letting them think that the ambassadors in Arras had let them down, and that he, Gloucester, could restore the situation.

Suffolk could see now why this would be. If for him, the story of the king's council was one of a lord back from France, setting out to heal the breach between Gloucester and Beaufort, and use his success as a stepping stone in his career at court, the story was not the same for Gloucester. Gloucester had little or no interest in the advancement of the earl of Suffolk. His interest was, of course, in the advancement of the duke of Gloucester.

He took seriously – very seriously – the instructions his dead brother, the much-renowned king, had laid down. True, when it came to Jacqueline of Hainault he had had no difficulty in overlooking his orders, but even the best men can be hypocrites sometimes. To work, for however long it took, to secure the crown of France for King Henry VI; to keep the dangerous French dukes as prisoners: these were canons for him, sacred texts, not to be questioned. And the most crucial of all – because the most abused – was the other instruction King Henry had given. Bedford should care for his conquests in France; Gloucester was to have England.

Of course he was bitter, angered to the core, that the lords on the council had not honoured this. And now was his chance to put it right. There was no duke of Bedford now to thwart him. Cardinal Beaufort was ageing, and had aged faster at Arras. Now Humphrey of Gloucester could step into the breach, and take his rightful place as the ruler of England. Although much time had been lost, there were still several years till the king would take full control. It was long enough, if he acted now. He hoped to take England, and Lancastrian France too, and do with them as he chose.

Suffolk could not reasonably have foreseen that the failure in Arras, and the disaster of the Valois-Burgundian treaty, would be coupled with Bedford's death. Bedford had not been an old and ailing man, he had only been in his forties, and his last illness had not been long. If it were not that Bedford was no longer there to be called on by the lords who opposed Gloucester, his brother would perhaps have been more circumspect. But he was not being circumspect now, he was moving to consolidate his power.

What was more, Suffolk must have realized now that for Gloucester too, the war in France did not look as it looked to him. Gloucester had been little, if at all, in France since the siege of Rouen. The story in his mind was of the great days of

Trinity Church, Vendome

Henry V's early campaigns. True, Rouen had been tough, but they had conquered it all the same. He had heard the news since, but he too had not taken in what it really implied. Told that they must try their utmost to negotiate with French lords such as Orleans to bring about peace, and that they if did not succeed, they risked losing much of their gains; that at the very best, they could do no more than hold on until King Henry VI was grown, and leave him to make a painful compromise – perhaps Gloucester had listened to men suggesting this, but they had necessarily said it in veiled words, and he had not heard their true message. One more push: that was what he believed. For preference, of course, it would be one more push headed by the duke of Gloucester, bringing to him glorious, immortal triumphs, and bringing to the English a permanent conquest of France.

It was too facile to call it naivety. From his perspective, perhaps he could have believed nothing else.

King Henry had not foreseen the outcome either. When the duke of Burgundy wrote to him after the congress, he addressed him for the first time as king of England, 'dear lord and cousin', but not his own overlord. Henry's response was to cry. If this was exasperating to his courtiers, they must have understood it to some degree: this was a boy of thirteen, accustomed from his first thoughts to deference. He had been brought up to believe he was the king of France, and it was not easy for him to realize now that this was by no means a title he would hold automatically. If he wanted to retain it, he would have to –

Not fight; Suffolk and his colleagues knew the king would not, could not do that. Negotiate? They must have feared the king would never really grow into the wisdom to do that either. Then he must be led to the understanding that others must negotiate for him, and that he should be grateful, and not angered, even if they did not gain for him all that he had once believed was his birthright. This would be a major task, and they could not look to Gloucester to help them in it. On the contrary, he would undermine them every step of the way.

Perhaps Suffolk thought, at this point, that it was too large a task. His grandfather had been destroyed in serving a weak king. There was no guarantee that he would escape the same fate. Perhaps he discussed with Alice whether this was the moment to withdraw to their estates. And leave Gloucester to destroy all that he had fought to achieve? He could not do it.

Gloucester made some changes in the king's court, but he did not remove Suffolk from his position as steward. He probably judged that Suffolk had been weakened enough by the criticism, the public hatred he had borne the brunt of. Suffolk was not his enemy, as Beaufort was; Gloucester must have believed he was a man who could be controlled, and used.

What he did, though, was to remove from Suffolk's custody the duke of Orleans. The duke was put under the control of Sir Reynold Cobham, Eleanor of Gloucester's father. A man might as well have said, under Gloucester's control, since that was so clearly the intention. It must have been tempting to read this as mean-spirited, but it was probably apparent to Suffolk that there was more to it than this. When

Gloucester accused him of having become too close to Orleans, these were not empty words. Gloucester believed it. He saw no benefit in a lord such as Suffolk becoming an English friend of the duke of Orleans. Rather, he saw it as only one step from treachery.

To understand this can have brought little comfort to either Suffolk or the duke. True, there was no immediate prospect now of using Orleans as a tool for peace, but Suffolk had clearly come to value him as a friend, and he does not seem to have been a man to whom friends came so readily that he could equably lose this one. And Orleans was left with no prospect of freedom, no prospect of communicating with Jean of Angoulême, no prospect of exchanging poems with an admiring English lord. Perhaps he had never quite believed that the outcome of Arras would see him freed, but he had dreamed of it, surely. He had set foot in France, even if only in Lancastrian France, then been hauled back to his English prison.

This was not the moment for Suffolk to suggest once more that he might be ransomed.

The duke of Burgundy's next action was to attack Calais. He claimed it was in revenge for the attacks on Burgundians in England.

The English had to respond. That was one point on which Gloucester, Beaufort, Suffolk and the other lords and churchmen were all in agreement. They could not leave Calais undefended. The Commons in Parliament agreed too, and voted through a tax that would provide some, at least, of the funds that would be needed. Cardinal Beaufort provided yet another loan. There was not sufficient for a great army, the kind that could realistically reconquer all the territory the Lancastrians had held at their high tide, but it would be sufficient, they must hope, to repulse the attack on Calais, prevent any further losses, and perhaps take at least some towns back. It rankled that Charles of Valois had bribed Burgundy not with his own resources, but with land that had been held by the Lancastrians. All the English would have liked to punish both him and Burgundy.

Gloucester announced that he was requesting appointment as captain of Calais.

And it had to be agreed: that was clear. Perhaps Gloucester was no great commander, but neither Beaufort, nor Suffolk, nor any other lord had the power at that moment to thwart him. The best they could do was to ensure that men who might be able to influence him should go to France with the army. The duke of York offered to lead it, and Suffolk was probably glad to let him take the role. York had been sidelined for years, but he was an experienced commander, a man of high rank and some stature, and no ally of Gloucester's.

He would have to go back himself; he can have seen no alternative. And he perhaps had a hand in the appointment of the third commander. This was the earl of Salisbury

Somme estuary

– Richard Neville, a nephew of Cardinal Beaufort's who had married Alice of Suffolk's stepdaughter and claimed her father's old title. The commanders' appointments gave them liberty to treat for peace, but realistically this was no time to do that, with an army in the field against them.

It was spring by the time the army had been raised, and they reached Calais in May 1436 – without Gloucester, who intended to follow afterwards. The delay must have been worrying, since it was quite conceivable that Calais would have surrendered before they reached it.

But fortunately it had not. The Burgundians had set an army round the town, but to starve it out they had to cut it off by sea as well, and they had not attempted this till that spring. Even then, they made a mess of arranging the blockade. They had sent four aged ships, laden with stones cramped together with lead, intending to sink them and stop up the narrow channel to the harbour. But the Calais garrison managed to scupper one vessel before it could get into position, and the Burgundian admiral positioned the others so badly that when the tide went out they were left high and dry on the beach. The people of Calais fell gleefully on them and broke them up for firewood. The English lords, arriving in the midst of this Burgundian débâcle, must have been thoroughly gleeful too.

The rest of the Burgundian fleet stood off for a while, then made a retreat. The English heard later that angry Flemings had grabbed the admiral when he came ashore and murdered him.

The English settled into Calais, and Gloucester's herald did as the duke had evidently ordered him to do: he headed out to the leaders of Burgundian army, which still encircled Calais to the landward side, and proposed that the whole issue should be settled by single combat. Burgundy had offered this over Jacqueline of Hainault, and Gloucester must have seen himself revenging the slights he had suffered then, as well as winning glory now. If the other English commanders sighed, this too was something they could not reasonably prevent. Perhaps it would not happen, they must have told themselves.

And it did not. Burgundy's troops were mutinying by this point, and English spies would have been working hard to ferment the brew. When Gloucester's ship belatedly docked at Calais, the Burgundians were already striking camp, preparing to head for their homes in Flanders.

We'll chase them, Gloucester announced, and Suffolk and the others would have been glad enough to do this. They were so hard on the Burgundians' heels that they had to abandon most of their supplies, and even their armour. When their enemies had dispersed, and it was clear there was no prospect of battle, they turned it instead into a chevauchée.

They were in the rich territories of Flanders now, where there were cattle to be rounded up, villages to be sacked, and plenty of booty to be taken. Alas, most of the cattle they took died of exhaustion before they got back to Calais.

Gloucester was annoyed at that. But it had been a triumph for him, as he had intended. And he had looked and listened enough, gauged the size of this small army well enough, that he probably realized it would be the best of the campaign. Perhaps he would have liked to reconquer France, but even he knew he could not do it right then. So with the victory at Calais fresh in his and all men's minds, he set sail back for England.

York and his men could not do the same: this army had been raised for a serious purpose, and they needed to use it for the full season. Burgundy's defection had sent ripples through Normandy and beyond, and a number of the French were openly in revolt against Lancastrian rule. They set about the slow task of quelling the unrest, and restoring order.

In England, an unhindered Gloucester was wrapping up his task of reshaping the king's council. But that could not be helped. All this was work Suffolk knew he could do well, and York and Salisbury were men he could readily do it with. They made plenty of places secure, and won back a few that the Burgundians had grabbed. He must have visited many of the garrisons, including some in places like Avranches and Pontorson where he still held the captaincy, though lieutenants had been doing the work for years now. All the men he talked to would have mourned the duke of Bedford. Who would be regent of France now, they must have asked? Would it really be Gloucester, or would York be given the post? And whichever man was appointed, would he spend much of his time in Rouen? When would the king come back to France?

There were no easy answers to give them. There will not be a regent, in England or France, he could have said. The king is crowned now, so it would not be appropriate. There will be powerful councillors, though, and for the time being, the duke of Gloucester will be chief among them. Will he come to France again? Most likely not. Will the king come? No, there was no likelihood of that. Will someone be appointed to head the administration in Rouen? Well, it was needed, there was no doubt of that. But he had no idea what arrangements would be made.

He could praise York, and assure them that the lords in England, and the people too, cared that this territory should remain their king's, but he could not tell them that they would be given the support, the resources, to keep it so, because he did not believe that this would happen. He could not tell them that Frenchmen would help them; they all knew that few Frenchmen would. He could not tell them peace would come soon, because he must have seen little prospect of that being achieved. When the king was grown, then efforts could be made; but there would be neither a final victory or a negotiated peace under Gloucester.

They lost Paris that summer. It had been won with the duke of Burgundy, and with Burgundy lost, they had had no real prospect of retaining it. But they must have known that in England it would be seen as a failure on their part. The people who still seethed at the treachery of Burgundy were not going to be appeased by a list of smaller places secured, skirmishes successfully handled, rebellions quelled. Gloucester was the only one of them who would return in glory.

Trinity Church, Vendome

50 Such fraud and subtle means

Suffolk must have chosen his tactics by the time he returned from France. In the council, he knew, Gloucester would be dominant. Suffolk had little enthusiasm for slowly taking over from Cardinal Beaufort as he sank into old age and retirement, and leading the opposition in the council, fighting Gloucester inch by inch to get approval for the policies he favoured. But he had thought of a better alternative: to build a different centre of power, one that focused instead on the king himself. It would take some time, but he believed it could be achieved. For all his wider popularity, Gloucester was not much liked by his nephew, and Henry did not seem to care greatly for his duchess either. There was an opportunity here, and Suffolk intended to take it.

Henry had not as yet had favourites in the way of some earlier kings. Gilles of Brittany had perhaps come closest, but he had gone back to France, and there was no one now at court, either of his own age or older, who could have been called the king's special friend. Perhaps that would change as he grew to manhood, but Suffolk probably judged that it would not. He could not see Henry turning into a lusty youth, surrounded by pretty girls or boys. Suffolk had not the temperament or the inclination – or the youth – to flatter and seduce his way into becoming a king's bedmate. But if there was no one else in that position either, why should he not become as close as any man to the king?

This was a path on which Alice could help him too. She could not have joined the council, but she could be much at court, listen, make friends, plan with him to surround the king with the men and women they chose. He still had his position as steward, and that gave him a foundation on which to build. And since Gloucester did not spend much time with the priests who clustered thick about the king, he could hope to consolidate his position before Gloucester began to notice.

So over the next three or four years, they pursued this plan. It was in its way a demanding one. A man who had learned of the nature of kings from Henry V did not approach even a patently less impressive king without caution. Henry VI might not have his father's martial spirit, but he did have some of his stubbornness, and his fondness for formality and display. He could not be dictated to, he had to be deferred to. He had to be flattered; all powerful men do. And the king was always surrounded, of course; Suffolk would rarely if ever have been alone with him, and was only sometimes in a position to speak to him without being overheard. Whatever he said to the king, it could not include anything he would fear to have repeated to Gloucester.

What he said had also to be simple, since Henry was not one for complex arguments. So it was perhaps not much more at this stage than: in time, sir, we must make greater efforts still to bring about peace in France. We must give much thought to how that can be achieved. The duke of Burgundy is not to be trusted. The duke of Orleans might yet be useful, should you agree to ransom him. You will need, in due course, to discuss the issue of peace with your uncle, Charles of Valois, the other man who calls himself king of France.

Henry listened, sometimes at least. He also talked to other men, and made decisions of his own. This was not a situation like the custodianship of the duke of Orleans: Suffolk could hardly read the king's letters, or veto his choice

Evreux Cathedral

of intimates. If other men, later, thought of the advisers around the king as a close cabal, it probably did not seem so to him. But he did have influence. In time, he grew to have much influence.

At the same time he continued to attend the council, and he did his best to stay on tolerable terms with Gloucester. They would not be friends ever again, but he had no wish to publicly make the man his enemy.

But it could not be avoided: the policy he wished to pursue was not one that Gloucester would support. It would be useful if Gloucester changed his mind, but it was not remotely likely. He would always regard any proposal for peace that left Henry with anything less than the crown of all France as a betrayal, and at some point his opposition would have to be confronted.

As Suffolk continued this process, inevitably Gloucester grew increasingly uneasy. He noticed that fewer decisions were brought to the council; that often it seemed the King was making them in the company of a few close advisers – who did not include his uncle. The council met in the Star Chamber at Westminster, but the king did not always attend. And it could recommend only; Henry now had the last word. Gloucester had his own spies. They must have told him that in the king's secret chamber at Kennington, and his private quarters in his other palaces – plus the abbeys and great houses where his servants encouraged him to make visits, to continue to save on his household expenses – Suffolk and other men who, it seemed, were in league with the earl, were meeting with the king, and encouraging him to act as they chose.

Henry could now make appointments, and did so. He was generous, if erratically so: he was known sometimes to give the same estate, or the same appointment, to two or more men. That tendency had to be watched, but overall Suffolk encouraged the king's generous streak. It would do no good for him to be so very generous that he fell into serious financial difficulties, and as Suffolk knew, his treasury was always close to empty; there were loans from Cardinal Beaufort, and from other men, that could never realistically be repaid. But he had seen what the Lancastrians' meanness with their allies had done in France, and he did not make the same mistake with his own men. Rewards went their way. And they went to him too: it was proper that the king should show gratitude for his steward's services. In April 1437 Suffolk was appointed steward of the Duchy of Lancaster north of the Trent. In 1440 he was made chief justice of North Wales and Chester, and of South Wales. In 1441 he was appointed to a number of royal commissions.

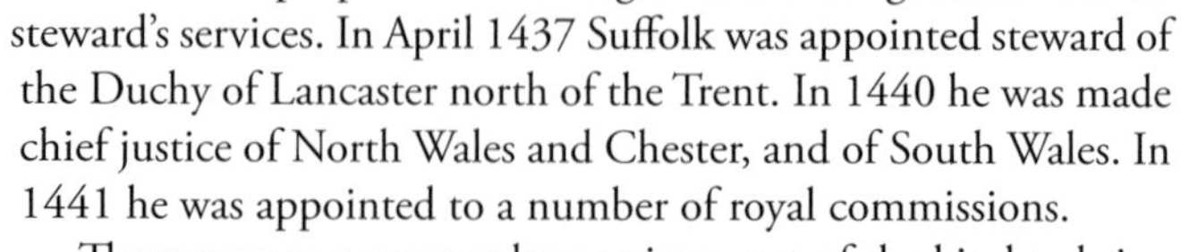

These were not spectacular postings, not of the kind to bring him triumphant cheers on his entry to London. But this was not what he looked for. They were useful positions, which enabled him to make contacts, and build networks of men to whom he could make it subtly clear that he was close to the king. He was careful not to be away from the king too much, though. He tried to leave no door open through which Gloucester might slip.

He spent some time in East Anglia, but not a great deal. There

Left top and bottom, St Mary's Church, North Tuddenham, Norfolk
Right, St Peter's Church, Ringland, Norfolk Photo Mike Dixon

was little to be gained by involving himself in disputes like the one between the prior and aldermen in Norwich. He had men in his service who could do this for him. He came when he was needed, to sit on commissions, and pass the judgments that Heydon, Tuddenham and his other retainers advised him to make, but he did no more than that. Lord Morley had died just before the Christmas of 1435, during the crisis over Calais, and if that cost him an useful ally in East Anglia, it also reduced his reasons for going there. His sister Isobel was a competent woman; she did not need too much of his support in her widowhood.

Catherine of Valois died in 1437. She had had several children by Owen Tudor, who were by then growing lads, half-brothers to the king. Catherine and Tudor had been rarely at the court, though, and Henry barely knew of these close relations. That was how it should remain: not just Suffolk, but all the lords reckoned so. Suffolk got the children sent to his sister Katherine, who was now the abbess of Barking Abbey.

This was a side-issue, though; there was nothing here that he expected to have repercussions. His focus was on ensuring that Gloucester's power in England was checked, by a king guided by more cautious and sensible men, and on paving the way for a peace in France.

And of course, he hoped to see the duke of Orleans go free. He had not made any attempt to regain the duke's custodianship. It was all too clear that this would have been unwise. Gloucester had spread the slur that his closeness to the duke was verging on treasonable, and this was not a period when he wished to give Gloucester any steel-tipped arrows to use against him.

He must have given much thought, at this time, not just to how a peace could be achieved, but also to how Orleans might play a part in it. If there were men who still believed that the duke must be made to swear firm allegiance to King Henry before he went free, Suffolk was most likely now not one of them. The duke's territory had almost all remained in Valois hands throughout the war, and it was firmly so now. This ageing man, returning to a country in which he was a stranger, could not single-handedly overrule men like his half-brother the bastard – a powerful captain still in the Valois army – and deliver his duchy to the Lancastrians, if there was no great movement of other French lords such as the duke of Burgundy to the Lancastrian side. It was beyond credibility that he could have achieved it. Suffolk's aim, surely, was to ensure that Orleans remained sympathetic to the cause of peace as a whole, and worked with both sides to bring about a negotiated peace in which both sides retained the land they now held.

Henry's land must be held in full sovereignty. Suffolk would not have tolerated an outcome which gave the king his territory only as duke, owing allegiance to an overlord – a Valois king of all France. There must be two kings of France, since both had been crowned, each holding his own separate territory.

Many men in France – both Valois-held and Lancastrian-held – would oppose this outcome, and many, probably most, men in England would do so too, so even this would not be easy to achieve. If he was to bring it about – and if he was to bring about peace, he must have seen its taking this shape – Suffolk would need help from good-hearted, rational men on both sides. So this was his purpose now for the duke. Orleans must agree to support Henry as king of the part of France that was in his hands.

In 1438 there was another peace initiative, and in 1439 yet another, but in neither could there have been any proposal along these lines from the Lancastrians. The king was not of age, and men in England were not ready. Suffolk was not appointed an ambassador either time, and probably was glad not to be. The negotiations were no charade, though: there were things they could achieve, albeit these fell well short of a peace treaty, and they could keep the idea of peace in men's minds, make the clear the difficulty of bringing it about: this was useful in itself.

Cardinal Beaufort took a major part. He had been building on his contacts with his niece, Philip of Burgundy's wife, and believed – with some justice – that although Burgundy would never now pay homage to Henry, still he was less unsympathetic than he had been a few years before. What Charles of Valois had offered him had not worked out well: the English had taken back most of the towns he had been granted, and the Valois had done nothing to help him regain them.

The chancellor, John Stafford, proved useful as well.

And Orleans played his part too. Although Suffolk did not travel to France, he perhaps met with Orleans as the man was prepared each time to join the negotiations should they reach a point when it seemed helpful for him to do so. It never did, but this was an opportunity to talk with him, and to reassure him that there were plans brewing that would in time have the right outcome.

St Peter Mancroft Church, Norwich
Photo Mike Dixon

The years were passing, though, and if they were bringing King Henry to full age, they were bringing Charles of Orleans to exhaustion and despair. Hopes raised, hopes dashed; trips to Dover, to Calais, and always the trip back again to his prison: poetry and courtesy could not have spanned the

Right: Wallingford Castle, Oxfordshire

chasm in his soul. Perhaps Suffolk felt sometimes that it was too late even to expect as little as he did from his friend.

In 1438 Beaufort believed he had got a deal that would see Charles of Orleans go free. But he had not; he and the duchess of Burgundy never quite agreed on what terms they had come to, and in any event, when a woolly-edged proposal was brought back to the king's council Gloucester stamped on it. But they got a ransom agreed for the earl of Somerset, after seventeen long years in his Valois prison. Once free, Somerset rejoined the army in France. Suffolk must have been glad of that: he knew the army needed strong commanders, and this man would be firmly on the cardinal's side, and therefore against Gloucester. But the whispers soon came back to England: Somerset was a broken man.

Cardinal Beaufort, and Suffolk too, worked in the king's council as well, and built up their network of connections. They were fortunate that for all Gloucester's power, he had few relatives on whom he could rely. Although the Beaufort lords were as closely related to him as to Alice, they were his enemies, most of them. The king was no supporter of his uncle, and Gloucester had no brothers alive, no sons except for an illegitimate one.

Suffolk, an earl with no surviving brothers, and his wife who had been an only child, were better equipped now than they once had been. As well as the chancellor, there were now other powerful Staffords, Suffolk's cousins. The earl of Stafford was particularly well regarded by the king. And the chancellor was perhaps responsible for introducing another bright churchman into the council: Adam Moleyns, who had written a well-regarded poem about English trade and sea power, the Libelle of Englyshe Polycye, clearly found common ground with Suffolk, and became a close associate of his.

Alice was perhaps responsible for fostering a friendship with Sir William Phelip, the brother of her first husband, who had become the chamberlain, another official in the king's household. The three of them – Alice, Suffolk and Phelip – were jointly given the constableship of Wallingford Castle in 1440. This was a stronghold not far from Ewelme, which Thomas Chaucer had once held for the king. It had been for a while in the possession of Queen Catherine, but she was dead now, and they moved into the vacuum she had left.

The Nevilles – the children of the cardinal's sister Joan Beaufort and her husband – were a numerous and powerful brood, and the earl of Salisbury was a reliable ally. Warwick had died in 1439, and his son was still a boy, a contemporary of the king – though a much more forceful and intelligent lad than Henry – whom Salisbury had got married to his daughter. York was mostly in France, as the king's lieutenant, and the earl of Somerset spent time in France too. But with the churchmen who were never Gloucester's friends, it was enough to hold the duke down. By 1440, they were ready to try again to ransom Orleans.

Much diplomacy – there had been much diplomacy throughout, working to bring Burgundy closer to them, to keep Brittany firm as an ally, to have King Henry start to write letters to his uncle of Valois – had produced a deal that Beaufort and Suffolk believed they could drive through. The ransom would be less than had been proposed two years earlier: 50,000 livres, not much for a royal duke, but importantly, a sum that could actually be raised. Isabella of Burgundy would play her part here. The duke's own estates could not do the job, so she had offered to lobby the other Valois lords. Her husband would not do much himself; Burgundy was one of those rich men who never put their hands in their pocket. Charles of Valois would not contribute, but that was as well.

Suffolk spoke with the king, and so did Cardinal Beaufort and other men. You believe in the cause of peace, sir. You have sympathy for the duke of Orleans, who has been for so many long years a prisoner. You will be glad to accept the commitments he makes, and allow him to go free to make your case for you in France.

King Henry did indeed believe these things, and not only because Suffolk had made the points too him many, many weary times. The king was a peaceable man, not cruel, but kind-hearted and generous. And if they had encouraged him – well, they had encouraged him to move down a path he was glad to travel down, put words in his mouth that had he had the eloquence, he might well have spoken himself.

All they had to do now was to get it past Gloucester.

Gloucester was opposed, of course. He would always be opposed to any agreement that ran counter to Henry V's dictates, and it could hardly be denied that this proposal did so, because there was no great peace to go with the freeing of the great duke. Suffolk and Beaufort could claim – and not only claim, but believe – that Orleans free would help them to achieve that peace, more than Orleans in captivity could ever have done. But freeing the man was not what Henry V had intended, and they all knew it.

So. Henry V had not always been right. He had had good fortune, and great skill and resolve as a commander, but his deathbed demands had been a long nightmare. Mind, Suffolk could never have said that to Gloucester.

Gloucester, though, did not use a wooden sword when he launched his own attack, which he made in the council, in front of the king. It started with Arras. What a disaster that had been, he claimed, and it was all the fault of Beaufort and Suffolk. What had they been dreaming of, hoping to reconcile Orleans and Burgundy? If they had not worked on this insane scheme, these two lords might have kept their quarrel going for ever. The Lancastrians could have kept the duke who was identified with the Valois safe in their captivity, and kept the duke who was his mortal enemy safely on the side of his jailers. But, dear God, this had not happened. The result of their utterly misguided endeavours was known by all men: because of 'such fraud and subtle means', the bulk of the French dukes had taken the Valois side at Arras, to the 'greatest charge and hurt of both your realms'.

He railed, too, against the present situation, the sidelining of the king's council, and the men who in clustering round the king, kept him from giving counsel to his uncle. This was an evil situation to him; what men said to the king, Gloucester knew, was not what he would have said himself.

It was vicious, and it would all be set down on the record. But they must have expected

Church of St Peter Mancroft, Norwich

something like this, and they had arguments to set against it. Most of all, they had the king to set against it.

Beaufort, Suffolk and other men spoke for King Henry. He did not speak for himself, but no matter: they spoke with his authority, and it was clear to all men, not just those who were there, but those would read the record, those who would hear from those who read the record, even those who heard from those who heard from those who read the record, that on this, the king and his uncle disagreed.

It was true, the king had chosen a different course from that which Gloucester was recommending. And there were reasons for it. 'Right other secret causes', that was how they phrased it. Causes not yet openly known, that 'moven the king greatly'. They did not need to spell them out, because they were the king's reasons, and this was enough in itself, but they added more. It had to be said now, if it was to be accepted later. There was no likelihood of the Lancastrians conquering a great country such as France city by city, fortress by fortress. Even if Henry V had lived on, they would not have had the resources to do it. Nor was there any realistic prospect of persuading the lords of France to bow, not even to the English king who had only partly conquered them, but to his son, who had not fought for this second kingdom at all. A negotiated peace was the only option, as indeed it had always been.

The choice of this course could not be set down to anyone other than the king himself. That had to be made clear, and the king was happy to let them make it clear on his behalf. Henry wished, his counsellors said, 'that it be openly felt and plainly known that that he has done in the said matter he has done himself of his own advice and courage for the causes aforesaid, moved and stirred of God and of reason as he trusteth fully'.

Charles of Orleans was delivered back to Westminster, to sign up to the promises he had agreed to make. He committed himself never to bear arms against the king of England, and to work to help bring about a peace between the Lancastrians and the Valois. It was not as much as had once been hoped, but for Suffolk at least – and for King Henry too – it was enough.

Suffolk met with his friend one more time, before the man went back to the territory of his enemies. He must have seen that if there was real hope now in the duke, there was not spirit, or drive; that was gone. It had taken too long: it was twenty-five years now since the battle of Agincourt. This was no longer a man who could take the jagged steel of the warring factions and forge it into a peace. To release him was still right, surely. Reason and justice, and the long years of real friendship, said it was so. And if he would not be a lion for the Lancastrians, he would not be one for the Valois either. But perhaps in the end, this would achieve no more than to give the duke a quiet old age spent not in England but back in France.

If he wanted to forge peace, Suffolk must have known, he would have to do it himself. But if all went well, Orleans would give him a little support when he did it.

Perhaps if Gloucester had seen how broken the Lancastrians' long-time prisoner was, he would have taken his defeat more gracefully. But he did not wait to see it. He had to stand there for the signing, but he did not stay for the celebration mass that followed it. He stalked off to his barge instead, and sailed away downstream to Greenwich.

Church of St Peter Mancroft, Norwich

51 The heavy lord and the good lord

Gloucester would look for revenge. His humiliation had been too complete and too public for it to be conceivable that he would not. Suffolk and his allies must have been wary in the weeks that followed the duke of Orleans' sailing to freedom in France.

Even so, he was wrong-footed when it happened. The duke of Gloucester and his countess went to Norwich. Suffolk's men must have reported to him that they had not done so on a whim: they had gone at the invitation of the aldermen of Norwich. The aldermen had held a great feast for them, and presented the duke with a purse full of coins: forty marks, so men said. Then the prior and the bishop had held another great feast, and Gloucester and Eleanor had enjoyed that one too.

It was perfectly proper of them. This was an invitation that would almost certainly have gone to the king, if the king had been minded to accept such invitations. But men were learning that the king was not; that although he was old enough now to receive men's petitions and mediate in their disputes, he was not willing (or perhaps, they whispered, but very quietly, not able) to do these things. What could be more reasonable, then, than to invite his uncle, Good Duke Humphrey, instead?

They could have invited the earl of Suffolk. But they had not.

This was his territory, though: the territory of all the men who had come with him to France, those who had died at Jargeau and elsewhere, as well as those who had come back – and, of course, more than a few who still remained in Normandy. East Anglia and its capital should have been the core of his support, the well from which he could draw when he needed to drink. He would have had to jostle for that support with the duke of Norfolk – that was how it had been for his father and grandfather – but he should have had his share of it. He could not afford to risk Gloucester poisoning that well.

And he must have seen now at least something of what Gloucester intended. If Suffolk had strengths in both his character and the position he had built up at court, Gloucester had his strong points too. He had his relationship to the king, as the one surviving uncle, whom men expected to keep a place at, or at least near, the centre of national affairs. And he had his popularity, his easy way with the common people. He had always been seen as the Good Duke. He not only meant to build on that: he meant to create a shadow to set his light in contrast, and he meant to put Suffolk in the black heart of it.

Suffolk should have known about the invitation to Gloucester in advance. No, he should have done more than that. He knew from men like Tuddenham and Heydon that there were problems in Norwich, and he should not just have been receiving the petitions, he should have ensured those problems were resolved. He should have been in a position to keep East Anglia firmly loyal to him, and not in one where men in Norwich were crowing about the interest that the man who had by now become his enemy was showing in them.

There were obvious reasons why he was not, and at the core of them was a lack of time. Attending on the king was his first priority, and this king was one who sucked in other men's energy, and gave out little or no light in return. If he was achieving things by all these hours spent at the king's side, they were not things that could be of immediate benefit to the aldermen of Norwich. There was Alice too, or at least there was Ewelme. Alice's estates still provided most of their livelihood, and it must have been Alice who insisted that they spend more time in Oxfordshire than they did in Suffolk. Cardinal Beaufort was near at hand, Ewelme Palace was new and comfortable: there were good reasons for favouring the place, but it did not alter the fact that he had neglected East Anglia.

Gloucester's visit did not lead to a resolution of the problems in Norwich. Perhaps Suffolk even thought cynically that this had not been his intention. Gloucester had spoken to both sides, bolstered the goodwill of both towards him, assured them he would do his best for them; he had not tried to create, and drive through, a compromise that could be made to stick. Other men would be left to do that, and to bear the anger that it left in the men who did not get all that they felt they needed and deserved.

Could he stand back himself? Suffolk must have asked himself that, but concluded that he could not. Men like Tuddenham and Heydon did not have the weight to drive through a resolution without public backing from him. The duke of Norfolk probably did not either – and even if he had, Suffolk might have hesitated to leave the matter to Norfolk. He must have realized he had no option but to go to Norwich, put time and effort into mastering the issues, and try to force a conclusion to the city's troubles before Gloucester put his bellows back to the fire.

Norwich Cathedral

Norwich is set in a valley, in which the rivers Yare and Wensum loop and drift before joining and heading east to the sea. In the centre is a hill – an artificial motte, built by the Norman conquerors of England, and surmounted by the huge square keep of their castle.

From the top of its walls – or even from the foot of them – a man can see all across the city, and perhaps Suffolk stood here at this time while his men reminded him of what he knew, and told him some of what he did not. He could see the city walls, built of flint like the dozens of towers of the churches within them, all of them the dull grey of stormclouds. He could see the spire of the cathedral, built in stark contrast in the white Caen stone the conquerors had imported, and the walls around the church and its vast abbey buildings, with their carved stone gateways blocked with sturdy wooden gates. The prior and abbot owned a great swath of Norwich, most of it green pasture, in contrast to the huddle of the city's alleys, the bustle of its markets.

This was a prosperous place, grown to be the second largest city in England, and one of the richest along with it.

He could see the chequered front of the Guildhall, where the aldermen had feasted the duke and duchess of Gloucester, an echo of the chess game he and Gloucester were playing for stakes even larger than the city. He could see King Street, and his own townhouse with its garden; across the city, the great palace of the duke of Norfolk. And he could perhaps see, upriver, the bulk of the new mills striding from bank to bank and blocking the stream. A corn mill and a fulling mill, for the use of Norwich's thriving cloth industry. His men would have told him there had been mills on that site since before the Conquest. But not ones like these, that prevented boats from getting upstream, dammed up the flow of water, and had caused floods all the way upstream.

He could not quite have seen from the castle, but his men would have taken him upstream and showed him the estates he had inherited from his father, grandfather and great-grandfather – those that he had not had to sell. This is your mill at Hellesdon, sir; as you see, it has lost its trade to the new mills in Norwich. These are your estates at Costessey, sir. You see where the land has flooded. And at Trowse downstream as well: all the flow in the river has changed, and it is men such as you who suffer.

He must have visited the abbey and spoken with the prior, and heard what the building of the mills had meant to him. The prior could no longer send boats from the moorings by the cathedral to his land outside the city at Holm. Suffolk must have gone to the Guildhall, and met with the aldermen and the masters of the guilds, and heard from them of their bitterness at the intransigence and greed of the churchmen – and the endless taxes to support the war, as well – and of the needs of the city, bursting out of the skin of its walls like a ripe peach.

He could see that, and see too that he had common cause with the prior in this dispute. But he must have been conscious that it was also important to pacify the aldermen, the guilds, the merchants. Some of them were powerful men, and they would make trouble if they were not allowed to retain their mills. And there were other issues that must also be considered. Heydon and Tuddenham might have hesitated to remind him about the ditcher

Near Hellesdon Mill, Norwich

who had been imprisoned, the petitions and pleas, the loss of Heydon's position as city recorder, but Suffolk had a memory; he would have recalled some of this.

Great Hospital Norwich

But he had been absent so much. Henry V's first campaign, Henry V's second campaign, and the years in France that had followed it; even the campaign that had been needed after Arras: it added up to many years not spent in Suffolk or Norfolk. It added up, too, to hundreds, thousands of men dead and buried in France, his brothers included, and too few living men who felt they owed him loyalty, let alone sympathy. Perhaps it was so long now that it was impossible for him to start to play the role that might have, should have been his. In a sense, he was in the same position as the duke of Orleans, returning to a country he did not recognize, and tangled in webs of men who were strangers; or the earl of Somerset, bewildered on the battlefield and unable to remember how to fight.

Absent in France, and absent in London and Oxfordshire too, he had depended much on Tuddenham and Heydon. These men were not fools, and would have kept close by his side on this visit. Perhaps Suffolk barely knew the city and its leaders, but Tuddenham and Heydon knew it well, and all the other places that Suffolk still owned in East Anglia, all the other hidden sores. It was scarcely in their interest to have Suffolk meet men who might have told him, your servants are corrupt and cruel, sir. Men regard you as a harsh and heavy lord, and much of this – almost all of this – is because of what these men do in your name.

So if he was cautious and wary, he was also perhaps even now not conscious of all that he had to be wary of. He listened to the arguments, spoke to some of the men who made them. Then he supported the setting-up of a commission to look into the problems. He ensured that Tuddenham sat on it. Heydon would clearly not have been a wise choice – he was part of the problem, and could not be part of the solution – but realistically Tuddenham was little better. Perhaps Suffolk did not know who else he might safely nominate. He told Tuddenham to ensure it found for the prior, and it did so. He perhaps told Tuddenham too to try to be moderate, to do so in a way that would not stir up more maggots that Gloucester could fish with. If so, he did not get what he wanted. The commission came down hard on the aldermen.

By the time the commission began their sittings, Suffolk was gone from Norwich. He was back in London, perhaps, hearing the news from France, and waiting to see what Gloucester did next.

Much of the news was as he must have expected. The duke of Orleans had travelled through northern France, and met with the duke of Burgundy, and Burgundy's wife who had worked to arrange his ransom. Burgundy had put on a fine reception, with parades, banquets and tournaments. The two great dukes whose ancestors had all but destroyed France had made their peace. Orleans had signed the Treaty of Arras, and joined the confederation of French lords who took the same line – which meant that they supported Charles of Valois, though in most cases without much enthusiasm. He had collected the insignia of the Golden Fleece, Burgundy's answer to the English Garter, and been found a new wife, since his last one was dead. This one – a young girl, decades his junior – was Burgundy's niece.

Then Orleans had ridden south to Bourges, to the Valois court, to present himself to Charles of Valois, the man who had called himself king of France for close on twenty years, during none of which the duke of Orleans had been at liberty to make obeisance to him. Charles knew he had come from the Lancastrians, and that if he had been their prisoner, he had nevertheless agreed to mediate at their request, and made promises – not just the promises Charles's spies and ambassadors had told him about, but for all the Valois knew, other secret promises as well. Why else had the English agreed to free him?

Men came out to tell the duke of Orleans that King Charles saw no reason to grant him an audience. He should ride on now, and go to eat quince marmalade and play at tables in his castle at Blois.

At this point, the pot in East Anglia boiled over. It was dramatic enough that messengers must have ridden hard to London, and gone straight to Suffolk, and to Gloucester too. When told of the fine the commission had levied, the order to demolish their mills, the men of Norwich had rioted. A man who called himself John Gladman had ridden through the town on a horse, with a paper crown and a sceptre and sword, claiming he would rule the town instead of the king. The ringleaders had rung the church bells, handed out swords, bows and arrows, and called on men to arm themselves and attack the priory. A huge crowd of them had done just that. The priory gates were holding, but only just. Fires had been lit, to try to burn them down. Help, help now! was the message from the monks.

The king's council met in emergency session. Men must have told Suffolk that there were protests against him too. Men were complaining of the rents and fines that Tuddenham and Heydon enforced in his name. But he had no time to dwell on it, and he was used to being unpopular from the years in France. At least Gloucester agreed, all men agreed, that action was needed immediately. They agreed, too, on who must take it: in these circumstances it could not be Suffolk or any retainers of his, and Gloucester did not offer to go there himself. So it would have to be the duke of Norfolk.

They must have waited anxiously then, to hear whether Norfolk had got there in time. They learned that he had, but only just. The troops that he had taken with him had put the insurrection down. He had promised an investigation, one that would look into all the claims and complaints, and this, it was clear, would have to be followed by firm action to enforce the decisions.

A paper crown. It could have been, perhaps should have been, taken as treason.

Henry V in these circumstances would have had men executed. This Gladman was not to be found, apparently. It had to be a pseudonym, and no one knew, or would say, who the man was. But this would not have deterred a man like Henry. He would have found a man who could be described as Gladman, and disembowelled him before anyone could say otherwise.

Well – this was not France, and the king was different now. And if Suffolk knew from long experience that Henry V's tactics had had their effect, he also can have had no wish to give Gloucester's men further ways to paint him as the heavy lord. Other men were saying differently. This had been no rising-up against the king. It was a pageant, one of the traditional parades that the guilds held in Norwich. True, it had grown out of hand, but at the root of it were images and words that men used often, in all innocence. A man could not be accused of treason for wearing a crown and carrying a sceptre in a play.

Suffolk took control. Perhaps he trusted no one else. He must have known that men from Norwich were calling on Gloucester, and being met with honey cakes and honeyed words too. But his had to be a different role. He saw the commission set up, and saw it drive through a decision that was mostly – as he had enforced before – on the side of the prior. No men were executed, and remembering the justice that had ruled in Normandy, he probably thought of this as lenient. There were fines levied on the aldermen and guilds of Norwich.

And when men grumbled, he saw more action taken. The mayor of Norwich was removed from his post, and a nominee of the king and his council ruled the city for the next nine years.

Church of St Peter and St Paul, East Harling, Norfolk
Photo Mike Dixon

52 Sir Roger and the Witch of Eye

If Suffolk thought at times, as he worked to restore a fragile peace in Norwich, that he had no option now but to try to take action to hobble Gloucester, he did not act on this thought – because he did not need to do so. Gloucester and his duchess brought about their own downfall.

It was, in a sense, Gloucester's learning that led to it. Knowledge is always a dangerous thing in an age of faith. Men of this era believed in God, almost without question, but to believe in the wrong article of faith could itself be a cause of a man's death – and had been, many times, over these men's lifetimes. They believed in the devil too, in dark forces. They believed in magic, things unseen and unknown. And they were both fascinated by and afraid of – and sometimes extremely cruel to – those who sought any kind of arcane knowledge.

It was only a step from the brilliant thinkers of Italy, with whom Duke Humphrey took so much pride in corresponding, to heretics, dangerous proposers of truths that threatened the powers of the Church, who questioned its monopoly of knowledge, and as a result must be destroyed. It was only a step from watching the stars and noting down their movements, to using them to tell fortunes. It was only a step from the white knowledge of medicine, of healing herbs and the control of the humours, to the black knowledge of poisons and abortients. At times it was no step at all.

In the spring and summer of 1441, these steps linked into a path for Gloucester and his duchess. It started perhaps with Marjery Jourdemain, the wise woman from Eye whom Eleanor of Gloucester, and quite likely Alice of Suffolk too, had consulted about their barrenness. Eleanor's childlessness had a particular importance because Bedford's death had made Gloucester the heir to the king. If Eleanor had a child, then the child would be heir to Gloucester, and at least until the king married and got a direct heir of his own, second in line to the throne of England – and the disputed throne of France as well.

One might move on to ask, then – would the king survive until this happened? Or might it be his fate to die too soon, like his father before him? Might there be ways – secret, arcane ways – of discovering these things? Might there be someone among the clever, eccentric men at Gloucester's manor of Bella Court who knew how to uncover them?

There were some such men, who if they did not exactly know, certainly claimed to have insight into such mysteries. Sir Roger Bolingbroke, 'a great and cunning man in astronomy', knew how to use the secret arts to look into the future. Master Thomas Southwell, a canon of St Stephen's at Westminster, was also a hanger-on at Bella Court. He might have been a man of God, but he

Church of St Peter Hungate, Norwich

was one who also studied things that no man learned in church. Urged on by Eleanor, and perhaps by Gloucester, they put on their shows, with candles and symbols and copper images. They produced a date when it seemed that the king might die, and told it to Eleanor. They also told it to others.

It was only when the date had passed, and the king was not dead at all, and they all breathed a little easier and believed a little less, than someone let the secret out.

Then it spread like Greek fire across the narrow alleys of London.

Church of St John the Baptist, Thaxted, Essex
Photo Mike Dixon

Suffolk would have known, as soon as these stories reached him, that they held the making of a treason charge. No man could admit to wishing the king dead. No man, or woman either, could admit to enquiring when he might die. This was no light dabbling in dreams. For him, it must have had its roots in Gloucester's greed – for money, power, fame – and in that part of Eleanor that had caused her to turn her back on her mistress and take her mistress's husband with her. It had its roots in Henry IV's ruthless usurpation of the throne of England, and his sons' destruction of half of France. It threatened a gentler king, and his dreams of peace. Other men perhaps would not see it in quite this light. But they too would know it was dangerous, and must be stopped.

He would have discussed with men such as Cardinal Beaufort whether they should move directly against Gloucester. Henry V had had less evidence than they had over this for the Southampton plot, and seen men who were his friends executed for it. But Beaufort and Suffolk lacked Henry's ruthlessness, and they knew too well of Gloucester's popularity, and of the king's soft-heartedness. They should move slowly, they must have decided; do what men called for, and no more.

Suffolk must have been conscious, too, that he and Alice had spent time at Bella Court, and knew some at least of the people who were named. The feud with Gloucester had distanced them, so they would have been there little if at all in the previous few years. However, Alice was still barren; there might have been whispers against her too.

So he waited and listened, and had other men listen for him too. Few spoke out in defence of the people who were named. There was self-preservation in this, but there was also shock and outrage. Good men and women did not plot against the king, and black magic was fearsome indeed.

The king must have been told of all this by his counsellors; he was rarely in public, and slow to hear rumours. His reaction was fear – to an extent that surprised even men who knew him well. Act, act now! the king demanded. Keep me safe!

So his men acted, in the king's name. They had Bolingbroke and Southwell arrested, and had it proclaimed that there was evidence these two men had conspired against the king. Bolingbroke was known to 'try to consume the king's person by way of necromancy', and Southwell had said masses in 'inconvenient places': more prosaically, in the lodge of Hornsey Park near London. On 25 July in that summer of 1441, the sergeants made Bolingbroke stand up in St Paul's churchyard, before the solemn mass began. They displayed a painted chair in which it was said he plied his craft, with a sword set at every corner, and a copper image hanging from every sword. Bolingbroke held another sword in his right hand and a sceptre in his left, and before a crowd of goggling Londoners, he swore to abjure the dark arts for ever more.

The next news was of Eleanor of Gloucester. She had fled by night, and was now at Westminster, claiming sanctuary in the abbey grounds.

Suffolk probably wished she had gone straight to France. Still, she had not, and the king when he heard was panicked again. So near! Keep her away from me! His courtiers calmed him as best they could. They took him to his manor at Sheen. It was far enough west that he could feel safe, though not so far that men like Suffolk could not ride between the king and the officers in Westminster who were doing all that must be done.

Suffolk must have known by now that this would be one of the hardest tests that he must face; as difficult, in its way, as the battles in France. He must keep the king's council solid and unified – apart from Gloucester. He must deal with the duke, and try to ensure he was weakened by this, but not by so much that it turned to sympathy and support from the mob. He must keep the king safe – from conspirators, but from the gaze of the public too. He must calm the king, and try to guide him to support the council in what wiser men chose. And not least, he must ride that untamed horse, the London crowd. Men knew what had happened in Norwich, only months earlier. It could not, must not, now happen in London.

With Cardinal Beaufort, and with other men in support of them both, he did all of this remarkably well.

Evreux Cathedral

The king insisted they must arrest Eleanor. Beaufort sounded out the bishops, and they must have agreed: if it was treason and heresy she was accused of, they could refuse her sanctuary and do just that. He and Suffolk talked to men in the council, and beyond, and got the sense that this would be given support. So men were sent in to the abbey, and the abbot and monks stood by as they led the duchess out. They took her to the Tower.

It could not be slow now. It had to be fast and firm, to keep down the shock waves rippling across the city. Suffolk and Beaufort perhaps sent men to Gloucester, and gave him the message: you know we are doing this because the king insists. But we shall try our best to leave you clear. There must have been men whom Gloucester valued enough to listen to, who pressed it home to him: you cannot save the Lady Eleanor now, sir, but you can save yourself. And Suffolk and Beaufort must have told themselves, we shall do well if we get all this dealt with, Gloucester weakened and no riots at all.

There was silence from Bella Court.

They would have waited anxiously for news from the Tower, where the serjeant's men were doing with Sir Roger Bolingbroke what all men knew had to be done. He had to be made to tell the truth, and there were time-honoured methods for forcing him. The messengers to Westminster and Sheen would have brought details of all that Bolingbroke confessed. Yes, he had done the magic that all men now knew he had created the tools for, and he had done it because Eleanor of Gloucester had begged him to do so. She wanted to know 'into what state she would come'. Would she become pregnant? More than that, was she ever to be queen?

Thomas Southwell was questioned too, but he died in the Tower before charges could be laid against him, which was unfortunate, but they would have to work with it. They had Marjery Jourdemain arrested, and questioned in her turn. She confessed that she had given Eleanor potions to persuade Gloucester to fall in love with her, and then to help her conceive.

All this was made known to the people of London, and beyond.

They burned the witch. It was to please the crowd, but it was more than that. They must all have sincerely believed that she had practised black arts; they all wished to see them gone in smoke.

Then the churchmen questioned Eleanor. The council drew up a panel of bishops – Canterbury, Winchester (the cardinal), York and Salisbury – and had the duchess appear before them in St Stephens' chapel at Westminster, where the dead Southwell had ministered. The charges they laid on her were witchcraft, heresy and treason, and Bolingbroke was their chief witness.

Suffolk and the other men of his household must have ridden many times to and from Sheen, telling the king all of this. Alas, it was clear the charges were true. All men were shocked and saddened, sir; no one wishes harm to come to you. Eleanor of Gloucester swears she did not intend that, but men now know she has asked questions she should not have asked, and dabbled with people who had ways of discovering answers to them.

If they thought of bringing the king out, they must have known they could not. He could not do, in public, what was needed. They must have thought too of bringing Gloucester to the king, and Gloucester's men must have asked for it. But the king refused to see his uncle, so Suffolk had to settle for sending messages to him. We are doing our best to persuade Henry to be moderate. She will be imprisoned; no worse.

News came from the sergeants: the duchess of Gloucester has tried to escape! But fear not, sirs, we have her secure still. She pretended to be sick, withdrew to her room, and got out of it and almost to the river. But we were on our guard, and captured her.

All Saints Church, Welbourne, Norfolk

They used this, since they had to. It was a further admission of guilt. The council must by then have come close to deciding – in private – how to deal with the duchess, and this would have firmed up those who were for a strong line. But they would keep Gloucester clear; that was agreed among them too.

There was a precedent, because Queen Joan, Henry IV's wife and Henry V's step-mother, had faced similar charges during Henry V's reign. She had been imprisoned for a while, and the king had taken advantage of her disgrace to plunder her inheritance, but she had suffered no lasting harm and had eventually returned to court. Many men remembered this, but the king would not have done so. Suffolk and others would have told him the tale, and perhaps suggested that it would be as well if the same were done for Eleanor of Gloucester.

And in time, be back at court? No. The king was adamant. She is guilty, she has admitted it. She must never come near me again.

More messengers must have gone to Bella Court.

Another commission was set up, of laymen this time. Suffolk was named as one of the commissioners, as was Lord Cromwell. They kept the rest of the council close behind them, and must have spoken often with the king. Henry was moving restlessly about southern England, as he had become accustomed to do. In the next few months he was often at Westminster and Sheen, but also at Eltham, Waltham, Hertford and elsewhere.

There had to be at least one execution. Men expected it by then. But they none of them intended Eleanor to go to the scaffold, so with Southwell inconveniently dead, that role was given to Bolingbroke. On 18 November he was dragged by a cart from the Tower to Tyburn, and there hanged and let down alive. His bowels were pulled out and burned, his head cut off and displayed on London Bridge. They quartered his body and sent the pieces to Oxford, Cambridge, York and Hereford, where they were set up as a warning to other men.

To Eleanor of Gloucester, they gave orders to do penance. She was taken to Temple Bar, and made to walk from there to St Paul's, dressed in a plain shift, carrying a pound candle all the way and then offering it at the high altar. A couple of days later she had to repeat the act, going from the Swan in Thames Street to Christ Church, and a third time she went from Queenhithe to St Michael's Cornhill. It was the kind of punishment given to common prostitutes. The dignitaries of London accompanied her, and a large crowd watched her carry out her punishment.

Eleanor made no protest, but did as she had been sentenced to do. And the crowd made no protest, but watched her do it. If they said in the taverns afterwards that it was hard on the woman, well, those at court might almost have agreed. But it could have gone harder, and they all knew it.

The council told Duke Humphrey that he must divorce her. If he was bitter – of course he was bitter – he must have known he could do nothing else. He severed himself from his disgraced duchess, and withdrew from the court to lick his wounds.

Then Eleanor was sent to prison, where she was told she must remain for the rest of her life.

Peterborough

53 Little John

There were slow months that winter. The pattern of power was changing, but it swelled as slow as a turnip in the earth: nothing was ready to be dug up yet. Gloucester had still to be watched. Suffolk must have wanted to press home his advantage, but he could not risk stirring sympathy for the duke. He needed rather to encourage men to conclude that Gloucester had been led a long way down a false path to a dead end in a dark wood. In the circumstances, the king's wise advisers might justifiably continue to keep him at a small distance from the king, and the king made it clear that this was what he wanted too.

St Mary's Church, Burnham Deepdale, Norfolk
Photo Mike Dixon

Although Suffolk could not expect gratitude from the Londoners, he got it from the king – and more than gratitude. Henry gave him the reversion of the earldom of Pembroke, and all the lands associated with it in the marches of Wales. This was one of Gloucester's titles, and it meant that if Gloucester died without an heir, all these lands would come to Suffolk. It was vinegar on Gloucester's wound, and the king must have known that, and chosen it. If men had thought King Henry incapable of being vindictive, they were learning different now. In his quiet, self-absorbed way, he knew how to work a knife between ribs.

News came from France. In time Charles of Valois had come around, and listened to pleas from the bastard of Orleans and other men. The duke of Orleans had been received at his court. He had his place now among the Valois lords; and he could speak to them of peace.

The king was of age now. He was corresponding with his uncle, Charles of Valois. He too spoke to his lords at court of his wish for peace.

What happened next was more good news for Suffolk. Alice hardly dared to hope; then she did hope; then she knew. She had done what the duchess of Gloucester would now never do, and was carrying a child.

It was too soon for euphoria, but time enough for joy. Eleven years, it taken them. Alice was perhaps thirty-eight. They could not hope it would happen again, so they had to pray she would carry the child safely to term, and that it would be a son and heir.

It would be an autumn child, like Suffolk himself, born when his father was close on forty-six. Alice must have rested much and ridden not at all, through a hot summer at Ewelme and Wingfield. And the child was born safely, on 27 September 1442.

It was a boy.

Suffolk called the baby after his brother: not Michael, but John. And although he had sold the estate a few years earlier, perhaps he now managed to buy it back, because he arranged for little John to be christened, just he himself had been, between the leaning columns of Cotton Church.

These were months to think of family matters: of young John and what could be done to prepare for his future, and also of the rest of the family. It was customary for the king to designate a guardian for a noble child, who would control the infant's upbringing and marriage. He gave this honour to the baby's mother, so Alice and Suffolk needed to consult no one else over what they arranged for their son – in law, at least. In practice, they needed to ensure that others were happy with what they chose, and they must have spoken to Cardinal Beaufort, and to other close associates.

Although he was still an infant, they must consider his marriage: a new alliance, to rebind old ties or forge new ones. They thought of the old earl of Warwick, and his daughter who was sister to the thrusting new earl. She died, though, before they could take it much further.

And they thought of the Beauforts. The cardinal had no legitimate children, of course, but he had had brothers and a sister, and they had had children and grandchildren. The earl of Somerset, the man who had been freed in 1438, seemed at this time to be recovering from his long imprisonment. Both Suffolk and the cardinal must have worked to help him rise, to tighten the Beaufort grip on power while Gloucester was still cast down. The king was happy to do what was needed. Somerset's earldom was raised to a dukedom. The earldom of Kendal was added to it, and he joined the knights of the Garter. He was appointed to lead a new army in France – to the dismay of York, who was still the king's lieutenant, and for years had not received the reinforcements he had pleaded for – but before he went, he got his wife with child. If it was a girl …

It was perhaps easier now for Suffolk to bring his bastard daughters within his family circle. He had had them brought up in Oxfordshire – perhaps not with, but at any rate near to, himself and Alice. And he gave some thought to his niece Margaret, Sir John's daughter. It was perhaps about this time that he saw her married, to Jean (or John), the son of a famous Gascon soldier of the period, Gaston de Foix, Captal de Buch. This was an archaic Gascon title, several of whose holders had been well-known soldiers. John de Foix was a soldier himself, and Suffolk watched out for him over the years that followed.

Somerset's child was indeed a girl, but that was the best of what he produced. Given an army to help keep France secure, raised at huge cost to the grumbling citizens of London, Norwich, Bristol and other places across England, he used it to attack the Bretons. Men looked on appalled. The alliance the Lancastrians had nurtured for decades teetered like an egg balanced on a fingertip, and looked destined to fall.

Then Somerset dragged his men off on a chevauchée, when York and other men would have had him invest towns that the Valois had retaken. What was this intended to achieve, his captains asked him? 'I do not divulge my secret to anyone,' Somerset told them. 'If my own shirt knew my secret I should burn it.' If he knew his own secret – which many men doubted – then it died with him, the following year.

Little Margaret Beaufort was his only child. She would be an heiress, and she had the blood of John of Gaunt in her veins. King Henry gave her wardship to Suffolk and Alice. They must have felt he might as well have said, this is my gift to you. Feel free to betrothe the child to your young son.

It was ambitious of them, and they knew it. For all they were rich and prosperous, for all they had achieved at court, men still knew what Suffolk's great-grandfather had been. And Alice, however grand she might act, had been a merchant's daughter, not even the child of a minor lord. It would take a tangled path indeed to bring this little Beaufort child much higher in the world, but men thought too that the king had no heir except Gloucester, and Gloucester had no heir at all. Perhaps the likes of Lady Morley murmured to them, is this wise? And perhaps in his cooler moments Suffolk thought, is any of this wise? The feud with Gloucester, the letters to the duke of Orleans, the men in Norwich who looked on him with the same dull veiled hatred as the townsfolk in Rouen and Avranches: was this how he had wished his life to be?

But he loved his son. He must have felt something not far off love for the duke of Orleans, and the dream of peace they had nurtured together. The king was favouring him, and Alice was warm with bliss. He could believe, at such times, that there were great things in store both for him, and for this son of his.

Outside St Clement's Church, Terrington St Clement, Norfolk

54 The captain of St Malo

Church of St John Maddermarket, Norwich

In the summer of 1443 Gilles of Brittany came back to England. He was now a handsome young man in his early twenties. It was nine years since he had left the Lancastrian court and returned to Brittany. Throughout all this time his uncle Arthur of Richemont had fought for Charles of Valois. And Gilles came now to protest at the earl of Somerset's sacking of the Breton stronghold of La Guerche, as well as to bring the new duke of Brittany's – his elder brother Francis's – offer to mediate between the Lancastrians and the Valois, when the diplomatic activity that was well under way led to a conference, and if all went according to plan, to peace.

Somerset was arguing that La Guerche was not Breton at all, it was a border town that had been held for the Valois, and the criticisms men had made of him were unfair. But Suffolk and the other Lancastrian lords could see that reparations would have to be made, and they were.

The offer to mediate was a little more tricky: it suggested the duke was more neutral than a Lancastrian ally, and although they all knew that he was steering a mid-course between the two sides, they had no wish to see it spelled out. Nor, however, did they wish to give Duke Francis all that he was hinting would be required to bring him to a warmer shade of neutral. The price tag was not just damages for La Guerche; the earldom of Richmond was mentioned yet again. As always, King Henry and his lords trod water on that claim.

They would have to hope that signing up young Gilles would be sufficient. As a younger son, he had not received much of an inheritance – the best of it was some lands on the Loire, that had been held for years by the Breton dukes – but as well as friendship, he had one very useful card to offer. His father had made him captain of St Malo, which was designated as a port favourable to the English, where the Valois ships were not permitted to dock, and King Henry's were welcome.

The king gave him a retainer – a thousand marks a year – and presented him with a cup of gold and a couple of missals for his chapel. If Gilles was happier with the first half of this offering than the second, he was diplomatic enough not to say so. He gratefully accepted, and headed back to Brittany as what his brother had not become, a sworn supporter of Henry of Lancaster.

Thank you, but no, was the answer to the duke's offer. The king was dealing directly with his Valois uncle, and no mediator was likely to be needed. Even if one were, it was difficult to see what Brittany could contribute, that men such as the dukes of Burgundy and Orleans were not in a better position to provide.

Gilles was barely back in France, though, when his messenger was back at Westminster. Help! was the core of the message he brought. The duke of Brittany had had no problem with the deal – it was what he intended, a relative tied to the English to balance out Richemont, and he must have guessed that the rest of his proposals would receive a thin answer – but Charles of Valois, when it had come to his notice, had reacted rather more forcefully. Brittany might claim to be independent, but Gilles owed allegiance to him for the lands on the Loire. To swear to King Henry amounted to treason; if the man chose to do this, he could not be treated as a lord of France.

So Valois troops had headed along to Gilles' estates, and repossessed the lot of them. The duke of Brittany was not willing to set his men against the Valois, so he was refusing to come to Gilles' aid. But the English would want to assist him, surely?

Henry was fond of young Gilles, but his lords did their best to ensure he was not tempted. They could not afford this, not now, when they had a real chance of negotiating for peace. Send messages of support, sir, Suffolk must have argued. Or let the lad come back to England. But no army – please, please, no army – to fight with the Valois on the Loire.

The king agreed, if reluctantly, and the crisis fell back from its high point. But Suffolk must have been uncomfortably aware that the one French lord who was sworn to King Henry was now landless and liable to keep causing problems.

St Mary's Church, Worstead, Norfolk

55 In the king's privy chamber

Nine years since Arras. Nine years in which the king had grown. He was of full age now, and although Gloucester might one day build back support in the council, the danger that he might rule England was gone, at least for Henry VI's lifetime.

And still no peace. Still the drain on men's lives and their purses in England that left the whole country fractious and edgy; still misery in Lancastrian France. The council in Normandy wrote a woeful letter to the king, which his English council would have read as well. 'Little diligence, or at least little effectual diligence, has been employed in bestowing care and medicine to relieve the affliction and to cure the grievous sickness of the state ... the hearts of your subjects are cast down and enfeebled, much chilled, and withdrawn from your love.' Other men who heard such words, and knew how little the king could do – or they themselves could do, or the duke of Somerset and the duke of York could do – were now agreed with Suffolk. Now that they could do so without acting treasonably, they must set behind them Henry V's great hopes, and settle for a peace in France on terms that were honourable, but necessarily lesser than had once been hoped.

Some negotiations had taken place; some of the ground had been prepared. Orleans was working for peace, and men well disposed to him might believe that Burgundy was too. Charles of Valois was perhaps less keen, but if it was offered on the right terms, he would surely agree.

As for what those terms should be, that had to be dictated by the reality: the solid possessions, and not the empty claims. The Lancastrians held all but a few fragments of Normandy. They held Gascony, as they had done since even before Henry V's first campaign. They had some of Picardy to the north of Normandy – and Calais, of course – plus some territory in the île de France to the east of it, and some in Maine and Anjou, farther south. They held Le Mans, the capital of Maine. Not Paris, not any more. This was not their high-water point, and there would always be men who said that if this was so, it could not be the right moment to negotiate.

But there was no prospect of the tide rising higher, as far as Suffolk could see. Somerset's army had achieved next to nothing, and there could be no new great campaign, since there was no money left to pay for it, and few lords willing to fight in it. The king still had a fine inheritance in France; now to secure it, let the land mend, and let England mend too.

They agreed, of course, that the king must hold the territory under his control (its borders perhaps tidied here and there, but carefully, with each concession traded for another) in full possession, and not as a vassal of the Valois. They could agree a title for him, surely: king of – not all France, perhaps, but some of it. It would be a fine thing if they could persuade the dukes of Brittany and Burgundy to pay homage to Henry as their overlord, although Suffolk might privately have thought this was asking too much. As for the Orleanais, the Bourbonnais, and all the other places the Lancastrians had never controlled – these could be left to Charles of Valois, or as they might call him if all was agreed, king of – also part, but not all of France.

If Gloucester loathed it, they could face him down, and other men too. For this, once more, Suffolk knew he could not expect cheering crowds in the streets. But if he gained this much, he could consider his life well spent.

A part of it would be a marriage for the king. That was what the king wanted, and what it was right for him to want. It could be – would be, if things went as they planned – a marriage with a Valois princess, one that would salve some of the raw wounds.

This would not be a daughter of Charles'. Although he had had eight, some had died, and others been betrothed elsewhere, and none had ever been what a sane man would have chosen for the king, or guided him to choose for himself. Nor did Charles seem inclined to offer one, so on that at least, they could all agree. Daughters of the count of Armagnac had been considered, but this had come to nothing. The duke of Burgundy could not offer a suitable candidate. So with help from the duke of Orleans and other men, they had settled now on a princess of Anjou.

This girl, Marguerite, must have seemed to Suffolk as good as they could hope for. She had been born in 1430, so she was younger than the king – and malleable, they must hope – but old enough to have children soon, and displace Gloucester as the king's heir for good. From all accounts she was reasonably pretty and intelligent. The girl was healthy too, not scrawny and half-crazed like so many of the Valois. With luck, she would bring to the king some of the backbone he lacked, some of the ability not just to sit on the throne, but to rule from it too.

There were drawbacks as well. Marguerite's father René was a learned man, well regarded, and a claimant to the kingdoms of Jerusalem and Sicily. But although he styled himself king of these places, he did not control them, so the titles were little more than a vanity. More problematically, he claimed Anjou, and his younger brother was count of Maine. The Lancastrian holdings became decidedly scrappy well north of Angers – which was René's capital, on the Loire downstream from Orleans – but they were not scrappy around Le Mans. On the contrary, it was firmly held. It had been suggested by the Valois – no, claimed; indeed, stated – that if Henry of England wished to marry this girl, he would have to concede the family's titles to these lands. But that could not be done, as Suffolk knew. Men in England would never have stood for it. Places in Anjou could perhaps be bargained for Valois-held places to the north, but Maine would have to remain with Henry. English captains had estates in the county. They had fought for these, won them hard, with blood and sweat. It could be argued that Henry's title to – to be overlord of Orleans, say – was as empty as 'King' René's title to Jerusalem, but the same was not true of his title to Maine.

René was also not rich. There could be no great dowry. This was unfortunate, but with so much to gain, if the Valois agreed to the marriage, and left a fair share of territory to the Lancastrians, it would have to be endured.

Perhaps the biggest problem of all, though, was the king himself. It was not that he was against the girl: on the contrary, he seemed very keen. He had not met her, but he had

St Michael's Church, Flordon, Norfolk

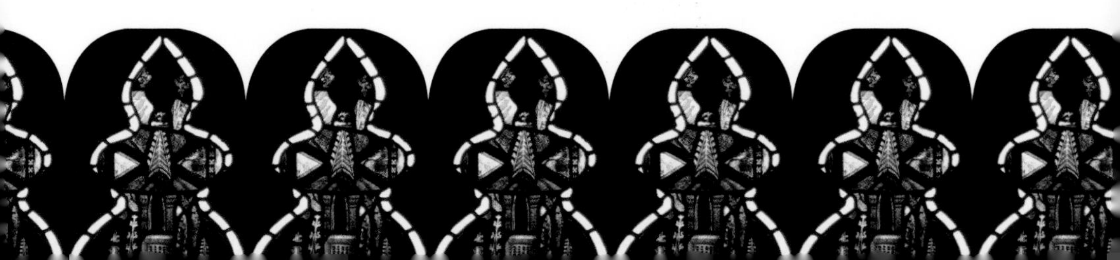

seen portraits of her, and pored happily over them. (She might be disappointed in him, but he was a king, of the very real country of England, and this was a marriage of state; she would have to live with that.) It was rather the question of what he was writing to his uncle of Valois. Suffolk neither wrote nor read the letters. Secretaries wrote them to the king's dictation, and he must have done his best to find out from these men what was in the letters. He probably did not find out much, but what he had learned must have made him uneasy. Did the king fully understand how one negotiated? That one held one's cards close, dealt them out one by one? That nothing must be revealed till it must, that one must work always to make the opponents lead? None of this came naturally to Henry's temperament. He was always too thoughtlessly generous. The message had to be put across, and Suffolk and other men had tried their best. You cannot give Maine to its Valois count, sir. You have given it already to your English lords.

Had the king heard this, he must have wondered?

Because in the end, it was not Suffolk who could choose the terms. The king was the king, and his counsellors owed him obedience. They could try to guide him all they wished, but they could not dictate to him; he dictated to them. They could not say to him, this princess, Marguerite, is tangled too stickily in a spider's web, let us forget her and look elsewhere – not now, when the king had seen her portrait, and was speaking of her as his intended bride. The ambassadors would be given their instructions, and Suffolk and his supporters could try to ensure before they left that those instructions were what they wished them to be. But if Suffolk were, say, to be handed a letter once he was in France, signed by the king's hand, with other instructions – no matter what the council believed they had agreed, the king could overrule them.

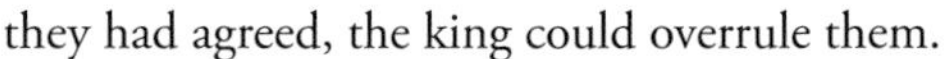

One other problem was personal to Suffolk, and that was the nature of his relationship with the Valois lords.

Gloucester had spread his poison wide. Many men must have thought by now that the earl of Suffolk was too close a friend to the duke of Orleans. Some also knew of his friendship with the bastard, whose brother had given him the county of Dunois after his release, so he was now a lord in his own right. And there were Burgundians to whom he had written, and counted as friends, and Bretons such as Gilles. To Suffolk, of course, these were useful contacts and not treasonable associations, but he knew they had always seemed otherwise to Gloucester. The duke was a wounded bear, withdrawn still but definitely alive. And it is the nature of a council or parliament that it breeds an opposition: by no means all men supported Suffolk and the cardinal, and he did not need to be told that some of those who did not were calling quietly on Gloucester at his country estates.

In these circumstances, it was an embarrassment to learn that the duke of Orleans and his brother the count of Dunois had written to the king, requesting that when an embassy was chosen to negotiate for the Lancastrians at the peace conference Charles of Valois was convening at Vendome, Suffolk should be part of it.

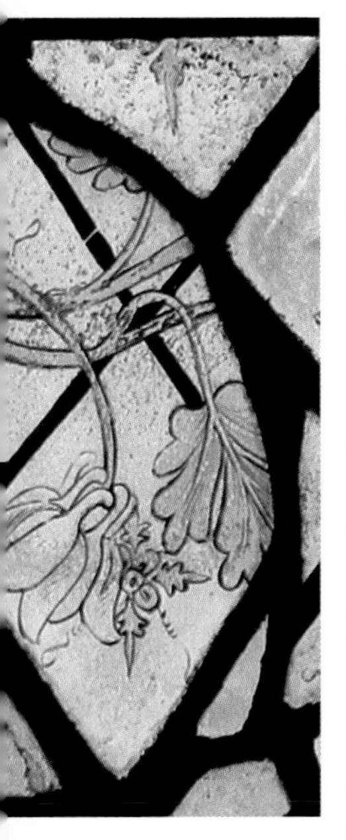

Much as he must have wished to see through the plans he had worked on for so long – and tempting though it would have been, too, to meet up again with Orleans and Dunois – he knew that he could not afford this. He must have given thought to how best to handle the situation, and taken soundings of other men, Cardinal Beaufort and Chancellor Stafford – newly raised now to be the archbishop of Canterbury – included.

They told him mostly what he already knew. This embassy must negotiate the king's marriage as well as the king's peace, and it must be led by someone who was close to the king and had his full trust. The king would never choose the duke of York for such a role. The cardinal was too old, and Chancellor Stafford was needed in England. There was no Beaufort lord with the skill and gravitas to play the part. Lord Cromwell had resigned the treasurership the previous year, after having made himself rich through it, and was focused on rebuilding his castle in Lincolnshire; nor was he particularly sympathetic to the peace proposals. Gloucester was out of the question. The king wanted Suffolk, the Valois clearly wanted Suffolk, so Suffolk it would have to be. What was more, although there were churchmen who could support him, there were none who could realistically lead the embassy, so he would not this time be in support of a bishop or archbishop; the weight of it would fall on him.

All he could do was to protect himself in advance, as best he could.

So this was what he did. When the council met in the king's privy chamber in Westminster, on 1 February 1444, he chose to make public his reluctance to take the appointment. He tried to draw Gloucester's poison by saying why. He mentioned his friendship with Orleans and Dunois. He emphasized too that he was no prince, but merely an earl. More exalted men than he had led negotiations and suffered for it; if an earl met with failure, the blame would fall harder.

The council set on record the fact that they had heard Suffolk's statements, considered his reservations, and decided to appoint him to lead their delegation. His reasons might be set on record, and he would be given an indemnity: whatever the outcome of the negotiations, any blame for it would not fall to him. Indeed, why should it, they pointed out? He was the mouthpiece of the king. He would and must negotiate as the king and his councillors dictated to him. They knew Suffolk for a reliable and cautious man, and whatever their doubts about his friendships with some of the Valois lords, they must have known he could be trusted to do just this.

The council agreed to Suffolk's request that himself should select the rest of the negotiating party. He must have given great thought to this, so it was by his choice that they were men of 'easy degree': not great lords, but men he could control. He looked for shrewdness and caution; he did not invite the reckless Beaufort lords or the increasingly powerful Neville men. He chose men he knew well, who were part of the king's household, or former retainers of his own.

He chose the churchman Adam Moleyns, who had been the clerk to the

All images, St Mary's Church, Gislingham, Suffolk
Photos Mike Dixon

king's council for some years, and was newly appointed to keep the privy seal. He took the king's secretary, the king's carver, his squire. And needing to pick a man from Lancastrian France, he picked the chancellor of Normandy, Thomas Hoo, a man who had served under him, and like the others, someone he knew well.

His other arrangements were more private. He remembered the riots that had followed Arras; knew that Norwich had exploded like a firecracker not so long before, and still fizzed and sparked under the foot of its royal controller. London had always been volatile; even Oxfordshire could be dangerous. He was leaving Alice in England, and their baby son. He must have wanted them secure.

So he made plans, probably at this time, for Wallingford Castle to be stocked and garrisoned. It was only a few miles from Ewelme, and Sir William Phelip, who shared its captaincy with himself and Alice, could be trusted to take charge of it in their interests. If there was unrest when men learned that the king was no longer to be thought of as king of all France, then Alice and John could retreat safely to within its stone walls.

This done, and the arrangements for the journey made, the necessary safe-conducts from the Valois issued, they set off. On 13 March they landed at Harfleur, where Suffolk's father had died half a lifetime earlier. He sent messengers from there to announce his arrival in France to the duke of Orleans.

Church of St Peter and St Paul, East Harling, Norfolk
Photo Mike Dixon

56 The Angevin daisy

Suffolk must have ridden many times from Harfleur to Rouen, since he had first come to France nearly thirty years earlier. He had never seen Normandy prosperous and at peace, and it was not so now. He had no army with him this time, but he needed the strong escort that he had.

En route, men would have asked him what was planned, and most likely been given the thin answers they always got from ambassadors who must keep their instructions secret. A peace would mean different things to each one. For a man at arms, the need to seek a new war somewhere else; for an English settler, the worry that a French claimant might return to dispute his lands; for a merchant, altered patterns of trade: it was too simple to say that they longed for agreement with the Valois, when they also feared change and wished to hold on to what they already possessed. But he must have got the sense, even so, that the time was right. Men did not say, fight on till we capture Lorraine and Provence. They said, bring an end to it, on terms that secure for us all we have gained. He could assure them that this was what he and his colleagues were hoping to do.

At Rouen they met up with Sir Thomas Hoo, and the other men from Normandy, both English and French, who would round out the delegation. Then in a large assembly now, they headed to the south and east.

Vendome is to the north of the Loire, and was on the border between the territories held by the Lancastrians and the Valois. Suffolk would have expected to find vast preparations under way, like those he remembered from Arras. They were not; and a first cloud must have drifted into the blue spring sky.

Excuses were made: Charles of Valois had fallen ill, and his chancellor had died unexpectedly. And the English had come sooner than was expected; always first to the venue, just like at Arras! It was no longer possible for the Valois embassy to travel so far to the north, but no matter, all was being rearranged. Rest, eat, drink, while we arrange your safe-conducts, and the remaining lords prepare to attend.

All this was wearily familiar, and Suffolk cannot have wished to travel well into Valois territory for a conference that should have been held on more neutral ground. Still, they had not come so far to ride home in pique; the Lancastrians settled in to wait at Vendome, and Suffolk Herald rode off to Blois to see whether they might learn more from the duke of Orleans.

He returned with an invitation. It would be weeks, perhaps, till the Valois were ready. But come to Blois, Orleans said, and meet with me now.

At such times, Suffolk was probably glad of his comrades of easy degree. These were men to whom he could say, we shall ride now to Blois, and they would agree.

So they rode on. The conference would not be at Blois, but this would be an opportunity to talk with Orleans and Dunois, without the rest of the Valois lords to watch them. That was useful in itself.

Part elegant chateau and part powerful stronghold, the chateau of Blois sits perched on a rocky spur above the Loire. Suffolk was met, most likely, in the Grand Hall, thirty metres long and eighteen wide, with columns and pointed arches dividing it into two huge spaces, and barrel vaults and walls painted with the lilies of the Valois.

And he was met with the grandeur and pomp of a French royal duke in his ancestral home.

Though impressive, it can have been no more so than the duke of Burgundy's court, or the great buildings of England – the Tower of London, Westminster Abbey, Norwich Cathedral and all the rest. He would hardly have been overawed, and the man who met him was not only a great noble, he was also a friend. But he would have noticed the luxury enjoyed by this man who had not paid his own ransom, and he would have noticed, too, the court officials deliberating – not rudely, but all too explicitly – how to deal with this embassy of easy degree.

An earl was a man of modest rank to head a delegation that would treat with a king, and none of his companions had even an earldom. There was not a drop of royal blood between them. From an English perspective, this was understandable. There were few dukes in England, now that all but one of king's uncles were dead, and all of them without direct heirs. But he perhaps sensed how it must appear to Charles of Valois, Philip of Burgundy, and some of the other great lords whose heralds and stewards were bargaining for lodgings at – it had been agreed now – Tours.

Nothing could be done about this now, and subtle questions later from Frenchmen who enquired after the duke of Gloucester and the duke of York, or even this king who had chosen not to come to France to meet the girl who might become his bride, could be given diplomatic answers. Meanwhile, he was able to tell Orleans his good news: the king and his council had agreed at last to release Jean of Angoulême. Thirty-one years he had been in prison, since 1413. It was far too long, and they all knew it, but at least his freedom could be celebrated now.

Suffolk would have met Orleans' young wife, Marie of Cleves, and of course his brother Dunois. He would have told his own news, of Alice and of his young son, and they would have drunk to his late-born heir, in the light Loire wines that Orleans had had brought to him throughout his years in England. Orleans had no son as yet, and Dunois, married for a second time, was childless too. But as Suffolk could have told them, hope kept alive can come late to flower.

There will have been feasts in the Grand Hall, and quieter meetings in the smaller chambers above. The first of the spring produce was in season around Blois, and there were the preserved fruits of the autumn before, the quince jam that the duke loved; fish from the river, beef and mutton from fields where no armies had fought. There were the poetry competitions that the duke so enjoyed, setting his comrades a first line, or a subject. Dean Moleyns was a poet too: the love of women was not his subject, but he could write of the love of God, the hope of peace, the joy of spring.

If they spoke of diplomacy, it would have been in general terms, since beyond the desire for peace, their interests in the negotiations were not the same, and nothing as yet could be revealed.

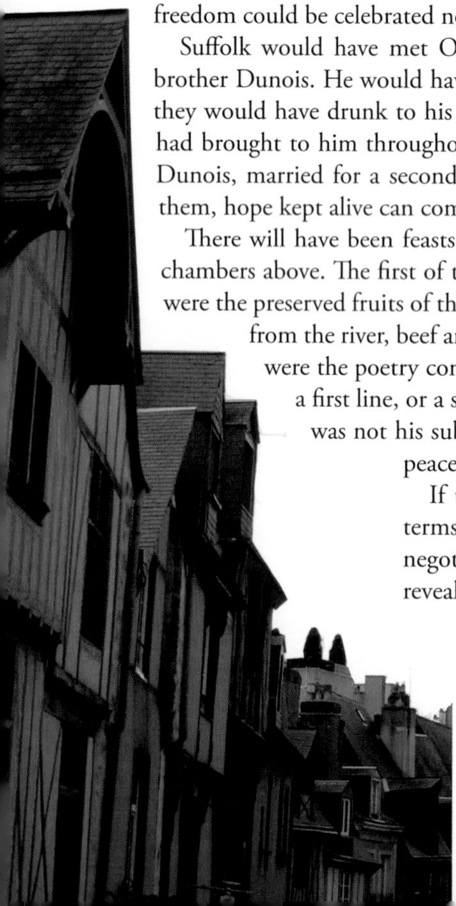

At last news came that they should travel to Tours. It was mid-April now, and the blossom would have been out, wildflowers in bloom in

Le Mans

the meadows, the birds singing as they were rowed down the river with the men of Orleans in their barges.

Tours was a great religious centre, and much like Arras, it was a double city, set on the flat southern bank of the great river. To the east was the cathedral, with its vivid glass and its echoing cloisters, and next to it the castle. To the west was a second centre, around the famous abbey of St Martin, with markets and shops, and between the two was a stretch of open fields and vineyards. Charles VII was not in the city, but at his chateau at Montils-les-Tours a short distance away.

Charles had not come to Tours to greet them, but there was a grand delegation all the same when they disembarked at the gates. They were met by the king of Sicily – this was how men referred to René of Anjou – and the duke of Calabria, his eldest son. The duke of Brittany was there, and the duke of Alençon, another of Suffolk's captors from Jargeau, although that incident would have gone unmentioned.

Arthur of Richemont he knew from the siege of Meaux, and from Arras. The frog-faced Breton had for many years been the Valois supporter among the Breton lords, while Gilles was the Lancastrians' man, and the duke stayed neutral. But the young duke of Brittany stood now among the Valois lords, at his uncle's shoulder. This was not good news. Prince Gilles was not there, but the estates on the Loire, not far from where they stood, that the Valois had taken from him and the Lancastrians had not helped him regain, would have had their place in Suffolk's mind.

They would have to wait to meet the prospective bride and her mother too. The duke of Burgundy was not present either. He planned to come to the negotiations, but would make his entrance later.

A game of precedence, that was what it was. Courteous, obtuse, carefully designed: to keep to the rules of chivalry, but in such a way as to wrongfoot the English. There was no easy degree to this reception; it was stiff with veiled intentions.

The heralds settled them into order for the procession into the city. Kings first – that meant René – then royal dukes, then lesser dukes, then other nobles in their order. The Englishmen were placed well back. For the churchmen it was no better: the papal legate who was to preside, the cardinals, the bishops of France, and in the tail, Adam Moleyns, dean of Salisbury. Give that man a bishopric! Suffolk must have muttered to himself.

The only cardinal in England was Beaufort, and he was not far off dying. He had not delivered what the pope had required, but had supported the Lancastrians with his fortune instead. There seemed no prospect of another English cardinal being appointed. The papal

The Grand Hall, Chateau of Blois

legate would preside over the negotiations, but the English knew all too well that the pope could not be regarded as neutral.

They settled into Tours, and spent another six days in feasts and poetry, masses and tableaux. This was a time to work, and since there were no other lords in the party, it fell to Suffolk to work on the French nobles, while Moleyns and the churchmen from Normandy did what they could with the bishops and cardinals, and the supporting laymen tried to forge links with the lesser men. There were meetings to which Suffolk was invited, but he must have known too that there were many meetings to which he was not. The duke of Brittany was probably elusive; it must have been clear that they had lost his allegiance. Suffolk had no authority to offer him the earldom of Richmond, and even if he had, it was years too late. Orleans was friendly as always, but not particularly useful. Suffolk must have come by then to the hard realization that the duke's reconciliation with Charles of Valois had not brought him great influence at court; that he had recovered his spirits but not the power that should have accompanied his position. Dunois clearly had considerable weight with the Valois as well as goodwill towards Suffolk himself, but he did not pretend to sympathize with the Lancastrian cause.

So it would be a hard peace they came to, with elements that would be resented by Englishmen. But it was in their own interests to agree that peace, he and his colleagues must have told themselves. And it was in the interests of the Valois as well. The churchmen, the nobles, the women at court: everyone assured the ambassadors they hoped for peace. And they knew what the Valois had offered at Arras, and knew that with the instructions they had now, they could agree such an offer. So it could be – surely it must be – achieved.

Six days later they travelled to Montils, and Suffolk got down on his knees before the Valois king of France, and presented him with the letters his own king's secretaries had given him, sealed with the king's signet and signed with his own hand. These public letters had been considered carefully, their wording discussed by the king's council. Charles was no longer addressed as the king's adversary of France, now he was his 'dear uncle of France'.

Charles was as Suffolk must have been told, a puny knock-kneed man who jumped at shadows. But he had changed greatly from the feeble dauphin whom men had expected to die as a boy. He had lived, married, sired a huge family, and kept reasonable control over his tumultuous flock of lords. He was famed for his mistresses, not least the notoriously beautiful and sophisticated Agnès Sorel, known as the *dame de beauté*. Moleyns must have been given a briefing: this is not the English court, where the king has never been known to have a mistress, just as his father did not either. Things are different here.

More than this was different. This was a court dedicated to pleasure, as the English court had not been in their lifetimes. The wine was richer, the food was better. The minstrels played. And the man they did not call king of France greeted the Lancastrian ambassadors graciously, and received the letters from his nephew.

The English were better fighters, they must have told themselves. This was a man who had lost half his kingdom. His nobles might be showing an united face now, but they had not put together a strong army and won it back for him. There might be a fine façade, but behind it, the Valois too were short of funds and low on hope. This king, like all kings, had to listen to his lords. Of course it would come hard to him to concede all claim to Normandy and the other lands the Lancastrians held. But Burgundy, Orleans and the rest had surely told him: you would have done it at Arras, and you must do it now.

Fontevrault Abbey, France

Then they went back to Tours. There was feasting and entertainment while they waited, but there was plenty of waiting too. On the first of May they returned to Montils to join the festivities as the dauphine – as the French called the wife of Charles of Valois' eldest son – rode out with 300 young gallants to bring in the may. The castle would have been thick with the scent of the heady white blossom. There was a marriage, young Charles of Anjou to Isabella of Luxembourg; there were archery contests between the English escort and the king's Scots guard. The Scots guards won, and claimed the prize. There were more poetry competitions as well. And there were plenty of cautious conversations, where men too schooled in diplomacy to reveal their honest thoughts would nevertheless probe, listen, speak in riddles and try to decipher them.

It was not till the third of May, a couple of weeks after the Lancastrians had arrived at Tours, that Philip of Burgundy put in his appearance. The next day they finally met Isabelle of Lorraine, René's wife, who called herself the queen of Sicily, and her younger daughter, Marguerite.

Twenty-three years earlier, Suffolk had been present when another King Henry met another French princess. Then the king had been a strong conqueror, and the girl a pale thin strip who had had little influence on him or his court. This girl was not the same: she was the envoys had described her, a pretty, plumpish girl with long fair hair and bright eyes. Her parents were proud of her learning, and rightly so: unlike Catherine of Valois she had been well educated and was intelligent enough to profit from it. This was a girl able to speak up for herself, who could be expected, young as she was, to hold her own in a foreign court. She was not getting the same kind of husband either, and it perhaps occurred to Suffolk that King Henry would find her a handful. But his orders were to bring the marriage about. She was as had been described, healthy and sane; there was no question of refusing her.

Once Marguerite had been shown off, she and her mother retreated to a nearby convent, and the negotiations proper began.

Perhaps Suffolk, Sir Thomas Hoo, Dean Moleyns and the rest had learned, or guessed, by then what the Valois had decided to offer. More likely they had not. They knew there would be little give from the Valois over Maine, Anjou or the duke of Brittany's allegiance; knew they would have to go to the limit of their instructions to agree the peace. But they perhaps thought still that if they went to this limit, offered all that had been requested at Arras, it was inevitable that the Valois would accept.

Not so. The papal intermediaries spelled it out: Henry might keep Gascony, Calais, and

a few smaller patches of land, but he would be granted none of these in full ownership; he must pay homage for all to Charles, king of France. He might not keep Normandy: if the English wanted peace, they must surrender this firmly held territory. There was no question of the English claiming Maine and Anjou: they must give up Le Mans, and every other place they held. Then, and only then, would the Valois agree a peace.

It must have seemed to them insane, outrageous. If the Lancastrians had been intransigent at Arras and since, they had had good cause; there was no more they could have conceded on behalf of a child king. But now it was not they who were being intransigent. They had moved to midstream, and the Valois had ducked the battle, and withdrawn behind their walls. This was not the basis of a hard negotiation, it bore no relation to the reality in France; it was, as every Valois lord must have known, bleak miles from anything within the Lancastrian ambassadors' authority to agree.

All this talk of peace, and all of it lies. If the Valois wanted a peace, they would have had to offer much, much more.

At Arras, Cardinal Beaufort had argued and sweated; now it was Suffolk who had to do it. He must have gone again to Orleans, to Dunois, to the duke of Brittany, to the duke of Burgundy, to many other men too, and worked on each one. What has changed since Arras? We hold still almost all that we held then. We ask now for what you would have given us then. A fair peace must mean that each side holds what it owns. We cannot surrender places hard-won; you know this, surely, as well as I. If you want a peace, you must accept these cold facts and agree a reasonable basis.

From many, he must have got little but shrugs and smiles. This is our king's position, and we support it. From Orleans and Dunois, perhaps he got more. Perhaps, late at night, under the stress and the disappointment, and with the consumption of much good Loire wine, the hard truths were said. But yes – things have changed. The English are disunited now, and the French stand side by side. And you know the reasons why. Men who would have taken Henry V as a harsh but fair king have no stomach for his halfwit son who does not fight or negotiate or rule even one country, let alone two. They might like the Valois little, but they like Henry of Lancaster less. When it comes to the hard core of it, they will not choose an English occupation. And they smell the discontent, waves of it from Normandy; the Valois might not be strong, but it is whispered now: the English are weaker. Why concede now what perhaps, one day, we will win back? The English in France are doomed. This is all we will give, but be warned: refuse it now, and next time you might be offered less.

Even if he could bring himself to hear this, he could not have accepted it. He was Henry of Lancaster's ambassador. He had fought in France for seventeen years. And he had not fought in order to give it all back to the damned, damned Valois.

The anger voiced – to the extent that it could be – they had to settle down again, and retrieve what they could. They had their instructions, and it would have achieved nothing to go home empty-handed, so they agreed on the lesser objectives. A truce was agreed for twenty-one months, and the Lancastrians insisted that the

Chateau of Angers

next round of peace negotiations would be held in England. Marguerite would marry the king she had never met, and with her would come her mother's claim – as empty as her father's claims to Sicily and Jerusalem – to the kingdom of Majorca, and 20,000 francs.

For this much, they would lose the chance to bargain a richer marriage for the king. But the king had to be married, and to get an heir. They were following their instructions. And the girl seemed promising enough.

A betrothal was the next step. Since there was no one more exalted on offer, it fell to Suffolk to play at being the king. The French were perfectly polite about this, but they were inflexible on the subject of precedence. Every man values his rank, the heralds would have emphasized; and of course he knew that for himself. So he had to stand and wait in the great church of St Martin at Tours, where the bones of the famed French saint were kept, while the lords and ladies of France filed into the church in their proper order. The dauphin and the bride's brother brought in Marguerite, and presented her to Charles of Valois, whom Suffolk still could not have called the king of France. Then Charles led her over to the papal legate, who had presided over the peace negotiations that in the end had not been peace negotiations at all, and who was to conduct the service. Finally the legate handed her to Suffolk, for the length of the service.

As soon as it was done, while the congregation was clapping and shouting 'Noel!', Marguerite was placed between the Valois queen of France and the queen of Sicily, and they paraded out of the church together, hand in hand, with Suffolk following on behind.

So this girl who had just bowed to one man who called himself king of France was tied now to another man who had been given no option but to continue to claim the same title. Two kings of France, neither with full possession of their kingdom; and a man who called himself king of Jerusalem and Sicily. René had never set foot in either of those places, he had no power in them, and no subjects who would have bent their knees to him. His wife had no queenly power either, but she was equal in precedence with the Valois queen of France.

This was a shadow game, but it was treated as real. From one perspective it was meaningless to claim to be king of a country that paid no attention at all to the claim, but from other perspectives it was not so. This was an acknowledgment of rights, of expectations, of the grandeur of a man's inheritance. Told that it made him ridiculous, King René would doubtless not have agreed. Told to surrender his title, he would have objected bitterly.

And the English had made it clear now that Henry's claim to the throne of France might be conceded. It had cost them no territory, but it had perhaps cost them, even so.

Even at the feast that followed, Suffolk was put on one of the side tables, while the new queen designate of England, who could also claim to be queen of France, sat at the top table between the other woman who claimed to be queen of France and the papal legate. Precedence, precedence! Everything the Valois were prepared to offer in the negotiations would have been decided before they ever sat down in session, but perhaps even so he might have wondered whether the Lancastrians would have fared better had the king himself come over, or a duke, or even an archbishop.

57 A truce was delivered at Tours

Durant les treves d'Angleterre
Qui ont esté faictes à Tours,
Par bon conseil avec Amours,
J'ay prins abstinence de guerre;
S'autre que moy ne la desserre,
Content suis que tiengne tousjours.
Durant les treves d'Angleterre
Qui ont esté faictes à Tours,

Il n'est pas bon de trop enquerre,
Ne s'empechier es faiz des cours;
S'on m'assault, pour avoir secours,
Vers Nonchaloir iray grant erre.
Durant les treves d'Angleterre
Qui ont esté faictes à Tours,

Charles of Orleans

A rough translation:

With England we came to agreement:
A truce was delivered at Tours.
Love gave us advice and its joy sent,
I abandoned warmaking for sure.
Others might plead disagreement:
In my mind, we need peace evermore.
With England we came to agreement:
A truce was delivered at Tours.

We agreed on some issues but then
went
Into silence; don't knock on that door.
Nonchalance is the path to
contentment,
We must honour our enemies more.
With England we came to agreement:
A truce was delivered at Tours.

58 An heiress and a bride

One last advantage of the low-key embassy was the scope it gave Suffolk to manage the news that came back to England and Normandy. Dean Moleyns and the rest had stayed solidly with him; they must all have agreed that in spite of their bitter disappointment, the outcome should be presented to men who had not been at Tours as a success.

And in its own way, it was. The truce was well received, both by men in Normandy who had longed for a respite, and by men in England who had no wish to be taxed for another great campaign. The king's betrothal was well received too. Suffolk downplayed the duke of Brittany's drift of allegiance, and as for the peace – well, it would be agreed in London in the next round of negotiations, people seemed to believe.

It would have been hard for him to believe that himself. But he knew too that there was no great might behind the fine Valois façade, and somehow, surely, a peace would have to come in time.

Meanwhile, he made it clear that although they could hardly create cardinals and royal dukes from nothing, they must do all that could be done to enhance the status of the English nobility, and in this the king was happy to oblige. Lord Stafford had royal blood on his mother's side; he was created the duke of Buckingham. The duke of Somerset who had threatened to burn his shirt was dead, but his brother in his turn was confirmed in the title, and since Suffolk and the men from Normandy must have stressed the need for reinforcements in the administration, lined up to go in his turn to France. The duke of York, still acting as the king's lieutenant in Rouen, might not like it, but it would suit the king's council for him to work alongside this rival.

At about this time Suffolk and Alice betrothed young John to Margaret Beaufort, daughter of the dead duke of Somerset, who had also been created earl of Kendal. There was no need for this title too to go to his brother: Suffolk pushed quietly for it to pass in a different direction, and although he had to wait eighteen months, in 1446 the earldom went to his niece Margaret's husband, Jean de Foix.

The king also rewarded Suffolk for his endeavours, by elevating him to a marquis, which put him in rank above the earls. It was a rare honour, and he must have savoured it.

Dean Moleyns got a promotion too: later in 1445 he became the bishop of Chichester.

Although men looked forward to the king's marriage and the coronation of a new queen, none took Marguerite of Anjou for a great heiress. It was Gilles of Brittany who won one of those.

No one offered her to him. None of the Valois, or his brother the duke, would have chosen to offer anything to Gilles at that time. In the uncomfortable position of being the sole French lord who remained a sworn supporter of Henry of Lancaster, he was something of an embarrassment to the duke, and an annoyance to the rest of the Valois. It might have been a wise moment for Gilles to abandon the English and join the rest, but he opted for a different course.

He needed considerably more money that Henry VI's modest pension. He needed lands, now he had been deprived of his inherited estates. So he picked out a girl who had them both, and set about making her his wife.

Her name was Françoise of Dinan, and her lands included the fine estates of Chateaubriant, La Hardouinaie and Montrafiland, and the good strong castle of Le Guildo, on the northern Breton coast, just west of St Malo. She was only eight years old. Gilles abducted her, married her – she was too young to consummate the marriage, but no matter there – and installed himself at Le Guildo. Then he sent envoys to King Henry, to assure him of his continuing support.

Hell, men must have said, good for young Gilles! If they were short of allies among the French, even better if the one they had kept had spirit and daring. He had picked his moment too, when the truce would make it hard to move against him. Perhaps, just perhaps, he would get away with it.

Suffolk's embassy had not brought Marguerite back to England: the marriage needed to take place first. They probably thought this no bad thing: a great expedition to bring home the queen, one that took a long course throughout the lands they held, could do still more to boost the morale of the Lancastrian French. Add Gilles and his new estates, hope for a quarrel between Richemont and the duke of Brittany – none too unlikely, from past experience – or even a quarrel between Charles of Valois and Burgundy, and it was not inconceivable that Lancastrian fortunes could surge. There was no reason to expect the tide of fortune to flow all in the Valois direction. Their task now was to ensure that it did not.

If Marguerite and her family had hoped the king would come in person for his marriage, they were disappointed. This must have been King Henry's decision. Suffolk can hardly have wanted to stand proxy again, or to spend more time away from England and the court. But this was what the king chose, and so this was what had to be done.

It would not be a hybrid expedition, like the king's French coronation, undertaken with an army. That was not an option because of the truce. It needed instead to focus on the kind of display that the Valois had put on in Tours, but that the English must have reassured themselves they could still do better. There would be women this time, as was appropriate to escort the new queen, and Alice of Suffolk would of course be among them. The widowed duchess of Bedford would come, and so would Lady Salisbury, plus the bishop of Norwich and other churchmen. By the time it was all agreed, the party to collect the queen contained five barons and baronesses, seventeen knights, 65 esquires and 215 yeomen to serve and guard them.

It took till mid-November of 1444 to put it all together. Seventy ships sailed across the Channel, carrying not just this host of men and women, but their best gowns, their jewels, their coaches and litters, and everything they needed to dazzle the French. They travelled right through northern France, heading not for Anjou but for Lorraine: to Nancy, in the far north-east. Marguerite's mother was a princess of Lorraine, and it was probably Charles of Valois' choice that she should be married there. Since his army no longer needed to fight in western France, he had diverted it to deal with trouble in the east, and was keeping court in Nancy while his men were laying siege to Metz. Quite a few of the English captains had come there too: they needed pay, needed a war to provide it, and the Lancastrians had no objection to their selling their services to either side.

The siege itself was a nuisance, since the Valois made it clear that the marriage could not take place till it was brought to a conclusion. The Lancastrians had to kick their heels in Nancy all through that winter. It had never been like this in Henry V's day, they must have grumbled. They had not even Marguerite to befriend, since the Valois had made no move to bring her from Anjou.

There was much they could have, should have, done in England. Men in England, meanwhile, were surely asking what they were doing in Lorraine. Gloucester and his supporters would seed rumours. Secret concessions in return for the marriage, close friendships and treachery with the Valois lords – this was a story Suffolk knew all too well.

One new piece of information did come to him in Nancy, from the English captains who were fighting as mercenaries for the French. There was a sharp man called Matthew Gough, whom Suffolk would already have known. There are good German siege engineers at Metz, he reported, and other good German mercenaries too. They are advising the Valois. We all know Charles of Valois is no fighter, but he has some strong lieutenants, as you know: Richemont, Dunois, a handful of others. They are persuading him now to do what he should have done years ago, and reform his army. A proper system of levies, professional advisers: when this truce is over, we shall face a different kind of enemy.

Suffolk listened. He sent messages back to the English council, to remind them that during the truce, the defences of Lancastrian France must be strengthened. But he knew even as he instructed his herald that there was neither the money nor the will in England to do this.

At last the defenders of Metz agreed to negotiate with the Valois; at last Marguerite was sent for. Finally, in March of 1445 Suffolk stood proxy again for his king. Alice sat in the congregation at Nancy Cathedral and watched as her husband underwent a marriage ceremony with Marguerite of Anjou. It was bizarre enough that we must hope they laughed.

Marguerite seemed overwhelmed, and wept to have to leave her family for this husband she had still not met. This was only the start, though: in time, if all went well, she would be a steadying influence, the public face the monarchy needed, and of course, the mother of the next king of England.

Eight days of festivities followed, then the new queen had to be escorted home. Each detail of this had been carefully negotiated, by two sides fighting for advantage, but in velvet rather than in steel.

St Mary's Church, Burnham Deepdale, Norfolk
Photo Mike Dixon

Charles of Valois escorted his niece a short way out of Nancy, then her father took her as far as Bar-le-Duc. Her brother and the duke of Alençon went with them on to Paris. The French capital was in Valois hands, so Marguerite was not treated there as queen of France, but she was queen of England nonetheless, and this called for a state entrance and yet more festivities. It was inconvenient that by now Marguerite was not well enough to cope with the ceremonies. Suffolk and Alice enlisted Lady Shrewsbury, who had to pretend to be the queen.

East of Paris, the Lancastrians took over. The duke of York and other men from the Lancastrian French administration met them at Pontoise. They went down the Seine to Rouen and then to Harfleur, dispensing bounty in the queen's name as they went. Not a lot – the cost of all this had been ruinous, and it was not yet clear how the king would pay for it – but enough that no one would recall the king's meanness in Paris. They needed goodwill, and although they must have wished the queen would revive a little and play her own part, it was going well enough.

Marguerite was still sick when they put out to sea, and more sick, much more sick, during the crossing. There was a limit to the circumstances in which a proxy could be used. She saw nothing of the trumpeters, rowed out on Genoese galleys to serenade her, and barely heard their melodies between bouts of retching. Still, Suffolk and Alice must have told themselves, these kind attentions were not only aimed at the queen: they were aimed at the chroniclers, the gossips, the London crowd.

By now they must have been desperate to get home, and when the damned girl came out in a skin rash, and her ladies agreed she was in no condition to meet with the king, it was frustrating to have to attend on her in Southampton while she recovered. It took a week, an endless week, and was followed by a low-key second wedding, this time with the proper groom. The king the English would not join with the Valois in calling a half-wit, and the bride with her tearful, blotchy face, were best not shown off to the London crowd, so this wedding took place in the abbey of Titchfield in Hampshire.

It was not done yet. They perhaps got briefly back to Oxfordshire, to little John, their home, their own affairs, then they had to rejoin the king and queen to ensure that all went well for the coronation. If Marguerite had not yet warmed to her husband, or resigned herself to life in England, still Suffolk and Alice had become familiar faces. She needed them at her side, and they had every reason to wish to be there.

The queen made a state entry into London, and this time she was well enough to make it in person. The lion that Henry had given her as a wedding gift accompanied her into the city. She sent it to the Tower, then made her way to Westminster Abbey for her coronation, on Sunday 30 May 1445.

They must have congratulated themselves at this point. The English did not only have the best army, one that had held onto much of France for all the long years since Henry V's death. They were also fine hands at ceremonial.

St Mary's Church, Mendlesham, Suffolk

59 The claim to Le Mans

Suffolk would have had news from his heralds, letters from his stewards and secretaries, throughout the months he had been in France, but even so he must have asked anxiously about the situation once he was back at Westminster. Any move from Gloucester? Any developments in the king's council? Anything to report of the king himself?

The answer was no. England was much as he and Alice had left it. The treasurer was worried, since although Suffolk had paid out much himself to meet the costs of the expedition, still the delays had driven them far above the budget. But this was a normal state of affairs: the king had been in financial difficulties ever since Suffolk had first joined the council – and before that too.

Still, best to be cautious, as he always tried to be. The king had summoned a Parliament, so Suffolk petitioned both the Commons and Lords to give him 'true acquittal and discharge, and honour of him in time to come', in respect of everything he had agreed in France. Gloucester found no reason to object, and Chancellor Stafford, the archbishop of Canterbury, assented in the name of the king.

Some men might have said that being absolved twice over was taking caution to a fault. Some might have asked whether there were agreements they had not yet learned about, that these elaborate absolutions were intended to cover. But he had always had enemies, and he knew he would have no fewer now. Before men had grumbled about his closeness to the king; now they would grumble about his and Alice's closeness to Queen Marguerite as well.

There was family business to deal with too, after his long absence from England. His daughters were grown now, and he needed to see them married. It was at this time, perhaps, that he put it in hand. He would not have looked for lords to marry his bastards, but he found them both respectable husbands, good Oxfordshire men whom he must have trusted to treat them well. Jacqueline of Hainault's daughter Beatrice probably married Drew Barantyne of Chalgrove, although the evidence is tantalisingly vague. Malyne's daughter Joan married Thomas Stonor of Pyrton, and lived to a good old age.

Although they had spent weeks with Marguerite on the journey from Nancy, Suffolk and Alice had perhaps learned less about her than they had hoped. Up till Paris there had been Valois relatives with her, and diplomatic blankness would have prevailed. After Paris she had been even more sick and nervous. When Queen Catherine had been brought to England Henry V had dismissed all her Valois attendants, but faced with this weeping child, Suffolk had not had the heart to do that. Although Alice was much with the girl, there were Angevin ladies with her too, and it was not a situation to encourage confidences.

Now, though, she began to settle into her new life in England, to lose her shyness, and to make her opinions known to the king and his counsellors. Now the Angevins were nudged back to France, and English noblewomen stepped into their place.

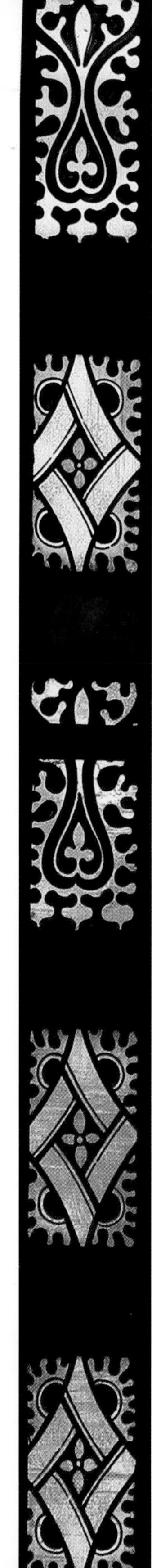

St John the Baptist Church, Thaxted, Essex
Photo Mike Dixon

So Alice would have started to get a real sense of what this queen was like, and Suffolk could add her information to his own. Marguerite's opinions were nothing he could not have guessed. She was related several times over to Charles of Valois. She had been brought up to support the Valois cause. She was honoured, if not exactly happy, to be married to the king of England, and regarded him as such. She did not regard him as the king of France. Charles VII was that; she had known this from her birth.

And her uncle was the count of Maine; that too was something she had never doubted. In her eyes it was unjust for the Lancastrians to have taken Le Mans from her uncle, and plenty of other places in the county too. She had been told by her Valois relations to make that clear to King Henry, and ask him to restore these estates to their proper lords. As for King Henry's claim to Anjou, that must have struck her as plain ridiculous. If he wished to have good relations with her family, he had to abandon it.

The Lancastrians needed to correct these erroneous impressions. Marguerite was one of them now. She had an obligation to support the king her husband. They were not willing to permit her to act as an agent of Charles of Valois and René of Anjou at the Westminster court. They needed her not only to speak differently, but to think differently as well.

Suffolk could have done with the king's support in this. He had learned by now to rely on the king for little, but he must still have hoped. It was in Henry's own interests to instill in his wife a sense of how she might – must – support his claims. But for all the efforts that had been made since his birth, by his tutors, courtiers, churchmen, his uncles, Henry had never seemed to understand the need to uphold his own interests.

And he was, of course, half Valois himself. He was a lonely man in a court made up largely of other men, and he was taken with his lively young bride. He listened to her. She had access to him that even someone as close as Suffolk could not rival – and nor did Suffolk want to limit that access, because it was important too that the queen should conceive a child. So he was faced with a difficult task. He dared not anger the queen, but he had at the same time to work to mould her opinions. He dared not anger the king, but he had at the same time to ensure that he understood that he could not – no, must not – do what his queen suggested.

It is never easy for kings, particularly kings who have been such from childhood, to understand and sympathize with the smaller concerns of other men. If Maine could not cheerfully be conceded to the Valois, it was not only – or even mostly – because it would have been a humiliating concession that there was no good reason to make. It was because a horde of Englishmen, Gascons, and other Lancastrian supporters had swarmed onto its estates and made them their own. This was their reward for their long arduous years of service in the king's army, fighting the king's war. They were not about to give up their lands in Maine to the bloody Valois. Henry was told this, often and in many words, but his lords must have had the sense at times that he was not hearing what they were saying to him.

Another suggestion that Marguerite made was a little (but only a little) less troublesome. She wanted her husband to come to France. It was years now since Henry had been in

France, and his queen was right that it would cheer his subjects for him to visit these lands that he claimed as his own. It would be useful for him to meet in person with his uncle Charles – well, useful after a fashion. Those who knew the king did not actually want it to be he who negotiated face to face with the Valois lords. And this was not the only objection; they had to think of the cost. After Suffolk's two expensive expeditions to France, the exchequer simply could not find the money to send Henry to France in suitable style.

Nor did Suffolk want to give the Valois an excuse to hold the next round of peace negotiations in France, even Lancastrian France. It was crucial that they be held in London, where the English could set the timetable, they could handle the protocol, the pope and his legates would be sidelined, and the king could be kept under discreet but tight control.

He could not afford to tell Marguerite no. She had as much sense of her own high dignity as the king; she had been brought up to condescend not just to earls, but to marquises too. It would be fatal to give her the sense that he was dictating to her, or trying to control her, and he knew that his position did not empower him to do either of these things. It was necessary to flatter, to seduce, and to prevaricate. She and the king were assured that this was a fine idea, but nothing was done to put it into practice.

The herald that arrived from Prince Gilles of Brittany brought news that made this delicate situation worse. Gilles had heard of his good friend King Henry's proposal to come to France, and had written to him in response. Do visit Le Guildo, from which I write, the fine castle I have acquired with my rich child-wife. Do, please do, keep paying my pension. And if there is anything I can do for you, to strengthen your position in relation to Charles of Valois – well, as you know, I have less reason than ever now to favour the Valois. You have only to ask me; I am yours to command.

The duke of Brittany's men had intercepted these letters. Charles of Valois had heard about them. He had accused Gilles of treason once already, and now he accused him again. The Bretons could be regarded as his allies now; the duke had signed to that effect at the Treaty of Tours. The duke was being pressurized to bring his brother into line. But as the English knew, the herald added, Gilles valued greatly his position as a sworn servant of Henry of Lancaster. He hoped his good lord the king would support him, and the king could be assured that such support would be repaid.

It must have been clear to Suffolk that the Lancastrians would have to do just that. It was bad enough that they had let Charles of Valois confiscate Gilles' inherited estates, and that the duke of Brittany had signed at Tours with the Valois lords. But these were not irreversible setbacks; they must have seemed to fit with the long ebb and flow of Breton relations. Signing for one side, for the other, for both at the same time: that was how the dukes of Brittany had always traced their road. The thing was to keep them on it, and this now meant ensuring the duke bent no further to the Valois side. If Suffolk thought that it would have been a damned sight easier to bribe the duke and forget his young brother, ten years and more of history with young Gilles meant this was not a realistic choice. The

Basilica of St Denis, Paris

thing now was to support Gilles, firmly enough that the duke would be kicked back to mid-path.

And without breaking the truce. That went without saying.

Heralds went back to Brittany, messages passed from side to side of the Channel. It was agreed that autumn that Gilles would surrender St Malo. This was a blow. But he kept his new estates, and the child-wife who had brought him them, and the duke let him keep his position as Henry of Lancaster's man.

All this had been achieved by the time the great Valois embassy that had been promised came to England, in a state as heavy as the English embassy that had gone to France the year before. Suffolk made sure he stood at the right shoulder of the king when it met with him. At other meetings he assured the ambassadors in a good loud voice 'that he wished everyone to know that he was a servitor of the king of France, and that with the exception of the person of the king of England, his master, he would serve him with his body and goods against all the world'. He told them the king felt just the same, and loved his uncle (whom he had never met) best in all the world, after his wife.

It was what diplomats said. These negotiations would not, could not, bring about peace. He had known that before they began. The French were offering even less than they had offered the year before. Even a man who wanted a peace as badly as he did would never have considered accepting the proposals. So the only option was to play for more time, in the hope that the Valois alliance would fracture, and a piece moved on the chessboard would transform the pattern of the game.

There was nothing agreed beyond an extension of the truce – nothing in public, that was. But something must have told him – the queen's private glee, the king's bashful evasiveness, the very blandness of the Valois ambassadors. The queen was pressing for the surrender of Anjou and Maine, encouraging the Valois to press for it too – and the king was listening to them all.

Evreux Cathedral

Do not do this, sir. Your subjects will not stand for it. There will be riots in London, and across the whole land. There will be riots in France. In Le Mans the English would withstand a siege, rather than bow to orders to hand over the keys. Suffolk must have said this; Chancellor Stafford said it; Cardinal Beaufort said it. If he had been close enough to the king – which he was not – the duke of Gloucester would have said the same.

So the king did not do it in front of his lords. It was in secret letters to his Valois uncle that he promised he would do what his queen had asked of him, and surrender to the Valois both Anjou and Maine.

60 The dead lane

Pretty, plump, stubborn, obtuse. Those were among the less ungenerous things he must have thought of Marguerite. He could have added, complacent too. Even now she did not seem to realize what she had done.

She did not understand that it would lead to blood. Perhaps she could not have done. Barely more than a girl, cosseted since birth, brought up with a fine sense of her own cleverness, she had never known hatred, never known riots. She probably did not realize it would destroy anyone's life, and least of all did she expect it to affect her own.

The king was little better. He had a touch perhaps, no more, of guilty awareness that Suffolk was angry and dismayed. But mostly he must have been defiant. Surely, my lord of Suffolk, you too want peace? My good uncle of Valois and my well beloved wife assure me that this is the route to bring it about. There can be nothing in this for you to fear.

But there was plenty to fear, and he knew it.

How does one handle a slow-witted king, one who does not know how to recognize his own enemies? He might well have asked his grandfather that.

But as that man had met his own downfall and death before Suffolk had even been born, he had to take his own judgement, which was that this king, however wrong-headed, must still be supported. He could only be told, let us hope you are correct, sir. Anything else would make it even worse.

They could drag their feet, and they did: both the men in London, and those in Le Mans. They took as long as they could before the private promises about Anjou and Maine turned into public announcements: indeed, so long that the Valois had long since announced it themselves. Then they took as long as they could again, dredged up every excuse they might find, to avoid handing over the keys to Le Mans. They had not even got peace in return for the promise to give the place up: all the Valois ambassadors had offered were further extensions of the truce. But Suffolk could not have seen how they could avoid an eventual surrender of Le Mans and the rest of Maine: not when the king had promised it, and was being pressed by his uncle of Valois to honour his promise, and still believed, even now, that what he had decided was the right thing to do.

What Suffolk must have dreaded most happened next. When the news got to Gloucester, he stirred himself from his self-imposed exile, and began to spread the word around. The blame for this lies with the men who surround the king. Did I not warn, long ago, that these men pursued the wrong course? Chancellor Beaufort, the duke of Buckingham, the bishop of Chichester, and most of all, as you know, that heavy lord, already so rightly hated in East Anglia, the marquis of Suffolk.

The rumours were clustering thick as bees on lavender. The friendship with the Valois lords, that Gloucester had complained about ten years before. The failures at Arras, when the Lancastrians had allowed those same Valois lords to unite. The suspiciously low-key embassy to Tours, which included no friends of Gloucester who might have kept these evil tendencies in line. And the months in Lorraine, when it if it had not been agreed at Tours – so men whispered now – the surrender of Anjou and Maine had surely been confirmed.

It was unthinkable to blame the king, and there was no one else Suffolk could blame.

For this, at least. For much else, he blamed Gloucester. And he became persuaded, over

Blackfriars, Norwich

the next few months, that he had no option now but to do what he had always avoided doing: he must bring Gloucester down. He must do it now, while some lords on the council might turn away when he approached, or smile uneasily without meeting his eye when he spoke to them, but none of them challenged him directly. He must do it now, before men dispossessed of their lands in Maine took ship back to England, and gave the fermenting crowds another shot of yeast. He had never been a ruthless man, but if he was to survive this, he would have to become one. Gloucester might be a wizened shadow of what he had been twenty years earlier, but he was powerful enough, and doing damage enough, that it was no longer sufficient to leave him alone.

The king had never been ruthless either. But he feared his uncle of Gloucester, as Suffolk knew. He had been truly frightened by the tales about Eleanor: he had believed then, believed now, that she and Gloucester had wanted his death. He had asked repeatedly, ever since, for reassurance that the duchess was still in her prison, for promises that she would never be freed. Gloucester's tirades against his policy awoke all this again in him. It was treason, was it not, he asked his counsellors? Did his subjects not have to do what the king had chosen?

True, sir. In theory, and often in fact.

And Queen Marguerite would support it too. The people who would not have dared to criticize the king were not quite so reluctant to blame his queen. The precious daughter of King René was now learning what it was to be hated. So when Suffolk said to her and the king, this is what must be done to keep you secure, she said with the king, then do it.

He planned it in the winter of 1446 – and planned it, as with all he did, with reasonable judgement and a great deal of care. There was plague about, and this too was making people uneasy. The aim of his plan was to quell the unease, and bring to the country some of the hard-edged certainty that Henry V had wielded so well. It would be public, not underhand. He meant to see Gloucester condemned in Parliament, shown before all men as a traitor. He meant to arrest, too, every man associated with the duke who had spoken out against the king's policy. They must all answer for their comments, and other men must see and feel the need for loyalty. Then if it had to be done, it would be done: Le Mans would be surrendered, but Lancastrian France and Lancastrian England would survive. And he would find a way next to force through a peace. Another French embassy was to come to England the next spring, and he must have believed he could achieve it then. The embassy would include Dunois, and he was working hard on Dunois and Orleans, and on others in France who still hoped for peace. After this disaster, the king would be forced to – and it could be hoped, would choose to – stand back; and it would be his counsellors who saw it through.

Beaufort would give support, but no more: he was dying, and could not take an active part. But there was a strong group of men on whom Suffolk could rely, not just to support him, but to lead in public. He persuaded them to do just this, because it had to be done by men who were not tainted by rumours, or known by all as bitter enemies of Gloucester. They included John Stafford, archbishop of Canterbury; the earl of Salisbury, the duke of Buckingham, the duke of Somerset – stationed in France still, but returned to England for the Parliament – and plenty of lesser men too. Suffolk had a majority of the lords, and with the king making it clear that these men were acting in his name, he would have been confident they could force the Commons to follow their lead.

Church of St Miles Coslany, Norwich

It was intended to hold the Parliament in Cambridge, but the plague reached there. Some men suggested Winchester, but Suffolk would not have chosen that. He got it called instead to a place firmly in his sphere of control, Bury St Edmunds in Suffolk. All men at court knew Bury, because the king had stayed several times at the great abbey of St Edmund. There was a large refectory and other sizeable rooms that could be used for the meetings. And Suffolk had an estate just outside the town, at East Thorp. He would have stayed there while he was seeing to the final preparations, and met there with the lords and churchmen in his inner circle: those would act for him, and for the king.

The king had said, protect me, and Suffolk intended to do just that. The king's usual bodyguard would be brought to Bury, but not only that: every lord who had sworn support was to bring his retainers. It would be a huge, a forbidding show of force. Perhaps 50,000 men would come to Bury, armed and ready – for what, most of them probably did not know. But no matter: the message to be given was that the king must be protected, and this was indeed the heart of their aim.

It was a bitterly cold winter, so it was in the snow that the lords and commons rode to Bury with this army. It lay thick on the fields and in the streets. Several poor people coming out to watch the nobles arriving froze to death along the road.

Gloucester had not arrived for the start, but that was as well; and he would have to come soon. The king's Parliament met for the first time in the abbey refectory on a Friday, 10 February 1447. Archbishop Stafford preached a sermon, and took as his theme good and bad counsellors. The text that he spoke on was 'To the counsellors of peace is joy.' This was an argument that had to be made, and made loud and often. All men wanted to cheer great victories, not to acquiesce in miserable compromises, but this was the path to peace, and there was now no other.

After the opening mass, they got on with the usual business of a parliament: the election of a speaker for the Commons, the appointment of other officials, the hearing of petitions. The king was much occupied with setting up a school at Eton and a college at Cambridge University, and there was business to deal with concerning these proposals. There was a petition by some sailors whose ship, the *Clement of Hamble*, bound from Normandy to England in December 1443, had been set on by twenty Breton ships, and plundered so extensively that the men had been stripped not only of their rudder, sail, candles and food, but even of their clothes. They were left at sea in terrible weather for three days and three nights, stark naked, until another ship came upon them and brought them to safety. This petition to help them get restitution was not orchestrated by Suffolk's men, but it was useful stuff to dwell on. It was this kind of unrest that the war had fostered. It was to prevent this type of thing that they were working for peace.

No mention was made of Gloucester. He must surely have had some knowledge of what was awaiting him. But most men see only what they want to see, and the duke of Gloucester was one of them. Perhaps he believed, even then, that if he stood up and made his case, men would back him.

And what case exactly was that, Suffolk might have asked? What could Gloucester offer now, a quarter-century after Henry V had died? It was no good insisting that the Lancastrians should fight to the end to win all of France. They had not the king for it, or the resources for it, or the goodwill in France for it. Too much had been lost, or squandered. They would do well now to salvage what they could. And with Gloucester gone, they could expect to do it.

He had to wait another week, then the message came. The duke of Gloucester had arrived in Bury. He had come with his retainers, but in no sense an army: about eighty of them, no more and no less than could have been expected. He had ridden into the town that morning through the South Gate, passed through the horse market, and turned into a filthy side street. There, apparently, he had feared he had lost his way and had asked a passer-by where he was. 'Forsooth, my Lord,' the man had told him, 'it is called the Dede Lane.'

This tale spread around. Well, let it. Men believed in fate, and they needed to be brought to believe that the duke of Gloucester's fate awaited him now.

The duke had been allocated lodgings in St Saviour's hospital, just outside the city to the north. Suffolk gave orders for men to ride there, and guard the duke. Gloucester might call it custody if he wished. He was to be told it was for his own safety. There was some truth in this, with the king so jittery and the horde of armed troops around the town.

This was achieved. Then he paused again. Men must know, word spread, at every stage of what was being done. Men must understand that this was no squalid coup. It was a group of great lords acting on the king's instructions, and in the king's name.

Two days, he gave it. Two days for Gloucester to sit and sweat.

Then he had more troops sent to Gloucester's lodgings. They arrived while the duke was at his dinner, and arrested about fifty men, more than half the duke's entourage. There were his servants, his retainers, his bastard son Arthur – men who could testify to what Gloucester had said, to each word of criticism he had made of the king. Suffolk had them sent out of Bury right away: to the Tower of London, Winchester, Nottingham. Men would see the soldiers marching them off, and more men in these places across the country would watch them being escorted to their prisons. Word would spread still further. This was what he intended.

A few days more. And then it was time.

It had to be lords who arrested a duke, so Buckingham, Somerset, Salisbury and their men did this. They rode to his lodgings, and demanded to see Gloucester. He was being arrested, they told him, in the king's name. Enquiries were now being made of his men. Evidence was building up, and he would be presented with it in due course, and asked to give his answer before Parliament.

Gloucester demanded to see the king. He might not do so, he was told. The king had ordered that he be kept apart. This was true, though they would not have added, he fears your berating him, and thinks still that you might kill him. In time, the king would come to Parliament; he would not see the duke until that moment.

The arrest made, they left the duke in his lodgings under guard, and must have met up with Suffolk, to share their news. They would have to wait now, till the questioners had done their work, and there was plenty of evidence to set before the king.

Then the messenger came. Terrible news, sirs! The duke of Gloucester has had a fit. He is lying unconscious in his lodgings. The guards want to know, sirs, what should they do now?

This was terrible news indeed. They none of them wanted Gloucester to die. It might have gone well up till then, but they knew, each one of them, that the country was like a great gunpowder store, and that the smallest spark might set off an explosion. Men might stand by and let them arraign Gloucester; might stand by again, and let them push through the peace. But if the whispers were that they had assassinated Gloucester, it was all too likely to cause a riot.

So there was frantic activity: doctors were called, the king alerted. Messengers rushed to Gloucester's lodgings, and back to East Thorp. The duke is awake! He has asked for a priest! Yes, one has been found, a reliable man. The duke has taken the sacrament.

The duke is dead.

It was on 23 February, five days after Gloucester had ridden into Bury, that he rode back into the Dead Lane. They must all have been stunned, Suffolk not least. From the laughing boy to the growling old man, he had stepped side by side with Gloucester almost all of his life.

They went to the king, and gave him the news. Henry took his uncle's death coolly. He made no move to arrange the funeral, and it did not seem to occur to him to visit the duke's lodgings and pay his respects to the remains. So Suffolk had to take the lead again, and plan with the other lords how to send out the news.

They had a lead coffin brought, the body prepared, and set naked within it. This had to be done respectfully, but it had still to be done, so every man could see there was no mark of violence. Then in the bitter cold the procession formed, and carried the last of Duke Humphrey through the streets of the town to the abbey church. The coffin sat there, in front of the altar, as the lords and commons all filed by. Candles were lit, masses were said. The king was pressed, all but forced, to appear. This was your uncle, sir, and your heir. Whatever we spoke of, no man found him guilty of treason. You must pray for him now, as well as for yourself.

It was not finished, of course. The rumours he had sent riding through England would curdle and turn sour. The Dead Lane. A death of shock and sorrow. A good duke, a loyal man, who wanted the best for England. Heir to the king. Poison, red hot pokers, all the vile deeds that leave traces only in the air, and on men's souls.

And there were the fifty men who had been arrested. His counsellors asked the king what he wished to be done with them, but the king seemed incapable still of any response, so Suffolk and the rest decided for him. They must not be too brutal, but they must be firm. This had indeed been a treason plot, and men must know it and believe it.

So they chose five men, and let the rest go free. Gloucester's bastard son Arthur was one of those held. They accused these men of assembling at Bella Court in Greenwich, and plotting to march to Bury, kill the king, free Eleanor, and proclaim Gloucester and Eleanor as king and queen.

If this was a piece of hokum, it was the best they could do. Men all have their own understanding of treason. Some men would believe it, and many of those who did not would realize all that was signified by it. Perhaps this would be enough.

Both photos, Norwich

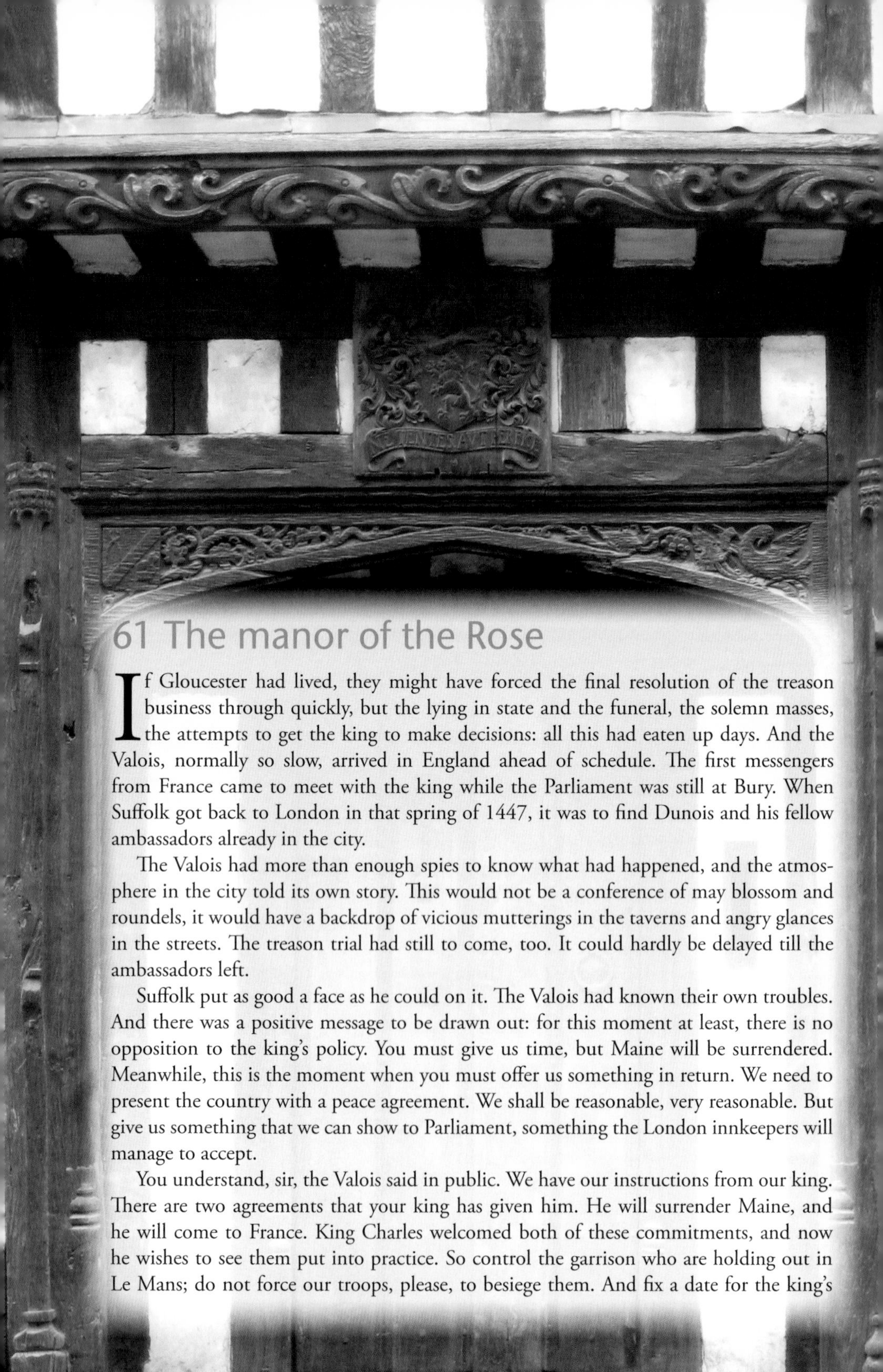

61 The manor of the Rose

If Gloucester had lived, they might have forced the final resolution of the treason business through quickly, but the lying in state and the funeral, the solemn masses, the attempts to get the king to make decisions: all this had eaten up days. And the Valois, normally so slow, arrived in England ahead of schedule. The first messengers from France came to meet with the king while the Parliament was still at Bury. When Suffolk got back to London in that spring of 1447, it was to find Dunois and his fellow ambassadors already in the city.

The Valois had more than enough spies to know what had happened, and the atmosphere in the city told its own story. This would not be a conference of may blossom and roundels, it would have a backdrop of vicious mutterings in the taverns and angry glances in the streets. The treason trial had still to come, too. It could hardly be delayed till the ambassadors left.

Suffolk put as good a face as he could on it. The Valois had known their own troubles. And there was a positive message to be drawn out: for this moment at least, there is no opposition to the king's policy. You must give us time, but Maine will be surrendered. Meanwhile, this is the moment when you must offer us something in return. We need to present the country with a peace agreement. We shall be reasonable, very reasonable. But give us something that we can show to Parliament, something the London innkeepers will manage to accept.

You understand, sir, the Valois said in public. We have our instructions from our king. There are two agreements that your king has given him. He will surrender Maine, and he will come to France. King Charles welcomed both of these commitments, and now he wishes to see them put into practice. So control the garrison who are holding out in Le Mans; do not force our troops, please, to besiege them. And fix a date for the king's journey to France. Then he can meet face to face with his uncle, and we can surely bring it to a conclusion.

This commitment too. Face to face negotiations. The wily Valois lord, and his disingenuous young nephew. Dear God in heaven, no! So he bowed and smiled, and said how admirable all this would be. And in private, he got to work on Dunois.

By now Suffolk had bought the mansion of the Rose, a great palace near to the Thames in eastern London. He had Dunois come there, and there were other places too, that his supporters must have made available to him, where the two men, and sometimes their associates, held meetings. This was how the French did it, as he knew so well by now. The public sessions were for show; what was agreed had to be decided by candlelight over cups of wine.

There is no record of what these men said, so we can only guess. Perhaps now, after years of correspondence, after Jargeau, and Orleans, and Blois, and Tours, they chose when alone to speak freely.

In that case, Suffolk might have outlined the problem that was at the core of his thinking now. After Tours, he no longer knew what shape a peace might take. And not knowing this, how could he press men to make concessions to bring it about? For other men could not see the shape of it either.

But you know it, Dunois might have told him. King Charles told it to you in Tours.

But those demands were not reasonable. Charles knew that the Lancastrians would not accept them.

And yet there can be no other peace. Think of what lands he offered the English. Calais, Gascony, a little more: lands that have been held by foreigners for generations. The land that living Frenchmen still claim must come back to us. Think not only of Le Mans. Think of Bricquebec, the manor you loved so in Normandy. And think of the family that built its castle, those generations of Bertrands whose bones lie buried in its church. Think of their successors, the Paisnels, who fled when the English came, but consider Bricquebec still to be theirs. There can be no peace until these families are living there once more.

This was too simplistic, as they both knew. Men have conquered each other's lands since time began. But perhaps he saw now what the united lords of France were seeking, and what they had pressed their king, one no more satisfactory than Henry of Lancaster, though his failings were not entirely the same, to demand in their names.

Dunois might have said more. You have conceded your king's claim to the throne. And what then is left? What you English fight for now is not the divine right of Henry of Lancaster to rule France. You fight for gain, as you have always done. You do not wish to keep Maine because your king has a right to be its overlord; you wish to keep it for the sake of the Englishmen who now claim its lands. You might profitably think back to the Treaty of Troyes. Two separate kingdoms: that was what Burgundy and the others agreed. France in no way subservient to the English. But this was not delivered, right from the start. Burgundy sold his country to the English, although in the end, thank the saints, he saw reason and came back. And now you dare to tell us you have right on your side, when you claim lands in Maine for English captains? You dare tell us that Englishmen will be angry – not because they care whom Frenchmen should have as their king, but because they have failed to keep France for themselves?

So his own seventeen years in France, a father and four brothers dead there – they counted for nothing?

With the English, perhaps, they counted. But to Frenchmen, even men he had thought of as friends, such as Dunois: no, they counted not at all.

It was not a quarrel, perhaps, but it was the end of a friendship. He would never see Dunois or the duke of Orleans again.

And there was something changed now, something broken in him. Perhaps it was the bitter knowledge that there would not be, could not be, the kind of peace he had worked so long for. Perhaps it was the impact of Gloucester's lonely death, with his divorced wife in one prison, his son in another, he himself in a third. Perhaps it was age, nothing more than that. He was fifty-one now: not ancient, but the battles, the injuries, the losses had taken their toll. There had been a kind of idealism in him up until then; but now it was gone.

This was something other men sensed too. Suffolk was used to being hated. All the English had been hated during his long years in France, and if he was blamed, not entirely fairly, for what was done in his name in East Anglia, it must have seemed to him more of the same. To himself, he could never have been detestable: he was a poet and thinker, a patron of churches and almshouses, a courteous and gentle knight. But now it was as if there was something in him that encouraged men's hatred. It was not that he was indifferent to it: he could scarcely have been that. But the loss of Gloucester had not removed the dark shadow, and brought him out into the light. It brought him power, but at a time when he can scarcely have known what to do with it. And it fixed him forever as the black and heavy lord.

At this time he must have hated the relentless unfurling pattern of his life. But he had to continue, nonetheless. He spoke in the king's council, and defended what he had done over Maine. That he had proposed to surrender territory to the Valois was nothing more than 'malicious rumours'. Everything he had done had been at the king's behest. The king must have agreed that he should make such a statement, and his own supporters would have believed him. Why should they not? What he told them was true. But there were plenty of other men who did not care who had made the first commitment to surrender Maine; they only cared that it had been done.

The repeatedly extended truces were creating their own problem. He can have had little confidence in Somerset: the man was better than his dead brother, but no great commander or administrator. There were no funds in England to send more troops to a Lancastrian France that was supposedly at peace, but its defences needed strengthening nevertheless. The men in France had not the resources to do it. And the warnings he had had in Lorraine were proving true: he had not needed Dunois to tell him this, although perhaps Dunois had done so all the same. There were many reports now that the Valois were actively reforming their forces. It would go hard with the Lancastrians if the truces came to an end without a firm agreement for peace. Suffolk knew this, but must have felt there was nothing more he could do.

The duke of York was in Ireland. With Gloucester dead, and no sign of Marguerite becoming pregnant, he had become King Henry's heir. This frightened the king, as Suffolk knew: York had as valid a claim to the throne as his own, and many men might have said, a better one. There was no looking to York for aid: the man would have to be kept in Ireland.

Prince Gilles sent his herald again. He had been summoned to his brother, told to answer to the rumours that he was planning to use his lands and men – his child-wife's lands and men – in the service of Henry of Lancaster. He had decided to ignore the summons, and tell the duke of Brittany that he believed he need answer to no one but the man to whom he was sworn servant. I think the truce will keep me safe, he wrote to the king, but it would be good to have your reassurances. Suffolk probably advised the king to tell Gilles to come to exile in England. He told Somerset in France to detail a small troop of men to guard the prince, and to make sure these bodyguards gave him the same message.

He saw the treason trial through as well. This too was necessary, and he gave thought, even now, to how it might best be done. But not quite enough thought: it was planned above all as a show for the London mob, but Suffolk had never really understood how to play the crowd, and he cannot have cared enough to learn those tricks at this late stage of his life. His plan was not brutal, since neither he nor the king were that: but there was a sick and angry edge to it, which perhaps reflected how he felt at this time.

Arthur of Gloucester and the four other men were tried on the charges of plotting to have the king killed. Evidence was offered – enough for the purpose. They were all convicted of high treason, all sentenced to die traitors' deaths. They were dragged on hurdles from the Marshalsea prison in Southwark across London Bridge to Tyburn, manacled and clad in velvet, while the crowd listened to them shouting their innocence.

The scaffold had been built, and they were led up the steps, the noose tied around their necks, the stands kicked away and their bodies left jerking. They were cut down, just barely alive, and the disemboweller unsheathed his knife.

Then shouts from the serjeants brought the executions to a halt. A way was cleared through the crowd, and through it rode the marquis of Suffolk and his escort. Stop it! he called out to the executioners. At this last minute the king has chosen to show mercy.

He had with him the charter that the king had signed, and he dismounted, climbed onto the platform and read it all out. The naked, shaking men had their hands unbound and rubbed their necks. The king had heard a sermon on the forgiveness of sins, Suffolk pronounced, and it had moved him to forgive each one of these men. This was a royal pardon; they might all now go free.

Free, but scarred beyond recovery.

What Dunois thought of all this is not recorded.

Bourges Cathedral

62 The Aragonese

The king was grateful, and it must have seemed to Suffolk that well he might be. And the king was always happy to show his gratitude. What Suffolk had had from the crown up to this point had been in proportion with the role he had played: reasonable, even modest if he compared himself with men such as Gloucester or Beaufort, or Lord Cromwell, who had grown fat from his years as treasurer. But he took now all that was offered, and angled for more.

He had been promised, years before, the reversion of Gloucester's earldom of Pembroke. The title and estates now came to him, and no matter what men thought, he claimed them. Men reckoned they brought him a thousand pounds a year. Henry offered him the role of chamberlain, an appointment – well paid, and not onerous – that had also been Gloucester's. He took it, and passed on the stewardship to another man. He became constable of Dover and lord warden of the Cinque Ports. In August 1447 the king made him admiral of England. More was to follow. It was a great slew, a torrent of appointments, all of them lucrative, all prestigious.

Men watched this, and scowled. Suffolk paid them no attention. He was grabbing land wherever he could: lands in Norfolk that belonged to the earldom of Richmond, lands connected to the duchy of Lancaster, lands with lucrative rents, that other men coveted, and could not be quite sure how he had acquired. Ten years before, he had been strapped to uphold the honour and obligations of an earl. He had been a poor man by aristocratic standards, saved by a rich wife. But now he was rich in his own right, and daily growing richer. It was as if he must seize all this, as a shield against men's hatred and contempt. But the hatred and contempt thickened as the shield thickened: a great festering brew of it, spiced with the rumours Gloucester had started. Treason trials, royal pardons, convenient deaths: men looked on all this, and all too many thought to themselves: there is something rotten now in England.

Suffolk's new riches must have changed his relationship with Alice, but perhaps the drive for riches of his own was less the cause of that change than its result. He must have been difficult to live with in the months following the Parliament at Bury. And

St Mary's Church, Mendlesham, Suffolk

his unpopularity would have been hard for her. She was a child of a rich man, but of one well loved, and if she had not quite inherited her father's gift of likeability, still she was used to the affection and admiration of others. Alice seems never to have been at her best in adversity. There is little evidence, but a sense comes across that in the next few years she and Suffolk were less close, less often together than in the past.

There was a coarseness in England now, a sense of looming danger. Perhaps Alice chose to be much at Ewelme, while Suffolk was forced to stay close to the king. Perhaps both of them checked on the garrison they had installed at Wallingford.

In these months Suffolk progressed the surrender of Le Mans and Maine, since he knew that it had to be done. On 28 July he was at Henry VI's side when the king signed the letter his secretaries had prepared, ordering two English captains to take formal possession of the county from the duke of Somerset, who had inherited the title of count of Maine, and hand the keys of Le Mans over to the representatives of the Valois. One of the captains was Matthew Gough, whom Suffolk would have met in Lorraine two years earlier: a sensible man whom he must have felt he could trust to do what was necessary. Somerset was to provide soldiers if they were required to effect the surrender. Suffolk sent the bishop of Norwich with a small embassy to Bourges, to reassure Charles of Valois that this had been done, and to negotiate another extension of the truce. And when Gough and his colleague Eyton, and Somerset's lieutenants, found reasons to claim the paperwork was incomplete, he had the king write angrily to Somerset, warning him that they could delay no longer, and made sure that Gough got the same message. The Valois were threatening seriously now to besiege Le Mans if the handover was not completed.

Gilles of Brittany was also a problem, because he seemed equally unwilling to take Suffolk and the king's advice. Instead of leaving Le Guildo and taking refuge in Normandy or England, the prince had chosen to raise the drawbridge and effectively challenge the duke to come and get him. I can do this, surely, he wrote to King Henry, since as you know I am covered by the truce.

The next news came from Gilles' English bodyguards. Valois troops had come to Le Guildo, they wrote. The prince told us to let down the drawbridge and admit them, thinking that he could trust in the truce. When they got inside the castle they arrested him, and we understand they have handed him over to his brother. They told him no truce can cover treasonous lords. We are sorry, sirs; we have done our best, but we could not have disobeyed the prince's orders – or come to that, defended him against a Valois army.

Gilles' herald came next. The Estates of Brittany had tried the prince. They had not found proof of treason, but the duke of Brittany had sentenced Gilles to indefinite imprisonment. He was being moved under guard between his young wife's strongholds: not Le Guildo, which was by the sea, but the keeps on her inland estates at Chateaubriant, Montrafiland and La Hardouinaie. He looks to you to rescue him, sir, the herald reported to King Henry.

We must do so, of course, King Henry said to Suffolk. Oh yes, do so! Queen Marguerite agreed.

There is a truce, he reminded them, even if it does not cover treasonous lords. We cannot storm a Breton castle and carry off a prisoner of the duke of Brittany without breaking it.

Then find some other way, the king pleaded with him. But we must do something for my good friend Gilles.

He must have found it difficult to keep his patience at this time. It was hard enough to manage the king, keep him from unwise words that would be repeated, from more secret promises to the Valois that would have in the end to be honoured. There was worse to come, he knew: there was the hard reality of the surrender that had not yet been made, and there would be the exiles from Maine, thousands of them, cast off with inadequate compensation for the lands they had lost, and complaining, begging, stealing right across England. He could not afford a daring rescue of a prince who would not listen to reason, and he also could not afford to have that prince creating mayhem in London.

But the king was still the king, and he could not say no. If the plan he came up with was cold and cynical, that was perhaps understandable. It was not that he disliked Gilles, he was probably fond of the lad, but the Lancastrians had lost too much already in support of reckless princes.

He chose to present the king with a scheme to take a stronghold that belonged to the duke of Brittany: not one of Françoise of Dinan's own strongholds, but another place, one in the marches, that could then be bartered for the prince. It had to be a credible scheme, one that would persuade both Henry and Marguerite that men were doing their best, but at the same time, it was probably his conscious intention that it should not be achievable. He must have envisaged long delays, followed by a valiant but doomed attempt: one that he could hope the Valois conservators of the truce would choose to ignore.

Somerset would handle the French end of this, and between them they needed a conscientious captain, who would diligently pursue the plan, and provide evidence to the king that he was doing so. If Suffolk considered taking the man into his confidence, he must almost immediately have realized it would be impossible. A man cannot be told he is being set up to fail. So this man would have to be offered inducements: real inducements, strong enough to make him willing to try, even if the task seemed immensely difficult. He would have to be promised support, and given sufficient to keep him to the task. But the support would never be quite enough, the challenge would be on the wrong edge of tough: it would be the kind of gallant failure the English have always done so well.

Although his contacts in Normandy were not as good as they had been twenty years earlier, it seems that Suffolk found the man himself, rather than trust this task to Somerset. Perhaps he enquired of Matthew Gough, whose stubbornness over Le Mans was understandable, even admirable in spite of its inconvenience, because the man he chose was a close associate of Gough's. He was not an English captain, but a mercenary, an Aragonese named François de Surienne. Surienne had fought with the English for years – for pay, naturally, but he was loyal and trustworthy. He had plenty of experience at capturing places, and some useful men among his troops, including a celebrated siege engineer, Thomassin Duquesne. Surienne, Duquesne and their men could discuss with great credibility their plans to do as the king required. Suffolk found his place too: Fougères, a castle in the Breton marches. It was an enormous fortress, one of the largest in France, with thirteen towers set around curtain walls. It was in good repair and extremely strong. There was a rumour, or he could create a rumour, that the Breton duke's treasure was being kept there.

He invited Surienne over to England, and told the king that this man, entrusted with a delicate and dangerous task, must be given rewards, great and glittering rewards. Henry obliged, and appointed the man a knight of the Garter.

It surely cannot have been what Suffolk had intended. He had always been chivalrous to a fault. The Garter fellowship was important to him, and he would have known it was unforgivable to betray a fellow Garter knight. And if Alice knew any of this, she would have found it hard too. She was a lady of the Garter; she owed Surienne her allegiance now, just as her husband did.

Perhaps Suffolk even thought at times, hell, let the man take Fougères if he can, and bargain young Gilles free. There will be enough lost: surely we can save this one ally?

But nothing would happen fast. That was not the intention. He and Surienne, brothers now in the fellowship of the Garter, met privately several times in London. Then he sent the man back to France, and left it to Somerset to take it from there. Messages were sent, poursuivants and heralds employed. They all reported that Surienne's men were progressing the task. There were earnest demands for equipment, particularly a pair of long pincers which Duquesne said were indispensable for cutting the chains on the defences. They were difficult to lay hands on, but the man was pointed to a supplier in Rouen.

Both photos, Chateau of Fougères

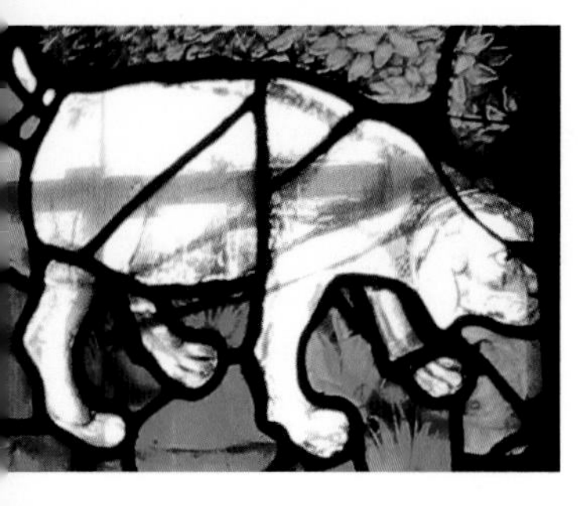

63 Laying in crossbows

Charles of Valois did not wait for the spring. His army began a siege of Le Mans in February of 1448. Lancastrian men from all across Maine had taken refuge in the city. About 2,500 of them settled in to defend the place. The Valois had brought perhaps 7,000 troops, commanded by Dunois, and their German siege engineers. There were skirmishes outside the city, and the Valois guns began to fire. Frantic messages came from Rouen, and Suffolk was forced to take fast action.

No point telling the king, so much for your plan for bringing us peace. He sent Bishop Moleyns at the head of an embassy to France, with orders to do all that was necessary to force a quick surrender of all the strongholds the Lancastrians still held in Maine. And this was done, as it had to be done. Matthew Gough and his colleagues demanded indemnities, and Suffolk ensured that the king and his council provided them. The men were not repentant over the delays they had fostered, they were only worried that they would be blamed for the surrender.

They would not be. For all the indemnities he himself had been given, it was Suffolk who would be charged with that.

The king was grateful. The king was always grateful. He told Suffolk in July that he intended to make him a duke.

There had never been more than a handful of dukes in England, and almost all were men with royal blood. It was unprecedented to make one of a man whose merchant forebears were still remembered. He would, of course, be hated for it, by every man who had to stand aside to let the duke of Suffolk precede him, and by every other man in England with any cause of grievance. A lawsuit going badly, an inheritance disputed? Blame the duke of Suffolk.

But he was hated already. He had set his course, to build his power and riches, and to use these as his defence, and he took the dukedom.

In the months that followed, the men from Maine started to come back from England. The rancour and desperation they brought with them that lay like a clammy fog across the country. Maine felt like a disastrous defeat, and it was the king and his chief counsellor who had inflicted it on them.

The king huddled away, as he had always done. Somerset was in Rouen, York was in Ireland. The bishops and archbishops, the duke of Buckingham, the lords: all good enough men in their way, but none of them born leaders. At the summit was Suffolk, and it must have been cold. It would have taken a great man, a Henry V, even a bigger man than he, to bring things right now. Suffolk might have tried to be a good man, but he was no great one, and he knew it. Nor had he ever been a man blessed with Henry V's kind of luck. When he tried to be firm, he was called harsh and cruel. When he tried to step gently, villains danced around him. The king loved and trusted him still. But he must have felt very alone.

In Norfolk Margaret Paston, wife to a good middling gentleman, and on visiting terms with Suffolk's sister Lady Morley, wrote to her husband about the estate they owned at Oxnead in Norfolk, but which one of Suffolk's men claimed was rightfully his. She

Above, Bury St Edmunds Cathedral
Right, Orwell estuary, Suffolk

begged her husband to try to get Suffolk's support himself, for if he did not, in those days, she reckoned, 'you can never live in peace'. These respectable people were laying in stocks of crossbows and quarrels (the darts to shoot from them), so that they might defend their claim to their lands.

William Tailboys, another of Suffolk's retainers, wrote at much the same time to Lord Beaumont, one of the lords who gone to arrest Gloucester at Bury. 'Hugh Wythom had said he would be at rest and peace with me, and not to malign me again,' but 'Monday last past', Wythom and three other men had attacked Tailboys' servant William Sheriff as he sat at work. They had stabbed him with a dagger, wounding him badly, then thrown him into jail. Wythom was a retainer of Lord Cromwell's, and another of Cromwell's men had come to take Sheriff out of prison, and bring him to Tattersall Castle, Cromwell's great stronghold. He had claimed that the man would be hanged, and as many of Tailboys' other servants as they could get hold of. Beaumont's and Suffolk's good lordship was needed, Tailboys wrote, to rescue his innocent men from the gallows.

But Tailboys and his men were a gang of thieves, according to Lord Cromwell: Beaumont's and Suffolk's good lordship was also needed to carry these men to the gallows. Loyal retainers on the wrong end of a feud, or lawless brigands? Suffolk most likely had not the slightest clue which was the case.

In Coventry the Stafford lords were fighting. On Corpus Christi evening (22 May 1448), Sir Humphrey Stafford was heading home with his man and his son after visiting with Lady Shrewsbury, when they met with Sir Robert Harcourt coming the other way. Richard, Stafford's son, was lagging behind, and Harcourt's men jostled him as they passed. Richard protested, Harcourt drew his sword and whacked him around the head, Richard pulled out his dagger, another of Harcourt's men pulled out his dagger too and stabbed Richard in the back. By this time Sir Humphrey and his men had pulled their horses round, and they joined in too. When they realized Richard was dead they set about killing Harcourt's men in revenge. And these were lords: relations of Suffolk's, and of the duke of Buckingham.

Such things had always happened, and they did not only happen in the counties where Suffolk held sway. There was lawlessness from Northumberland to Devon and Cornwall. Suffolk made efforts to deal with it, but he had little enough time, plenty of pressing calls on it, and every man's story contradicted the other.

When William Tailboys took things further, Suffolk probably thought of it as just one more damned incident: regrettable, but no different from dozens of others. Tailboys and his men, their arms hidden, came to the Star Chamber at Westminster and lingered there, hoping to catch Lord Cromwell. One of Cromwell's men recognized them, sent for reinforcements, and had the lot of them arrested.

Suffolk and Beaumont had not acted over Tailboys' jailed servant, but Tailboys was Suffolk's own retainer, so he had an obligation to intervene. He protested to Cromwell that the man had done nothing; and if perhaps he had come to Westminster hoping to do something, well, it was designed to get his jailed servant free. Not so, said Cromwell; this was an attempt at assassination. He hustled the case to court, and got the man fined 3,000 pounds and committed to the Tower. Suffolk hauled it back to court, and got the fine reduced.

It was Cromwell who would lead the lords who worked from then to bring him down.

64 Bon Désir and a broken truce

March 1449. And here was François de Surienne's herald, Bon Désir – good hope, an ironic name if ever there was one – standing before the duke of Suffolk in Westminster Palace, and bringing him what he described as great good news. His master had done the all but impossible, and captured the stronghold of Fougères.

And broken the truce.

Somerset had been obliged in the end to give Surienne men – the king had been querulous, what was being done about his poor friend Gilles? – but only 600 of them, which should not have been remotely enough to take a place the size of Fougères. Somerset and Suffolk had probably been convinced he would not even attempt it. And now the Aragonese and his engineer Duquesne had achieved a great triumph.

It could at least briefly be painted as that. The king would be pleased. And it was not Surienne's fault that, clever and experienced captain as he was, he had not been quite clever and experienced enough with the wiles of politicians to realize that he was not actually expected to capture Fougères. Suffolk sent his congratulations. What else could he do? The duke of Somerset in France did the same. He was more delighted to hear it, he said, than if someone had given him 'a hundred thousand crowns of gold'.

What should Surienne's men do now, Bon Désir enquired? That was a good question. Suffolk let the king answer it. Hold the place, of course! Henry said. And send him reinforcements. Suffolk passed this instruction to Somerset, who duly sent some bows and culverins. Not men: there were no spare men in Normandy.

The king was intending to negotiate with the duke of Brittany. If he had only known it, he scarcely needed to negotiate at all. Brittany had no desire to see the truce broken, and even less desire to keep his not quite treasonous brother a prisoner for ever. He sent his heralds to Fougères and offered to swap the place for Gilles. But François de Surienne had received no instruction to compound for the place in return for Prince Gilles, so he turned the offer down.

Meanwhile, the news spread. And the Valois captains told their king, it is time. Our army is disciplined, trained, ready for action. Lancastrian France is stretched as taut as a bowstring. Now to let it loose, and see the arrow slice through the air to bring us freedom.

Somme estuary, France at dawn

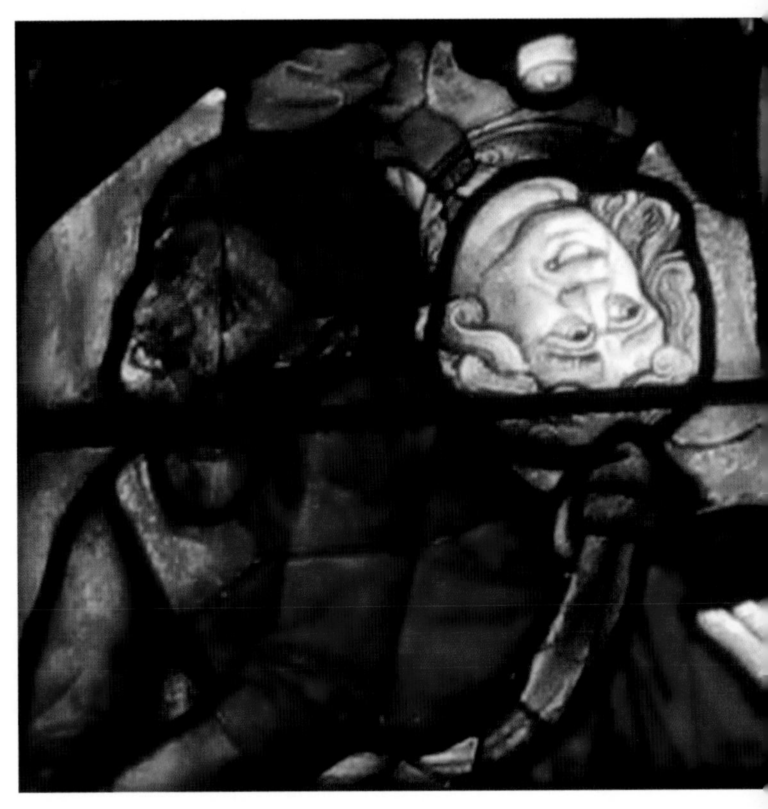

Evreux Cathedral

He must have known this would come, and he knew too, how it would end. More than thirty years now since Henry V's men had first rampaged through Normandy, and Lancastrian France was still a half-empty land of sullen men and women held down by a fragile lattice of garrisons. Neither these, nor the scattering of English settlers, could resist the army he had been told of: at least 30,000 men, set under captains like Dunois.

Still, it had to be tried. The king and his council agreed on that. They put together about 2,500 men: more than a token force, but much less than was needed. It was not easy to raise them, not least because it was muttered that the king had no funds to pay them with. By the time the musters had been completed and the men assembled, it was coming on to winter, and the winds were against them. So while the towns of Normandy opened their gates one by one to the Valois, the English reinforcements sat at Portsmouth, waiting to sail.

That brisk wind from France brought the news. The huge Valois army had been divided up, since they knew there was no great Lancastrian army to oppose them. Charles of Valois taken to the field himself: not to fight, admittedly, but to be among his men and give them encouragement. He attached himself to Dunois's contingent. They made their way steadily to Rouen, and in October 1449 they reached the city. Charles installed himself in the monastery of St Catherine, which the earl of Salisbury had captured a generation before, and watched as Dunois, his army and the Rouennais mob drove the duke of Somerset and the Lancastrian administration back to the castle that Henry V had built. Then he came to harsh but decent terms with Somerset, and watched the Lancastrians march out of the city.

Lancastrian Normandy was all but gone.

65 A garter returned

Bon Désir came back to London, and this time he brought with him a garter. There was a message with it, from François de Surienne, eloquent with fury and disgust. He and his men had held on in the fortress of Fougères, as the autumn wore on into winter. The extra troops they had been promised had never come. The further instructions they had been promised had never come either. The news from Normandy had certainly come, and so had the Breton army, determined to force them out.

By November 1449, they had decided they could hold out no longer. Nor could they see why they should, when all Normandy was falling around them. So the Aragonese captain had compounded with the duke of Brittany, and made an orderly surrender. There was no mention of Gilles of Brittany.

Betrayal, disgrace – but not my disgrace, wrote Surienne. It is the disgrace of you, your council, the Garter lords in England. I wish no part any more of this honour, no part in the Lancastrian venture in France. I am headed now towards Spain.

Betrayal, disgrace. No man wishes to see himself in those colours, and Suffolk must have thought it unfair even now. Bad luck, perhaps some misjudgement, but good intentions – mostly, even now.

He cannot seriously have contemplated exile. That is not what an honourable man does when his king has need of him. So he continued, like the troops in Normandy, to do his inadequate best. Reports were coming from Portsmouth that the army which had festered there ever since autumn, and not received its pay while it did so, was close to mutiny. This at least could be dealt with. The money was found – much of it most likely his own, since the treasury was empty. He sent the bishop of Chichester to Portsmouth to pay it over.

And the news came back, but the bishop of Chichester did not. The soldiers had not waited for him to hand the moneybags over. They had grabbed him at knifepoint. What is happening, and why? We hear from the men who are coming from France. The following wind that hinders us is filling their sails, and every boat is packed to the rim. Normandy lost, men escaping from the massacring French. But why, how? Normandy is ours, and has been for all of our lifetimes. This cannot be. Who is to blame?

It was hard for Suffolk, when he heard the tale, to criticize his old friend the bishop. What else could the man have done, with a knife at his throat? He could not have said it was the king's fault, so he had blamed it on the duke of Suffolk. When they had heard this, the soldiers had killed him.

Church of St Mary the Virgin, Pulham St Mary, Norfolk
Photo Mike Dixon

No instructions came to La Hardouinaie either, where in a castle in a Breton forest, young Gilles had sat a prisoner for two years. His jailers had not been paid, and they were beginning to think the best thing might be to let their prisoner die of hunger. But Gilles charmed enough people to somehow get himself food. So they strangled him, on 25 April 1450. His brother the duke had not intended that. The men who did it were arrested and tried, and sentenced to die.

Little Françoise of Dinan was now a rich widow. The Bretons married her off to an elderly lord.

Evreux Cathedral

66 The fear of the Tower

A week after Bishop Moleyns' death, Suffolk wrote his will. It was not long. He left his soul to the highness and mercy of God, and requested that on his death, his 'wretched body' be buried not at Wingfield, nor at Ewelme either, but in the burial place of his long-back ancestors, the Charterhouse in Hull. His image in stone was to be made there, and his 'best beloved wife' might have her image beside him if she chose. There he wished that 'pore creatures' might pray for him, 'in no pomp nor pride of the world'. Alice was to be his sole executor, 'for above all the earth my singular trust is most in her'. His son he left to his mother's care, wishing there to be between them 'love and al good accorde'. He did not trouble to itemize his possessions; Alice must have known what they were.

At the same time, he gave the orders that the king would never be able to give for himself. The army at Portsmouth was dragged back into order, given out its pay, and told to set sail for France as soon as the wind turned. The Lancastrians still held some land in and around the Cotentin. Somerset was holed up at Bayeux with the men who had retreated from Rouen: these reinforcements could join up with those men, and put up what resistance they could.

He had to do what he could for himself, as well: not only for his own sake, but for Alice's and John's. He had always been a man who set store by words. There was little point now in drawing men's attention to the minutes of the king's council. They might save him from a treason charge, but they would not save him from taking the blame in the country. Nothing could save him now from that. But he must have seen no better option than to make more statements, spell out with careful logic what had been done in the king's name, and why.

Parliament had been sitting since the previous November. He asked to make a speech before it, and this was granted.

He feared the Tower. It was what the fortune teller had warned him of years before.

He believed in such predictions, in the workings of fate: not as men imagined those fates would unravel, but in a way that twisted what was foretold, spoke it in an echo chamber and made the words sound different, and yet still brought the prophecy to fruition. So perhaps it was at this time that he said to the king, promise me this. You will do largely as your council advises, but still you have choices to make, so this is what I ask. Do not sent me to the White Tower.

Perhaps another part of him believed that however it came to pass, his Jerusalem would in any case not lie there.

On 22 January 1450 the duke of Suffolk stood up in the Painted Chamber at Westminster, before the king, lords and commons, and set out his case.

There was no denying the mood in the country, so he acknowledged that first of all, as his main reason for thinking this statement necessary. 'Most high and dread Sovereign Lord' – he addressed himself, as was conventional, to the king – ' I suppose well that it be come to your ears, to my great heaviness and sorrow, God knoweth, the odious and horrible language that runneth through your land, almost in every common's mouth, sounding to my highest charge, and most heaviest slander.'

He spoke of the bishop's alleged dying confession, and said that the king knew it to be untrue. Then he reminded the king and his lords of all that his family had done in their service. He began with all that his father had done for Henry IV, 'in all the voyages in his days, by sea and land, that were made out of this land, in the which he was at.' He spoke of his father's death at Harfleur, his brother's death at Agincourt. His other two brothers, lost at Jargeau, 'the day that I was taken; but as a Knight ought to be, I trust to god, and paid £20,000 for my ransom.' His fourth and last brother, 'lying there for me in

hostage, died also in your enemy's hands'. And not least, his own service: 'Myself hath been armed in the King's days your father and yours, thirty-four winter, and of the fellowship of the Garter thirty, and continually within the time beforesaid abiding in the war there seventeen year, without coming home, or seeing of this land.'

He reminded them of his service since, and his great affection for the king. And he added: 'And if it ever shall like our Lord, that I die otherwise than in my bed, my blood unshamed, I beseech Him, for the weal of my soul, I may die in that quarrel, that I have ever been true to you, Sovereign Lord, and to your land, and to your prosperity and welfare, and so might He at mine end save me, and none otherwise, and so will ever be with His great mercy.'

It was conventional in many ways, but it was eloquent, and it was all at least broadly true. It was never going to be enough. Three days later the commons petitioned the king that since Suffolk had admitted himself that there were 'heavy rumours' against him, he should be taken into custody while they were investigated. The lords consulted with the judges and announced that since no specific charge had been laid against him, they had resolved that this should not be done.

White Tower, Tower of London

This must have heartened him. He had supporters still; the majority of the lords, indeed. The men who had stood firm with him and confronted Gloucester at Bury, who had fought with him in France and argued with him in England, were not all turning their backs on him now.

But the commons came back with a specific charge. The duke of Suffolk, they said, had conspired with the French to invade England. He had prepared Wallingford Castle, and stocked it with arms for their use.

That must have pained him. True, the place had been fortified, but never for that purpose. And if there was blame owing, it was not for conspiring with the French. But he knew how treason charges are made. They are set on the solid ground that plain men understand, and not in the shadow world of whispers and hints. This was what he had done over Gloucester's men; it had a kind of brutal equity that men were doing it now to him.

There was a charge to be answered now, and on 28 January 1450, Parliament agreed that while it was investigated further, the duke of Suffolk must be remanded as a prisoner to the Tower of London. King Henry said nothing.

Traitors Gate, Tower of London

67 Misprisions not criminal

Suffolk had been a prisoner before, in France. Now he was a prisoner in England. For the next two weeks he was kept in a chamber in the White Tower, the forbidding keep at the core of the fortified complex that was the Tower of London, with armed guards at the door and the ravens pecking at the winter grass outside the barred windows.

The Valois did not invade, brandishing the keys of Wallingford Castle, unload its stores of arrows and gunpowder, and attempt to take England. But the Channel was not wide, and the friends who came to speak with him would perhaps have told him that some men truly feared this would happen.

Meanwhile, the commons put together a further set of charges. Suffolk was taken out of his prison and brought back before Parliament, and they were read to him a fortnight later.

There were eight allegations. First, he had married his son to Margaret Beaufort, knowing that the king still had no direct heir, and plotting that Margaret, with her royal blood, might become heir to the throne, and his son become king.

Second, he had worked for the delivery of the duke of Orleans from his custody in England, and plotted with him to help the Valois recover the English conquests in France.

Third, he had agreed to concede the king's title to Anjou and to surrender Maine, in secret and without the council's knowledge.

Fourth, he had disclosed the king's counsel to the count of Dunois, bastard of Orleans, and others of the French nation.

Fifth, he had betrayed to the French the strength of the king's ordinance and munitions beyond the seas.

Sixth, by disclosing the king's secrets, he had caused the peace to be broken.

Seventh, he had prevented sundry arms from passing into the hands of the army, and supported the king's enemies by doing so.

And eighth, he had weakened the king's cause by deliberately omitting from his list of allies in the Treaty of Tours 'the King of Aragon, who is almost lost; and the Duke of Brittany, who is wholly so'.

This must have frightened him indeed. And angered him too, since where there was a kernel of truth behind any of these allegations, it was so twisted and distorted that it had become something else. It spoke not only of enemies he had known, but of enemies at whom he had not even guessed; of men who had watched him for years, noted down every move, every word, kept their knowledge tight and secure, and waited till they could use it to bring him down.

Margaret Beaufort did have royal blood in her. She had never been regarded as the heir to the king: few men questioned that the duke of York was that. But if York's lineage were ruled out, through usurpation and the taint of the treachery Henry V had uncovered at Southampton, then it was not inconceivable that if the king had no son, men would turn to the Beauforts. Not inconceivable, but hardly likely. This was not the whole argument, though, and he knew it. This was about the descendant of a ferry keeper on the Humber, looking to marry his son to a child closely related to the king. This was the dukedom, this was the precedence. This was the shadow truth, the claim to a title that was empty and yet not empty. This was jealousy and revenge.

This was men watching in the street, or even spies in his own household, reporting to men he could not yet even identify. He had met with Dunois, these articles claimed, on 16 July 1447, 'at London, in the parish of St Laurence Pulteney, in the ward of Candlewickstreet'. That was the address of his mansion of the Rose. They had met again 'on 20 July… in the parish of Holy Sepulchre, in the ward of Faringdon within'. And there were men who had known it, and kept note of the dates, and perhaps genuinely worried about what he and his friend had said in these private meetings.

This was someone who had access to the minutes of the king's council, or even someone who had been at its meetings. Someone, or several someones, who could remind the king of his 'sitting in your council in the Star Chamber in your palace of Westminster, openly [declaring] before the lords … that he had his place in the council chamber of the French king, just as he had there, and he was as well trusted there as he was here, and could remove from the said French king the most trusted man of his council if he was so minded.' Most likely he had done so. He would never have conceded that he had done it 'to move, counsel, stir and provoke [Charles of Valois] to come into this your realm to levy, raise and make open war against you sovereign lord with a great might and army to destroy your most royal person and your true subjects'. But the men who believed, or wished to believe, that he had intended this, had taken the care to find truth on which to erect their card-tower of allegations.

The king of Aragon? He perhaps had to ask himself which of the men with their shadow titles and their real titles who had drifted around Tours and Charles of Valois' court at Montils this had been. Was this another title of 'King' René's? Or was really it a powerful king of whom neither he, or Bishop Moleyns, or Sir Thomas Hoo, had taken note? Was this a man he had met, whose hand he had kissed? It was no man who had come to him and assured him of support for the Lancastrian cause, of that he must have been sure. Should he have courted this man, should his embassy have done more? They had been absolved for everything they had done. But that was a shadow now, and these new allegations were the reality.

There was more yet. The 'misprisions not criminal' followed. This was every thing that could be held against his retainers, every bribe men believed he might have taken, every appointment another man had coveted, every piece of land another person wished also to claim. This was Lord Cromwell, angry that Suffolk had supported his retainer William Tailboys and his men, and not let the huge fine that Cromwell had had levied against them stand. This was the Pastons in Norfolk and their friends, convinced that their title to their manor was valid, and not the title of the man under Suffolk's protection. This was someone – no, many someones – who had kept note of his relations, his retainers, his friends, and each favour he had done to benefit them. His niece's husband John de Foix had been appointed earl of Kendal: seen through this prism of fear and hate, it had been done 'for the sole enrichment' of the pair of them, and to the damage of other men.

Chapel of St Nicholas, Gipping, Suffolk
Photo Mike Dixon

Left: Norwich Cathedral cloisters

Men had done the sums, and laid them out. As they reminded the king, at his last Parliament, when his accounts had been laid out, it had been discovered that he was in debt to the tune of £372,000, 'a great and grievous sum' indeed, and that his core annual income was only £5,000 – at least £19,000 less than his household expenses. They knew who to blame for this: it was the king's steward, who had leaned on the king, ever since he had first become close to him, to make grants to himself and his cronies. The result was that the king's household had been impoverished, his more menial servants' wages had gone unpaid, his charges had not been met. And the king's common subjects had been squeezed to make up the difference, 'so unbearably charged, that they have come close to their total destruction'.

St Nicholas's Church, Blakeney, Norfolk

Lord Cromwell was behind some of this. Cromwell for long years had been the king's treasurer, responsible for the king's accounts. Suffolk would have remembered Cromwell, seventeen years earlier when he himself was newly back from France, laying out his statement of the king's affairs. The king had been in debt then, disastrously (albeit not quite so very disastrously) so; just as had his father before him. And the king's councillors had been rich: Cardinal Beaufort, Gloucester, Cromwell himself, creaming off money to build his great castle.

If Suffolk feared what he heard, he would also have been beginning to find cause to hate.

And there was more still. Not laid before Parliament, but in the allegations that were being circulated, was the claim that he had been a coward at Jargeau, that it was his 'sinful abandonment' of his post that had caused his brothers and other men to die. A man in his garrison must have had sores to pick here, because it went on, 'The night before he was captured, he lay in bed with a nun whom he took out of her holy orders and defiled. Her name was Malyne de Cay, by whom he had a daughter who is now married to Stonor of Oxfordshire.' He had not even paid a ransom of £20,000, it was rumoured. The sum had been much lower, and he had made up the difference to Dunois in underhand ways.

So they had watched and listened here too. These were not just men unknown to him, but men in his garrisons and in his household.

He must have seen it now ending in the Tower.

And he fought back still, both publicly and privately. On 9 March the king had Suffolk brought from the Tower to the parliament chamber, where he was read the charges, and given three days to prepare his answers to all of them.

He must have made his private plea again. Because when he was led away, it was not to return to the White Tower. He was lodged now in the Jewel Tower, in Westminster and not in London: a smaller, less threatening place, and nearer to the king and to those he might wish to consult in drawing up his answers.

He will have consulted everyone who had access to him, in the days that followed. He will have heard that the spring tides had come and the army on the south coast was headed for France. But this would not save him, not when so many men had built up so much hate, and not when there was so much need for someone to bear the blame.

So as well as fighting, he must have pleaded and bargained.

It was March 13, with the spring beginning, when he was brought out again to appear before the king and his lords spiritual and temporal. He went down on his knees before the king, and gave his answer to each of the eight articles of treason in turn. He denied all these completely. They were 'false and untrue, and … he would provide sound proof how the king's will ruled him', he said. It was 'contrary to reason' to think Margaret Beaufort so close to the crown, there was no evidence at all that he had plotted to bring her closer, and anyway he had mentioned to several lords that he had been considering the duke of Warwick's daughter as a wife for his son, until she had died still a child. As far as Anjou and Maine were concerned, the agreement to cede them had been made in the king's council and 'other lords were as privy to it as he'. The bishop of Salisbury had lied, or the men who had reported his words had, and the slanders claimed to have been made against him were 'false and untrue'. And if he had boasted unwisely in the Star Chamber, it was not in the words attributed to him, or with the intent that men had read into them.

All this was necessary, and all this meant nothing. Some of his answers were framed to blame others, but none of them were, or could have been, phrased so as to blame the king.

What mattered then was what the king would do, and there Suffolk must have been more hopeful. His grandfather had been in a similar position, and not made to face a traitor's death; he had been sent into exile by a merciful king.

He was taken back to the Jewel Tower, and he waited yet again.

Four days later he got his final summons. There must have been debate throughout this time, between the king, his lords and his lesser advisers, about how this affair should best be handled. In the end, the king would have made the decision.

So this time Suffolk was brought to the king's inner chamber, with had a gable window looking over a cloister of Westminster Abbey: only a few yards from the Jewel Tower, which it seemed was also not to be his Jerusalem. It was crowded with every lord who was within reach of London; archbishops, bishops, dukes, earls, viscounts and the rest. Suffolk knelt again, and the chancellor, Archbishop Stafford, delivered the verdict. The king had chosen to make judgement himself, 'by his own advice and not resorting to the advice of his lords', so the archbishop said on behalf of the king.

On the 'great and dreadful charges' which amounted to treason, the king found the duke of Suffolk 'neither declared nor charged'. So he was no traitor, whether men wished to think him so or not. On the misprisions not criminal, the king did not deliver a finding of guilty or not guilty, but he did pronounce a sentence. Suffolk was to be banished from all his realms. He must leave England by the first of May, and remain absent for the next five years. And he should do nothing to avenge himself on any man for the claims that had been laid against him.

Church of St John Maddermarket, Norwich

Church of St Peter Hungate, Norwich

68 A pursuit and a farewell

There is no record of any word from Alice.

His gaolers probably warned him, when they let him out of the king's inner chamber, and he was able to order his servants to fetch his possessions and prepare to leave Westminster, that he should beware of the anger of the crowd. He can scarcely have needed them to do so. He knew what had happened to the bishop of Chichester, knew what anger there was in the country, and knew that he had been marked out as its target. The death of Gloucester, the French queen, the heavy taxes: it was not just Normandy, it was all of this. More blood would be lost before people calmed down.

He would not die a traitor's death in the Tower of London. But there are many different kinds of tower.

So he left by night, as unobtrusively as he could. Even so, men who had heard of the pronouncement pursued him and his men. They got his horse, and seized some of his servants, chasing him as far as St Giles without Holborn. He got away from them there, was found a new mount – perhaps he took one of his servants' horses – and rode for his life.

He must have done so many times before, in France. But this was England, and he was not now a young man. He was a man in middle age, whose actions good and bad had all come together to define him – and in the eyes of his enemies, condemn him.

But only his enemies. The king had not condemned him. The lords had not condemned him, and if there were some, like Cromwell, who harboured hatred, there were still other men who had stood by him, and helped to make the verdict less bad than it might have been.

He could not stay at his manor of the Rose: strong as it was, it was not secure enough, and he had no wish to be besieged in London. Nor could he go to Ewelme, or to Wingfield; men knew these places for his estates, and they would lie in wait for him there. So he went to East Thorp, near Bury St Edmunds, the manor from which he had plotted the destruction of Gloucester.

He got there safely, and sent men off to the duke of Burgundy, to ask for a safe-conduct. He was forbidden from staying in France, so it was to Burgundy's lands in the Low Countries that he planned to go, at least initially. He had contacts there; he had had Burgundian servants. Five years was not so long, and he could wait the time out, he must have thought, then see whether it was safe enough to return to England and his wife and son.

The news from France probably came while he was there. The relieving army had landed at Cherbourg, and joined up with Somerset's men from Bayeux. This brought it up to about 4,000 men. It was Arthur of Richemont's men who marched to engage them, and Arthur of Richemont's men who won a victory at the battle of Formigny that April, and destroyed the last hope that these men could save anything of Lancastrian France.

Suffolk was still a great lord. He would travel in some state. In early April the king's serjeant at arms was commissioned to arrest two ships and a pinnace – a small boat – which would be used for the transport of him and his servants to France. He had his safe-conduct from Burgundy, and he obtained a safe-conduct from King Henry as well, so that he could travel safely through England. He had been able to stay securely at East Thorp while all this was being prepared, and he arranged a strong escort for his journey to Ipswich, from where he intended to set sail.

These days of waiting he spent putting his affairs in order. Then he set off for the familiar streets and quays of Ipswich, where the king's ships were waiting to take him to exile.

While he was in Ipswich he wrote to his son. It was a long and careful letter, and he let copies of it be circulated. Perhaps there were private letters too, but this was meant for public knowledge. Suffolk could write well, and he knew it, and if these words were as conventional in their way as the poetry he had once written, they were also heartfelt. He must have believed that they would show him in a kinder light than the lists of allegations which men were still circulating and adding to.

He called God's blessing on John, and begged him to love and dread his God, 'by the which ye shall with his great mercy pass all the great tempests and troubles of this wretched world'. Next, he must be a true liege man, 'in heart, in will, in thought, in deed' to the king, their most high and dread sovereign. He must be willing both to live and to die to defend his king. Third, he must love and worship 'your lady and mother', and trust to her advice in everything, since she would be 'best and truest to you'.

'Furthermore' Suffolk went on, 'I charge you in any wise to flee the company and counsel of proud men, of covetous men, and of flattering men, the more especially and mightily to withstand them.... And I will be to you as good lord and father as my heart can think.'

He wrote this in his own hand, on 'the day of my departing from this land'.

The men of Suffolk who had served him, and many of them grown rich themselves under him, gathered around him on the quay. A chaplain gave him the holy sacrament, and he swore before God that he was guiltless of the treasons he had been accused of. Then he boarded ship, and set off first for Dover.

Orwell estuary, Suffolk

69 The rowing boat and the rusty sword

Suffolk's men ordered the sailors to moor their ships off the straits of Dover, and the two larger ships waited there while the little pinnace, carrying a couple of his servants, went on ahead. He probably wanted to get up-to-date news, from Calais most likely, before finalizing his route into exile.

The pinnace never got there. The little boat was intercepted in mid-channel by a larger ship, the *Nicholas of the Tower*. The master asked its captain what his mission was. He was told about the ships in the Dover Roads, and the duke of Suffolk, waiting there for news. So he turned the *Nicholas* and set its sails for Dover.

Suffolk's ships did not flee; he perhaps did not order them to flee, or the sailors did not wish to flee, or they none of them knew what they might be fleeing from. But when he saw the name painted on the larger ship's stern, he maybe knew what kind of tower he had arrived at.

He was called to board the *Nicholas,* and he took the small boat from his ship, and went across to it. The master greeted him with the words 'Welcome traitor.' Suffolk showed the king's safe-conduct. But these were words that to those men meant nothing.

They gave him a common man's trial of a kind, as the ship rocked gently on the waves of the Dover Roads. They found him guilty of treason, and told him to prepare himself for death. He was given a day, and allowed to have his chaplain with him. He must have prayed.

The following day he was taken off the ship, and into a rowing boat, where a sailor with a rusty sword waited for him. In Dover Roads, in a place called the Scaleshif, he lay his head down on the gunwale. And the rusty sword brought his life to an end.

St Mary's Church, Erpingham, Norfolk

Notes, acknowledgements and references

A postscript

After his death, at the hands of a sailor called Richard Lenard, Suffolk's body was discarded on Dover beach, with his head set upon a pike. His final burial place is unknown. No action was ever taken against his assassins. There were rumours that they had influential backers, but nothing was proven.

Alice lived on for almost 25 more years, till 1475. She never remarried. Her body was interred – separately from Suffolk – in a great tomb that still survives in Ewelme Church. Her and Suffolk's son John lived to adulthood. His marriage to Margaret Beaufort was annulled, and instead he married Elizabeth of York, whose brothers became kings Edward IV and Richard III. John never achieved the same distinction (or infamy) as his father and great-grandfather, and although he and Elizabeth had at least 11 children, the family was never as prominent again.

A comment on sources

It would be cumbersome to provide line-by-line sources for a book such as this. It is not intended as an academic biography, and I have not done so. The bibliography below lists the written sources I have used. Should any readers wish for more information, I will do my best to assist them.

To the best of my knowledge there has been no previous full-length biography of Suffolk published, but there are fairly full accounts of his life (on which I have drawn heavily) in two sources: the *Dictionary of National Biography*, and the Rev. Napier's *Historical Notices of the Parishes of Swyncombe and Ewelme,* written more than 150 years ago. This brings him one-quarter nearer to Suffolk's era. Mostly I have trusted him, although when placed the third earl of Suffolk's tomb in Ewelme Church I failed to be convinced.

My title comes from a 1911 article in which H. N. McCracken published a number of Suffolk's poems: with a firm sense of proportion, he entitled it 'An English friend of Charles of Orleans'. Of course, it also applies to other friendships described in this book.

Inevitably authorities disagree on some issues, including the fine details of genealogies and the presence of minor lords, including Suffolk in his younger days, at different battles. I have made my best guesses from the available information. Not all sources mention that he was at Cravant, and some historians would perhaps question his relationship with Jacqueline of Hainault, but I think both are more likely than not. Some authorities claim that Alice had two further children with Suffolk after John's birth; I think that less likely. Confusion about the all too many women called Katherine de la Pole is also common. My best judgement is that Suffolk had both a sister and a niece of that name who became nuns, though it is also conceivable from the evidence that his niece Katherine died young, and only his sister took vows.

The taking of Fougères in 1449 is often described as incomprehensible or a major strategic blunder. I have not encountered elsewhere the thesis that Suffolk and his colleagues did not actually intend it to be taken. I think it is more credible than alternative explanations, but it is my own interpretation of events.

General notes and acknowledgements

I first studied Suffolk's life for my novel *The Heron's Catch*, published by Collins in 1989, and Professor Peter Ricketts kindly translated Charles of Orleans' poem that I have entitled 'No game for dicers' for that book. The rhymed translations here are my own, but would not have been possible without that precursor.

I owe an enormous debt to Mike Dixon for permitting me to reproduce his fine photographs of East Anglian stained glass. The photo of Wingfield Castle is taken from a guidebook dating back to the days in the 1980s when it was open to the public (it is so no more); no publisher is given, so I have been unable to obtain formal permission to reproduce it, but I will gladly make the necessary arrangements should the copyright holder contact me. The other illustrations for which no source is given are all my own photographs.

Some of the original buildings of Bricquebec Castle are now a hotel; Hambye Abbey too is open to the public. Many other buildings mentioned here no longer survive. Geographically, it should be noted that Le Havre was not a place of any significance in the fifteenth century; Harfleur, though now barely more than its suburb, was then the substantial port on the north bank of the Seine estuary.

My husband Paul Simmonds has trailed patiently with me around many churches, cathedrals and other locations in both England and France, and read and commented on a number of drafts of the book. My biggest debt is to him. Much thanks also to those others who read and commented on various drafts of the book, and in some cases loaned me material: Chris Carr, John Woodhouse, Keith Razey, Barbara Searle, Meg Norman, Stephen Dudley and Sylvia James. Robert Short kindly obtained an elusive article for me; Jackie Hunt gave me advice on publication. This book could not have been written without them, and without the information provided by the authorities mentioned below. The responsibility for errors is, of course, mine alone.

Susan Curran
Norwich, UK and Lasse, France
April 2011
susan@curranpublishing.com

Written sources

Allmand, C. T. (ed.) (1972) 'Documents relating to the Anglo-French negotiations of 1439', *Camden Miscellany* vol. 24, London: Royal Historical Society.

Anon (nd) 'Battle of La Brossinière <http://yomi.mobi/egate/Battle_of_La_Brossini%C3%A8re/a> (accessed 8 November 2009).

Anon (nd) 'Le chateau de bricquebec' <http://chateauducotentin.unblog.fr/tag/le-chateau-de-bricquebec/> (accessed 6 November 2009).

Anon (nd) 'Medieval price list' <http://www.maisonstclaire.org/resources/pricelist/pricelist.html> (accessed 14 August 2010).

Anon (nd) 'Earls of Suffolk' <http://fmg.ac/Projects/MedLands/ENGLISH%20

NOBI LITY%20MEDIEVAL2.htm#_Toc196023998> (accessed 5 November 2009).

Anon (nd) 'Guide to St Mary's Church Ewelme and to the Almshouse and the School', leaflet.

Anon (1980s) 'Wingfield Castle: Suffolk's only inhabited castle' (guidebook).

Anon (nd) 'Wingfield Castle', leaflet.

Archer, Rowena E. and Walker, Simon (eds) (1995) *Rulers and Ruled in Late Medieval England: Essays presented to Gerald Harriss*, London and Rio Grande: Hambledon.

Aston, Margaret (1968) *The Fifteenth Century: The prospect of Europe*, London: Thames & Hudson.

Barker, Juliet (2009) *Conquest: The English kingdom of France,* London: Little, Brown.

Bennett, H. S. (1922) *The Pastons and their England*, Cambridge: Cambridge University Press.

Binchois, Gilles, lyrics <http://www.google.co.uk/search?hl=en&q=lyriques+mon+souverain+desir+binchois&start=10&sa=N> (accessed 27 November 2009).

Blomefield, Francis and Parkin, Charles (1809) *An Essay towards a Topographical History of the County of Norfolk*, London: William Miller.

Bolton, J. L. (1980) *The Medieval English Economy, 1150–1500*, London: Dent.

British History Online (nd) 'Houses of Carthusian Monks, 43: The Priory of Kingston-upon-Hull' <http://www.british-history.ac.uk/report.asp?compid= 36257> (accessed 26 July 2007).

Brown, A. L. (1969) 'The King's councillors in fifteenth-century England', *Transactions of the Royal Historical Society*, 5th series, vol. 19, London: RHS.

Brown, John and Brown, Elizabeth (2000) 'The de la Poles, earls and dukes of Suffolk', leaflet.

Burne, Lt. Col. Alfred H. (1956/1991) *The Agincourt War*, London: Greenhill.

Carpenter, Christine (1997) *The Wars of the Roses: Politics and the constitution in England, c. 1437–1509*, Cambridge: Cambridge University Press.

Castle UK (nd) 'Wallingford Castle' <http://www.castleuk.net?castle_lists_south/175/wallingfordcastle.htm> (accessed 20 March 2008).

Chrimes, S. B. (1966) *An Introduction to the Administrative History of Medieval England*, 3rd edn, Oxford: Blackwell.

Contamine, Philippe (1985) *War in the Middle Ages*, trans. M. Jones, London: Guild Publishing.

Cook, T. A. (1899) *The Story of Rouen,* London: J. M. Dent.

Curry, Anne (2006) *Agincourt: A new history*, Stroud: Tempus.

Davies, J. S. (ed.) (1856) *An English Chronicle of the Reigns of Richard II, Henry IV, Henry V and Henry VI, written before 1471 (the Brut),* London: Camden Society.

Dictionary of National Biography: Chaucer, Thomas (c. 1367–1434) <www.oxforddnb.com>.

Dictionary of National Biography: Cromwell, Ralph, third baron Cromwell (1393?–1456) <www.oxforddnb.com> (accessed 15 November 2009).

Dictionary of National Biography: Pole, Sir William de la, Called in English William atte pool (d 1366) <www.oxforddnb.com> (accessed 15 November 2009).

Dictionary of National Biography: Pole, Michael de la, first earl of Suffolk (*c.*1330–1389) <www.oxforddnb.com>. (accessed 15 November 2009).

Dictionary of National Biography: Pole, William de la, fourth earl and first duke of Suffolk (1396–1450) <www.oxforddnb.com> (accessed 15 November 2009).

Dockray, Keith (2007) *Warrior King: The life of Henry V*, rev. edn, Stroud: Tempus.

Duby, Georges (1991) *France in the Middle Ages 987–1460*, trans. J. Vale, Oxford: Blackwell.

Earle, Peter (1972) *The Life and Times of Henry V*, London: Weidenfeld & Nicholson/Book Club Associates.

Encyclopedia Britannica (nd) 'Thomas de Montagu, 4th earl of Salisbury <http://www.britannica.com/EBchecked/topic/519368/Thomas-de-Montagu-4th-earl-of-Salisbury> (accessed 5 November 2009).

Erlanger, Philippe (1931) *Marguerite d'Anjou: reine d'Angleterre*, Paris: Emile-Paul Frères.

Evans, Joan (1957) *Life in Medieval France*, rev. edn, London: Phaidon.

Ewelme Trust (nd) 'Ewelme Trust' <http://apmf.clo.uk/ewelme/EwelmeTrust.htm> (accessed 20 March 2008).

Favier, Jean (1980) *La guerre de cent ans*, Paris: Fayard.

Fords Farm (nd) 'Ewelme' <http://www.fordsfarm.co.uk/Ewelme-I.html> (accessed 12 December 2009).

Fryde, E. B. (1988) *William de la Pole, Merchant and King's Banker*, London: Hambledon Press.

Gairdner, James (1904) *The Paston Letters, a.d. 1422–1509, Vol. II*, London: Chatto & Windus.

Gatehouse, The (nd) 'Duke of Suffolk's Palace, Kingston upon Hull' <http://homepage.mac.com/philipdavis/English%20sites/1679/html> (accessed 26 July 2007).

Gray, Robert (1979) *A History of London*. New York: Taplinger.

Greene's biographical encyclopedia of composers, 'Binchois (or De Binche), Gilles' [online] http://books.google.co.uk/books?id=m3S7PIxe0mwC&pg=PP9&lpg=PP9&dq=BINCHOIS+GILLES+GREENES&source=bl&ots=KU4KzTM4T6&sig=tUirowY66lfa8HVqpAy4yg9Ged8&hl=en&ei=bMOpTY2JO4XX8gOK_KG5Ag&sa=X&oi=book_result&ct=result&resnum=1&sqi=2&ved=0CBYQ6AEwAA#v=onepage&q&f=false (accessed 16 April 2011).

Griffiths, R. A. (2004) *The Reign of King Henry VI*, Stroud: Sutton.

Hallam, Elizabeth (ed.) (1988) *The Chronicles of the Wars of the Roses,* London: Weidenfeld & Nicholson.

Hallam, Elizabeth (ed.) (1990) *The Plantagenet Encyclopaedia,* London: Guild Publishing.

Harriss, G. L. and Harriss, B. A. (eds) (1972) 'John Benet's Chronicle for the years 1400 to 1462', *Camden Miscellany* vol. 24, London: Royal Historical Society.

Harvey, A. S. (1957) *The de la Pole family of Kingston upon Hull*, East Yorkshire Local History Society.

Hibbert, Christopher (1964) *Agincourt*, London: Pan.

Hicks, Michael A. (1991) *Who's Who in Late Medieval England,* London: Shepheard-Walwyn.

Holmes, George 1974) *The Later Middle Ages 1272–1485*, London: Sphere.

Holy Trinity, Hull (nd) website <www.holy-trinity.org.uk>.

Horrox, Rosemary (1983) *The de la Poles of Hull*, East Yorkshire Local History Society.

Hunting, Penelope 1981) *Royal Westminster*, London: Royal Institute of Chartered Surveyors.

Jacob, E. F. (1961) *The Fifteenth Century 1399–1485*, Oxford History of England, Oxford: Oxford University Press.

Jambeck, Karen K. (1998) 'The library of Alice Chaucer, Duchess of Suffolk: a fifteenth-century owner of a 'Boke of le Citée de Dames', Misericordia International <www.leedstrinity.ac.uk/.../5%20Jambeck,%20Karen%20K.%20(1998)-The%20Library%20of%20Alice%20Chaucer,%20Duchess%20of%20Suffo...> (accessed 14 August 2010).

Kent, Sheila (based on Aldwell, S. W. H.) (1999) 'Wingfield Church history and guide', leaflet.

Kent, Sheila (2000) 'Alice de la Pole, Duchess of Suffolk', leaflet.

Kett, John (nd) 'St Agnes Church, Cawston: notes on the history of the Church', leaflet.

Koch, H. W. (1978) *Medieval Warfare*, London: Bison.

Lewis, P. S. (1985) *Essays in Later Medieval French History*, London: Hambledon.

Lucie-Smith, Edward (1976) *Joan of Arc*. London: Allen Lane.

Lydgate, John, 'At the departing of Thomas Chaucer' <http://xtf.lib.virginia.edu/xtf/view?docId=chadwyck_ep/uvaGenText/tei/chep_1.0283.xml;chunk.id=d170;toc.depth=100;toc.id=d167;brand=default;query=chaucer#1> (accessed 12 December 2009).

McCracken, Henry Noble (1911) 'An English friend of Charles of Orleans', *Proceedings of the Modern Language Association*, vol. 26, pp. 142–80.

McFarlane, K. B. (1973) *The Nobility of Later Medieval England*, Oxford: Oxford University Press.

McFarlane, K. B. (1981) *England in the Fifteenth Century: Collected essays*, London: Hambledon Press.

McKisack, May (1939) *The Fourteenth Century 1307–1399*, Oxford History of England, Oxford: Oxford University Press.

McLeod, Enid (1969) *Charles of Orleans: Prince and poet*, London: Chatto & Windus.

Mesqui, Jean (1991) 'Le pont médiéval de Jargeau sur la Loire', *Bulletin de la Société Archéologique et Historique de l'Orléanais*, vol. xi, no. 91 (January).

Miller, Michael (nd) 'Wars of the Roses: an analysis of the cause of the wars and the course which they took,' Ch. 38, The murder of William de la Pole, Duke of Suffolk 1450 <http://www.warsoftheroses.co.uk.chapter_38.htm> (accessed 29 April 2007).

Monro, Cecil (ed.) (1863) *Letters of Queen Margaret of Anjou, Bishop Beckington and others, written in the reigns of Henry V and Henry VI*, London: Camden Society.

Montherlant, G. Millon de (1898) 'La siege de Montargis en 1427', *Revue des Questions historiques*, avril <http://pagesperso-orange.fr/gatinais.histoire/siege_Montherlant.htm> (accessed 2 December 2009).

Napier, Henry Alfred (1858) *Historical Notices of the Parishes of Swyncombe and Ewelme in the county of Oxford*, Oxford: James Wright.

Nash Ford, David (nd) 'Royal Berkshire History: Donnington Castle' <http:www.berkshirehistory.com/castle./donnington_cst_html> (accessed 29 April 2007).

Neillands, Robin (1990) *The Hundred Years War*, London: Routledge.

Norfolk and Norwich Archaeological Society (1847) *Miscellaneous Tracts Relating to the antiquities of the county of Norfolk, Vol. I*. Norwich: Charles Muskett.

North Country Wills, Surtees Society, vol. cxvi (1908), pp. 50–1. Leeds.

O'Donoghue, Rod (2009) *Medieval Stained Glass in Suffolk Churches*, Milton Keynes: Authorhouse.

Oman, Sir Charles (1924/1991) *The Art of War in the Middle Ages, vol. 2: 1278–1485*, London: Greenhill.

Orleans, Charles de (1982) *Poesies, vol. 1: La retenue d'amours, ballades, chansons, complaintes et carolles*, ed. Pierre Champion, Paris: Librarie Honore Champion.

Orleans, Charles de (nd) Poems <http://www.gutenberg.org/files/14343/14343-h/14343-h.htm> (accessed 14 August 2010).

Owen, L. V. D. (1891) 'The connection between England and Burgundy during the first half of the fifteenth century', Oxford <http://www.ebooksread.com/authors-eng/leonard-victor-davies-owen/the-connection-between-england-and-burgundy-during-the-first-half-of-the-fifteen-hci/page-5-the-connection-between-england-and-burgundy-during-the-first-half-of-the-fifteen-hci.shtml>. (accessed 12 March 2011).

Parliament Rolls of Medieval England, various extracts, British History Online (accessed 15 January 2010).

Pernoud, Régine (1953) *Vie et mort de Jeanne d'Arc, les témoignages du procès de réhabilitation 1950–1456*, 26th edn, Paris: Hachette.

Raby, F. J. E. and Baillie Reynolds, P. K. (1959) 'Framlingham Castle', London: HMSO.

Radford, Lewis B. (1908) *Henry Beaufort: Bishop, Chancellor, Cardinal*, London: Pitman.

Renshaw, P. (1987) ‘A guide to the memorials and brasses of Ewelme Church’, leaflet.

Richardson, Douglas (nd) ‘William de la Pole’s illegitimate daughter, Joan, wife of Thomas Stonor, Esquire’ <newsgroups.derkeiler.com>archive>Soc>soc.genealogy.medieval>208-9> (accessed November 2009).

Richmond, Colin and Scarff, Eileen (eds) (2001) *St George’s Chapel, Windsor, in the Late Middle Ages*, Windsor: Dean and Canons of Windsor/Maney.

Russell, Jocelyne Gledhill (1955) *The Congress of Arras, 1435: A study in medieval diplomacy*, Oxford: Oxford University Press.

Rutherford, C. (1915) ‘The forgeries of Guillaume Benoit’, *English Historical Review*, vol. 30, pp. 193–215.

Schnerb, Bertrand (2009) *Armagnacs et Bourguignons: La maudite guerre*, rev. edn, Paris: Perrin.

Seward, Desmond (1978) *The Hundred Years War*, London: Constable.

Sheppard, Thomas (1912) *The Lost Towns of the Yorkshire Coast and Other Chapters Bearing upon the Geography of the District*. London: A Brown & Sons. <http://www.archive.org/details/losttownsofyorks00sheprich> (accessed 27 August 2009).

Sherborne, James (1994) ‘The defence of the realm and the impeachment of Michael de la Pole in 1386’, pp. 99–117 in *War, Politics and Culture in Fourteenth-Century England*, ed. A. Tuck, London and Rio Grande: Hambledon Press.

Shirley, J. (1868) *A Parisian Journal*, extracts on <http:mw.master.ca/scriptorium/paris1.html and http:mw.master.ca/scriptorium/paris2.html> (accessed 7 January 2010).

Sitwell, O. R. (1970) ‘Framlingham: a short history and guide’, booklet.

Smith, Anthony (1995) ‘The greatest man of that age: the acquisition of Sir John Fastolf’s East Aglian Estates’, p. 137–53 in R. E. Archer and S. Walker (eds), *Rulers and Ruled in Late Medieval England: Essays presented to Gerald Harriss*, London and Rio Grande: Hambledon Press.

Smith, Robert Douglas and De Vries, Kelly (nd) ‘The artillery of the dukes of Burgundy, 1363–1477’ <http://books.google.co.uk/books?id=UAL0SfuyUGQC&pg=PA91&lpg=PA91&dq=siege+le+crotoy+1423&source=bl&ots=u_PgW1Nsxm&sig=qp3kkSPreq_iHWTe4V4_6eNd0NY&hl=en&ei=RV1HS7v2LaPUjAeF6tGABw&sa=X&oi=book_result&ct=result&resnum=1&ved=0CAcQ6AEwAA#> (accessed 7 January 2010).

Stevenson, Joseph (ed.) (1861/4) *Letters and Papers Illustrative of the Wars of the English in France, during the reign of Henry VI*: Vol 1, 1861; Vol II Part I, 1864; Vol II, Part II, 1864 (includes William Worcester’s collection of papers). London: Rolls Series.

Stevenson, Joseph (1863) *Narratives of the Expulsion of the English from Normandy, 1449–1450,* London: Longman, Green, Longman, Roberts and Green.

Storey, R. L. (1986) *The End of the House of Lancaster*, Gloucester: Alan Sutton.

Strutt, Joseph (1799) *A Complete View of the Dress and Habits of the People of England,* vol. II, London: J. Edwards and others.

Thompson, James Westfall and Johnson, Edgar Nathaniel (1937) *An Introduction to Medieval Europe 300–1500*, New York: W. W. Norton.

Thompson, John A. F. (1983) *The Transformation of Medieval England 1370–1529*, London and New York: Longman.

Thompson, Peter E. (trans. and ed.) (1966) *Contemporary Chronicles of the Hundred Years War from the works of Jean le Bel, Jean Froissart and Enguerrand de Monstrelet*, London: Folio Society.

Tricker, Roy and van der Does, Rosemary (1999) ‘Short history and guide to St Andrew’s Church, Cotton, Suffolk’, leaflet.

Vaughan, Richard (2002) *Philip the Good: The Apogee of Burgundy*, rev. edn, Woodbridge: Boydell Press.

Virgoe, R. (ed.) *Illustrated Letters of the Paston Family*, Basingstoke: Macmillan.

Virgoe, Roger (1997) *East Anglian Society and the political community of late*

Medieval England: selected papers of Roger Virgoe, ed. Caroline Barron, Carole Rawcliffe and Joel T. Rosenthal, Norwich: Centre of East Anglian Studies, University of East Anglia.

Waley, Daniel (1985) 'Burgundy, The great duchy of the west', Chapter 9 in *Later Medieval Europe: From St Louis to Luther*, 2nd edn, London: Longman.

Ward, Jennifer (1995) *Women of the English Nobility and Gentry 1066–1500*, Manchester: Manchester University Press.

Westminster Abbey (nd) Information on tombs of Henry V and Catherine de Valois <http://www.westminster-abbey.org/our-history/royals/burials/henry-v-and-catherine-de-valois> (accessed 6 November 2009).

Wikipedia (nd) 'La bataille de Cravant' <http:..fr.wikipedia.org/wiki/Bataille_de_Cravant> (accessed 7 November 2009).

Wikipedia (nd) 'Edmund_Beaufort,_2nd_Duke_of_Somerset' <http://en.wikipedia.org/wiki/Edmund_Beaufort,_2nd_Duke_of_Somerset> (accessed 14 August 2010).

Wikipedia (nd) 'Jacqueline, Countess of Hainault' <htto://en.wikipedia.org.Jacqueline,_Countess)_of_Hainault> (accessed 22 May 2009).

Wikipedia (nd) 'Michael de la Pole, 2nd Earl of Suffolk' <http://en.wikipedia.org/wiki/Michael_de_la_Pole,_2nd_Earl_of_Suffolk> (accessed 6 November 2009).

Wikipedia (nd) 'William de la Pole, 1st Duke of Suffolk' <http://en/.wikipedia/.org/wiki/William_de_la_Pole,_1st_Duke_of_Suffolk> (accessed 26 July 2007).

Wikipedia (nd) 'John Stafford' <http://en.wikipedia.org/wiki/John_Stafford_%28arch bishop%29: John Stafford (archbishop)> (accessed 12 June 2010).

Wikipedia (nd) 'Knights and ladies of the Garter' <http://en.wikipedia.org/wiki/List_of_Knights_and_Ladies_of_the_Garter> (accessed 5 November 2009).

Williams, Benjamin (ed. and trans.) (1850) *Gesta Henrici Quinti, Angliae Regis*, London: Sumptibus Societatis.

Williams, E. C. (1965) *My Lord of Bedford, 1389–1435, being a life of John of Lancaster, first duke of Bedford, brother to Henry V.* London: Longmans.

Williamson, Allen (nd) 'Biography of Joan of Arc' <http://www.joan-of-arc.org.joanofarc_life?_summary_victoire.html (accessed 22 May 2009).

Wilson-Smith, T. (2006) *Joan of Arc: Maid, Myth and History*, UK: Sutton/History Press.

Wolffe, Bertram (1983) *Henry VI*, London: Methuen.

Trinity Church, Vendome

Subject index

Note: Noblemen and women are indexed under their final title (of the period covered), with cross-references from family names and other titles in some instances. Queens and kings are indexed by first name.

B

Church of St Mary the Virgin, Yaxley, Suffolk
Photo Mike Dixon

Church of St John the Baptist, Thaxted, Essex
Photo Mike Dixon

Index of illustrations

In France:

St Nicholas's Church, Blakeney, Norfolk